STATE TRUST LANDS

DEVELOPMENT OF WESTERN RESOURCES

The Development of Western Resources is an interdisciplinary series focusing on the use and misuse of resources in the American West. Written for a broad readership of humanists, social scientists, and resource specialists, the books in this series emphasize both historical and contemporary perspectives as they explore the interplay between resource exploitation and economic, social, and political experiences.

John G. Clark, University of Kansas, Founding Editor
Hal K. Rothman, University of Nevada, Las Vegas, Series Editor

STATE TRUST LANDS

History, Management, and Sustainable Use

Jon A. Souder
Sally K. Fairfax

University Press of Kansas

© 1996 by the University Press of Kansas
All rights reserved

Published by the University Press of Kansas (Lawrence, Kansas 66049), which
was organized by the Kansas Board of Regents and is operated and funded by
Emporia State University, Fort Hays State University, Kansas State University,
Pittsburg State University, the University of Kansas, and Wichita State
University

Library of Congress Cataloging-in-Publication Data

Souder, Jon A.
    State trust lands : history, management, and sustainable use / Jon
A. Souder, Sally K. Fairfax.
        p.   cm. — (Development of western resources)
    Includes bibliographical references and index.
    ISBN 0-7006-0731-5 (alk. paper)   ISBN 0-7006-0939-3 (pbk.)
    1. School lands—West (U.S.)—Management—History.   2. Public
lands—West (U.S.)—Management—History.   3. Natural resources—West
(U.S.)—Management.   I. Fairfax, Sally K.   II. Title.   III. Series.
LB2827.S65   1995
333.16—dc20   95-31165

British Library Cataloguing in Publication Data is available.

Printed in Canada

10 9 8 7 6 5 4 3 2

The paper used in this publication meets the minimum requirements of the American
National Standard for Permanence of Paper for Printed Library Materials Z39.48–1984.

CONTENTS

FOREWORD

Jon Souder and Sally Fairfax have produced the first systematic study of state land management in the West. Even though I have spent twenty years closely involved with issues of the public lands, I found the book to be filled with surprises. I did not know, for example, that state trust lands total 135 million acres—more than two-thirds of the total land area in the lower forty-eight states managed by either the Bureau of Land Management or the U.S. Forest Service. In a sense there are three major public land systems in the West: the national forests, the BLM lands, and the state trust lands.

Yet, the state trust lands—lands whose revenues are dedicated to education or other special purposes of a state trustee—have gone virtually unnoticed in academic and popular discussions of public land management. This book is important and exciting because it opens up a whole new field for investigation at a time of rapidly expanding interest in the future of federal land management and in the capabilities of state governments to manage land.

For researchers in the field, the state lands have the great virtue that there are often wide variations in policies from state to state. Grazing fees in 1994, for example, ranged from $1.48 in Arizona (well below the federal fee) to $6.42 in Colorado (more than three times the federal fee). With only one federal fee for all the West on BLM and Forest Service land, there has been a limit to what could be said with any confidence about the impacts of different fees. Now, however, as Souder and Fairfax have made it impossible any longer to ignore, there is a whole range of fees in the states to be studied.

Higher grazing fees are not the only area where state land managers have taken policy initiatives over the years that could never get beyond the discussion stage for federal lands. For example, I was shocked to discover the extent to which the states have already been serving their long-touted function of laboratories for policy experimentation, in this case in land management. The federal government has debated for years the possibility of a new mining law. Little has happened because Congress has never been able to agree on whether a leasing system would work in place of the claim/patent system of the Mining Law of 1872, while the mining industry has asserted that any significant royalty would be economically devastating. Yet, as *State Trust Lands* describes, some states already have had leasing systems for "hardrock" minerals for years and most have royalties. Future mining law debates will have to begin with the recognition that many options have already been tried out on state trust lands.

Perhaps because state land management has been so lacking in visibility, the states have been less susceptible to the gridlock of interest group conflict and ideological controversy. The Forest Service has regarded allegiance to "even flow" timber policies as virtually a religious test of fealty to principles of sustained yield, but Souder and Fairfax point out that state forestry departments long ago recognized that varying harvest rates according to economic conditions in the market offered major practical advantages. Selling any parcel of federal land has been regarded by many participants in public land debates as a virtual declaration for the political and economic philosophy of James Watt. Meanwhile, a number of states have put into place financially lucrative programs of making limited amounts of their land available for intensive recreational and other commercial development. For them it was not a matter of capitalism versus socialism, but simply of making money for the state trustee and contributing to state economic development. As Souder and Fairfax explain, such efforts offer "a chance for new and interesting answers to fundamental questions about public resource management."

While the federal government has not responded much to the many proposals over the years for wider use of the market mechanism in land management, this book shows us that the states have been more innovative here as well. Some of them have been actively exploring options for allowing environmental and other groups to buy out grazing rights in wilderness and other environmentally sensitive areas. Recreation has always suffered in the budget process at the federal level because the federal government collects so little from the large numbers of recreational visitors to public lands. Souder and Fairfax show how Montana has established a program to limit hunting use in selected areas and improve the conditions for hunting, and to collect substantial fees.

Among its many claims on our attention, this book is also timely in that there is growing interest today in the question of whether the federal government should continue to own 48 percent of the land area of the eleven westernmost lower forty-eight states. From welfare, to Medicaid, to the Clean Water Act, to a number of other tasks of government, proposals are currently emerging to devolve federal responsibilities to the states. After a century of growing centralization of power in Washington, since its beginning in the progressive era, suddenly there is a new level of interest in the basic state role in the U.S. federal system. Legislative proposals to transfer portions of federal lands to state ownership are sure to be on the agenda of possible devolutions of federal authority.

Souder and Fairfax do not attempt in any comprehensive way to say whether this would be a good thing, but they do offer important evidence of the capabilities of state land managers. They provide counterweight to the common impression that the states have grossly abused their lands and that state land management has been inferior to federal efforts. Indeed, they find that in some respects the states have done a better job. Reflecting the imperative to earn positive revenues for their trustees, the states financially have had much better results than the large drain that the federal lands have been for the U.S. Treasury. Moreover, the need to maintain future earning capacity gives the states a strong incentive to maintain the lands in good physical condition. If overgrazing damages the range and thus reduces future grazing capacity, it is not only an environmental problem for society but a financial problem for the state trustee.

Souder and Fairfax argue that the very presence of the state trustee as a "residual claimant" acts to promote management for long-run sustainability. For one thing, the courts have felt much greater freedom to act on complaints of the trustee, when state legislatures or land managers have behaved in harmful ways. In some states, for example, courts have ruled that low subsidized fees for ranchers are not consistent with the trust responsibility of the managers to maximize the long-run returns from the lands and have overturned the legislature. The authors explain that the "explicit enforceability of the trust . . . has potential for protecting long-term resource commitments from politically pressured legislatures and managers and provides another tool in managing for sustainability."

A further basic objective of this book is to describe a set of economic principles that should guide future investigations of land management options. Souder and Fairfax not only devote chapters to the basic circumstances of grazing, forestry, and mineral management on state trust lands but also present a number of specific analytical methods suited to the study of each of these resource areas. I have said less about this aspect of the book because there is less that is surprising here—at least for someone trained as an economist, as I am. I should also say that readers who do not have much economic background may find these sections heavy going, and may be content to gather the gist of the argument. The book then shows how to apply some of the economic methods presented and develops some important new research results of its own. With the large body of information on state lands that they provide, Souder and Fairfax have opened the way for many future analysts and researchers to contribute further new studies.

For any researcher, it is rare to find a whole new dimension of his or her field that has escaped attention. In this major contribution to the field of public land management, Souder and Fairfax have opened up a brand-new line of inquiry. It now falls to others to take further advantage of the rich body of data and information on the state trust lands that they have given us.

Robert H. Nelson
School of Public Affairs
University of Maryland

ACKNOWLEDGMENTS

One critical but frequently overlooked criterion for picking a research topic is to focus on something that will enable you to go beautiful places with good people. Our inquiry has been extremely successful in this regard; it has taken many, many years to accumulate a basic understanding and basic data regarding twenty-two diverse state programs. We have unusually rich, long-term data to show for our effort. It would be an error, however, for readers to think we pulled it all out of musty libraries in the lonely pursuit of scholarly abstractions. We could not have done this work long enough to do it right if we had not been having fun all over the West with great friends.

We are thankful that the Western States Lands Commissioners Association puts so much effort into organizing its biannual meetings. It is traditional that at each gathering of that tribe, the local hosts take enormous pains to arrange field trips that give their visitors a sense of the region and its resources, as well as the commissioners' management problems and aspirations. Some of this is delightfully goofey—we have enjoyed wine from Arkansas, salsa from Oregon, and honey from Wisconsin, and we both have almost complete WSLCA outfits—many hats, T-shirts, tote bags, croakies, not to mention the fabulous briefcases that show up from time to time. But we have also spent important time with very knowledgeable resource managers in places we would have had no other way of getting to. There are a lot of numbers and charts in this volume (far too many for the taste of one of us), but we hope that there is also a sense that beyond the offices and the files there is land and people. There is probably a boondoggle element in our travels—if that is what a cynic wants to call enjoying your work—but we have also seen wonderful, diverse places that are important to the state, the folks who manage it, and the folks who live there. The land we have been shown is very much worth worrying about.

We also have many old friends as a result of our inquiry, some who we have now known for ten or fifteen years. We met most of these folks through the Western States Lands Commissioners Association and have been hanging around their conferences for so long that we are now on the organizational roster under the heading "Miscellaneous." We are pleased and proud about that designation, which we take to be indicative of extraordinary good fellowship, when we imagine alternative descriptions that could be attached to academics who have, for more than a decade, sent out questionnaires, follow-up questionnaires, and requests for information, soon followed by drafts, articles, and endless charts and chapters to review. Perhaps worse, having made their acquaintance at the WSCLA, we have then showed up in the state land commissioners' offices at odd times to paw through the files, chat and probe endlessly, borrow the photocopier and the phone, and then, having finally decamped, call back with more questions and new queries. Once when we showed up for a site visit, one of us had a newly broken arm. On another occasion, the entire research team came to town with food poisoning. That trip included two visiting undergraduate interns, Chris Ortiz of Cornell and Scott Tang of the University of Arizona, who worked with us one summer. Several generations of lands commissioners, their colleagues, and staff have welcomed us with warmth and guided, educated, assisted, and corrected us beyond what any researcher has any reason to hope for. The footnotes, which acknowledge the help we have received, frequently say "personal communication." It would be more fun, and more accurate, to say "we called up Kevin, or Bill, or Pam to find this out, and thanks." This work has taken up a big chunk of our lives, and we are deeply appreciative to have spent it in the company of such fine human beings.

The Harris Trust, administered by the Institute for Government Studies on the Berkeley campus, gave us our first seed money to start this project when other funders were turning back proposals on the grounds that the trust lands no longer existed. Fred Kisabeth of Idaho got us to our first WSCLA meeting, without which nothing else would have happened. During our initial steps in examining trust land issues, Jan Stevens, Deputy Attorney General for the State of California, and Rowena (Roe) Rogers, former President of the Colorado Board of Land Commissioners, provided the moral support (plus some very fine meals) that allowed us to proceed. Had either of these two been less encouraging, our work might have faltered in its early stages. Paul Klein and Gretta Goldenman, both students at Boalt Hall School of Law, also worked assiduously, as we were first starting to locate enough case materials to figure out if the trust lands existed as a meaningful category. Later we were fortunate to work with Jim Phillips, then of Texas and head of the WSCLA Legal Committee, to produce a small volume of historic trust cases.

Surveys and questionnaires were a major tool in our early efforts to understand trust management. Karma Pippin organized our bibliography and taught us the joys of Pro-Cite. Karen Bradley joined us from the History Department to conduct the major historical research on the states' accession processes. Our first public presentation of the material in Chapters 1 and 2 was at a 1990 meeting of the Western Political Science Association in San Diego. David Olson of the University of Washington took his role as commenter with unusual seriousness and gave us a wonderful boost just as we started writing.

Our theoretical treatment of trust management and the relationship between trustees and beneficiaries was enhanced through discussions with Bill Cook, Ernie Rushing and Paul Silver, Jim Rinehart, Margaret Bird, John Duffield, Madalyn Quinlan, Stephanie Balzarini, and Jay Gildersleeve. Gail Llewellen first made us pay attention to the issue of standing, regarding who could defend the trust.

Pat McElroy had the bad fortune to wander into San Francisco on vacation just as we put the finishing touches on the forestry material, which cost him several days as he tried, yet again, to straighten us out on the finer points of the crucial Washington program. He took up, to be sure, where Don Lee Frasier left off in the time-consuming job that falls to public servants of educating scholars.

Our studies on trust land grazing management were advanced as a result of conversations over the years with Bob Langsenkamp (N. Mex.), Keith Kuhlman (Okla.), Jeff Kroft and Burt Lewis (Oreg.), Lee Otteni (N. Mex.), Pat Hennessey (Wash.), Jeff Hagener (Mont.), and Mike Brandt (S. Dak.), and especially Dick Leblanc, who also had to tell us the ZIP code abbreviation for Nebraska ("NB"). Pat Flowers (Mont.) served on a panel at the 1990 Western Forest Economists meeting in Wemme, Oregon, to discuss trust forestry issues. Ross Gorte of the Congressional Research Service provided valuable comments on sustainability in the context of trust forest management. Our understanding of minerals management has been strengthened by discussions with Jeff Kroft (Oreg.), Doug Morgan and Pary Shoftner (Okla.), Mike Price (Ariz.), Rick Larson (N. Dak.), and Walt Rosenbusch and Billy Farr (Tex.). Our discussion of emerging resources benefited from conversations with Kevin Carter (Utah).

Our work on water management was made possible by a grant from the USGS, and has been undertaken primarily by Elizabeth Soderstrom. The initial inquiry was highlighted by a mini-conference of diverse colleagues who sat with us one day and critiqued our preliminary results. Helen Ingram, Lyle Manley, Michael Hanemann, Gary Weatherford, and Bob Mailander started us thinking about federal reserved water rights, with good cheer and good food. You really cannot ask for much more than that. Well, actually, we could ask that Elizabeth finish her dissertation, but certainly the best is yet to be.

Biologists study frogs for what they can teach us about animals in general. We have dissected state trust lands management programs, albeit with considerably more cooperation on the states' part than biologists generally receive from their frogs, both because they are intrinsically interesting and important, and because they have much to teach us about public resources. Our goal has been to make these lands accessible for public consideration and further academic study. For far too long the instructive comparisons that are available on the state trust lands have been overlooked. We hope that state trust lands will provide a focus for a new and fruitful path of inquiry into public resources and resource management. And while frogs do not usually directly profit from their dissection, we do especially hope that state trust lands and their managers will benefit from the enhanced attention and analysis that their efforts so richly deserve. With that hope, we dedicate this volume to the state lands commissioners, their co-workers, and staff whose support made it possible.

INTRODUCTION

State trust lands exist in a quiet corner of public resource management, only occasionally coming into view. Their obscurity conceals important lands and resources, as well as the opportunity to extract from their management significant lessons for public resource management more generally. This book has two goals. The first is to provide sufficient information and analysis to raise the visibility of state trust lands and land management. The second (and frequently implicit) goal is to use the array of management techniques and priorities found on the state trust lands to diversify our thinking about the hows and whys of all public resources, especially on federal lands.

The state trust lands ought to be more visible: they are important, valuable, and fascinating. The history of the grants—which states got how much land and where, and how the program has evolved—contains rich and wonderful questions. School lands policy began before the federal Constitution was adopted. These are the famous "section 16s"[1] in each township first promised to states in the General Land Ordinance of 1785. School lands were granted by Congress to the states at the time each new state joined the Union, beginning with Ohio in 1803 and ending with Alaska in 1959.[2] The states made clear and specific promises in return for the granted lands, cementing each statehood bargain. The land grants were originally made for a single, explicitly stated purpose—to support common schools and similar public institutions—and that purpose continues to be controlling at the end of the twentieth century. Very few programs in this or any other nation have such a deep, clear past or such a consistent core.

But the current management of the granted lands is even more fascinating than their history. The state trust lands are particularly instructive because of what many regard as a peculiar management mandate. The granted lands, in combination with the revenues and permanent funds they produce, are generally viewed as a trust; hence, trust land managers approach their management responsibilities under the same array of rules and enforcement mechanisms that surround any trustee, such as a banker managing funds for a client's grandchild. Thus, they provide myriad opportunities for comparative analysis that could expand our thinking about public resources in general. Those rules—establishing clear priorities and requiring strict accountability and disclosure—make it interesting and relatively easy to assess whether state officials are choosing management tools and allocating resources in a way that contributes to achieving trust goals. Another ba-

1

sic rule of trust management—requiring preservation of the productive capacity of the trust—is less easily defined and evaluated. Nevertheless, this
commitment to perpetuity is a clear and enforceable component of trust
land administration.

Understanding the trust mandate is crucial to achieving both of our
goals for this book. Therefore, we begin with a brief discussion of what constitutes a trust, and how that is translated into a land management mandate.

DEFINITION OF A TRUST

We begin with some legal definitions of fundamental terms:

- A *trust* is a fiduciary relationship with respect to property in which the
  person by whom the title to the property is held is subject to equitable du-
  ties to keep or use the property for the benefit of another.
- A *fiduciary relationship* places on the trustee the duty to act with strict hon-
  esty and candor and solely in the interest of the beneficiary.
- The *settlor* of a trust is the person who creates the trust.
- The *trustee* is the person holding property in trust for the beneficiary.
- The property held in trust is the *trust property.*
- The *beneficiary* is the person for whose benefit the trust property is held in
  trust.
- The *trust instrument* is the "manifestation of the intention of the settlor"
  by which property interests are vested in the trustee and beneficiary and
  by which the rights and duties of the parties (called the trust terms) are
  set forth in a manner that admits of its proof in judicial proceedings.[3]

When a trust is established, it invokes an enormous range of legally enforceable rules, defined over centuries in British common law and more recently in American common law, codified with some state-by-state variations. Most of the rules, and certainly the ones most pertinent here, define
the obligations of the trustee. Without the deep veneer of case interpretation, the trustee's obligations sound not unlike the Girl Scout oath: to proceed with undivided loyalty to the beneficiary; to deal with the beneficiary
with fairness, openness, and honesty, and to disclose fully to the beneficiary; to exercise prudence, skill, and diligence in caring for the trust; to
make the trust productive; to preserve and protect the trust property. Where
the duty to make the trust productive might conflict with the duty to preserve and care for the trust, the rule is that the trustee must act as a prudent
investor.[4]

Although it is not essential to have a formal document or agreement explicitly stating that a trust exists,[5] neither do courts presume that a trust is

implied.[6] For example, neither the absence nor the presence of the word "trust" in the language that allegedly establishes the trust is dispositive of the issue.[7] Moreover, courts decline to find an intention to establish a trust in mere "precatory words"—that is, in words that express "a suggestion or wish that the transferee should use or dispose of the property in a certain manner" or "impose merely a moral obligation."[8]

For a trust to exist, three elements must be present. First, there must be an expression of intent. No trust is created unless the settlor "manifests an intention to impose duties which are enforceable in the courts."[9] Second, there must be a beneficiary. "If the beneficiary cannot be ascertained, no trust is created."[10] Finally, there must be a property interest that exists or is ascertainable and is to be held for the benefit of the beneficiary.[11]

We translate the foregoing legalese into four general principles that guide trust land management: clarity, accountability, enforceability, and perpetuity. A key characteristic of trust principles is clarity of the goal: the trustee is obligated to manage trust resources for the benefit of the beneficiary. *Benefit* is typically defined in terms of monetary returns to the trust. The trustee must exercise prudence, skill, and diligence in making the trust productive for the specified beneficiary.[12] The principle of undivided loyalty states that the trustee is strictly forbidden from diverting trust resources to others.[13]

Clarity of goals facilitates the second characteristic of the trust mandate; *accountability.* The trustee must keep property records and accounts of receipts and disbursements, and must furnish this information to the beneficiary.[14] The trust's goals are *enforceable* because trust doctrine allows the beneficiary[15] to sue to enforce the terms of the trust. Trust obligations are fully elaborated in common law, and statutes and many centuries of judicial experience offer guidance in enforcing the trust requirements. Again, the clarity of the purpose of the trust facilitates evaluating whether the trust goals have been achieved. The final component of trust land management is *perpetuity.* Preserving the productive capacity of the corpus of the trust is one of any trustee's fundamental obligations. Trusts are not necessarily perpetual: a trust might be liquidated, for example, at the instruction of the trustor, when a beneficiary reaches a certain age or when the purposes for which the trust was established are achieved.[16] The trust purposes can also be changed or the trust terminated if the purpose for which the trust was established is no longer reasonable.[17]

The school land trusts' peculiar emphasis on perpetuity arose in the 1840s. The original school land grants did not clearly establish a perpetual trust, or even a trust.[18] Indeed, early state programs frequently utilized the granted lands for such purposes as paying teachers' salaries.[19] Perpetuity became a component of the school trust when the "permanent school funds" were established. Congress began the school lands program by granting section 16 in each township to the townships to support township schools. In 1849, during the Michigan accession, the state became the grant recipient. This arrangement required the state to establish a school fund to receive and disburse the funds to the schools. This fund evolved into an explicit embrace of perpetuity: the funds became known as permanent or perpetual school funds,[20] and states enacted increasingly elaborate provisions for supplementing the fund and for protecting it against loss and diversion.[21]

Trust land management obviously proceeds on a strikingly different footing than federal land management. The singularity and enforceability of the mandate differ radically from the enormous discretion conferred on federal land management agencies. We will make most of our comparisons between the trust mandate and the multiple-use language to which both the U.S. Forest Service and the Bureau of Land Management adhere. However, the trust's emphasis on making the trust productive for a specific beneficiary represents a point of divergence from the mandate of the National Park Service, and discussions of recreation access and preservation of amenities are germane to NPS policy as well. Like the federal land management agencies, school lands managers are occasionally accused of wasting trust resources or of running them into the ground. However, the trustee does not have discretion to assert that objectionable programs or practices somehow meet the needs of the people. Strict standards of accountability and of full disclosure inherent in the trust mean that the issue of protecting the corpus of the trust can be defined— within certain clear parameters—and answered.

There are limits to the answers we can present. Accountability in this context is, like benefit, discussed primarily in terms of money. This is not as comprehensive a standard as advocates of wilderness preservation or biodiversity would like to see. However, we believe that it is more generally useful than might first appear to opponents of commodity development. The conservative, rather standard analyses of state lands that this trust mandate invites and requires are both radical and useful. Indeed, most of the analyses offered in the rest of this book cannot be made regarding federal land management because the multiple-use mandate is so flaccid and because data regarding costs and returns are not collected. The contrasting clarity and strict record keeping of the trust management regime permit auditors to be clear and specific about whether the managers are meeting their obligations. Monitoring and enforcement are therefore possible.

GOALS OF THE BOOK

The trust principles—clarity of goal, accountability, enforceability, and perpetuity—are the core of achieving the goals of this book: to raise the visibility of state trust lands and land management, and to diversify our thinking about the hows and whys of all public resources.

The state trust lands are worthy of attention just for themselves.[22] Because they are unfamiliar, observers tend to assume that the resources involved are insignificant. This is incorrect. Some round numbers are useful for comparison: the U.S. Forest Service manages about 192 million acres; the BLM, about 270 million acres; the National Park Service, about 80 million acres; and the U.S. Fish and Wildlife Service, about 90 million acres. The state trust lands total about 135 million acres, a figure that goes up to about 153 million acres if you include the severed mineral estate. This is more than half again the Park Service total, and near what the Forest Service manages. The permanent funds produced by those resources currently exceed $27 billion, from which about $3 billion are distributed annually to the beneficiaries. An additional $1.5 billion are distributed annually directly to the beneficiaries as a result of land management revenues.[23]

Moreover, because twenty-two states are involved in trust land management, opportunities for informative comparisons abound. What is the relationship between sustainability and the trustee's obligation to preserve the productive capacity of the trust? What grazing lease terms appear to be most effective in encouraging responsible land stewardship? What are the options for funding improvements on the leasehold, and who owns these improvements when the lease expires? Who owns, and who should own, the water developed by a lessee on a school lands parcel? More recently, how can the trust be compensated for managing for resource preservation, and when is it necessary? What uses ought to be subsidized, and which pay full market value? Trust lands provide many different answers to these questions, and offer an opportunity to compare the outcomes of different policies.

Unfortunately, debates over these questions are frequently pursued on the basis of limited knowledge about the trust lands' unique history, management constraints, and role in the economic structure of state and local finance. The primary goal of this book is to provide sufficient information and analysis to enhance the ability of people—state and local officials, school superintendents, environmentalists, lessees and resource developers, and students of public resource management—to discuss state trust lands.

These lands also provide a wonderful lens for looking at public resources management more generally. Understanding even the rudiments of the twenty-two state programs provides a basis for exploring alternative public resource management strategies and philosophies. This volume will not always make direct comparisons, but it invites and provides grist for such explorations.

Managing public resources to maximize returns appears to be antithetical to what many regard as the basic purpose of public resources. It is therefore important to underscore that the state trust lands are in fact an integral part of our experience with public ownership and management of resources. The school land program reflects, and is clearly a product of, the land disposition emphasis that dominated congressional policy toward the public domain throughout the nineteenth century. The federal shift to land retention is interestingly mirrored at the state level: throughout the twentieth century, both state trust programs and congressional policies toward the public domain evolved gradually toward a commitment to retention and land management.

This knot of common history is tightened by the fact that much of the school land is still held in the separate sections originally granted, scattered like measles across lands now retained in federal ownership. Conflicts over management of trust lands arise in part as a result of changes in the policies governing neighboring federal land. The states and the federal agencies also frequently conflict over fees for access. One state official, noting that the federal government charges neither rent nor royalty for hardrock minerals extracted on federal mining claims, grouses: "It is difficult for the states to sell what the feds are giving away." Similarly, citizens accustomed to relatively free access to hunt and recreate on federal lands pressure state trust land managers for the same privileges.

The gradual shift toward retention explains why our analyses focus on a selection of western states. In line with the assumptions and practices of the early nineteenth century, most of the early joining states have sold or otherwise disposed of their granted lands. Although they were initially involved in trust land management, many states of the "Old Northwest" no longer have school sections. We identified our study states based on the membership of the Western States Land Commissioners Association (WSCLA).[24] Not all of those states manage granted lands, however; Arkansas, for example, has not been able to identify school sections still in state ownership, but has joined the association because it faces on its sovereign lands many of the management problems of the other states in the association. Nevada traded its section grants for selection rights and therefore has virtually no granted land left; consequently, it does not appear in our analysis. Nevertheless, Nevada is a member of the WSCLA for the same reasons as Arkansas. Similarly, many of the upper midwest states in the association (Minnesota and Wisconsin) manage sovereign lands or lands private owners lost in tax defaults during the Depression in part as a trust for schools. While focusing on the granted lands, we will provide data for these states when it is appropriate and interesting to do so and will omit them otherwise. The fifteen core states in our analysis are Arizona, California, Colorado, Idaho, Montana, Nebraska, New Mexico, North Dakota, Oklahoma, Oregon, South Dakota, Texas, Utah, Washington, and Wyoming.

Texas, Alaska, and Hawaii require special comment. All three manage trust lands, and all three are members of the WSCLA; but their unusual histories make it difficult to include them in the discussion in a consistent way. Texas was a republic prior to joining the United States and did not receive any granted lands from the federal government. However, the Texas constitution was based on the U.S. pattern: Article 10 of the 1845 state constitution provides both for school land grants and for a permanent school fund. In addition, Texas manages enormous on- and off-shore petroleum resources, which produce significant revenues for the permanent fund. Data from Texas are therefore included in the discussions that follow—most particularly in the discussion of oil and gas leasing.

Alaska and Hawaii joined the Union much later, in 1959. Hawaii, like Texas an independent nation prior to annexation, has peculiar trust lands that reflect the traditions of its earlier monarchy and are less relevant to the issues discussed herein than the trust nomenclature might suggest. Alaska's granted lands are more similar to the prevailing pattern, but the lands were granted as selection rights rather than as particular sections in a township. Moreover, Alaska's programs have been confused in recent years by subsequent statutes granting Alaska natives and federal agencies selection rights and by complex litigation about which lands are in or out of the trust. Unraveling the trust in those states is a book not yet researched. We will include Alaska and Hawaii as appropriate in the hope of inspiring a subsequent scholar to take up this task.

A major goal of our discussion of state programs is to establish a context for comparison between and among federal and state programs by focusing on leasing. Observers frequently overlook that the common core of most federal and state resource management programs is the lease; but access for most resource development on federal *and* state trust lands is in fact defined by some form of leasing arrangement. States approach most leasing situations with strikingly different assumptions and techniques than the federal agencies employ. Lacking the accountability and disclosure requirements that help guide the state managers, the federal agencies do not keep data in degree and format that allow direct analysis of the efficiency of federal programs. However, simply noting the diverse ways in which states do precisely the same things that the Forest Service and BLM do should expand our range of alternatives for resource management. The text, footnotes, and appendices, especially in the chapters covering timber, minerals, and agricultural land leasing are laden with details about different state leasing arrangements. In these tedious details, alternatives for federal land management are hibernating.

In spite of a rather narrow and restrictive management mandate, the states' managers appear to be more flexible than their federal counterparts in approaching their resources. They manage for all the "traditional" uses—

grazing, timber, oil, gas, coal, and hunting. But they also take an aggressive approach to developing alternative resources that might benefit the trust. State managers are inclined to think of their holdings in terms of a portfolio of assets. This requires state trustees to evaluate repositioning their assets in order to achieve their stated goal. The resulting flexibility among state trustees contrasts interestingly with public and agency assumptions at the federal level.

This juxtaposition provides many opportunities for reflecting comparatively on alternative management regimes. What (if anything) ought to be given, and what sold, is a basic conflict throughout federal resource management. The trust lands management philosophy constitutes a clear and important alternative to the multiple-use mandate that operates on most federal lands. And as we struggle now to balance efficiency and subsidies, economic sense and biological sustainability, the issues that arise on the granted lands seem ever more enlightening.

OVERVIEW

We address these issues in the following sequence. Chapter 1 briefly reviews the historical and legal evolution of trust lands policies. We describe the enormous diversity of the grants as they evolved over nearly 150 years, and then we focus on recent trust case law to explain why these lands are now collapsed into a single program category. Because the grants were made during each state's territorial and statehood negotiations, we briefly review the key 1785 and 1787 Land Ordinances, which defined that process. Then, briefly summarizing the accessions, we emphasize that the lands were not just "given" to the states by the federal government.[25] Instead, they were reserved and then granted through a bargaining process between state and nation that evolved over time. Lessons were learned and forgotten. Some states got better deals than others. Earlier states refined their constitutional language to incorporate advances made by subsequent states. It is important to understand why some states received more or less than others, and what has happened to the lands and funds.

Chapter 1 also develops the present chapter's abbreviated introduction to trust principles, to clarify how state trustees differ from either federal or private land managers. This discussion covers the effect of litigation (largely initiated by beneficiaries) on the evolution of policy. Although cases relating to specific resource management policies and procedures are discussed in subsequent chapters, the information in this chapter establishes the key features that the courts examine when deciding on specific issues.

Chapter 2 builds on the trust notion by treating the trust as a system with four parts: (1) lands and resources, (2) land management, (3) revenues produced and distributed to the beneficiaries, and (4) the permanent fund. There is a tendency, especially among aficionados of federal land management agencies, but also noticeable among state trustees themselves, to begin and end discussions with the land. Chapter 2 provides a general overview of which states have what different types of lands and resources. However, land is but one part of the trust system. Accordingly, we also focus on the resources produced from state trust lands—how much revenue each resource produces, why the source of the money matters, where the revenues go, and how the state agencies allocate funds and personnel to achieve the revenues. The discussion, while presenting only a single year's data, is based on a comparative set of states' revenues, leased areas, and permanent fund performances over the last twenty years.

Standard methods to analyze the management of trust resources are described in Chapter 3. Our goal in the chapter is to provide a theoretical basis to answer both conceptual and practical questions about trust lands management. If that is not your goal—if, for example, you just want to look at different ways to lease grazing and crop lands—you may not need to labor through Chapter 3. Some of what appears in subsequent chapters may then make less sense than it otherwise might, but if you are primarily interested in individual or specific resource programs, go directly to the general information in Chapters 1 and 2 and then proceed to the appropriate resource chapters. The goal of Chapter 3 is to provide enough theory and technique to enable the interested bystander to answer two general questions. First, are the day-to-day and lease-to-lease decisions efficient? Second, has the manager tied resource management and capital management together in a way that serves the overall goals of the trust?

The first section of Chapter 3 uses the production function as a way to describe the management (land and permanent fund) and the revenues as a trust system. It starts with the fundamental but frequently unstated observation that the trustee does not develop resources to produce a return for the trust; she *leases* the resource to a private developer who intends to make a profit. The discussion focuses on the use of leases to allocate risk and reward between the landowner and the resource developer, and it uses portfolio theory as one method to analyze the mix of risks faced by the trust.

The second section introduces tools for evaluating whether the manager is efficiently managing the trust's assets. It identifies two important measures of agency performance: (1) revenues received per acre leased for a specific use; and (2) revenues received per full-time employee in each program. Because personnel expenses are the major outlay of all state trust lands offices, the second criterion is particularly useful in assessing the efficiency of each operation. It is a short hop from asking about efficient allocation of lands and personnel to inquiring whether the state land office is overfunded, underfunded, or funded just right.

Finally, Chapter 3 discusses the states' permanent funds, asking how the trustee makes tradeoffs between short-term and long-term priorities. The discussion emphasizes first the role of interest and discount rates, and second several models from macroeconomics that portray choices between the preservation versus the consumption of trust resources. The goal of this rather dense discussion is to achieve some insight into tradeoffs between current and future development.

The first four chapters are, in sum, introductory. They provide a smattering of history and historical context; a descriptive overview of lands, resources, and management programs; and the general analytic tools necessary for analyzing of specific resource management programs, which are the subject of the rest of the volume.

Chapters 4, 5, and 6 focus on the management of familiar commodities in the trust context. Each chapter presents the same basic information about the state programs: revenues produced, returns to the beneficiary, number of leases, and acres involved. In addition, each chapter has a different theme and a different emphasis. Grazing and cropland leasing focuses on the relationship between the government and the lessee. Implicit in this discussion is a contrast between the evolving state–lessee interaction and the long-standing relationship between federal agencies and grazing permittees. Because one of the points of this chapter is to demonstrate the importance of lease terms in allocating risk and benefits between landowner and resource developer, we will pay detailed attention to lease specifics in this context. The timber discussion in Chapter 5 concentrates on forestry programs in four states and explores the tension between benefit for the beneficiary and benefit for the general public. This chapter deals less with the minutiae of timber sales than with interpretation of crucial litigation. Several cases, most specifically the dispute over timber contract buyouts of the early 1980s, raise interesting questions about who benefits when a bureaucracy has sufficient legislative discretion to pursue its own definition of the "general public benefit." Chapter 6 focuses on minerals management and analyzes long-term versus short-term benefits in the context of permanent fund management. Because federal statutes have colored so much of the discussion of minerals management, Chapter 6 pays extensive attention to simple concepts of minerals development that prevail regardless of the controlling legal regime. Chapter 7 plunges into less familiar territory to discuss new management strategies and emerging issues in state trust lands management. The Epilogue concludes with speculation on the lessons of these analyses for improved trust lands management and for rethinking public resource management more generally.

Grazing and crop land leases are the subject of Chapter 4. The story of state lands leasing is dominated, not unlike federal leasing, by tension between the lessor and the lessee. One factor that makes state cropland and grazing land leasing so interesting, however, is that the pattern of control has radically shifted in many states: whereas lessee needs, preferences, and priorities dominated state leasing programs for much of their history, following major litigation, recent emphasis has shifted toward procuring maximum benefit for the beneficiary. It is instructive to notice which specific aspects of the leases have been altered to achieve that result.

Cropland and grazing leasing programs are important for three other reasons, as well. First, these leases cover the vast majority of the surface acreage in all the trust land states. Second, the grazing lease fees and procedures that the states use are directly comparable to those used by the federal government. Third, all the detail on apparently obscure lease terms underscores the diversity of important tools available to grazing land lessors and, by implication, highlights the aridity of the discussion at the federal level, which focuses almost exclusively on fees. In many cases in the west, state lands are virtually undifferentiated from surrounding federal lands; yet the states charge anywhere from less to more than three times what the federal government does for grazing. This chapter examines the states' leasing programs to gain insight not only into federal systems but also into the differences—perceived and actual—among the states' programs and between the states and the federal government. The material in this chapter provides perspective for those analyzing crop and grazing leases on all types of public lands.

The chapter begins with a general theory of crop and grazing leases. It is followed by a descriptive overview of contemporary crop and grazing lease programs. Because of the contours of the debate at the federal level, we pay close attention to current fees and the systems used by the states to determine the fees charged. Each of the lease provisions (lease term, renewal procedures, subleasing) in this section has been identified in other studies as affecting both the value of the lease to the lessee and the fair market value of the resources leased. The final section uses the theoretical models from Chapter 3 to determine where the states have been successful in meeting their trust obligations, and where (and in what types of situations) the states have fallen short. Then, with an eye toward protracted attempts at the federal level to reform grazing leasing, we proffer an "ideal" leasing system based on the strengths and weaknesses of the states' experience.

The states' trust land forestry programs are analyzed in Chapter 5. Although most state trusts include a forestry component, timber management is only a major program in four states: Washington, Idaho, Montana and Oregon. Not surprisingly, much of the debate mirrors the issues at the federal level. Tension between the trustee's efforts to manage for the benefit of the beneficiary and increasing pressure to manage to achieve "general public benefit" is the dominant theme of the chapter. The issues revolve around protecting existing stands of old-growth timber, the practices on production forests, cumulative effects of state timber harvests in combination with those on federal and private industry lands, and the protection of habitat for endangered species.

Although the debate has familiar contours, state trust land forestry provides a perspective to trust lands management different from that of other trust resources. The state trust timber lands are unlike agricultural lands because they frequently are held in contiguous or consolidated areas instead of in dispersed sections. This pattern is a result of in-lieu land selections, land exchanges with the Forest Service in the 1920s, and lands managed by the state as a result of tax forfeitures. With these aggregated parcels comes increased public awareness of noncommodity values associated with these lands. Further, because of the relatively high value of these lands to the trust, both in standing inventory and productive capability, the beneficiaries are often more observant of their management.

The first section of the timber chapter provides a descriptive overview of the states' timber programs. The second section introduces the tension between general public benefit and benefit for the beneficiary, by focusing on recent litigation that appears to draw rather clear lines that preclude consideration of general benefit in relation to trust lands. We then begin to erode that clarity by focusing on specific wording regarding the beneficiary in relevant state constitutions and specific mandates about forest management in state statutes. The third section further erodes the hard lines by looking more closely at specific decisions made in timber management programs. Even when the decision is made to manage a parcel for maximum profit, choices about the nature of the product to be sustained, the time frame and periodicity of returns, and the discount rate to be employed all create opportunities within an income-maximizing regime for general public benefits.

Minerals—hardrock and energy resources (primarily oil, gas, and coal)—are discussed in Chapter 6. New Mexico, California, Texas, and Wyoming derive the largest portion of their revenues from subsurface resources, and most states have at least a small minerals program. In this discussion we focus on two themes: the interplay between federal and state regimes; and intergenerational equity. The trust resource system, which includes both the land and mineral resources *and* the permanent fund, provides a wonderful opportunity to discuss the tension between short-term and long-term priorities. In the context of the trust system, we can ask whether it makes any sense to develop minerals when the receipts from such development wither in the permanent fund. A leitmotif is a substantial broadening of the familiar federal toolbox for achieving minerals policy goals.

Hardrock minerals are treated in the first part of the chapter. Hardrock minerals, sometimes called metalliferous minerals, can generally be thought of as those that glitter (copper, gold, and silver), although states have—or have had—about forty different minerals in either prospecting or production leases. These resources are not major revenue producers except in Arizona, Utah, Wyoming, and Montana. But the field is ripe with alternatives and comparisons, nonetheless. State hardrock minerals programs are quite different from the equivalent federal programs, which proceed under the much lamented 1872 General Mining Act. In fact, the state hardrock programs are similar to the federal energy minerals program defined by the Mineral Lands Leasing Act of 1920.

Energy minerals—oil, gas, coal, and geothermal—are treated in the second part of the chapter. Oil and gas are the most productive resources in four states: New Mexico, Oklahoma, Texas, and Wyoming. Coal revenues are important in Colorado, Montana, North Dakota, and Utah. California receives the vast majority of its trust revenues from geothermal steam. We examine the states' experiences in an attempt to gain insight into the critical decisions that the state as trustee must make when allocating benefits between present and future generations. The states' energy minerals programs provide an excellent study of the tension between generating present revenues versus future ones. Using the notion of the trust corpus as the repository of asset values, we ask whether the trust is better off if the minerals stay in the ground or if they are converted into money and placed in the permanent fund. Finally, plucking provisions from all the states, we identify principles for an "ideal" mineral leasing system.

Chapter 7 departs from what might be considered traditional resources—grazing and cropland lands, forestry, and energy and hardrock minerals—to discuss emerging strategies and issues in state trust lands management. Many of the emerging issues involve strategies for more aggressive management of trust resources and the new controversies that those strategies have inspired. Forced by increased emphasis on returns for the beneficiary, changing politics, and alterations in public taste, trustees are reviewing traditional programs and developing new resources. Our discussion focuses first on several programs that illustrate this newly aggressive posture of most trustees. We begin with a discussion of permanent fund management, introducing its size and extent, relating fund management to land and resource management, and then discussing its role as a repository to maintain asset value from nonrenewable resources. Inflation and restrictive investment rules are discussed in detail. A second resource currently receiving increased management attention is water. State trustees are emerging as significant players in state water adjudications in several states. Finally, states are developing diverse programs for managing what might be considered "new" resources. Some, traditionally regarded as "minor," such as harvesting of mushrooms, cones, ferns, and boughs, have the potential to become important revenue producers. Of all the new and nontraditional uses, perhaps the most difficult for students of federal land management to think about is the states' aggressive entry into commercial and urban land development. The trustee has a number of options for balancing risk and returns in designing a commercial lands program. Our discussion cannot explore this topic fully, but it emphasizes the options and choices a trustee must make. Telecommunications sites are a major resource for commercial development. A brief discussion of the current status of debate in this area highlights the conflict between the federal government's tendency to subsidize development and the state's attempts to make the resource productive for the trust.

A second set of discussions in Chapter 7 deals with the response that these more aggressive management strategies have elicited, especially from environmental groups. We consider the trustees' responsibilities under the Endangered Species Act, the growing controversy over providing recreation and hunting access to trust lands, and management of trust resources for preservation purposes. When we inquire how the trust might be compensated, as it must be, for such management, we again confront the issue of general benefit versus benefit for the beneficiary. This time it cuts to the core of central federal land management debates: Who actually benefits from, and who pays for, preservation policies? What ought to be paid for at fair market value, and what subsidized?

The unifying theme of this chapter is the concept of the trust lands as a portfolio of assets. Contemporary state trust managers are less and less likely to be trained and steeped in the forestry tradition and the biology orientation that dominates at the federal level. The state managers view their resources as "assets" and are willing to reposition them, to alter land uses, and even to trade in land holdings, as a result of changing public priorities. Land exchanges, sales, and transfers are of growing importance in managing these portfolios. This does not necessarily lead to economic efficiency or profit, and it is not likely at first blush to find favor among environmentalists. However, the results of such proclivities have had some interesting and clearly salubrious effects in some states. Differences and changes in perspective regarding what constitutes a valuable resource and what constitutes a public resource are well explored in this context.

Three Levels of Discussion and Analysis

The book addresses state lands at three levels of analysis. The first level consists of a descriptive overview of the trust lands—a general introduction to the lands, their resources, their history, and their management—sufficient to allow the uninitiated reader to understand the basic system. Most of this very general material is contained in Chapters 1 and 2. A second analytical tier examines resource management issues and techniques in detail, using state-by-state comparisons. Interested citizens, practitioners in state lands management (such as land office staffs), legislators, and beneficiaries will find this material useful in any effort to understand the pros and cons of current management alternatives. Simply understanding that public resource managers do similar things—such as leasing pasture or defining access to minerals—with an astounding variety of provisions and goals is an important step toward expanding the vocabulary we use in describing and debating public resource priorities and practice. Topics covered include the nature and extent of leasing procedures and how leasing is conducted at the operational level; we also set out the comparisons needed to analyze the states' practices in relation to federal and private arrangements. This discussion proceeds resource by resource, in Chapters 4 through 7.

The third level of analysis is primarily conceptual: school trust lands are different from but more deeply rooted in the history and political traditions of the nation than federal lands and resource management. We should know this and think about what it means. In so doing, we encounter vital questions relating to what the lands are for, the tension between short- and long-term management, and the spectrum between private and public management techniques. These fundamental questions emerge frequently in contemporary state land management debates: episodic pressure on state land commissioners to sell trust lands to lessees; the role of the lands and their permanent funds in state educational finance; the importance of profit maximization in their management; and the stresses between rural areas, where the lands are located, and the increasingly urban areas that benefit from their revenues. They are also at the heart of contemporary debate about federal land management. These questions are woven into the discussion throughout the book and are emphasized in the concluding Chapter 8.

We have been misinterpreted in the past, so, having gone on at some length about what we are trying to say, we wish to emphasize what we are *not* saying. We are not advocating that federal lands be turned into state land trusts. We think about such things in the shower but have not analyzed such an unlikely future step in any detail. Our starting point is that we should know more about *all* of our public lands and land management traditions in order to choose the tools and perspectives that are most appropriate for meeting the diverse needs of a diverse citizenry in the next century.

CHAPTER ONE

History of the School Land Grant Program

The history of the school land grant program is long, complex, and important. It is woven deeply into the process by which the nation was formed. Debate over western lands began during the Revolution, and the fundamental statute establishing the school lands program was enacted under the Articles of Confederation in 1785.[1] We have no intention of telling the whole tale here. This chapter summarizes just enough of the story to make two seemingly contradictory observations credible. First, we introduce the great variety among the twenty-two state programs. Second, having emphasized the diversity, we explain the peculiar mandate—trust management—that causes all these lands and programs to look alike, or at least similar, to the casual observer.

To achieve these purposes, the chapter proceeds in three major parts. The first two underscore the roots of the diversity of the land grant program. We begin by placing the land grants into the context of the times in which they were debated, by offering a brief overview of the Articles of Confederation, the General Land Ordinances of 1785 and 1787, and the process by which territories were formed and became states. By dividing the accession process into four periods, we emphasize changes in the evolving land grant program, concluding with a comparison of the rather barren language of the initial Ohio accession (1803) and the long and complex history and provisions of New Mexico's accession (1910).

With that context established, the second part of the chapter identifies specific differences that emerged as the land grant program unfolded over more than a century. It focuses on the evolution of the language affecting key aspects of the grants: how much land was granted, to whom and for what, whether the lands were to be leased or sold, and how the permanent fund emerged. It is inconceivable that a policy that was defined and implemented incrementally over the whole of the nineteenth century would not vary enormously from start to finish. The first two discussions associate that variation with the political debates of the day—most particularly, slavery and the gradual evolution from federal land disposition to land retention and management—and establish the details and implications of the resulting diversity.

The third part of the chapter focuses on the apparent similarity of the grants, emphasizing the most pervasive commonalty: the trust mandate. We argue that viewing the school land grants as trusts arises out of the New

Mexico and Arizona accession and has gradually been applied retrospectively (and with increasing clarity) to all the grants. That background having been established, the rest of the book explores the meaning of the trust mandate for managing school and granted lands.

ROOTS OF DIVERSITY: THE ACCESSION PROCESS[2]

Developing a Formula for Admitting New States: Land Ordinances of 1785 and 1787

The idea of land grants for schools was just one of a number of concerns revolving around the western lands before, during, and after the Revolution. The need to resolve some of those issues was given urgency in the early 1780s by several major events, the most pertinent here being the acceptance of the Virginia land cession[3] by Congress in 1783. Congress was obliged[4] to announce policies governing the disposition of the lands that had been ceded. In two statutes remarkable for their brevity and durability, Congress did so.[5]

The General Land Ordinance of 1785 provided for the rectangular survey[6] and sale of western lands. It also initiated the program of land grants for schools, providing that lot number 16 in every township would be reserved "for the maintenance of public schools within the said township." The Northwest Ordinance, passed two years later, provided a system for territorial governance and transition to statehood. As set forth in the Northwest Ordinance, the path to statehood was to be marked by logical steps and cooperation between the federal government and the state-in-making.[7] After a region had been explored and settled, it was to be "organized" by an act of Congress, at which point it would become a United States Territory. A governor, a secretary, and three judges would then be appointed by the President. Once the population of free adult male settlers reached 5,000, the Territory could elect a legislature and send a delegate to Congress. The territory was still controlled by the federally appointed officials at this point, and its delegate could speak but not vote.[8] A Territory could not be admitted to the Union until its population reached 60,000, according to the ordinance. At that time, popular opinion willing, people of the Territory could send a petition to Congress through the Territorial legislature or its delegate in Congress, or both, requesting admission.[9] If the petition was favorably received, Congress would pass an *enabling act* authorizing a constitutional convention in the state-to-be. Then the state constitutional convention had to meet and draft a governing document, which would be subjected to a popular referendum in the Territory. If that passed, the constitution would be sent to Congress for its acceptance, after which the state would be admitted on an equal footing with all others.[10]

Among the most important elements of the new states' constitutions were the articles outlining the method of distribution of specific quantities of public land. Land grants to new states were an important component of Congress's efforts to keep control of the accession process while resolving a host of concrete difficulties. The cost of policing the territories was considerable; and the larger the territories, the bigger the cost. Who would foot the bill? What would prevent the West from breaking away to form a new nation? How were the many land claims to be dealt with, from Indian tribal claims to those of squatters and miners? How could these claims be reconciled with the demands of large-scale capital ventures such as those of the land speculators? If new territories were to be developed, who would benefit from that development? Was there any way to guarantee a return to the original states? Not only did the states from which the western lands had been ceded expect some return for their cession, but the federal government had every intention of making the distribution and administration of the public domain a self-supporting, even lucrative project.[11]

These crucial issues were resolved differently in different phases of accession. The timing and contours of states' admission was colored by continually changing national politics. Describing the admissions process briefly in terms of phases reminds us of the political issues surrounding the development of school land grant programs.

The Four Phases of Statehood Accession

PHASE ONE: ORIGINAL COLONIAL STATES

The first phase of statehood accession began in 1785 and ended in 1803. This phase concerns us least. During it, the thirteen original colonies became states in the Union, and three others (Vermont, Tennessee, and Kentucky) were soon added.[12] This first phase is chiefly relevant to our discussion of school land grants because the western land cessions that occurred created the "original" public domain.[13] Seven of the original states had colonial charters granting them lands extending to the Pacific Ocean.[14] The federally controlled public domain originated from the western lands that these seven states ceded to the federal government soon after the Revolution. None of the original thirteen colonies contained any federal public domain lands, and none of the phase-one states received any land grants at accession.

PHASE TWO: NORTHWEST TERRITORY AND
MISSOURI COMPROMISE

Table 1-1 summarizes key aspects of the next three phases of the accession process, showing when each state joined the Union, how much school land was granted to each state, and some basic detail about grants and acces-

TABLE 1-1. Phases in the Development of State Trust Land Grants

Phase	Entered Union	State	Acres Granted*	Historical Notes
Phase II: Northwest Territory and Missouri Compromise	1803	Ohio	724,266	(a) Part of NW Terr.
	1812	Louisiana	807,271	(a)
	1816	Indiana	668,578	(a) Part of NW Terr.
	1817	Mississippi	824,213	(a) Part of GA cession
	1818	Illinois	996,320	(a) Part of NW Terr. and VA cession
	1819	Alabama	911,627	(a) Part of GA cession
	1820	Maine	0	(e) (1) (2) Missouri Compromise 1820
	1821	Missouri	1,221,813	(a)
	1836	Arkansas	933,778	(a) (1) (6)
	1837	Michigan	1,021,867	(a) (1) (5) Part of NW Terr.
Phase III: Sectional divisions and territorial expansion	1845	Florida	975,307	(a) (1) (6) Same enabling act as Iowa
	1845	Texas	0	(e) (1) (3) Annexed by U.S. in 1848
	1846	Iowa	1,000,679	(a) (1) (5) Same enabling act as FL
	1848	Wisconsin	982,329	(a)
	1850	California	5,534,293	(a) (1) (4) (5) Admitted as part of Comp. of 1850
	1858	Minnesota	2,874,951	(a)
	1859	Oregon	3,399,360	(b) (1) (5)
	1861	Kansas	2,907,520	(b) (1) (5)
	1863	W. Virginia	0	(e) (1) (2) Admitted as a free state during Civil War
	1864	Nevada	2,061,967	(b) Admitted with low population in 1864 to ensure Lincoln's victory in national election.

TABLE 1-1. Continued

Phase	Entered Union	State	Acres Granted*	Historical Notes
Phase IV: The Arid West	1867	Nebraska	2,730,951	(b) Originally part of LA Terr.
	1876	Colorado	3,685,618	(b)
	1889	Montana	5,198,258	(b) (1) (7) (8)
	1889	N. Dakota	2,495,396	(b) (7)
	1889	S. Dakota	2,733,084	(b) (7)
	1889	Washington	2,376,391	(b) (7)
	1890	Idaho	2,963,698	(b) (1) (5)
	1890	Wyoming	3,472,872	(b) (1) (6)
	1896	Utah	5,844,196	(c)
	1907	Oklahoma	2,044,000	(d) (1) (9)
	1912	New Mexico	8,711,324	(c) (9)
	1912	Arizona	8,093,156	(c) (9)

Notes:
a. Received section 16 of every township for common school grant.
b. Received sections 16 and 36 of every township for common school grant.
c. Received sections 16, 36, 2, and 32 of every township for common school grant.
d. Oklahoma got 2 sections and then indemnity for Indian lands to be used for common schools.
e. Did not receive common school grant lands from the federal government.

1. Organized and incorporated territories, but no enabling act.
2. Previously parts of other states or territories; no enabling act.
3. Previously an independent republic.
4. Previously unorganized, under military rule.
5. "Tennessee Plan" states; elected Senators and Representatives before admission to statehood (none were allowed to take their seats before admission).
6. Drafted state constitutions before admission, but did not elect Senators and Representatives.
7. In 1864, these "Omnibus States" were organized by a single act of Congress.
8. Parts of MT Territory belonged at one time to OR Territory, ID Territory, and Dakota Territory.
9. Numerous enabling acts for these territories, starting with Compromise of 1850.

Source: M. N. Orfield, Land Grants to the States 44–45 (1911), and P. Gates, The History of Public Land Law Development 804 (1986).

sions in individual states. The notable increase over the course of the period in the acres granted is discussed in the next section.

The second phase of the statehood process is critical because, during this period, a "formula" for the rest of the statehood process was established. None of the phase-one states had received land grants as provided in the Ordinance of 1785, so the formula is key to our topic: until Ohio it was unclear whether the promise of lands for schools made twenty-eight years earlier would be honored.[15] The 1803 admission of Ohio was later seen as the "proving ground for statehood."[16]

Slavery played an important role in the admissions histories of phase-two states, especially in connection with the timing of admissions. Slavery had been forbidden in the Northwest Territory; but in 1818, when the citizens of the territory adjacent to Illinois applied for admission to the Union under the name of Missouri, the slavery issue deadlocked Congress.[17] The impasse was eventually broken by the Missouri Compromise of 1820, a formula that attempted to preserve the balance of power between slave and free states. Arkansas and Michigan were the last pair of phase-two states to enter the Union under the Missouri Compromise.

PHASE THREE: SECTORAL DIVISIONS AND TERRITORIAL EXPANSION

The Civil War and territorial expansion defined the third phase of the state-making process, which extended from 1845 to 1864. The Missouri Compromise did not hold, partly because the dramatic territorial gains made during this period were predominantly in the South. In its settlement with Mexico after the war of 1846–1848, the U.S. acquired territories that later became the states of California, Nevada, Utah, Arizona, New Mexico, and Texas. The debate over slavery in Mexican Cession lands, which culminated in the fragile Compromise of 1850, had hardly subsided when it erupted anew in the Kansas and Nebraska Territories.[18] While the slavery issue sped up the process of statehood for California and Nevada, it slowed it down for Texas and Nebraska. California was admitted without an enabling act as part of the Compromise of 1850, and Nevada was admitted in spite of its sparse population in 1864 to ensure an electoral victory for the Republican party.[19] Texas, by contrast, was ready for statehood as early as 1836, according to historian Paul Gates, but was not admitted to the Union until 1845 because the debate over whether slavery would be allowed there was so acrimonious.[20] Texas as a former independent republic included no federal public domain lands and hence received no school land grants.

PHASE FOUR: THE ARID WEST

After the Civil War, the fourth and final phase of the statehood process played out. The eradication of Native American rights was accelerated during this period as well, with the relocation program of the 1830s setting a precedent for the later, even more brutal military campaigns on the Great Plains. Movement by settlers to the West accelerated, with towns sprouting up on the Pacific Coast and railroads itching to complete the tracks from New York to San Francisco. The process of "closing of the frontier"[21] led to significant changes in congressional attitudes toward its western domain. The long-held presumptions that federal land ownership was temporary and that federal authorities were confined to determining the shape of land disposal programs eroded under two forces: eastern pressure to retain and manage apparently dwindling national resources, and growing recognition that some areas of the arid west were not susceptible to family farming.

That four of the new states—Montana, North Dakota, South Dakota, and Washington—were admitted under a single "omnibus" enabling act might suggest that the admission process had nevertheless become routine.[22] For other states, however, admission in this phase was far from simple. Four of the states that had not gained statehood by the 1880s had been locked for decades in a struggle with Congress for "equal footing" within the Union.[23] In New Mexico and Arizona, a significant component of this struggle involved the large Hispanic and Native American populations in the territories; in Utah, a major hindrance to statehood was the territory's Mormonism.[24]

POSTSCRIPT: ALASKA AND HAWAII

After a forty-two–year interlude, Congress voted to admit Alaska and Hawaii to the Union in 1958 and 1959, respectively. The first statehood bill for Alaska had been introduced in 1916, and for Hawaii in 1919, but World War II was over before both states held plebiscites that showed strong support for statehood. Not until 1956 did both adopt state constitutions. Old ugliness reared its head: southern members of Congress, locked in final battles to defend segregation, were unenthusiastic about admitting racially diverse states unlikely to support their position.[25]

Throughout the pendency of Alaska's statehood quest, the federal government continued to own more than 99 percent of Alaskan land. Moreover, although the normal federal land disposition statutes were ostensibly in effect in Alaska, in reality much of the land had been reserved or withdrawn from entry and was unavailable for settlement. Instead of granting sections in townships, the statehood bill for Alaska gave the state twenty-five years to choose 102.5 million acres of unreserved land and fifty years to select an additional 800,000 acres of national forest land near communities. The value of those selection rights was significantly reduced when state selections were halted and both the federal government and the state's Native Americans moved to the front of the land-grab queue with almost 200 million acres of selection rights, as a result of the Alaskan Native Claims Selection Act.

Hawaii joined the United States after half a century as an independent constitutional monarchy and another 50 years as a territory of the United States. The statehood act ratified a trust established on royal lands to support schools and returned to the new state all the lands held by the U.S. at the time of statehood. Hence, Hawaii has a school land trust, but it is not based on the cadastral system so familiar in the lower forty-eight, finding its roots and traditions rather in the Great Mahale of 1848. The trust lands held for the benefit of schools are the result of royal prerogative and bequest and will not be treated here.[26]

Ohio and New Mexico Compared[27]

Ohio was the first state to go through the process described in the Northwest Ordinance; and for most purposes important to this book, New Mexico can be considered the last.[28] We use a review of both the process and the land grant program in these two states to illustrate the complexity of any individual state accession and the changes that occurred over time.

OHIO

Ohio's enabling act was passed by Congress on April 30, 1802, just as its population reached 60,000.[29] Delegates drafted a constitution, which was approved by Congress; and after some negotiation, Ohio's admission was approved on March 3, 1803. Section 16 in every township, was "granted to the inhabitants of such township, for the use of schools." And in language that became a fixture of future compacts, "where such section has been sold, granted, or disposed of, other lands equivalent thereto and most contiguous to the same" were to be selected.[30] In addition, one-twentieth of the net proceeds from lands sold by Congress were to be used within the state to build roads laid out by Congress.[31] This early revenue sharing also became a fixture, although later in the process states received the 5 percent grants outright.

Throughout the process, in return for these grants, Congress required that the state pass an ordinance "irrevocable without the consent of the United States" stating that all land sold by Congress within the state would remain exempt from state taxation for five years from the date of sale. Subsequent irrevocable compacts required in addition that the state waive all title and interest in public domain lands within the state, and that it never interfere with congressional plans for the "primary disposal of the soil."[32]

The Ohio formula only became known as such after the fact. Ohio's experience was disputed and complicated, underscoring issues that were live in the 1780s and not resolved by the beginning of the nineteenth century. Some people opposed the whole idea of granting parts of the federal public domain to individual states. Their position rested on the argument that the public lands belonged to all American citizens equally, and that giving them to individual states amounted to expropriation. To the Federalist governor of the Ohio Territory, the debate over section 16 in each township for schools was meaningless, since the grant had already been made in the Ordinance of 1785.[33]

For many states, in fact, the statehood formula as outlined by the Northwest Ordinance and Ohio's precedent was either insufficient or inapplicable. Fifteen states entered the Union with no enabling acts at all.[34] Utah, by contrast, had five enabling acts and argued for nearly fifty years with Congress over Mormon priority in Utah government and over polygamy in Mormon society before it finally gained admission in 1896.[35] New Mexico, caught in the crossfire of national politics, had to wait more than sixty years following its initial 1850 enabling act before it joined the Union with Arizona in 1912. California and Texas were independent republics before they joined the United States; and a number of states, including Utah and Texas, had to resolve boundary questions before the Territories could become states. Thus, while the Ohio precedent was vital, it was merely the foundation upon which the evolving statehood formula could be built.

NEW MEXICO

New Mexico's admission history is exceptional. New Mexico made eleven bids for statehood before it was finally admitted. It wrote three separate constitutions, and fourteen other states overtook New Mexico on its path to statehood. New Mexico finally came into the Union under the same enabling act as Arizona. While the terms under which it finally achieved statehood reflect the standard provisions that had endured and evolved during the process, it also shows more clearly than most the interference of national political issues that complicated implementation of the Ohio formula.[36] The seemingly endless delays led State Delegate Fergusson to request Congress to give some of the newly available land to the schools, even before New Mexico was admitted as a state. Accordingly, the Fergusson Act of 1898 allowed New Mexico to select and make use of half its school land grants immediately, while the other half would be reserved until New Mexico was officially admitted to the Union.[37] When its land grants were finally selected, four sections per township were designated for the support of public schools. This amounted in total to 8,711,324 acres (compared to Montana's 5,198,258 acres and Ohio's 724,266 acres).

In contrast to the brief provisions relating to school land grants to Ohio, Congress considered New Mexico's grants in six lengthy sections of the enabling act.[38] The school lands figure most prominently in §§ 6, 9, and 10 of the act. The § 6 grants, in addition to setting aside the previously reserved sections 16 and 36, included sections 2 and 32. Mineral lands were excluded, and sections included in national forests were to be administered as part of the forest, with the appropriate portion of forest receipts going to the common school fund, until indemnity lands were selected. The act's § 9 made the ancient grant of 5 percent of the proceeds of sales of public lands lying within the state.[39] Finally, § 10 specifically provided that lands granted to the state were to be held "in trust" and declared that it was the duty of the Attorney General of the United States to enforce in court the provisions relating to the application and disposition of the lands, the products thereof, and the funds derived therefrom.[40]

Perhaps because New Mexico's enabling act contained uncharacteristically lengthy provisions regarding the school lands, the New Mexico's state constitution added little on the topic.[41] The state constitution described the management of the school fund in less detail than the enabling act and established a formula for its distribution.[42] Article 13 established a minimum price of $10 per acre for school lands not contiguous to other state lands and prohibited their sale for ten years after statehood. Meanwhile, § 2 provided for a Commissioner of Public Lands to have "direction, control, care and disposition of all public lands, under the provisions of the acts of Congress relating thereto and such regulations as may be provided by law."

Adoption of the New Mexico enabling act and constitution marked the end of the accession period. The early enabling acts had merely granted the land, and the early state constitutions had left major issues to the legislature to sort out. Halfway through the nineteenth century, the states were concerned merely to provide for the establishment and preservation of a permanent fund whose income was to be devoted to supporting common schools. Later state constitutions made provisions regarding the sale price of school lands, the securities in which the proceeds of the sales could be invested,[43] the management of the fund, and the like.[44] Although a clear core to the accession process and the land grant program is discernable across the decades, it evolved differently in the bargains struck by states over time.

DIVERSITY ON THE GROUND: THE EVOLVING
PROVISIONS FOR SCHOOL LANDS

The changing context surrounding the phases of accession is reflected in the evolving provisions for school lands. Beneath the constant reiteration of basic themes—the reservation and grant of land to support common schools, and the compact irrevocable between the federal and state governments—considerable change occurred in language and focus. We will look at the emergence of that diversity by exploring the evolving program, emphasizing significant changes in four key aspects of the grant: the amount of land granted, the recipients and beneficiaries named, the rights of subsequent disposition conveyed, and the permanence of the trust established. The accession process consisted of a series of hard fought and carefully negotiated bargains.[45] In every instance, as the "compact irrevocable" language underscores, statehood was an actual exchange whose terms and conditions were explicitly stated in the documents.[46]

How Much Land Was Granted?

Because the courts and others have tended to interpret the grants on the presumption that Congress was constantly guarding against state mis-and malfeasance with ever more stringent grant requirements, it is well to begin with the most obvious pattern in the program: increasing federal generosity to the states.

As the nineteenth century progressed, school land grants to the states became larger and larger. Ohio and all phase-two states thereafter until the Oregon enabling act in 1848 received one section per township. After 1848, starting with California and Oregon, all states received two sections per township. Then, at the Utah accession near the close of phase four, four sections per township were granted. That standard continued through the 1910 grants to Arizona and New Mexico.[47]

Table 1-1 shows the dramatic increases in acres granted that accompanied the shifts from one to two and from two to four sections. One could argue that generosity had little to do with the shift from two sections to four—that Utah, Nevada, Arizona, and New Mexico were given four sections because the land was arid and more of it was needed to achieve the purpose of the grant (namely, support for schools). Certainly the land is more arid and less valuable for the style of family farming idealized in the nineteenth century.[48]

Perhaps a more accurate explanation than generosity involves the growing political power of the new western states. Nevertheless, Congress was granting more and more land in an ever-expanding variety of land grants and donations. Salt licks were included in the Ohio grant; and soon swamplands and land to support colleges, universities, hospitals, schools for the deaf and dumb, and other public buildings were added. Beginning in 1841, middle-aged states and all new ones received selection rights for 500,000 acres of land. In many states this land was added to the school trust. Many states also voluntarily added to the fund the land they received from salt spring grants and from the swampland drainage program.[49] It is difficult to describe succinctly this pattern of increasing openhandedness, because grants to states were so munificent, so frequent, and so frequently made retroactive. Further, many grants were made to the states to be regranted to developers of internal improvements, such as railroads.[50]

A variation on the increasing federal generosity theme manifested toward the end of the grant/accession period involved Congress's inability to protect the federal government's growing interest in western land from the states. In at least two areas, Congress clearly abandoned the effort to protect what were, as the decades wore on, increasingly viewed as its own resources.

The first area, "in lieu selections," did not vary over the accession period. As early as the time of the sale of land to the Ohio Company in 1785, which first put the Ordinance of 1785 into operation,[51] experience with squatters[52] was extensive. In every school grant, Congress provided that, if the land in the designated section(s) was previously occupied, the grantee was authorized to select land nearby in lieu of the granted land.[53] Initially, Congress tried to exempt from the school land grant process the growing federal land reservations for forests, parks, and Indians. The omnibus enabling act for North and South Dakota, Montana, and Washington, and the later Utah enabling act, clearly state that the provisions granting sections in every township do not apply to federal land reservations.[54] This provision cost those states a good deal of land. In 1910, Arizona and New Mexico were successful in having that provision specifically disavowed. Hence, as we have seen, New Mexico and Arizona were able to select land in lieu of sections contained in national forests.

Second, Congress was not particularly effective in protecting its rights to minerals. Not until 1866 did Congress first exempt mineral lands from the school grant provisions. Thereafter, Utah and Oklahoma successfully bargained with Congress to procure minerals as part of the school land program.[55] Moreover, Congress rejected the Supreme Court's aid in covering its tracks. Although Congress did not reserve minerals in the California school grants, the courts did so anyway. In 1880, the Supreme Court ruled that, since Congress routinely exempted mineral lands from all other grants—be they for railroads, public buildings, or some other development—the justices were "forced" to conclude that "Congress did not intend to depart from its uniform policy in this respect in the grant of those [school] sections to the state."[56] In January 1927, however, Congress granted to the states all mineral school sections then not in controversy, with the proviso that the states should reserve the coal and other minerals lands.[57] This tale had an unhappy ending for Utah, which we discuss in Chapter 7 under the heading of land exchanges.

Although the amount and mineralization of land granted constitute an important data point, the pattern of land grants shown in Figure 1-1 is probably more significant to present-day managers. Many states continue to hold the majority of their trust lands in the dispersed pattern of two or four sections per township in which they were granted. This pattern is typical of the state school lands throughout the west and has significant consequences for management of those *and other* lands. Obviously it is difficult to plan for and administer scattered parcels of land.

6	5	4	3	②	1	6	5	4	3	②	1
7	8	9	10	11	12	7	8	9	10	11	12
18	17	⑯	15	14	13	18	17	⑯	15	14	13
19	20	21	22	23	24	19	20	21	22	23	24
30	29	28	27	26	25	30	29	28	27	26	25
31	㉜	33	34	35	㊱	31	㉜	33	34	35	㊱
6	5	4	3	②	1	6	5	4	3	②	1
7	8	9	10	11	12	7	8	9	10	11	12
18	17	⑯	15	14	13	18	17	⑯	15	14	13
19	20	21	22	23	24	19	20	21	22	23	24
30	29	28	27	26	25	30	29	28	27	26	25
31	32	33	34	35	㊱	31	32	33	34	35	㊱

6 Miles ↑ — Township Boundary ↑

←— Township Boundary —→

State trust lands for the support of public schools (common school lands).

Additional two sections for public schools in Arizona, New Mexico, and Utah.

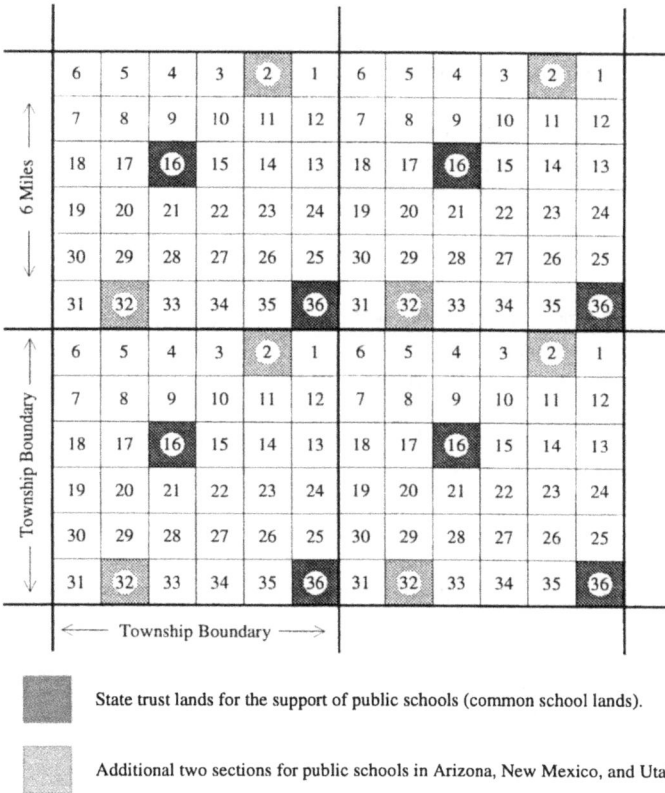

Figure 1-1. State trust land ownership patterns in each township for public school grants.

To Whom and for Whose Benefit Are the Lands Granted?

Clearly, Congress granted more and more land, but to whom? Although these lands are known ubiquitously as *state* school lands, the state was not always the recipient. Congress resolved this issue in a number of different ways during the first half of the nineteenth century before settling into a standard pattern.[58] When Ohio applied for statehood, it proposed that the townships receive section 16 or equivalent for the use of schools. Congress rejected that idea and, after a series of concessions and counterproposals, provided instead that all sections for the use of schools be vested in the state legislature.[59] Thereafter, however, the mixture of recipient, administrator, and purpose remained unsettled until the close of the second phase. The pattern evolved as follows: initially after Ohio, Congress granted land to the township for use by schools in the township. Later, the lands were granted to benefit schools in the township, but the grants were to be managed by the county. Then Congress, while continuing to make schools in the township the beneficiaries, assigned responsibility for administration to the state. Finally, Congress granted the lands for the benefit of schools in the state, to be administered by the state.[60]

This gradual shift from township-centered allocation to state-based allocation to state-based administration made sense for several reasons. First, the township did not always exist as a government; and in any event, the local level was not always adequate to administer the resources. Second, the townships were not equally endowed by the grants. In some townships, the section represented valuable or marketable land, in which case there was support for schools in the township. In other areas, the resource was not marketable, but the township still needed support for schools.[61]

One inevitable result of this change in policy was that phase-three states began operating their school systems with a centralized source of funds. Early in phase three, the states began to write into their Constitutions conditions under which money would be distributed to the localities. One of the first was that no school district that offered less than three months of schooling would qualify for what were by then *state* funds.[62] Perhaps at some future moment in the evolution of K–12 education, some persons might wish that the federal government had not established a system that was centralized within each state. They clearly did so. But it was accomplished at the behest of and in close and constant negotiation with the joining states.

Lease/Retain or Sell

A closely related issue is what the recipient ought to do with the granted lands. As the grant program evolved, Congress offered surprisingly little guidance in that area. The Ohio accession is far more typical than the New Mexico one in this regard, since virtually all of the restrictions and directions regarding disposition of the lands are contained in the enabling act of the latter state. Prior to 1910, the reverse was true: state constitutions contained an elaborate array of protective restrictions. Early in phase two, Congress presumed that the grants were to be leased and the receipts used to support the common schools. Various leasing systems were tried in each of the five states of the old Northwest, however, and "in every case it was discarded as a failure."[63] States learned from each other's experience: Thus, in discussions in Indiana regarding the advantages of sales as opposed to leasing, the arguments drew "from the experience of Ohio and other states."[64] In 1827, Ohio petitioned Congress for authority to sell rather than lease the lands. Thereafter, Congress passed special legislation making the same authority available for all states, and it included the sale authority in the new grants.

On the other hand, the federal government did not impose sales restrictions as grant conditions on states until 1875. The Colorado enabling act provided that school property had to be sold "at a public sale for not less than $2.50 per acre. All states entering since that time have done so with restrictions on the sale of the school allotments. The states, however, began imposing sales restrictions on themselves in their own constitutions much earlier. For example, the original Kansas constitution, and several subsequent ones adopted between 1861 and 1868 provide for minimum sales prices. The education article of the 1868 version of the Kansas Constitution provides that "the school-lands shall never be sold until such sale is authorized by free and fair vote of the people of Kansas. . . ."

By the mid-1830s, state constitutions authorized legislatures to make rules to sell, lease, or otherwise dispose of granted lands. No apparent shift in language heralds the return to the original lease-based approach to retention and management of the lands. How then, did the western states initiate the practice of retaining and managing the granted lands? Evidently, the shift toward reservation was accomplished gradually at the state level, in much the same way as it was accomplished at the federal level. Over time, the assumption that the federal government would dispose of all public domain lands eroded under diverse pressures.[65] The states were carried along in this same national reorientation.

Currently most states have authority to lease, sell, and (largely by implication, until quite recently) retain and manage the school lands. Deciding among these options has been complicated by the fact that many parcels, long regarded as grazing or agricultural lands, are now surrounded by cities or are otherwise quite valuable for commercial development. State programs evolving to deal with these new and unanticipated realities are discussed in the Epilogue.

Permanent School Funds

The existence of permanent school funds sharpens the contemporary definition of the old issue of sell or hold. The permanent funds appear to have developed as a logical concomitant of the shift to state-level management of the land grants. Michigan appears to be the first state to set up a permanent school fund in connection with the receipt of school land grants. Its 1835 proposed constitution provided that the "proceeds of all lands that have been or hereafter may be granted by the United States to this State, for the support of schools, which shall hereafter be sold or disposed of, shall be and remain a perpetual fund, the interest of which, together with the rents of all such unsold lands, shall be inviolably appropriated to the support of common schools throughout the State." This concept was rapidly picked up by other states. Eventually even the old and new old states had established the same kind of fund to facilitate administering the retroactive land and cash grants they bartered for. For example, Louisiana, which had been admitted in 1812, revised its constitution in 1845 to establish a permanent school fund for dealing with the proceeds of retroactive land grants.

Not until 1875 did the Congress get around to requiring a state to set up a permanent school fund—this in the enabling act for Colorado. And the Colorado constitution, adopted at statehood in 1876, contained pages of requirements for how the school fund should be administered, by whom, how invested, and how distributed. These grant terms and constitutional requirements continued to grow more elaborate until the state-making process was concluded.[66] Among the most important elaborations regarding the permanent school fund are restrictions in state constitutions regarding investment of the funds. It is quite common for phase-four states to restrict permanent school fund managers to investing in first farm mortgages and/or government bonds. Generally the goal of such restrictions appears to have been to require a conservative investment strategy that would support a farm economy. As we discuss in Chapter 2, however, such restrictions now constrain permanent fund management to the degree that many funds cannot keep pace with inflation.

Summary

The early enabling acts and constitutions, to paraphrase Swift, left major issues to the legislature to sort out, providing merely for the establishment and preservation of a permanent fund whose income would be devoted to the support of common schools. Subsequent constitutions made provisions regarding the sale price of school lands, the securities in which the proceeds of the sales could be invested, the management of the fund, and the like.[67] The pattern for the spread of permanent school fund and fund management requirements is familiar: the states initiate such provisions, which become very elaborate; the federal government picks up variations on the state language as grant conditions; and subsequent states elaborate and specify the conditions further. The direction of the process is clearly toward more stringent standards for preservation and operation of the school fund. However, the initiation and "testing" of the provisions took place at the state level.

Given all this variation, the grants obviously meant or ought to mean different things in different states. Yet we have also argued that they are clearly treated as trust in all twenty-two states. Why, and what does that mean to managers, beneficiaries, and the land and resources? To answer those questions, we turn away from nineteenth-century accessions and constitutions and focus instead on twentieth-century litigation regarding the meaning of the grants.

E PLURIBUS UNUM: THE TRUST MANDATE AND THE HOMOGENEOUS TRUST LAND GRANT

Because of the trust mandate, school trust lands are unique among public resources. It is reasonable to wonder how this doctrine came to be applied to the lands. The notion of a "trust" was not present at the beginning and did not become a clear part of the federal/state bargain, as we have seen, until the Arizona and New Mexico accession. Yet all these lands are currently referred to as "trust lands." After carefully exhuming all the diversity in the historical bargains between state and nation, we must clarify why this is so. Our inquiry involves two slightly overlapping topics: first, key rights-of-way cases, which show that the application of the trust doctrine to the school lands is rather recent; second, a single case, *County of Skamania v. State of Washington*, which illustrates diverse forces acting to round the edges of diversity to make all the grants appear quite similar.

When Did the School Land Grants Become Viewed as a Trust?

The rise of the trust notion is best seen in a series of school lands rights-of-way cases. Each involves state and federal agencies seeking uncompensated access across school lands. Over time, the basic theme has altered dramatically from fairly unfettered granting of rights-of-way without compensation—and indeed without any reference to a trust—to strict invocation of trust principles. In state cases from the 1920s and 1930s,[68] state courts did not find either state constitutional *or* enabling act provisions regarding appraisals, public auction, and similar requisites to disposition of school lands to bar state agencies from using school lands for diverse state purposes. The Arizona Supreme Court's 1965 decision in *State v. Lassen* is crystal clear about early state interpretation of the Enabling Act: "For over fifty years the state and county highway departments of Arizona have obtained rights of way and material sites without compensation over and on lands granted to the State of Arizona by the federal government. . . ."[69]

Early cases involving federal agencies seeking rights-of-way across school lands produced the same result. Two 1920s and 1930s federal courts found the school land grants no barrier to an uncompensated state grant of right-of-way across school lands for federal irrigation projects. In *Ide v. United States,* the Supreme Court found that a Wyoming statute granting rights-of-way over "all lands of the state for ditches 'constructed by and under the authority of the United States'" to be lawful without ever mentioning or discussing the trust notion.[70] Several years later, the federal district court in Idaho reached the same result, noting an 1866 federal statute and a 1905 state statute that permited the granting of rights-of-ways across school lands without regard to any restrictions on alienation of granted lands. Again, the trust notion was not mentioned in resolving the issue.[71]

The worm turned radically in 1966, when the U.S. Supreme Court reviewed and overturned *State v. Lassen. Lassen v. Arizona Highway Department*[72] is the starting point for a series of modern cases that rely on trust principles to answer ancient issues about the granted lands. Contemplating the methods by which the state of Arizona might obtain trust lands for "purposes not included in the grant"[73] and the standard of compensation that Arizona must employ to recompense the trust for land it acquires,[74] the Supreme Court relied throughout on trust terms and obligations: "The Enabling Act unequivocally demands both that the trust receive the full value of any lands transferred from it and that any funds received be employed only for the purposes for which the lands were given." The Court concluded that the state must "compensate the trust in money for the full appraised value of any material sites or rights of way which it obtains on or over trust lands."[75]

State cases from all over the West embrace the Supreme Court's analysis in Lassen. In *United States v. 78.61 Acres of Land in Dawes and Sioux Counties,* a federal district court confronted essentially the same question: "whether the Nebraska Legislature had the power to grant to the United States a right-of-way over school lands without compensation."[76] Citing *Lassen* and invoking the trustee's duty of undivided loyalty to the beneficiary, the court concluded that "a sharing by the trust property in the general benefits to the state of an irrigation project is not sufficient compensation to the trust."[77] Further, the court concluded that the fact that the United States is the grantee does not "alter the principle that the *res* of the trust may not be depleted."[78] Similarly, in *United States v. 111.2 Acres of Land in Ferry County,* another federal district court held that the state could not donate school land to the federal government.[79]

Creeping Uniformity—The Supreme Court in the Southwest

Once the Supreme Court decided *Lassen,* state courts all over the West, irrespective of the language of their particular enabling act or state constitution, fell into line. Thus the least typical of the accession bargains has become central in defining all of them. A number of factors have contributed to this result. The first is the routine observation that, when any aspect of the diversity we have so carefully exhumed results in a dispute, the issue is usually defined at some point by courts. Lawyers and judges have, not unpredictably, looked to familiar trust principles[80] and previous decisions to unravel claims and counterclaims about the school lands.

Two familiar judicial procedures have inclined the decisions, on balance, to simplify around a few tractable themes. These procedures are not peculiar to school lands cases. First, one effect of school lands obscurity has been a blurring of the distinctions that arose historically and a tendency for the familiar (the trust principles) to dominate the unfamiliar (the peculiarities of public lands history and policy). Second, normal deference to U.S. Supreme Court decisions has given this blurring a particular flavor in the school lands setting. Unique provisions in the Arizona and New Mexico Enabling Act authorized the U.S. Attorney General to enforce the provisions of the act.[81] Cases from Arizona and New Mexico have, therefore, dominated Supreme Court discussion of school lands, and precedents from Arizona and New Mexico have become central in interpreting the grants in other jurisdictions.[82] Nevertheless, as indicated by the rights-of-way cases, the unanimity is of relatively recent origin. Although the notion of a trust has been mentioned in connection with the lands since the 1850s, the frequency of the references to and the dominance of trust principles become most apparent as the twentieth century advances.[83]

To suggest the validity of these observations about the process of simplification without becoming mired in 150 years of cases, we will discuss but one: a major recent case from Washington State, *County of Skamania v. State*.[84] Two things interest us in this context: the admixture of citations from diverse jurisdictions without adequate reference to differences in state obligations, and the centrality of U.S. Supreme Court decisions without apparent awareness that importations from Arizona and New Mexico were occurring.

The state court in *Skamania* began by announcing the relevance of trust principles: "Every court," it asserted, "that has considered the issue has concluded that these are real, enforceable trusts that impose upon the state the same fiduciary duties applicable to private trustees." The *Skamania* court cited, "for cases in which courts have applied private trust principles to federal land grant trusts," decisions from Oklahoma, Alaska, and Nebraska. Later, the court concluded that "divided loyalty constitutes a breach of trust," and argued that its holding "is consistent with a host of cases from other jurisdictions. To our knowledge, every case that has considered similar issues has held that the state as trustee may not use trust assets to pursue other state goals."[85] Trust land cases are not indexed by any of the major reporting services. Hence it is not surprising that judges and attorneys are not aware of their full breadth and complexity. Judicial reliance on simplified versions of precedent from other states is characteristic of the school lands cases in general.

This process has been exacerbated by reliance on decisions of the U.S.

Supreme Court. This is well illustrated by the *Skamania* court. For authority for the notion that the trusts are real and enforceable and "impose upon the state the same fiduciary duties applicable to private trustees," the *Skamania* court relied on *Lassen v. Arizona*.[86] The *Skamania* court embraced *Lassen* fully, noting that "[a]lthough *Lassen* involved a different enabling act, the principle of *Lassen* applies to Washington's Enabling Act." This assertion was supported by reference to a Washington case, *United States v. 111.2 Acres of Land*,[87] that presumably ought to have been interpreting Washington law but that in fact merely cited *Lassen* again.[88]

In Washington, the trust is unquestionably "real." Washington entered the Union under the Omnibus Enabling Act, which did not establish a trust; but Washington's state constitution clearly did so. Its specific provisions are especially relevant to the issue of "undivided loyalty," about which the *Skamania* court was so emphatic. The state constitution states unambiguously that "all lands granted are held in trust *for all the people*."[89] That language does not obviously justify using trust resources to support stability among timber purchasers or in local economies, which was at issue in the particular case. However, if the trust is to benefit all the people, not just school children, it is far from clear how undivided loyalty to all the people ought to be defined, or how loyalty to the common schools is affected by loyalty to the broader group of citizens. The *Skamania* court never addressed that issue, to which we shall return in Chapters 5 and 7.[90]

The point here is a simple one. Trust principles, especially those enshrined ambiguously[91] in a few U.S. Supreme Court cases interpreting the Arizona–New Mexico accession, have come to dominate judicial understanding of school grants. The difficulty of obtaining alternative information has combined with the standard reliance on precedent and higher court rulings to erode appreciation of differences in state accession bargains. A gradual process of accreting judicial decisions has rounded the angles and left the courts with the operating assumption that the grants are trusts that are basically the same.

Much of the diversity of the nineteenth-century grants is preserved in management programs that vary considerably from state to state, depending on the peculiarities of state constitutions and statutes. The trust mandate in common makes comparisons possible and informative with regard to a broad range of public resource issues. The trust mandate also makes it feasible and reasonable to think of the trust lands, revenues, funds, and management as forming a system designed to achieve trust goals. We will use that approach in describing the trust lands and resources and their administrative structures.

CHAPTER TWO

Using a System Orientation to Understand Trust Lands and Resources

This chapter starts with the idea that the trust is a system to produce revenues for the beneficiaries. It describes the component parts of the system in sufficient detail so that readers unfamiliar with state trust lands can obtain a basic understanding of the nature and magnitude of the resources, the revenues, and management regimes involved. The system orientation is useful because, like the trust principles discussed in the Introduction, it brings the enormous and diverse detail of state programs together into an approachable analytic focus. The chapter describes the lands and their variation and then examines the goals of the system—principally the production of revenues for the beneficiary—and how the various parts of the system fit together to contribute to the goal. Focusing on the overriding trust goals allows outsiders to critique the management of any single part or resource in the system based on how well it contributes to the overall goal, rather than on how it is managed in isolation.

Although much political hay has been made throughout the history of the trust land program on the proposition that the states are wasting or dissipating their resources, the system as a whole is (as noted in Chapter 1) an impressive one. Both the lands and the revenues they produce are substantial. This chapter views the trust as a system that has three parts: management, the trust properties or assets (sometimes called the "corpus"), and the revenues produced by managing the trust corpus. The trust corpus includes the trust land base and the states' permanent funds.[1] Each of these three system components is discussed in detail separately.

The final section of this chapter focuses directly on revenues, emphasizing their sources, the amounts produced in each state by each resource, and the distribution of the revenues. We pay special attention to how receipts from trust lands are divided among annual disbursement to the beneficiaries, placement in permanent funds, and allocation to land office management funds.

Because the trust doctrine requires accountability, we can follow revenues and expenditures through the system to show where the receipts from various development activities go and how management expenses are paid.[2] Trust land managers make many hard decisions, complicated by the fact that the land manager is rarely the fund manager. Institutional arrangements for trust management frequently cloud viewing trust management from the system perspective. For example, in several states the trust's forest resources are managed by the same office that fights forest fires on rural private lands. Since fighting forest fires is an all-consuming task, foresters working on trust management are often diverted from administering trust programs to fighting fires, with the result that either needed trust management is not carried out or the offices are overstaffed in relation to what would be needed to manage only the trust's forestry activities. In another example, prices for oil and gas rose extremely rapidly in the late 1970s. Yet revenues from the production of oil and gas from state trust lands are put into the states' permanent funds, which in many states suffer from restrictions on the types of investments allowed. As a result, the dividends from the permanent funds have been much less than the increase in value of the oil and gas resources, had these been left in the ground.

Looking at the management of the individual resources in these two examples, you could say that each was being effectively managed: rural areas were being protected from forest fires, and the oil and gas being produced from trust lands brought vast amounts of money into the permanent funds. Nevertheless, to evaluate trust land management—as we do in Chapter 3—we must view the whole system. By looking at the trust as a system, rather than at the management of the individual resources, one observes that the forestry programs were not paying their way, and the state might have been better off to leave the oil and gas in the ground rather than lose its "real" value in the permanent funds. Persons attempting to assess a state's land trust management are often tempted to proceed piecemeal with their analysis, identifying a specific component of the trust and examining how well its management stands up "on its own." The most appealing aspect of this approach, obviously, is that it breaks the task up into seemingly coherent blocks without imposing an artificial order on the whole system. Unfortunately, however, piecemeal analysis neglects the interconnectedness of the trust's components. Even a component that is managed with exemplary skill and efficiency may mesh badly with other trust components; if so, the trust as a whole suffers, and the prevailing approach to management of the overall system and of the various subdivisions in place needs rethinking.

TRUST LANDS AS A PRODUCTION SYSTEM

Visualizing the Production System

The trust lands were granted to the states to provide support for public institutions. Because they have this purpose, the managing agencies, the lands and resources, the permanent funds, and the revenues these produce can be depicted as a single system geared toward attaining that goal. A diagram representing this general system is shown in Figure 2-1.

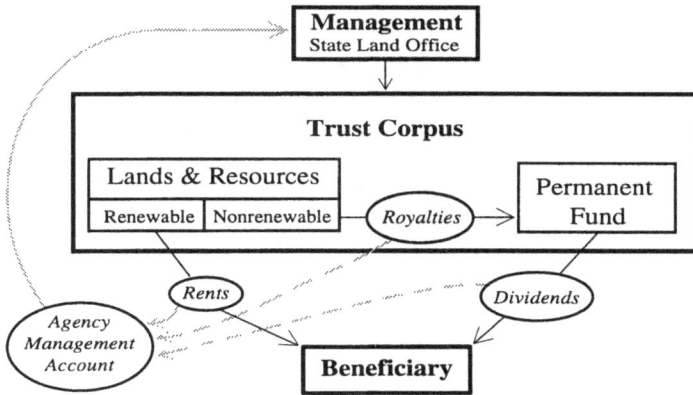

Figure 2-1. The trust production system.

Revenues from land and resources are treated differently depending on whether they are generated from the development of renewable as opposed to nonrenewable resources. We have therefore divided the lands into those two categories. Receipts from these resources are similarly divided into rents, royalties, and dividends, each emanating from a different part of the trust corpus, as shown by the arrows. The ultimate goal of trust management is to generate revenues to be received by the beneficiaries.

Figure 2-1 shows the components and flows of the trusts' production system in a very general sense. The exact path through which money travels before reaching the beneficiaries varies in different states according to three factors: the source of the revenues; the beneficiary of the lands that produced the revenues; and the deduction for managerial expenses, which varies among land types and beneficiaries. Funding for management of the trust resources also varies tremendously among the states, both as to amount and as to source. This ambiguity is represented by the ghostly gray arrow. In some (but not all) states, funding for trust resource management is deducted from receipts. This clearly colors management styles, priorities, and staffing levels in the different programs. The important thing is the relationship between the revenue flows in any specific resource and the overall management of the trust.

STATE LAND OFFICE ORGANIZATION, STAFF, AND FUNDING

State land offices[3] serve as the managing trustees for the land and resources depicted in Figure 2-1, and occasionally (or partially) as managers of the permanent funds. There is wide variation among the states in how management is organized. Three aspects of organization seem most significant: structure of the state land office (what kind of a board, if any, is in place, how the agency head is selected, and where is the agency located within the state's natural resources bureaucracy); the amount and distribution of staff devoted to management of the various trust resources; and the level and source of funding for management activities. We set the stage for discussing the influence of organizational structure by describing the variation in how the trustee agencies are organized in different states.

Organization in the State Government

In the basic model for trust land management, a board of land commissioners acts as trustee to oversee the operations of the state land office. Boards may range from a collection of ex officio constitutional officers (such as the governor, the state treasurer, and/or the superintendent of education) to panels composed entirely of members of the public who have been appointed in various ways. Some states do not have a board of land commissioners at all, but instead delegate sole authority for management of the trust lands either to an elected land commissioner or to an executive director appointed by the governor.

THE BOARD

Most states have some form of board of land commissioners to oversee state trust land activities. Figure 2-2 summarizes the composition and role of boards in the various states. We have found it difficult to relate patterns of management decisions to particular institutional arrangements. It appears that the most important factor is the degree of beneficiary involvement in the decision making. In six states, the board is composed of ex officio elected officials (usually including the state treasurer and/or state auditor). Three states—California, Oklahoma, and Washington—have boards composed of both elected and appointed officials, with the appointed member(s) designated by the governor. In four other states—Colorado, Hawaii, Nebraska, and Utah—the entire board is appointed by the governor.[4] Members of Utah's board represent specific groups, including oil and gas and ranchers, with only one ex-officio member representing the beneficiaries.

The boards' role and level of activity vary among the states, ranging from almost complete noninvolvement to active participation. The extreme hands-on case is Colorado, where there is no land commissioner and where the three board members serve essentially full time, running the office on a day-to-day basis. In Wyoming, the board (composed of the state's five elected officials), meets monthly but is largely uninvolved in the day-to-day matters of the land office; and in Washington the board's involvement is

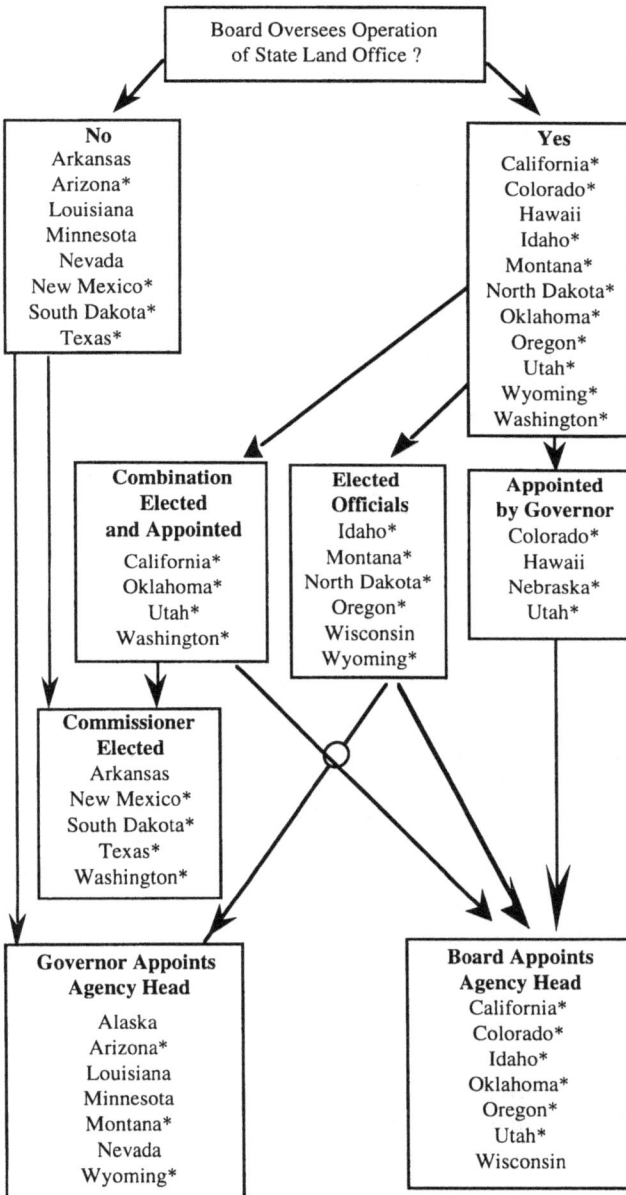

Figure 2-2. Institutional relationships in state land office organization. *Source:*
Souder & Fairfax, Western States Survey Responses (State Lands Project,
Department of Forestry and Resource Management, University of California,
Berkeley, December 1989), and WESTERN STATES LAND COMMISSIONERS ASSOCIATION,
DIRECTORY (1992).

confined mainly to approval of land transactions. Arizona's board meets only to hear appeals of land office decisions, and has no other powers. In Texas and Washington, the commissioner of state lands must obtain board approval for certain types of decisions (primarily land sales and exchange) but cannot be removed by the board. At the other end of the spectrum, in New Mexico and South Dakota, the elected commissioner acts without board oversight.

THE AGENCY HEAD

The agency head may be elected, appointed by the board, or appointed by the governor. Again, it is difficult to trace particular outcomes to particular methods of selection for commissioners. The power of the commissioner to influence decisions varies widely among the states, and the means of selecting this officer appears to be only one of the relevant variables. Figure 2-2 indicates which states proceed by which selection method. Five states— Arkansas, New Mexico, South Dakota, Texas, and Washington—have elected land commissioners. In states where the commissioner is appointed, some responsiveness to the appointer is to be expected. Where the governor appoints (Arizona, Montana, and Wyoming), the state land office can be seen as an instrument of state executive control. Where the commissioner is appointed by the board (Nebraska), the power of the executive head depends on the amount of oversight exerted by the board.

The line of authority above the agency head may also be significant in the choice of management strategies. New Mexico's commissioner is elected, has no board oversight, and has an independent agency, giving that official a large measure of autonomy.[5] The commissioner may be directly responsible to the executive or may be indirectly responsible through intervening agency heads. The latter situation prevails in Colorado, where the board has fought turf battles with its umbrella agency over staff positions, oversight, and other administrative issues.[6]

WHERE THE LAND OFFICE FITS IN STATE GOVERNMENT

Another variable affecting the trustee's ability to focus on trust management is state administrative structure: is the state land office an independent agency, or is it included within the structure of another, larger agency? Three administrative patterns emerge in the various states: the state land office is totally independent of other state agencies; the state land office is independent but is administratively overseen by a larger agency; or the state land office is functionally integrated into another agency, sharing facilities and staff. In every state except Washington, the land office is independent of other agencies. Only in New Mexico, however, is this independence complete (except for oversight by the attorney general); all the other states impose some administrative superstructure over the land office.

Power and management emphasis may be diffused if the agency managing state trust lands has other responsibilities as well. Diversion of trustee attention may occur when an activity that the state land office manages requires significant commitments of personnel who would otherwise be contributing to trust land management activities (such as fire fighting) or when personnel staffing decisions focus on an area other than trust land management and these people subsequently move into positions of responsibility for the trust.[7] States combine various other resource programs with state trust land management. Arizona, Colorado, Idaho, Montana, Utah, Washington, and Wyoming all combine private forest regulation and management responsibilities with trust land management; and with the exception of Colorado, all these states' land offices are also responsible for forest fire protection. Similarly, four states—Idaho, Montana, New Mexico, and Washington—include oil and gas drilling permits and accounting, and mining regulation and reclamation in the state land office. In Wyoming, the state land office manages farm loans; while in Arizona, California, Idaho, Oregon, Utah, and Washington, sovereign lands (which include the beds of navigable waterways, lakes, and the inner coastal shore) are managed by the trust land office.

The relative power of the land office in state policy decisions compared to other state agencies is important. Total independence, while it allows focus on trust goals, may weaken the trustee politically. Thus, while New Mexico's land commissioner is independent, the office appears not to be terribly powerful in disputes with the state engineer over water management. This is a characteristic feature of trust land water management, which we discuss in Chapter 7. The question here is one of balance: a small, independent agency that deals exclusively with trust lands issues may be focused on beneficiaries but lacking in bureaucratic allies and therefore vulnerable in state-level administrative politics.

Staffing in State Land Offices[8]

Although the structure and organization of the different state offices are important, staffing is probably the most interesting and informative variable to look at. Because it constitutes by far the largest operating expenditure, staffing provides an important measure of management priorities in our analysis in the next chapter, when we move from a production system to a production function. Here, we simply discuss the allocation of staff to different resource management functions.[9] Table 2-1 shows the staffing amounts and patterns for the various states.[10]

Resource-specific staffing patterns for the states are provided in Table 2-1 for each of four broad staffing categories: renewable resources; nonrenewable resources; land sales and exchanges; and administration. The table

TABLE 2-1. State trust land office staffing patterns, expressed in terms of full-time equivalent employees (FTEs)

Program	AZ	CA	CO	ID	MT	NB	NM	ND	OK	OR	SD	TX*	UT	WA	WY
Renewable resources															
Cropland and grazing															
Professional	15.5	1	5	12	10	15	4	3	24	2	1	2	7	46	5
Clerical	5		5	2	2	1	9	1	5	0.5		0	4	4	5
Forestry															
Professional	38.5	2	1	51	48					65.3	0.1		1	358	7.5
Clerical	3	1		8	6									40	6
Commercial leasing and development															
Professional	8	1	1	4	1.5		4		1	2		3	7	16	
Clerical	2		1	1	0.25		4		0	1		1	4	2	
Nonrenewable resources															
Mining leasing															
Professional	8	3.3		3	1						0.5	1	2	6	
Clerical				1	1						0.5	0	1	0.5	
Oil and gas leasing															
Professional		0.2	2	3	1	1	6	1	8	1	1	14	2	6	14
Clerical			3	1	1		8	2.25	4	0.5		1	1	1	10
Land sales and miscellaneous															
Land exchanges															
Professional	10	2	5	3	2.25		3			14	0.75	6		1	
Clerical	2	0		2	0.75	1	3				0.25	0		1.5	
Other program management															
Professional	26	3.5	1		4.5						0.5	21			
Clerical	2		2.5		2						0.5	0			
Administrative															
Revenues management															
Professional		2		2	1.5	2	6	2	20	6	1	2	4	5	1.5
Clerical		4		4	2.25	2	4	0.75	16	2		0	4		1.5
Overall administrative personnel															
Professional	25	6.6	1	4	2.5		15	1	10	9	1	8	7	104	1.5
Clerical	5			4	1.5			1	5	2		2	2	15	1
Civil service exempt	5	1	0	3	0		8		1	8			1	0	4
Total FTEs	150	25.4	37	104	84.5	25	66		93	110.3	8.1	61	59	736	53

*Texas data is for headquarters office, trust land management only. Field positions are not included. Total General Land Office staff is 542 FTEs.

reports the number of full-time equivalent (FTE) employees in professional and clerical positions in each of the four categories. The renewable resources category provides staffing information broken down into three resources: cropland and grazing, forestry, and commercial leasing and development. The data for nonrenewable resources management fall into one of two subcategories: oil and gas leasing, and mineral leasing. Oil and gas leasing was separated from other mineral leasing activities because of its importance as a source of revenues in many states. The second category—mineral leasing—includes all other subsurface leasing activities, such as for coal, hardrock minerals, and geothermal. Staffing in land sales and exchanges is also reported in two subcategories: land exchanges and appraisals, and other program management. Land exchanges are very staff-intensive and typically do not produce immediate revenues for the trust. "Other program management" refers to staff working in land sales and easements, and various land-based record-keeping activities. The final program area—administration—comprises two specific areas: revenues management, and overall administrative personnel. Revenues management includes accounting and auditing staff. Overall administrative personnel generally includes the "front office" staff—usually the director and commissioner, public relations, and shared secretarial and other support staff.

The patterns in Table 2-1 show that in many states staffing is focused on a single resource. In Idaho, Oregon, and Washington, this resource is timber; in Texas, it is oil and gas. This is to be expected, since these resources provide the bulk of the revenues in these states. In Chapter 3 we emphasize the amount of staff relative to the revenues received as one way to judge the effectiveness of trust management. Viewed as part of the production system, the amount of staff in each resource management program indicates how important the management of that resource is in relation to others within the trust.

Funding State Land Office Management

How the agency is financed affects and is affected by the resource revenues from the trust land base. States use variants of four basic processes for funding state land office activities: all land office functions may be funded by appropriations from the state legislature; management may be funded by a percentage of trust land surface revenues; management activities may be funded by a percentage of both surface and subsurface trust land revenues; or management may be funded by a combination of receipts and general fund appropriations. Table 2-2 shows the mechanisms each state uses to fund its land office management.

The most common method of funding management is for a percentage of revenues from renewable resource receipts to be deducted prior to distribution to the beneficiaries.[11] In Oregon, only renewable resource revenues are used to fund the operations of the Department of Forestry (and the Oregon Division of State Lands, for nonforested state trust lands). The split in revenue between county trust lands and state school and institution trust lands in Oregon differs. The Oregon Department of Forestry receives 36¼ percent of the revenues from the county forest lands,[12] but it recovers only administrative costs for forestry man-

TABLE 2-2. State land office funding mechanisms

Funding Mechanism	AZ[a]	CA[b]	CO[c]	ID[d]	MT	NB	NM[e]	ND	OK	OR[f]	SD	TX	UT[g]	WA[h]	WY
Funding from revenues?	No	Yes	Yes	Yes	Yes	No	Yes	Yes	Yes	Yes	No	No	Yes	Yes	Yes
% of disbursable income			10%	10%	2.5%		100%	10%	6%	36¼%			20%	25%	25%
% of royalty income		10%							6%				20%	25%	
Land sales income included?		10%											No	25%	
% of permanent fund interest								10%	6%	Yes			20%		
Cost recovery (net distributed)		Yes								Yes					
State land office funded by direct appropriation?	Yes		Yes		Yes	No					Yes	Yes		No	Yes
Appropriated by legislature?		Yes	Yes	Yes				No[j]	Yes	Yes		Yes	Yes	Yes	No	Yes

Notes:
a. Based on Arizona's response to survey.
b. California P.R.C. § 6217.5 and § 6217.7 for revenue types and cost recovery.
c. Based on C.R.S. § 36-1-145. Funds appropriated by legislature, § 36-1-145(2b).
d. *Evans v. Van Deusen* 31 Idaho 614, 174 P. 122 (1918). Idaho management account's 10% must be used for the same program where the funds were generated—i.e., timber for timber—and can't be shifted among programs.
e. N.M.S.A. § 19-1-11, Amended 1989, ch. 15 § 1. Previously 20% of disbursable income was available for management expenses.
f. Part of permanent funds can be used to improve land values. Oregon Constitution Article VIII § 2 and O.R.S. § 273.115. The 36¼% management fee is for county forested lands, on a cost-reimbursable basis between the Department of Forestry and the Division of State Lands (OREGON DEPARTMENT OF FORESTRY, FOREST LOG 59(1) [1989] at 6). Other state trust lands are managed on a cost recovery basis.
g. Based on U.C.A. § 65A-5-1.
h. Up to 50% of revenues from county forest lands obtained by gift or purchase (WASHINGTON DEPARTMENT OF NATURAL RESOURCES, PROPOSED FOREST LANDS MANAGEMENT PLAN 1984–1993 [1983], at 29).
i. W.S.A. § 9-4-305(c) designates the income fund; § 39-4-307 says that 25% goes to the general fund with the exception of the university and fish hatchery trust lands. The legislature then appropriates operating funds for the state land office from the general fund.
j. Expenditures from maintenance account at sole discretion of the State Land Office (1953–54 Op. Att'y Gen. No. 5781).

Source: Western States Survey Responses at 4, and state statutes.

agement on the common school lands.[13] In the case of county forest lands, receipts from land sales and rights-of-way are used to purchase other lands or are returned to the county of origin.

In other cases, such as Washington, agency management expenses are also funded through a percentage of nonrenewable resource receipts.[14] In Washington, the Department of Natural Resources receives up to 25 percent of the revenues from both renewable and nonrenewable resources, including land sales, for its operational cost accounts for the state trust lands.[15] On Washington's Forest Board lands, up to 25 percent of revenues from reverted lands and up to 50 percent of revenues from board lands obtained by gift or purchase by the board can be used for management expenses.[16] The receipts in these accounts must be appropriated by the legislature before they are available for expenditure. Proceeds from sales of Washington Forest Board lands are used to buy replacement lands.[17]

Finally, agency management costs may be met directly from the state general fund, as is the case in Idaho and Montana (with small exceptions). Management cost recovery in Idaho includes a forest improvement program to maximize the revenue production from state-owned forest lands, which levies a 10 percent fee on gross revenues from timber sales on these lands to fund the program.[18] The remainder of the funds are deposited in the endowment fund; management operations of the Idaho Department of Lands are funded from direct legislative appropriation.[19] Montana's resource development program is funded by an amount not to exceed 2½ percent of the income received from trust lands, which, while primarily used in range and cropland development projects, may also be applied to timber improvement projects.[20] The remainder of Montana's forestry management activities are funded through direct legislative appropriations of general funds.[21] The Arizona and Wyoming land offices receive all their operating funds from annual appropriations; consequently, they must work first through the executive office with budget requests, and then through the legislature for appropriations. In Wyoming's case, the state land office budget has been reduced by 30 percent in the last three years, irrespective of the effects this may have on trust responsibilities.

THE TRUST CORPUS

A crucial distinction between state trust land and other public resource management programs is that the states' assets have two components: granted lands and resources that remain in state ownership; and permanent funds that were established (frequently at statehood) to hold in trust receipts from land sales and leasing of nonrenewable resources. We look at these two components individually in the subsections that follow.

Trust Lands and Their Uses[22]

LAND OWNERSHIP

In Chapter 1 we discussed the original grants of land to the states. Here we look at what remains after almost 200 years of management. Figure 2-3 shows the current surface land ownership in trust land states and the percentage of the original grants still in state ownership. Three fairly distinct groups of states can be differentiated on the basis of the extent of land ownership. Alaska, Arizona, Montana, and New Mexico are the major holders, each retaining title to more than 5 million acres.

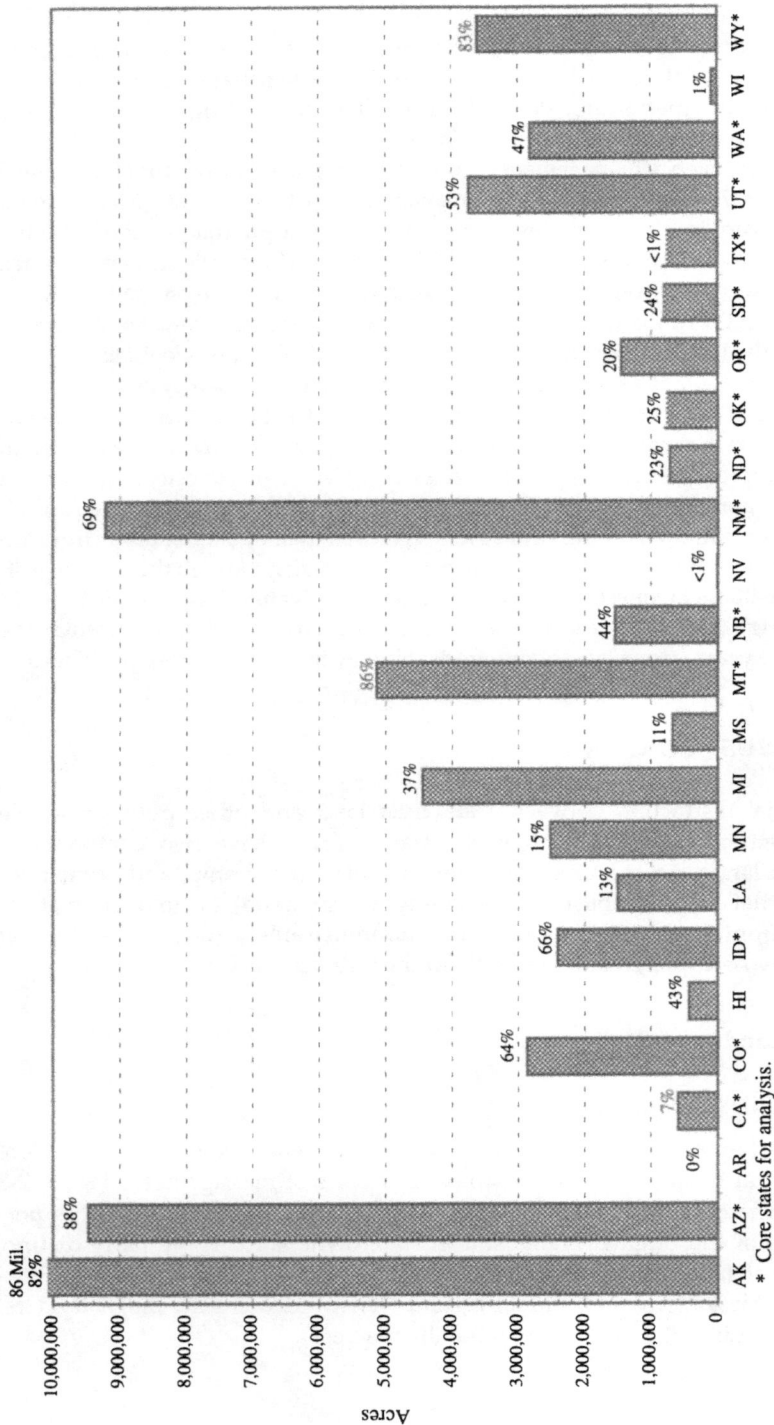

Figure 2-3. Current state trust surface land ownership and percentage of original grants. *Source:* WESTERN STATES LAND COMMISSIONERS' ASSOCIATION, DIRECTORY (1992).

Clearly the last states to receive their trust lands—Arizona, New Mexico, and Alaska—still have the largest amounts. Those states also received the most to begin with. Arizona and New Mexico both received four sections per township, and their lands were difficult to sell because of the poor quality of the land and because of constitutional constraints on sales. The states that sold most of their lands now have the least: California and Oregon. The middle group of six states includes three that have sold some or much of their lands (Utah,[23] Montana, Colorado) and three that were smaller states and thus received less land in the first place (Washington, Idaho, Wyoming). In Washington and Oregon, forested lands returned to public ownership through tax reversions—over 600,000 acres in each state—and are now managed by the state.

Table 2-3 shows the amount of surface land ownership held by the various beneficiaries. The common schools (K–12) hold the vast majority of the acreage managed by the states.[24] In Chapter 1 we discussed how the common school grants were originally made "in place"—through the granting of specific numbered sections of land within each township. This was the predominant state ownership pattern unless these sections were already claimed by homesteaders or reserved by the federal government for National Forests or Indian Reservations. In such instances, "in lieu" lands were selected, usually in larger blocks than the original single-section parcels. In contrast, the other beneficiaries received "quantity" grants of land—for example 200,000 acres for a university—which were then selected by the state from the unappropriated public domain. The quantity grants and in lieu lands were often selected in blocks, or settlers and speculators were told to apply to the state for lands that they desired; and as a result, much of the acreage from the original grants to beneficiaries other than the common schools has been sold.[25] In some cases, it was anticipated that lands granted to fund the construction of a state capitol or university would be sold.

States typically hold larger acreage of lands in mineral rights than they hold in surface ownership. Not infrequently, states have sold the surface land but retained title to the minerals beneath; less frequently, they have acquired the surface estate without minerals. We discuss the implications of these "split estates" in Chapter 6, but it's worth noting here that millions of acres of mineral rights are owned by the states in situations where the surface is owned by others, and that some surface acres (albeit a much smaller number) are owned by the state without the subsurface estate.

SURFACE LAND USES

Knowing how much land a state owns is probably less important to understanding the trust system than knowing what the land is good for. Table 2-4 shows each state's uses of these trust lands in acres.[26] There are three traditional land uses: grazing, timber, and agriculture. In most western states,

TABLE 2-3. Acres of state trust lands owned by each beneficiary

State	Common Schools	Colleges and Universities	Public Buildings	Hospitals	Asylums	Prisons	Deaf and Dumb Schools	Reform Schools	Charity	Saline Lands	Internal Improvements	County	Other	Total
Arizona	8,255,377	738,848	66,609	92,887	76,901	80,036	82,122	78,427						9,471,207
California	586,917													586,917
Colorado	2,635,589	34,566	4,075			8,211				16,063	159,089			2,857,593
Idaho	2,054,292	210,681	6,812	30,348		28,550			73,330					2,404,013
Montana	4,597,691	236,502	186,227	1,276		10	36,236	73,744						5,131,686
Nebraska	1,519,774	10,444								1,385			197	1,513,800
New Mexico	7,004,959	1,088,370	88,726		216,695	114,616	197,573		74,864		431,196			9,216,999
North Dakota	635,885	39,823	9,981	5,118			8,233	4,349					19,684	723,073
Oklahoma	388,565	356,386	36,946						3,281					785,178
Oregon	785,868											652,000		1,437,868
South Dakota	666,375	92,864	14,168	18,790		10,487	13,569	4,676	74					821,003
Texas	809,389													809,938
Utah	3,590,236	54,778	3,359	10,668		79,549	25,354	1,593			52,923			3,738,911
Washington	1,836,986	156,011	108,926	38,515			17,949	23,085				622,498	8,107	2,812,077
Wyoming	3,139,814	105,971	82,890		28,266	20,217			144,953					3,601,660
Total	38,507,717	3,125,244	608,719	197,602	321,862	341,676	381,036	185,874	296,502	17,448	643,208	1,274,498	27,988	45,911,923

TABLE 2-4. State trust lands uses (in acres)

State	Cropland	Grazing	Timber	Commercial and Special Use	Other Non-commodity	Minerals	Oil and Gas	Coal	Geothermal	Other Commodity	Water Rights	Land Sales	Right-of-Way	Exploration Permits
Arizona	160,992	8,456,525	35,000	736,106	11,311	20,995	60,954	0	0	8,670		3,800	20,817	84,069
California		73,500	30,000											
Colorado	127,181	2,538,627	71,001	124,831		91,384	1,517,829	39,580	0	8,650		273	52,685	
Idaho	7,172	2,016,284	881,000	17,877		54,683	346,271		1,095	7,501		1,164	178	
Montana	559,954	4,090,430	500,000	18,000		5,847,866	6,353,350	6,189,150						
Nebraska	1,526,796						141,997							
New Mexico		8,700,000		18,000			4,874,854	4,874,854				183		
North Dakota		716,494					480,924	4,240					146	
Oklahoma	769,303						30,133					2,842		
Oregon	50	620,000	754,498	43			30,000							
South Dakota		819,067	4,978			40	25,073							
Texas		614,800		2,400			755,805				42,308			1,425
Utah	11,725	3,560,502		91,328	40,065	244,823	1,777,077	71,788	16,640	23,193		3,281	75,244	
Washington	164,325	1,044,083	2,078,090	156,682	3,349	68,664	240,967	720		227,978		23,067	797	
Wyoming	9,894	3,639,925		17,158		68,475	1,713,040	317,317		1,115				
Total	3,337,392	36,890,237	4,354,567	1,182,425	54,725	6,396,930	18,348,274	11,497,649	17,735	277,107		34,610	149,867	85,494

grazing is the dominant use of most of the state trust lands. Virtually every state has a grazing program. In its constitution, North Dakota limits the surface use of its trust lands to "pasturage," or grazing; but the more pervasive reason for grazing dominance is the type and location of granted lands still in state ownership. Lands not sold during the disposition era of state land management are frequently dry and situated in isolated sections, many of which were soon surrounded by federal lands.

Where lands are of better quality and water is present, cropland use predominates. As we discuss in Chapter 4, croplands occupy a smaller acreage than grazing lands but bring in higher revenues. States with major croplands programs include those in the eastern tier—South Dakota, Nebraska, and Oklahoma—but Arizona, Colorado, Montana, and Washington have important programs, too.

While grazing lands and croplands are likely to be held in the original scattered parcels, the major timber resources on state trust lands are far more likely to be held in large blocks. Lands selected in lieu or exchanged for state sections reserved for national forests typically occur in large parcels of land along the boundaries of the national forests. In some states, the institutional beneficiaries' block grants were also selected from forested lands. Finally, due to tax and mortgage foreclosures, many states in the 1920s and 1930s received into the trust corpus lands that were burned or cut over. Many of these lands have since been reforested. For these three reasons, most states have some sort of forest management program. Timber revenues, however, are significant in only four: Oregon, Washington, Idaho, and Montana. We discuss the states' timber management programs in Chapter 5.

SUBSURFACE LAND USES

Most trust lands that have mineral rights are leased for one subsurface use or another. The states own approximately 153 million acres of mineral rights. As we discuss in Chapter 6, much of this land is unproductive and much of the states' mineral leasing programs are speculative. Arizona, for example, has an active oil and gas leasing program but has never had a producing well. Lease terms average about ten years, and the amount of acres under lease shifts depending on the expectation of future higher prices. As expectations are dashed—because of either price drops or dry holes—these leases are abandoned by the current holders only to be re-leased during the next wave of speculation.

Several states, however, have a long history of productive mineral leases, from which royalties are received over a long period of time. In 1989–1990, the states received about $2.3 billion in revenues from mineral leases, the vast majority resulting with oil and gas production. New Mexico, Oklahoma, Texas, and Wyoming have been particularly well-endowed with oil and gas, as can be seen both from the acreage leased for these uses in Table 2-1 and from the revenues received. Colorado, Montana, New Mexico, Utah, and Wyoming have leased large areas for coal production, with the difference among the states being that the coal in Colorado and Utah is mined underground—resulting in smaller acreage leased—while coal in Montana, New Mexico, and Wyoming is strip-mined.

NEW AND EMERGING USES

Various other surface uses occur on trust lands. And in addition to pursuing traditional commodity uses, state trust land managers are becoming increasingly active in developing "transition lands" for commercial purposes.[27] Commercial uses run the gamut from shopping centers to ports to residential developments to communication tower sites. We address the variety of these programs in Chapter 7. The acreage devoted to commercial uses varies tremendously among the states, as is seen in Table 2-1, and the actual numbers recorded often depend on how the state classifies "Special Use."

The received wisdom about state trust lands is that the grants were frittered away, that not much remains and that what does remain probably is not worth talking about. We have seen, to the contrary, that the states' holdings are extensive and extremely valuable for a number of important uses. Both the amount and the location of land each state owns reflect the extent and timing of the original grant and the sum total of state actions to date. What remains in state ownership is in many locations as much a reflection of water availability as of any frittering. But understanding the management of the lands hinges on understanding the trust system of which they are a part. We turn therefore to the permanent funds.

Permanent Funds

If state trust lands are obscure, the permanent funds are the hidden corner of state trust land management. In most states neither the beneficiary nor the state land office is influenced by revenues passing from the trust lands into the permanent fund. This disconnection results from two factors: first, neither the state land office (except in Oklahoma and North Dakota) nor the beneficiaries has direct control over management of the permanent fund; and second, short-term revenue fluctuations that might attract the attention of the beneficiaries and/or the land office are moderated by the nature of the permanent funds investments. Yet the permanent funds are a crucial part of the trust management system.

PERMANENT FUND AMOUNTS

Like everything else we have looked at, permanent funds vary considerably from state to state.[28] In one state (Oregon) all revenues from the trust

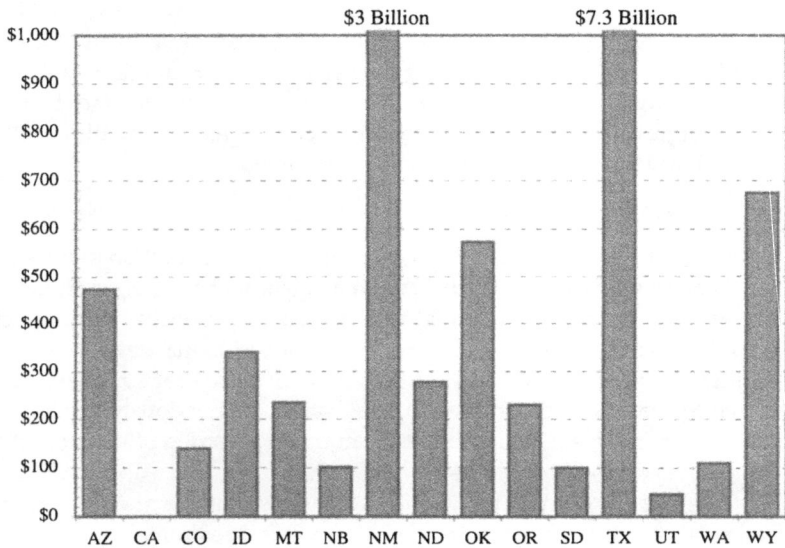

Figure 2-4. State permanent fund levels, 1990 (in millions of dollars).

lands go into the permanent fund; but another state (California) essentially has no permanent fund.[29] Generally speaking, state permanent funds are the repository of revenues received from the sale of trust lands and from royalties on nonrenewable resources, usually from oil, gas, and coal leases.[30]

The differences today in the amounts of states' permanent funds are chiefly traceable to two factors: the amount of lands sold for low prices in the early days of statehood[31]; and the amounts of mineral royalty income accruing to the permanent funds since the 1970s. That the states have widely varying amounts in their permanent funds is shown in Figure 2-4. This variation is due both to the nature of their resources and to legislative and fiscal actions affecting the funds over the years since statehood. California has the least amount of permanent funds because its were liquidated by constitutional amendment . Utah has the next lowest amount of permanent funds because, in the early 1980s, faced with a state budget cut of one-third, the beneficiaries were allowed to liquidate their permanent funds to maintain their programs.[32]

New Mexico, Oklahoma, Texas, and Wyoming have high levels of permanent funds due to oil, gas, and coal royalties. Arizona's large fund is less easily explained: it has no significant oil, gas, or coal royalties, its mining royalties were set below fair market value until recently,[33] and it still retains almost all its originally granted lands (91.6 percent). In 1987–1988, however, the land office received almost $24 million in land sales, mostly from high-value lands surrounding urbanizing areas. Washington's land sales revenues are similar to Arizona's. However, its permanent fund came primarily from land sales prior to 1920. Washington's recent policy of not decreasing its trust land base means that money from current land sales does not go into its permanent fund, but instead is used to buy replacement lands. The other states with smaller amounts of permanent funds either have sold many of their lands (Idaho and Oregon) or have received smaller amounts of royalty income than the top producers (Colorado and Montana). Table 2-5 shows the amount of the permanent fund, the amount of revenues flowing into the fund, and the amount of dividends and interests disbursed to the beneficiaries—each divided into two categories: the total amount, and the amount in the common school account (which makes up the bulk of the states' permanent funds).

PERMANENT FUND INVESTMENT CRITERIA AND DIVIDENDS

As Table 2-5 indicates, the states with large permanent funds (Arizona, New Mexico, Oklahoma, Texas, and Wyoming) have similarly large amounts going into the funds—the input category—and going back out to the beneficiaries—the net payments category. Net payments from the states' permanent funds reflect two factors: first, the amount of the permanent fund; and second, the rate of return on investments of the fund. Rate of return can be calculated simply by dividing the revenues distributed from the permanent fund by the amount of the permanent fund, and then multiplying by 100 to convert to a percentage. Calculating the rate in this manner yields the "effective" rate, since it is what the beneficiary sees, but it does not consider investment costs or growth in the capital value of the fund. As the last column of Table 2-5 makes clear, the rate of return on investments varies greatly among the states—at least it did in 1990, ranging from a low of 8 percent to a high of more than 19 percent.

REVENUES AND THEIR DISTRIBUTION

Types of Revenues from Trust Lands

Because different kinds of revenues travel different routes to the beneficiary, it is important when discussing revenues produced from trust lands to note not only the amount of revenues but how they were produced and how they are distributed.

States typically do not produce revenues directly from their trust lands. Instead, they transfer use of these lands to others who, for example, use them to graze cattle, cut timber or drill for oil and gas. The people who use these lands pay the state a fee. The use and the amount of the fee are deter-

TABLE 2-5. States' permanent fund performance, 1990

State	Year	PERMANENT FUND PRINCIPAL AMOUNT		STATE LAND INPUTS TO PERMANENT FUND		NET PERMANENT FUND PAYMENTS TO BENEFICIARIES		Rate of Return (Percent)
		Total	Common Schools	Total	Common Schools	Total	Common Schools	
Arizona	90	$473,633,597	$441,487,799	$62,623,927	$60,893,004	$39,133,212	$36,116,216	8.3
California	90	None	None	N/A	N/A	N/A	N/A	N/A
Colorado	90	$139,365,114	$189,701,129		$9,906,262			
Idaho	90	$340,308,539	$233,989,594	$22,797,838	$15,910,128	$28,643,517	$19,757,403	8.42
Montana	90	$235,329,000	$222,019,000	$14,790,238		$23,423,000	$22,094,000	9.95
Nebraska	89		$99,646,314	$682,943			$6,775,182	6.8
New Mexico	90	$2,927,073,719	$2,408,706,612	$104,922,166	$83,632,662	$258,960,574	$213,199,034	8.85
North Dakota	90	$277,945,132	$246,850,470	$15,007,367		$54,079,244		19.5
Oklahoma	90	$573,019,765	$419,232,674	$20,753,968	$14,846,155	$43,463,448	$31,320,790	7.58
Oregon	90	$230,351,774	$229,916,141	$12,790,279	$12,790,279	$19,957,239	$19,914,732	8.66
South Dakota	89	$98,771,630	$82,062,557	$2,128,583	$1,726,644	$9,886,322	$8,002,538	10.0
Texas	90		$7,328,172,096		$178,515,921		$674,634,994	9.21
Utah	91	$45,764,956	$43,904,659	$5,117,554		$3,535,962		7.7
Washington	89		$110,313,000	$16,405,154	$1,172,427		$7,165,000	0.9
Wyoming	90	$674,551,983	$610,460,433	$32,060,515		$95,477,815		14.2

mined by a lease executed between the state (the lessor) and the user of the resource (the lessee). Three types of payment are generally received from state trust land leases: rents, royalties, and bonus payments.

The payment type is important for two reasons. First, it usually determines whether the payments are distributed directly to the beneficiaries or go into their permanent funds, as well as whether the state receives a portion of the receipts for its office management. Second, the existence and magnitude of the various payments can be used in some cases to determine whether the state is receiving fair market value for its resources. For purposes of our discussion in this chapter, the category of revenues is important for the first reason: where the money goes after it is received by the state. The second reason is discussed in more detail in subsequent chapters.

The first category of payment for leases is for the rental of the land surface. For grazing, surface rental is the predominant compensation to the state. Users of the state's mineral rights also pay a surface rental, which serves as a "holding fee" until the minerals are developed. The second category of payments consists of royalties. The traditional concept of royalty is that it is the portion of the revenues due to the sovereign, or royal authority, for use of the land. In the contemporary trust lands case, *royalty* refers to the portion of the profit from use of the land's resources due the owner. Royalties are collected on the value or amount of the physical production of resources from trust lands. The royalties most commonly thought of are from oil, gas, coal, or hardrock minerals, although the proceeds from timber sales—which are priced according to the amount harvested—could be (and in some states are) considered royalties. The third category of lease payment is the bonus. Bonus payments are generally received, during the leasing process, if competitive bids are solicited by the state. Usually the surface rental rate is fixed, and the royalty percentage value is predetermined. Hence, what distinguishes one bidder from another is the amount of the bonus, a lump sum to be paid when the lease is awarded. The qualified bidder that offers the highest bonus wins the lease.

After leasing or sale, revenues begin to flow into the state land office. Revenues are received from three basic sources: use of renewable resources, including grazing fees, timber sales, commercial or special-purpose leases, and the surface rentals received for oil, gas, coal, and mineral leases; royalties from the sale of nonrenewable resources, again usually oil, gas, coal, and minerals; and revenues from the sale of trust lands.

As shown in Figure 2-1, receipts from surface and renewable resource leases or sales are generally channeled directly to the beneficiaries, in some cases after the state land office deducts its operating expenses. These are generally classed as "rental" income in land office financial statements. Revenues from mining royalties and land sales usually go into an inviolate permanent fund, with only the interest disbursed to the beneficiaries on the

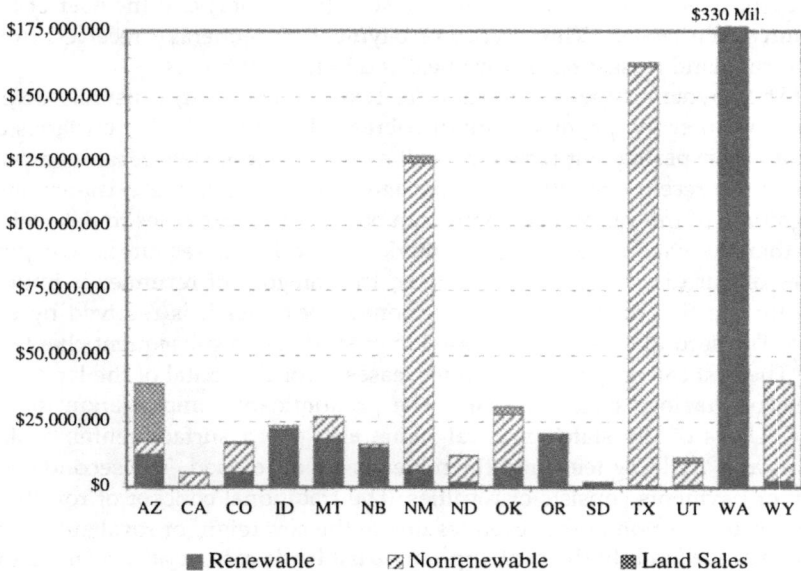

Figure 2-5. Composition of trust revenues by source.

basis of their contributions to the fund.[34] Revenues from nonrenewable sources are usually categorized as "royalties."

Amount of Revenues from Trust Lands

Revenues received from leases are constantly in flux. Revenues from some uses, such as the traditional ones of agriculture and grazing, are relatively stable year-to-year. Annual revenues for other uses—particularly ones where royalties and bonus payments provide the bulk of the receipts—vary tremendously. We focus on a single year's revenues in our discussion here, because displaying and discussing multiple years' worth of data is too complex for this introduction. In later resource-specific chapters, we look at revenue flows and prices over time.

As can be seen from Figure 2-5, revenues received from trust lands vary considerably among the states. States can probably be divided easily into three categories: those that receive a very small amount each year from trust lands—less than $3 million per year (Arkansas, Nevada, and Wisconsin) or between $4 million and $20 million per year in revenues (California, Colorado, Nebraska, North Dakota, South Dakota, and Utah); those that receive between $20 million per year and $80 million per year (Arizona, Idaho,

Montana, Oklahoma, Oregon, and Wyoming); and those that have very high levels of trust revenues (New Mexico, Texas, and Washington).

Revenues from specific resources are shown by state in Table 2-6. By any measure, New Mexico, Texas, and Washington are in a category by themselves, receiving substantial annual revenue from their trust lands. In the case of New Mexico and Texas, the revenues are primarily from oil and gas; in Washington, the renewable revenues are mostly from timber, while its high land sales receipts are from a one-time sale of environmentally sensitive lands to the state parks. States in the second category—receiving between $20 and $80 million per year—have high-valued lands and resources (Idaho, Oklahoma, Oregon, and Wyoming) or just lots of land (Arizona and Montana). States in the first category typically either have lots of land but receive little revenue from it (Colorado and Utah), or have smaller amounts of land that have higher-valued uses (California, Nebraska, North Dakota, South Dakota, and Utah).

The levels and types of revenues are significant for two reasons. First, some states emphasize management of their major revenue source (such as oil and gas in the case of New Mexico, Texas, and California, and timber in the case of Washington and Oregon). Other states focus less on management of their major revenue earners than on traditional resources such as grazing. Similarly, resources that return revenues to the operating expenses of the state land office may gain priority in use over other uses.[35] For example, the land office may emphasize grazing programs that return operating funds to it instead of programs involving sale of the lands (such as commercial development), even if the latter would be better for the permanent fund. For this reason, the differentiation in how revenues are disbursed to beneficiaries may be significant in identifying potential inefficiencies in state land office management.[36]

Distribution of Revenues

Revenues flow to the beneficiaries by two routes, as shown in Figure 2-1: revenues directly distributed from renewable revenues, and dividends earned on investments of the permanent fund. In this section we go into greater detail about which types of revenues are directly distributed, based generally on whether they are rents, royalties, or bonus payments. Variation in distribution patterns among the states will be highlighted. Ultimately, the success or failure of state trust lands to produce revenues for the beneficiaries can be judged by the amounts of revenues they provide. Figure 2-6 shows the relative magnitudes of the revenues dispersed to the beneficiaries from each of these two sources.

Land-based revenues (identified as Resources in Figure 2-6) flow from renewable resources (the left-hand side of the Lands & Resources box in Figure 2-1), minus agency funding deductions (see Table 2-2, represented in Figure 2-1 by the "ghost" arrow), and divided by type of resource (see Table 2-7

TABLE 2-6. Revenues from use of state trust lands, 1990 (includes rent, royalty and bonus payments)

State	Agriculture	Grazing	Timber	Commercial, Special Use	Other Non-commodity	Minerals	Oil and Gas
Arizona	$2,158,043	$1,609,168	$209,498	$8,393,269		$3,212,509	$44,313
California	$52,565	$4,500	$25,044	$63,190	$389	$64,468	$22,273
Colorado	$1,280,075	$2,690,432	$49,329		$1,685,258	$138,129	$8,065,469
Idaho	$124,803	$1,073,666	$19,470,946	$949,363			$480,666
Montana	$7,350,754	$4,133,290	$6,642,118		$331,382		$5,917,233
Nebraska	$15,192,562						$1,133,070
New Mexico		$6,039,779	$13,200	$456,489	$116,087	$1,203,834	$115,467,705
North Dakota		$2,082,765					$9,182,216
Oklahoma	$7,175,471				$211,683		$20,296,320
Oregon	$16,349	$197,216	$20,047,558	$135,495		$69,349	$36,834
South Dakota		$1,671,267				$1,425	$96,531
Texas		$674,111				$16,218,346	$143,791,850
Utah		$372,000	$31,979	$358,739	$32,219		$8,676,267
Washington	$4,449,891	$459,248	$260,699,866	$880,059	$117,263	$79,414	$66,837
Wyoming	$50,184	$1,911,765	$104,781	$298,975	$275,844	$8,275,815	$23,913,436
Total	$37,850,697	$22,919,207	$307,294,319	$11,535,579	$2,770,125	$29,263,289	$337,191,020

below). Dividend payments are ultimately the result of resource revenues that go into the permanent fund (Table 2-7), are invested, and subsequently return interest payments to the beneficiary, net of administrative costs.[37]

Distribution of revenues varies state-to-state and by whether the trust beneficiary is the county or the public schools and institutions. Table 2-7 shows this variation among the western states. All the states' nonrenewable revenues for public school and institutions are placed in permanent trust funds. Other sources of revenues commonly placed in permanent funds are land sales and rights-of-way, although some states (California and Washington) use a "land bank" account, where receipts from land sales are placed to await purchase of replacement land. In Montana, net receipts from timber sales go into the income fund of the institution whose lands generated the revenues.[38] Idaho is unique in placing receipts from the sale of timber, along with land sales, easements, and mineral royalties, into a permanent endowment fund.[39] Montana, unlike the other states, disburses only 95 percent of the renewable resource revenues, and only 95 percent of the interest on the permanent funds to the public schools; the remaining 5 percent of each of these funds is placed in the permanent fund.[40]

How the revenues get to the beneficiaries once they are earned also varies by state. Use of trust lands revenues is only specified in two states: California and

TABLE 2-6 *(Continued)*

Coal	Geo-thermal	Other Commodity	Water Rights	Land Sales	Right-of-Way	Fees and Permits	Total
		$1,865,052	$126,312	$21,091,728	$741,193	$915,914	$40,366,999
	$5,090,616			$308,066	$18,245	$1,936	$5,651,292
$2,653,673		$158,399		$334,632	$308,914	$56,291	$17,420,601
				$1,328,944	$72,169		$23,500,557
$2,302,504		$108,725		$69,032	$105,350	$174,195	$27,134,583
				$6,900	$27,153		$16,359,685
$471,523	$1,000	$636,543	$138,203	$1,686,436	$1,213,994	$259,822	$127,704,615
$778,723		$8,607		$204,802	$152,219		$12,409,332
		$64,098		$2,894,862	$181,867	$377,124	$31,201,425
		$5,146		$11,900	$2,175		$20,522,022
		$45		$408,021			$2,177,289
$549,004		$547,296		$96,958	$1,394,280		$163,271,845
		$50,834		$1,782,854	$129,326	$20,206	$11,454,424
$1,800		$647,060		$58,291,970	$4,115,018		$329,808,426
$5,356,483		$344,633	$33,155	$98,396	$41,187	$95,083	$40,799,737
$12,113,710	$5,091,616	$4,436,438	$297,670	$88,615,501	$8,503,090	$1,900,571	$869,782,832

Washington. All revenues, except receipts from land sales, go to the State Teachers' Retirement System in California. Both renewable resource receipts and the interest on the permanent funds from the public school trust lands go into the common school construction fund in Washington, traditionally the only state source of funds for school building construction.[41] Receipts from public school trust lands in the other states are not restricted in purpose and constitute only a portion of the states' contribution to education, usually apportioned to the school districts according to student numbers. The South Dakota Office of School and Public Lands distributes trust land revenues directly to the beneficiary school districts.[42]

SUMMARY

The theme of this chapter is that trust management is a system set up to fulfill trustee goals: to generate revenues for the beneficiary, to protect the corpus of the trust, and to make the trust assets productive. The system includes the lands, resources, and permanent funds; the revenues; and the management system and personnel. States exhibit variety in the extent and the types of lands managed, in the resource uses leased from these lands,

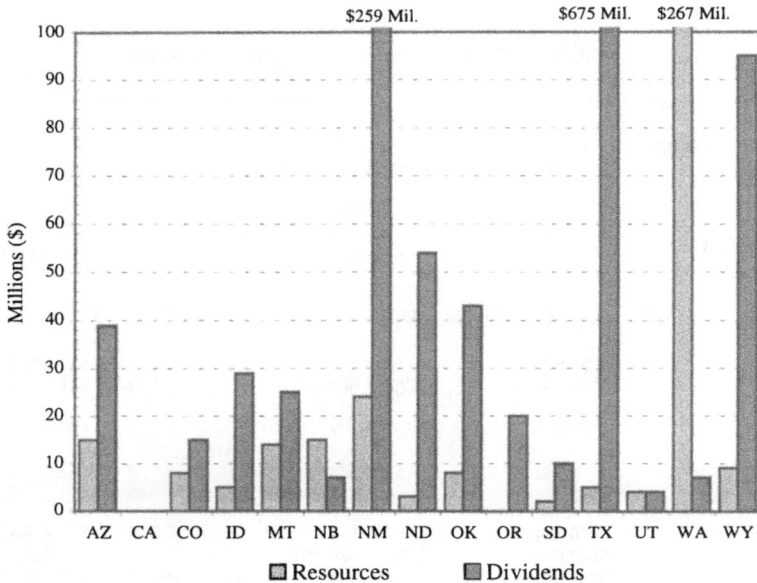

Figure 2-6. Payments to school and institutional trusts by revenue source.

and in the distribution and management mechanisms they set up to account for the management of the lands and revenues.

First we examined how the trust manager organizes—that is, whether there is a board of land commissioners, and if so, its composition, whether the agency head is elected or appointed, and where the land office fits in the larger state government. How the board is organized and how the agency executive head is selected influence the insularity of the agency in managing trust resources without interference from outside political forces. Board composition also reflects the influence of the beneficiaries compared to other interests. Although these variables ought, according to conventional wisdom, to be connected to outcomes, such connections are hard to demonstrate. Clearer lines can be drawn between personnel allocation and outcomes and between funding mechanisms and outcomes. The amount of funding and the ways that the offices are funded both influence how the staff is apportioned to manage the various resources. We saw that the number of employees varies among the states, and that the proportion of each state's employees assigned to manage specific resources also varies tremendously.

The amount of the lands that the states own varies considerably, and the uses of these lands are equally varied, although all states lease lands for agriculture and grazing. Other significant surface uses are for forestry (in

BLE 2-7. Division of revenues between direct disbursement to beneficiaries (net of land office expenses, if applicable) or placement in beneficiaries' permanent fund

Revenue Source	AZ	CA	CO	ID	MT	NB	NM	ND	OK	OR	SD	TX	UT	WA	WY
Renewable																
Cropland	B	B	B	B	B	B	B		B	PF	B	B	B	B	B
Grazing	B	B	B	B	B	B	B	B	B	PF	B	B	B	B	B
Timber	PF	B	B	PF	B		B		B	PF	B	B	B		
Water	PF	B			PF				B	PF	B	B			
Commercial	B	B	B		B	B	B		B	PF	B	B	B	B	B
Other noncommodity	B	B	B				B			PF	B	B	B	B	B
Nonrenewable																
Minerals																
Surface rental	B	B	B	B	B		B	B	PF	PF	B,PF	PF	PF	B	B
Bonus bids		B	PF	PF	B			B	PF	PF	B,PF	PF	PF		B
Royalties	PF	B	PF	PF	PF		PF	PF	PF	PF	B,PF	PF	PF	PF	B
Oil and gas																
Surface rental	B	B	B	B	B	B	B	B	PF	PF	B,PF	PF	PF	B	B
Bonus bids		B	PF	PF	PF	B		B	PF	PF	B,PF	PF	PF		B
Royalties	PF	B	PF	PF	PF	PF	PF	PF	PF	PF	B,PF	PF	PF	PF	PF
Coal																
Surface rental	B	B	B		B		B	B	PF	PF		PF	PF	B	B
Bonus bids		B	PF		B			B	PF	PF		PF	PF		B
Royalties	PF	B	PF		PF		PF	PF	PF	PF		PF	PF	PF	PF
Geothermal																
Surface rental		B,OT		B	B		B			PF		PF		B	B
Bonus bids				PF											
Royalties		B,OT		PF	PF		PF			PF		PF	PF	PF	PF
Other commodities																
Surface rental		B	B	B	B	B	B		PF	PF		PF	PF	B	B
Bonus bids						B			PF			PF			
Royalties		B	PF	PF	PF	PF	PF		PF	PF		PF	PF	PF	PF
Lands and miscellaneous																
Right-of-way	B,PF	B	PF	PF			PF		PF	PF	PF	PF	B	PF	PF	PF
Land Sales																
Interest	B	LB	PF	B				B	B	PF	B	B	PF	LB	B
Income	PF	LB	PF	PF	PF	PF	PF	PF	PF	PF	PF	LB	PF	LB	PF
Fees and permits	B	B		B,PF					B	OT		B		B	B	OT

Codes: B = disbursable to beneficiary; PF = permanent fund; OT = other; LB = land bank.

three states) and for commercial leasing (in another four). The distributions of leasing and production for subsurface uses are very uneven. Some states—specifically, Oklahoma, Montana, New Mexico and Wyoming—received lands with significant oil and gas reserves, as can be seen both in the areas leased for this use and in the revenues received. Coal is produced largely in six states—Colorado, North Dakota, Montana, New Mexico, Texas, and Utah—but even within these states, the amount of lands leased for this use varies according to whether strip or surface mining is used. Hardrock mineral leases are most varied, primarily because mineralization occurs in small discrete areas. Only in Arizona, Texas, and Wyoming do they produce significant revenues.

The other component of the corpus is the permanent fund. The beneficiaries' permanent funds serve as a repository of revenues received from nonrenewable resource uses and from land sales. In some states, other sources of revenues are also deposited in the permanent funds. Instead of simply treating such funds as a "sink" or "black box" that receives revenues and disburses interest, we spent some time describing the nature of the various states' funds, providing information about the amount of each state's fund and the flows of revenues into and out of each.

The distribution of revenues between annual disbursement to the beneficiaries and placement of revenues in permanent funds varies depending on the resource, on what type of payment is received, and in which state it is received. Significant variation also exists in how the state land offices are funded. In Chapter 3, we ask whether either of these two variations among the states affects their resource management; and if so, what the effect is on the trust. But the state land offices do not exist in a vacuum within the larger state government.

We can use this information on the historical evolution of the trust lands and their guiding principles, together with the view of trust management as a system that is supposed to act in the best interests of the beneficiaries, as the basis for evaluating management. Chapter 3 provides necessary tools for beginning that task.

APPENDIX: SOURCES OF INFORMATION

Information on the amount of revenues received and the extent of state leases is available in a variety of places, depending on the state. These should be mentioned before we continue our overview of trust lands and their resources. Most state land offices publish some sort of annual or biennial (depending on the legislature) report. The level of specificity and information varies from a single page in Montana to hundred-page-plus reports in other states. Trust principles require at a minimum that the amounts of revenues received, their destinations, and the amount spent on land office activities be disclosed. Again, the degree of specificity varies by state. Management of the permanent funds is frequently handled by another state agency or by a quasi-agency sometimes called the "State Investment Council" or something similar; accounting reports are generally provided by these organizations. Very few states provide information on personnel allocations within the land offices; however, this information can sometimes be found in the budget requests that the governor submits to the legislature. Other potential sources of information on state land office revenues and management expenses are reports of the state treasurer's and auditor's offices. These reports, usually in the form of accounting tables, sometimes provide information at a greater level of specificity than does the land office report; in other instances, they provide additional parts to the puzzle. For broad comparisons among the trust land states, the Western States Land Commissioners Association publishes an annual directory that provides summary statistics. Your state land office should have a copy available for inspection. The amount and location of information available vary by state. Experience and persistence are the best available tools.

CHAPTER THREE

Evaluating Trust Lands
Management Decisions

This chapter provides a structure and tools for evaluating whether trust lands management decisions meet the trustee's obligations to the beneficiaries. We take the components of the trust system, introduced in Chapter 2—the lands, revenues, and permanent funds—and use production economics and portfolio theory to explain basic trust land decisions. We look at four areas where we think crucial decisions affecting the efficacy of trust management are made.

The first and most fundamental question a trustee must address is whether it is better for the trust beneficiary to sell the lands and invest the receipts or to retain and manage the lands. Although one might think that American society decided at the turn of the last century to retain and manage public lands, such is not the case. Whether or not to "privatize" or otherwise dispose of federal public lands is a hardy perennial of debate and advocacy. In the trust lands context, the question also arises frequently. Many state legislatures have directed or forbidden the trustee to reduce their land holdings. Throughout the remainder of this book, we discuss specific proposals and programs for disposing of or repositioning trust assets. Evaluating that decision—making an informed determination regarding the best interests of the trust—continues to be an important analytical task. The state trust context differs from the federal land context, however, because the manager's obligations to the beneficiary provide a standard for assessing the decision reached.

Second, once the trustee has made the decision to retain and manage state lands, three systems can be used to produce revenues from these lands: the state can produce the commodities itself, by hiring labor and providing its own capital; it can rent or lease the lands to others to produce commodities, receiving a fixed amount in return; or it can share costs, responsibility for production, and returns with the producer. One of the least discussed and most frequently overlooked decisions in public resource management—one that pervades virtually all state and federal agencies and programs—is the decision to forgo the first option. In the United States, government landowners do not typically develop the resources that they own by, for example, hiring government loggers to cut trees which they sell at the road head. As a result of this strategy, government managers generally lease the resources to others who produce commodities. Thus the decision to lease is absolutely central to state trust resource management. Analyzing lease provisions carefully, to understand the structure of the lease and the specific balancing of risk and return that it entails, becomes crucial to evaluating the trustee's day-to-day operations.

Third, in evaluating trust management, we are concerned about the expenditure of funds and the allocation of land, personnel, and management resources. Because personnel costs are the largest single component of trust manager's budgets, they provide an appropriate focus for evaluating whether trust assets are being efficiently managed.

Fourth, managing the receipts from resource development—the permanent fund—is crucial to day-to-day resource management decisions. This aspect of the analysis is complicated by the fact that only in Oklahoma and North Dakota does the trustee have responsibility for managing the permanent fund. However, if the goal is to raise revenues for schools, it makes no sense to develop resources to produce revenues if the funds are poorly managed and lose value to inflation. The trust would be better off leaving them in the ground. The issue of the permanent fund also sharpens questions about the time scale of management, focusing on tradeoffs between short-term and long-term management decisions and strategies.

The goal of this chapter is to provide an analytical framework and tools for assessing the decisions that a trustee makes in these four areas. We do not take them up in the order just presented, but rather follow a path that makes more sense in terms of building analytical concepts. The chapter's first section describes the trust lands and assets as a production system to fit the various parts of the system together and describe how they work together to produce revenues for the beneficiaries. The lease as a system for allocating risk and rewards lies at the core of this discussion. Once the state decides to let lessees develop its resources, various arrangements are possible that have different advantages and disadvantages. The risk associated with varying returns from resource production are identified as a key determinant affecting different leasing arrangements. Risk also plays a role in determining the optimal mix of various types of resources produced—or invested in—by the trust. The section uses portfolio theory as a method to analyze this mix and their associated risks.

Building on production theory and portfolio models, the second section looks at ways to evaluate whether the trustee is efficiently managing the trusts' assets. We evaluate efficiency in two ways. First, using commonly available information from the states (remember the trust's accountability requirements), we identify two useful measures of agency performance: revenues per acre leased for a specific use; and revenues per full-time employee (FTE) engaged in various resource management programs. The former criterion provides a useful measure to incorporate into portfolio theory, while the latter criterion indicates whether sufficient emphasis is being placed on programs that serve the beneficiaries' interest. We then go from the efficient allocation of lands and personnel to ask whether the state land office is underfunded, funded just about right, or overfunded. The discussion of funding is necessarily conceptual, but it brings forth the notion that an optimal percentage of receipts provides the greatest net return to the beneficiary. Identifying exactly where this point is located however varies by state and by resource.

We then ask the question, "how does the trustee make decisions about the tradeoffs between short-term and long-term management decisions and strategies?" The third section discusses the range of choices that trustees have faced and continue to face in setting broad policies. Economic development theory is used to focus particularly on decisions trustees make that have the potential to consume, rather than perpetuate, the trust corpus.

While consuming the value of the trust corpus is explicitly prohibited in most states, the implicit structure for trust management in many states nevertheless leads to this result. Our discussion displays an array of possible scenarios that have this consumptive effect, as well as ways to ameliorate it. We emphasize two areas: the role that the interest and discount rates (really the same thing) play in these decisions; and the various models from macroeconomics that portray the choices that the state has (or has had) in the preservation versus consumption of trust resources. The interest and discount rate(s) that a state uses constitute the most explicit recognition of the tradeoffs between the present and the future they make. We briefly review the effects that interest and discount rates have on that choice. Building on this, we then look at the larger-scale tradeoffs between current development and future retention. Possible development scenarios are described, using a variety of conceptual models. Our goal is to make explicit the choices that the state makes when it decides to develop or to dispose of trust assets.

The chapter concludes with a case study analyzing the effect one state's decision had when it diverted assets from the trusts' permanent funds to meet a budgetary crisis. We identify a range of possible situations where such use seems acceptable. By tying the conceptual models to a real issue, we hope to demonstrate the applicability of the analytical models and tools described in this chapter.

RISK AND RETURNS: INTRODUCING THE PRODUCTION FUNCTION AND THE LEASE AS A TOOL FOR SHARING RISK

The easiest way to visualize how commodities are produced from natural resources is to imagine that various types of inputs are combined to produce

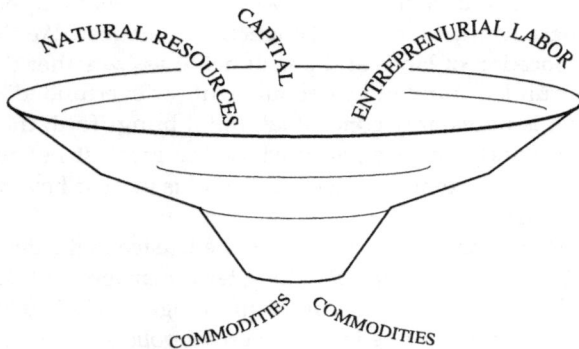

Figure 3-1. Conversion of inputs into outputs in the production function.

outputs. Outputs are the products of natural resources, whether they be cattle, coal, or recreation days. Inputs—called "factors of production" or "factor inputs"—are usually discussed under two or three broad headings. For most purposes, land, labor, and capital are common input categories. The production function is a standard analytic tool of economics used to describe how different combinations of inputs are mixed to form outputs.[1] Figure 3-1 shows this in graphic terms.

Within each of the broad categories of factor inputs, numerous specialized components exist. For example, the land factor can be subdivided into various types and different qualities of lands of a given owner. Similarly, clerical, professional, field, and hired or contracted labor are different types of labor inputs. Capital inputs can also be differentiated into subcategories such as equipment, investments, and even plans and intellectual expertise. The boundaries between different types of factor inputs are not precise. For example, current land capability is frequently the result of the previous application of varying amounts (positive or negative) of labor and capital. Similarly, capital in the form of intellectual expertise may have required considerable expenditures of money and labor to develop. Depending on the product desired, different amounts of the different types of factor inputs are required. The amount of a specific input factor used is called its *intensity*. As the intensity of a specific input is varied, the amount of the commodity produced varies. In many cases, one input can also be substituted for another.

Whether any one production input can be substituted for another is determined by physical, biological, and/or mechanical processes. Knowing when the factors are most effectively balanced is a key to managing resources efficiently. For example, to produce the same amount of wheat, one can either farm a large land area extensively or a smaller area intensively (using additional labor and other inputs such as fertilizers and irrigation).

Of course, the costs of the factor inputs and the prices received for the commodities produced affect the appropriate intensity of use of any specific factor, the optimal mix of factors, and the amount of production. Whether it is efficient to substitute one input—or to vary the intensity of use of an input—is also a function of costs and returns. However, the capability of one factor to substitute for another is limited and usually declines as the intensity of use of that factor increases. Thus at some point, the cost of applying more fertilizer equals the value of the wheat it will produce. Once that point is reached, any additional use of that specific factor is unproductive.

One way to look at the factor inputs is to view them as being "owned" by someone. In this framework, someone owns the land, the labor is owned by its providers, and individuals, corporation, or banks own capital. Here, too, the boundaries are not always clearly defined, but the general picture is useful. The key issue becomes how to apportion the revenues and risks resulting from production to the various input owners.

The Lease: Apportioning Risks and Returns

Landowners can produce commodities themselves by hiring or using their own labor; or they can lease lands to others to produce the commodities; or they can share the production responsibilities with the labor's owner. In the first case, all revenues go initially to the landowner, who also decides what to produce and how intensively to use various inputs. But the landowner also incurs all production risks. In the second case, where the landowner leases, the lessee determines the amount of other inputs to use to produce commodities and is responsible for paying the costs of their use. Thus, the lessee incurs all production risks. The third system, where the landowner and labor supplier share production risks and returns, has been known as "sharecropping" in agricultural contexts. The landowner provides the lands and may share in providing other inputs, such as managerial expertise or capital (in the form of improvements such as roads, utilities, and fences) or other inputs. The tenant or lessee, sometimes called the *cropper*, provides labor and may provide a portion of the other production inputs. The division of the proceeds from the production—and the sharing of risks—is determined by agreement between the parties, which often varies according to who provides the inputs.

The choice of production arrangement often reflects the factor providers' willingness to risk their resources, since commodities production is inherently risky. Prices received for the products depend on market demand, which usually lies beyond the producer's control. Weather frequently affects the quantity produced as well as production costs. In minerals, the extent, quality, and even existence of the desired ore is frequently unknown prior to exploration or sometimes even production. Each production arrangement apportions risks and returns differently. But before going into detail about how risk is apportioned, we need to understand it; then we can discuss leasing as a mechanism for managing and apportioning risk.

Risk and Variations in Lease Returns[2]

Risk in business activity is the difference between the expected revenues and the actual revenues received. Revenue expectations are usually based on past occurrences projected into the future, called the *trend*. *Variance* is the difference between the actual and the expected revenues along the trend— that is, the shorter-term fluctuations around the longer-term trend.[3] Three important types of variance affect natural resources leasing: the larger, macroeconomic cycles in the economy as a whole; the variations in the prices of the specific commodities produced by states; and the variance due to particular aspects of an individual, firm, or operator.

Highly complex models can be used to explain the movement of demand and commodity prices and their effects on the overall economy. Basic (but still useful) knowledge can be gained by using the simple procedures we develop here. First, we want to know the general trend in prices for commodities produced from state lands, and the variability in prices around the trend. Then we want to know the covariance between one commodity's price fluctuations and other resources important to the trust. Using the variance and covariance information, we can determine the risk inherent in the trust portfolio to understand both the likelihood of revenue fluctuations and the means to incorporate that risk into management.

MEASUREMENT OF RISK

The measurement of price fluctuations provides an indication of the variability, or risk, of the activity. For each of the three types of variability, it is important to know not only the individual variance for any single component, but the interactions—or covariance[4]—among the different components of risk.

Beta. When judging potential leasing activities, we often find it advantageous to compare how the risk of one activity compares to the risk of other possible undertakings. Standard parlance uses the term *beta*[5] to identify the risk of one activity as compared either to a risk-free activity or to the market as a whole. For example, states generally lease for the production of a number of different resources—such as timber, grazing, and minerals—while at the same time they invest some or all of the proceeds in permanent funds that may also include various other types of investments, such as government bonds, Treasury bills, and equity stocks. The total of all these activities—which we call the state's portfolio—has an average risk determined by the total risk, or covariance, of each individual activity's risk. Beta provides a measure of the risk of a single activity versus the average risk when weighted as its proportion of the whole.

Risk Premiums and the Capital Asset Pricing Model. The only rational reason for choosing a risky activity involves the possibility of gaining an additional benefit from it compared to a lower-risk venture. The difference in the return between these two activities—one risky and one less so—is called the *risk premium.*[6] If the risk premium is high enough, then the *potential* return from the activity may offset the additional risk associated with it. Risk premiums typically are calculated by using a method called the *capital asset pricing model.* This model asserts that the risk premium varies in accordance with the beta of the activity.

TYPES OF RISK

Careful differentiation of the three types of risks—or revenue variations—inherent in production from natural resources[7] is crucial, since certain types of risks can be moderated by mechanisms that the state controls, while others are uncontrollable but nonetheless should be incorporated into decision making. After describing each of the three broad risk categories, we discuss how leasing procedures can generically be used to moderate the various risk types.[8] But although we divide risk into these tidy categories, feedback mechanisms frequently cause consequences of one type of risk to spill over into others.

Macroeconomic Cycle Variation. Most of us are painfully aware that the economy of the United States goes through cycles that are impossible to control. Two effects of these large-scale cycles—which economists call *macroeconomic cycles*—are periods of recession and inflation that occur even when the economy is growing over the long term. We can describe macroeconomic cycles in relation to the trend by using such indicators as the unemployment rate and the consumer price index. When these indicators are higher than their long-term trend, a recession occurs; when they are below their long-term trends, expansion occurs.[9]

States face the same problem individuals do in dealing with macroeconomic effects. Recessions affect states by causing a general slowdown of the economy as a whole, thus reducing demand—and prices—for the commodities produced from the trust lands. And while demand and prices for trust products fall, the revenues received from trust assets become more important to the beneficiaries because, during recessions, alternative income sources are also reduced. Inflation, which is usually (but not always) countercyclical to recession, occurs when the government prints too much money, thereby devaluing it, or when society creates too much demand for too few consumables, thereby increasing their prices. In either case, inflation has two effects on trust assets that should be factored into planning. First, it reduces the value of the state's permanent fund, since the dollar value of the fund stays the same while its purchasing power is reduced. Second, inflation has vastly different effects depending on whether the increase in the price of a commodity—or in the total portfolio of goods—produced from trust lands rises in value at a rate greater than the rise in the cost of goods purchased by the beneficiaries. We discuss the effects of inflation in more detail later in this chapter.

Commodity Market Variation. Macroeconomic cycles also interact with the second risk category: commodity market variations. Demand for and prices received for commodities produced from trust lands are closely linked to macroeconomic cycles. In some cases, commodity prices influence the inflation rate. For example, the rise in oil prices in the mid- and late-1970s contributed to high overall levels of inflation during these times. In other cases, the general state of the economy affected the prices received for other commodities, as occurred with timber prices in the early 1980s when a recession-depressed housing market reduced the demand for lumber. To analyze these variations adequately, we must first characterize cycles in commodity prices, then distinguish them from macroeconomic cycles, and finally factor their variation into leasing procedures.[10] But as we saw in our portfolio theory discussions, even more important is the covariance between commodities. Are increases in timber prices related to oil and gas price increases? If their covariance is low—or if one goes up when the other goes down—they can reduce overall variation by balancing each other's price fluctuations.

Unique Lease or Lessee Variation. The final risk component is associated with the specific lease or lessee. Each lease has characteristics that allocate varying degrees of uncertainty to the resource owner, to the potential lessee, or to both. This is especially the case with regard to subsurface resources, where the extent and value of the ore deposit is frequently unknown prior to leasing. Uncertainty also occurs in surface leases, where one party in the transaction may possess less information about the value of the property than the other. In grazing leases, for example, the state may not have inspected the property thoroughly prior to initiating or renewing a lease, while the new or existing lessee may have considerable knowledge of the value of the property to his or her operation. Weather frequently produces variations in the revenues and/or costs associated with leases—especially agricultural leases, but also timber sales where access is problematical during wet weather or where fire hazards prevent work in extremely dry seasons.

The quality of the lessee and, to some extent, the quality of the state land-managing agency are also risk elements. Some lessees have the experience and capital to manage leased properties better than others can. Further, the behavior of individual lessees may affect the revenues received from the lease. For example, the lessee may default on rent payments, may abuse the land and waste assets, or may cheat on accounting. From the lessee's point of view, the state may be similarly burdensome, requiring expensive documentation prior to allowing improvements on the lease, failing to provide services at a level commensurate with private lessors, or unilaterally changing rules and regulations during the term of the lease. All these factors—from both sides, both known and unknown—influence how much revenue is received from natural resources leases and leasing mechanisms.

Neither party has perfect knowledge of the risk, but significant "information asymmetries" arise when one party knows more than the other about certain aspects of risk. The classic way to describe information asymmetries involves the traditional method for purchasing a car. The dealer knows how much the car cost from the manufacturer and how much additional money is required to cover the dealer's costs and profit. The buyer typically only has the information on the sticker—or list—price but hopes that the dealer will take less. The information asymmetry in this case benefits the dealer, who has an idea of the minimum acceptable price, while the buyer only knows that the price is reducible but not by how much. If the purchaser knew how much the car cost the dealer, and what additional amount the dealer required to cover expenses, then the two parties could negotiate a reasonable profit or markup. But since this isn't the case, the purchaser pays more than the dealer's minimum markup in practically all cases as a result of the information asymmetry.

If neither party is certain about the variability in a lease or about the lessee's behavior, then risk can be shared through a number of processes. First, risk can be reduced through contractual provisions between the state and the lessee. Such contractual provisions may specify how uncertainties are to be dealt with. Second, either party's risk can be reduced by dividing costs and revenues, as in share-cropping. Third, the risks can be placed entirely on one party in the transaction, with the expectation that the rent paid will reflect the concentration of risk in one of the parties.

Apportioning Risk in Leasing

If both parties involved in the lease want to reduce their risk—or the variation in returns—then analysis of leasing procedures is a matter of determining who bears the risks, and how this is reflected in the division of the returns from the lease. Risk can be reduced in different ways, depending on whether you are the landowner, the lessee, or the lender of capital. Here we focus specifically on the allocation of risk between the landowner and the lessee; however, the role of the provider of capital is also important for developing several resources, as we discuss in following chapters.

MECHANISMS TO OVERCOME OR REDUCE RISK

There are limits to what the parties to a lease can do to reduce each of the three risk types. Neither party can do much to overcome general macroeconomic cycle risks. The owner of the resource may be in a position to reduce the commodity market risk by not putting all of its investment eggs in the same basket, through diversifying or becoming involved in a number of commodities that are subject to different market cycles.

Resource owners also want to reduce the risk unique to each lease. Various strategies permit this. First, the "law of large numbers" reduces overall risk: because the state usually has large numbers of leases and lessees, performance tends to average out between the good ones and the bad ones. One way to increase the odds of success is to identify and terminate leases with lessees who fail to perform. Lease terms and conditions permitting relatively easy lease revocation are a risk reduction strategy. Resource owners commonly require minimum bidding qualifications and institute rules and regulations governing the conduct of the leases. This risk-reduction strategy is not, however, cost- and risk-free: the owner is then required to expend effort monitoring to ensure that the lessee fulfills the lease terms.

Lessees, too, have an interest in reducing the risks they face. Their market risk can be reduced by having a low fee, since, if the lease fee is nominal in comparison to the potential return, the risk that the market will fall while the rent remains high is reduced. An alternative strategy, which also works well for the owner, is to allow the lease payments to vary in response to market conditions. Such tying of the rent to market conditions is called *indexing*. If the price for the product is high, the rent rises; but conversely, if the price for the product drops, the rent is also reduced. This risk-reduction strategy is inherent in sharecropping.

But lessees bear other risks. For example, many agricultural lessees view the agreed-upon lease, under which the period of the lessee's tenancy is spelled out, as encompassing a risk that they will not be able to continue the lease at the end of the current term. This makes it difficult for them to establish a stable allocation of resources in their total operation. Lessees try to reduce this risk, which is especially important when the lease fee is below market, by establishing a system of preferential rights for lease renewal.

The decision to share risks by leasing resources to others for them to develop is one fundamental decision that a trustee can make. Although lease terms can be negotiated to achieve a reasonable balancing of some of the risks, some risk is unavoidable. Trustees make diverse decisions that allocate risk in production and management more or less efficiently. Having obtained a flavor of the lease as a mechanism for spreading and sharing some of the risks, we now turn to methods for evaluating the manager's decisions.

CONDITIONS FOR EFFICIENCY IN PRODUCTION AND MANAGEMENT

Our ultimate goal in examining decisions associated with the production of resources from trust lands is to develop concepts and tools for evaluating the overall effectiveness of trust land management. A major step in accomplishing this is to explore some of the complexities involved in defining "overall effectiveness." We begin by examining different interpretations of what "for the benefit of the schools" means in economic terms. We contrast three different goals that the trustee might choose to pursue: profit maximization, revenue maximization, and cost-constrained maximization. Each of these notions of overall effectiveness fits comfortably within the trust obligation, yet each has different implications for management and for the beneficiary. Unfortunately, trust documents and most legislation are not clear as to which criterion the trustee is supposed to meet. Sometimes one can discern clues to the state's priorities in different decisions regarding state land office funding mechanisms, which we therefore explore closely. We then discuss a set of criteria that can be used to evaluate whether trust resources are efficiently deployed among the various resources managed by the state. These criteria measure the performance of land office management in terms of revenues returned per acre of land managed for a specific resource use and revenues generated by each employee of the agency in their various management capacities. We point particularly to the role that land office funding mechanisms play in the allocation of personnel.

We then combine notions of risk and uncertainty with concepts of efficient allocation of resources to introduce portfolio theory. Portfolio theory—a familiar tool of financial management—describes the efficient allocation of resources through diversification to reduce risk in the form of fluctuating revenues. Part of portfolio theory requires that a guiding rate of return on investments be identified; we discuss this in connection with the trust's permanent fund. Since an optimal portfolio of resources and investments cannot be achieved without some costs, the concept of transactions costs is introduced and applied here with respect to changing portfolios and (in subsequent chapters) with respect to specific leases. Transactions costs and portfolio theory are then linked by discussion of the time frame for adjusting an optimal resource management strategy to prepare for the section of the chapter dealing with development alternatives.

Approaches to Benefiting the Trust

Trust principles are, as we saw in Chapter 1, utterly unambiguous that the primary obligation of the trustee is undivided loyalty to the beneficiary. The trustee must manage the trust lands to produce benefits for the beneficiary. Those notions and phrases are not, unfortunately, self-interpreting. Enabling acts, constitutions, and state land office management objectives do not provide specific guidance as to what *benefit* means.[11] In this section we describe three different but completely reasonable ways to define "benefit to the trust," presenting each in theoretical terms as well as in terms of its effects on the trust.

THREE DEFINITIONS OF "BENEFIT TO THE TRUST"

The production function describes how land, labor, and capital are combined to produce commodities. Implicit in the production function, therfore, is the capacity to substitute one factor of production for another. Assuming that each factor has a cost—which may change as more or less of it is used—then theoretically some optimal mix produces the highest monetary return. In reality, however, reaching this optimal combination may be subject to a number of constraints. The amount and type of land available, the amount and type of labor available, and whether the state or the tenant can make investments to increase production are typical constraints that managers encounter. When deciding on the mix of inputs to use in producing commodities, managers can use economic theory to distinguish among three possible definitions of benefit to the trust: profit maximization, revenue maximization, or cost-constrained maximization.

We should first define some terms. *Revenues* are the monies received from selling commodities produced from trust resources. Commodities are typically priced on the basis of a standard measurement—for example, pounds of beef, board-feet of timber, or barrels of oil. Revenues equal the unit price times the quantity of units produced. Because most states do not produce enough of any commodity to affect market prices, revenues are related directly to how much is produced. Because the state does not affect the price, the *marginal revenue*—the amount of additional money received from producing an additional unit of the commodity—is usually considered to equal the price of a unit of the commodity.

Costs are usually divided into *fixed costs*, which are incurred regardless of the amount of the commodity produced, and *variable costs*, which result from the amount produced. *Marginal cost* is the cost of producing an additional unit of the commodity. Marginal costs are generally high initially, when small amounts are produced, because they incorporate both the fixed and the variable costs; as production levels increase, however, the fixed cost per unit produced (fixed cost divided by the number of units) decreases, and the variable cost may remain the same over a range of production. Eventually, marginal costs usually increase, either because the production based on the initial fixed costs increases—for example, because each additional unit of input such as fertilizer becomes less effective—or because additional capital (a fixed cost) may be required to increase production. *Profit* is the revenues received from selling the commodity minus the cost of production. Because both the revenues and the costs vary according to the amount produced, the amount of profit also varies by the amount produced.

Using these concepts, we can discuss three definitions of "benefit to the trust": profit maximization, revenue maximization, and cost-constrained maximization. *Revenue maximization* entails receiving the largest amount of money from the production of commodities, irrespective of the costs of production; that is, it means maximizing the *gross* amount of money received. In contrast, *profit maximization* implies generating the largest *net* amount of money after the costs of production are subtracted. The third possible financial management objective, *cost-constrained maximization*, involves maximizing the revenues subject to a limit on the amount of costs that can be incurred in their production.

EFFECT OF DIFFERENT MANAGEMENT OBJECTIVES ON THE TRUST

Although the preceding three terms relating to maximization are all in the same ball park and are frequently used as though there were no significant differences among them, they can support very different policies. We illustrate four possible cases regarding management objectives by exploring the state land management office's labor inputs and their effect on trust revenue generation. The four cases are roughly but not precisely analogous to the three different definitions of benefit discussed earlier. In our illustrations, we assume that the amount of land is fixed, while the amount of labor and capital can vary over short time frames. Figure 3-2 shows the three different objectives in graphic format. In this figure, P equals the price of a unit of the commodity, C equals the cost to produce the commodity, MC is the marginal cost to produce an additional unit of the commodity, and MR is the marginal revenue received by the state from producing an additional unit (in this case, assumed to be equal to the price). The vertical axis of the graphs represents the price and costs in dollars (increasing from bottom to top), while the horizontal axis represents the quantity Q of the commodity produced (increasing from left to right). Multiplying the price times the quantity gives the revenues received from producing a given quantity Q of the commodity (represented in the graphs by the area under the $MR = P$ line and to the left of the vertical Q line). The total cost of producing a level Q of the commodity is represented by the area (integral) beneath the MC curve to the left of the Q vertical line, shown in the graphs as the loosely

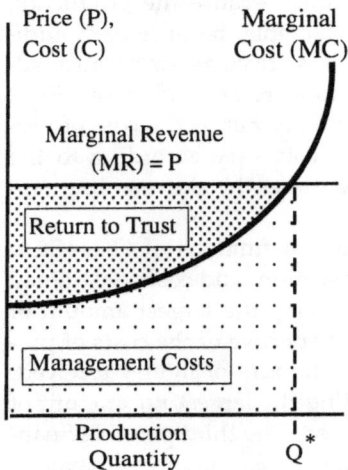

(a) Profit maximizing production.

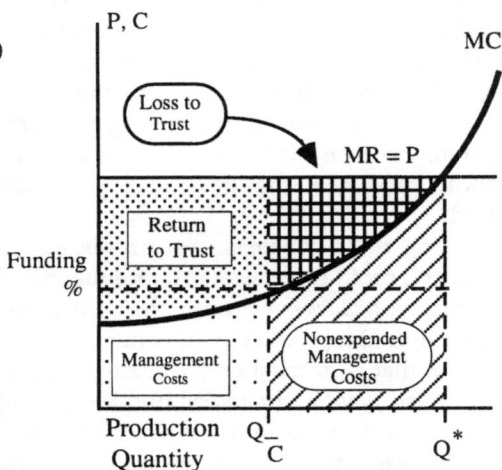

(b) Management cost-constrained (Funding %) production effects.

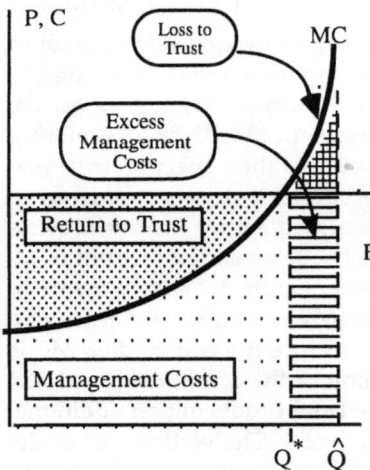

(c) Potential overproduction in net revenues management.

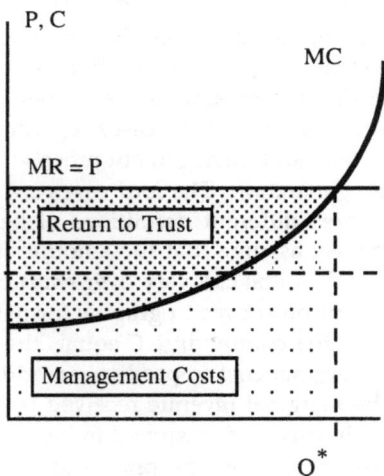

(d) Unique case where percent cost recovery equals profit maximizing production

Figure 3-2. Effects on trust returns from profit maximization compared to cost-constrained and net revenues management financing.

stippled area. Profit, called "Return to the Trust," is shown in the graphs as the closely stippled area.

Figure 3-2(a) represents the profit maximization objective. In this case, the land office has the flexibility and the determination to manage at an economically efficient point so that the marginal cost of operations equals the marginal revenues (as price) received for all the outputs from the trust lands. When the quantity of output equals Q^*, (optimal output) returns to the trust are maximized. Figure 3-2(b) shows the cost-constrained option. If the land office is constrained to operate at a level below the optimal labor input—whether because only a percentage of the revenues being returned or because the operating budget is limited by small legislative appropriations—the trust will receive lower revenues than it would under less restrictive conditions. The effects on the trust of the cost-constrained revenue maximization case is a considerable loss to the trust due to underinvestment or nonexpended management costs.

A third possibility exists where the state land office returns only net revenues—after deducting its operating expenses—to the trust beneficiaries. The land office may manage past the point of optimal economic efficiency due to lack of knowledge of the operation's cost structure, lack of differentiation between trust management and program areas, or simple inefficiency. This situation, involving the revenue maximization objective, is represented by the graph in Figure 3-2(c). The quantity produced is above the optimum level, so the marginal cost of production is greater than the price received for the output. Losses to the trust are represented by the crosshatched area in the graph, while the horizontal lines represent the added land office costs of overproduction. Notice that the immediate loss to the trust equals the area under the marginal cost (MC) curve above the price ($MR = P$) line. Depending on the resource, the loss to the trust could be still greater if resources with increasing value are used to subsidize the added costs of production above the efficient level.

Figure 3-2(d) shows an economically efficient funding arrangement for state land office management expenses, permitting profit to be maximized. The optimal point occurs when the percentage of revenues allocated for land office operations exactly equals the economically efficient amount of revenues—that is, when the integral of the management cost curve in Figure 3-2(d) equals Funding %* times PQ^* (where Funding %* represents the optimal funding level). The determination of this exact percentage, however, requires knowledge of the exact marginal cost curves for the agency. The cost curves, if represented as a percentage of revenues, fluctuate annually if the labor component is fixed, because the percentages depend on prices received for the outputs. To determine an exact percentage to use in legislatively mandated expenditure restrictions, one must take into account the short-term fluctuations in revenues, as well as the time periods for adjusting staff and resources to optimal program-specific expenditures. Figure 3-2, however, provides the theoretical basis for visually displaying the effects of fixed and variable land office expenditures on returns to the trust.

We have demonstrated how various objectives affect trust returns, and how these objectives are related to the way the state land office's management is funded. That an efficient point in management maximizes the net revenues to the trust is simple in concept but more difficult in application. Simply stated, states should apply sufficient management up to the point where an additional dollar of expenditure equals a dollar of additional revenues received from the management activity. But to apply this concept in practice, the states need to have a mechanism to assess whether their management is efficiently allocated for present funding expenditures and for adjustments (either increases or decreases) in funding.

Efficient Allocation of Resources and Personnel

Luckily, economic and business administration theory provides some relatively simple and straightforward criteria for determining whether resources are being efficiently allocated. Following from the production function, an input into the production of a commodity is efficiently applied up to the point where its marginal cost equals the marginal return from its use. In relation to the trust's production system, this implies that lands and personnel should be managed—optimally—up to the point where the revenues received from additional acreage and/or employees equal their cost. However, this criterion assumes that the states have the capacity to vary their land holdings and staffing levels; and neither of these is the case in reality, certainly not in the short term. So, given the constraints resulting from current land ownership patterns and legislatively limited staffing levels, how can states and beneficiaries determine whether resources are efficiently allocated? We first describe measures to evaluate management efficiency, and then subsequently discuss whether the mechanisms that the states use to fund their state land offices affect how efficiently resources are managed.

PERSONNEL EXPENDITURES

By far the largest management expenditure in the state land offices goes for personnel—costs that either could be used for other activities or could be passed on to the beneficiaries. Efficient personnel allocation is critical for trust management. There are two commonly used measures of performance: the return per employee required to produce a commodity; and the revenues per acre of land dedicated to a specific use.[12] The efficient personnel allocation criterion asserts that, all other things being equal, the return per employee should be similar across management programs within a state.[13]

These two efficiency measures—return per employee and return per acre—are derived from what is called "activity analysis." Activity analysis problem formulation is essentially descriptive; that is, the amount of input of each factor used in producing each output is fixed, based on empirical evidence. In the activity analysis production function, factor prices do not play a role in determining the optimal intensity of use of a factor compared to the intensity of use of another factor of production.[14] The intensities of factor use do come into the optimality condition in the determination of overall levels of production of a specific output, given the proportions of inputs specified in the intensity coefficients.[15]

The efficient condition in activity analysis is that the marginal rate of transformation of inputs into outputs is equal among the activities. For example, the marginal rate of transformation of labor into output should be equal among all the activities. The difference between the average rates of transformation, as calculated previously, and the marginal rates—which are theoretically stronger criteria measuring small incremental changes—is the difference between analyzing an individual project comparison and examining a statewide programmatic allocation of labor: it is a matter of scale. While changes in production processes at some point will yield differences in marginal rates of transformation, the marginal and average rates will be the same over the range of values incorporated in the activity analysis's average rates, since the rate of transformation is fixed.

An analysis conducted on the labor side should show equivalent valuation among the resource management programs within the state land office. This means that the return per FTE should be equal among programs.[16] If this is not the case, an overriding benefit to the trust that may not be measurable in direct, current, financial terms should accrue.[17] The adjustment to optimality question becomes important at this point. Given that certain lower-valued activities are taking place, and with the expectation that alternative uses of the trust lands and their assets could occur, then the choice of which activities have the highest return to the trust for a given amount of land and labor can be seen from the activity analysis coefficients.

We used information provided in the states' annual reports, similar to that provided in Chapter 2, to calculate the activity analysis coefficients for various resources that states manage.[18] Table 3-1 shows how personnel are allocated in relation to revenues received. The percentages in the table represent the amount of revenues returned per employee in one program (the left-hand side) compared to the returns per employee in another program (the right-hand side).[19] Efficient personnel allocation criterion requires that the ratio of labor productivity between any two programs should be approximately equal to one; that is, it requires that their relative value be equivalent.[20] Significant divergence from 100 percent indicates potential problem areas.[21] For analytical purposes, we examined the data on an individual re-

TABLE 3-1. Comparative revenue returns from the allocation of personnel among resource programs (by percentage)

	AZ	CA	CO	ID	MT	NM	OR	UT	WA	WY
Program Level Percentages*										
Renewable → Nonrenewable	18	3	24	234	1,424	2	24	3	388	8
Lands → Nonrenewable	139	3	30	2,084	5,611	25	487	134	6,239	
Renewable → Lands	13	89	80	11	25	10	5	2	6	
Renewable → Grand total	30	10	59	80	156	5	24	10	99	12
Nonrenewable → Grand total	168	335	243	34	11	215	99	314	25	153
Resource Level Percentages										
Agriculture → Timber	2,038	450	60	33	11		100	120	19	2,346
Agriculture → Commercial	31	92	336	41		363	131		200	
Timber → Commercial	2	20	561	124			130		1,041	
Commercial → Land sales	28	82	24	21		4	4,226		1	
Commercial → Land program	74	144	31	10		4	4		1	

*Percentages are determined from the ratios of the labor factor coefficients. A percentage of 100 means that equivalent revenues per employee (FTE) are received from the program to the left of the arrow compared to the program on the right. Percentages higher than one hundred indicate the relatively greater amount that the program on the right receives compared to the one on the left. The converse is true for percentages less than one hundred.

Source: J. A. Souder, Economic Strategies for the Management of School and Institutional Trust Lands (Ph.D. dissertation, University of California, Berkeley, 1990), table 4-6 at 85.

source basis as well as aggregated into surface, minerals, and land sales programs.

The results in Table 3-1 show that labor factor return ratios at the aggregate program level differ by orders of magnitude among states. Relative contributions from renewable versus non-renewable programs range from 2 percent in New Mexico to 1,424 percent in Montana. This means that New Mexico receives fifty times more revenue per employee in its mineral leasing programs than in its program for managing surface resources. The converse is true in Montana: the return per employee in surface management is twenty-six times greater than the return per employee engaged in mineral resource management.

At an individual resource management level, the results are also informative, particularly in the surface management programs. The agriculture and grazing program and the forestry program show a better balance in return per employee between each other than occurs between the overall surface management and overall mineral management programs. The differences in return per employee balances among the states are also interesting. Oregon, Utah, and Colorado are relatively well-balanced in personnel allocations between these two programs. Arizona, California, Montana, and Wyoming put many more employees in their forestry programs—when compared to agriculture and grazing—than the revenues appear to justify. In Idaho and Washington, the returns per employee in the agriculture and grazing programs are much less than the revenues per employee managing their forestry programs.[22]

Application of the efficiency criteria to land is less direct than for personnel, even though the same optimality condition holds: the value of output from one acre of land should equal that of another if their prices are equal. The prices of land vary relatively directly, however, according to the value of what can be produced from them. Efficiency criteria are therefore modified to account for the difference among land prices. This is done by requiring that the returns as a percentage of land value be equivalent across the different resource programs. For example, if the coefficient for grazing land was 0.001 and the coefficient for commercial land was 0.1, then the commercial lands provide 100 times greater return per acre than grazing lands, and their value to the trust should reflect this. But because the prices of some types of land increase faster than others (recall the discussion of trend), we further modify the efficiency criteria to take these potential future price increases into account. The desired optimality condition is to produce to the point where the marginal cost equals the marginal revenue product for all inputs and outputs.[23]

The trust obligation requires that states manage lands that give them the biggest return in terms of the beneficiaries' objectives.[24] Clearly, the magnitude of the differences in revenues produced per employee among the various states' programs is considerable. This imbalance may be a coincidence of fluctuating annual revenues and "sticky" staffing patterns. But states should at least be cognizant of the situation and understand how it may be affected either by their past "agency culture" or by ongoing funding mechanisms. But it is also as a result of the trustee's duty of full disclosure that this information is available, so this tool can be used to ask intelligent questions about the level of investment in different programs.

FUNDING MECHANISMS

The influence of funding mechanisms on personnel allocation led us to wonder whether the way the land offices receive funding affects their programs. State land offices are funded in three different ways: the office may expend as much of its receipts as needed to manage lands, with the remainder going to the beneficiaries or to the permanent fund; managers may expend either a fixed percentage of the office's surface lease revenues or a percentage of its total revenues; or managers' expenditures may be determined by the legislature and appropriated from the state's general fund. We wondered whether an objectively unjustified imbalance between surface and mineral program expenditures occurred in land offices where funding was received on the basis of revenue sources. We found that a significant difference in personnel allocations occurred as a result of funding procedures: where offices were funded only by a percentage of surface revenues, a statistically significant imbalance between surface and mineral management prevailed. This suggests that tying budgets—and hence agency activities—to the accomplishment of objectives is crucial for effective management.

It is clear from our analysis that the information available from the trustee should suffice to allow beneficiaries, the legislature, or interested citizens to determine whether the trust is being efficiently managed.[25] By managing only productive lands, the trustee reduces the likelihood of overmanagement. Sufficient information should be collected to permit a determination of the point at which additional management expenditures are not worthwhile to the trust—that is, the point at which marginal lands should be sold or only custodial management should occur.[26] However, state restrictions on management funding and land purchases lead to a situation where the state is required to maximize revenues subject to constraints on both the labor (as determined by agency funding levels and state personnel policies) and the land factors of production. The optimal mix of land and labor for profit maximization is the same as the optimal mix for the revenue maximization when inputs, input prices, and output prices are specified.[27] In the case of state trust lands, the state can be assumed to be a price-taker in its outputs,[28] and in the short-term (at least) the land production factor can be assumed to be fixed. Thus, the only input factor that can be varied (within limits) to maximize output in the short-term is the labor component.

Adjustment to Optimality: Portfolio Theory and Transaction Costs

States obviously cannot immediately or continually adjust their existing land ownership and staffing patterns. Nonetheless, an optimal mix of resources within the trust corpus would go a long way toward fulfilling the trust's obligations to the beneficiaries, whether they be high annual dividends or low to moderate risk. The description of this optimal mix builds on the discussion in the section on variability and risk, and it includes the previous discussion in this section on measures of efficient management. Portfolio theory allows for explicit tradeoffs between various resources, based on their levels of return adjusted for their risk. How one reaches this optimal mix can be described by transactions cost theory. In this application, transactions cost theory looks at the costs of moving from the existing pattern of ownership and staffing to the optimal one. It recognizes that actions to attain the prescribed shift incur costs, and that these costs can sometimes be substantial enough that alternative objectives make more sense. In this part, we describe both portfolio theory and transactions cost theory, and then we specifically link the two as adjustments over time; this leads to the explicit discussion of development objectives in the third section.

PORTFOLIO THEORY

States can use portfolio theory to adjust the composition of their trust corpus to achieve maximum returns subject to an aggregate risk level that they can accommodate. The first step in applying portfolio theory is to determine the beneficiaries' risk tolerance. The amount of risk that any state can tolerate is related to the importance of the trust revenues to the beneficiaries and the availability of alternative sources of income for the beneficiary. If the trust revenues are crucial for the beneficiaries, the resulting risk level should be comparatively low. If they are not crucial to the beneficiaries, however—and particularly if revenue fluctuations do not imperil them—the amount of risk in the trust portfolio can be comparatively high.

It is a relatively straightforward matter to determine an optimal portfolio once the amount of risk that the beneficiaries can accommodate has been determined. Various portfolio models have been developed by financial managers; states are probably already using them for their permanent funds or other state investments. But these models need to be adjusted to integrate the trust lands and their resources into the portfolio. The returns from each type of land can be calculated by means of the tools previously described. The risk of variation in returns can be determined similarly. On the basis of each resource's beta, its rate of return can be adjusted for risk. The proportions of each type of resource held in the trust corpus can then be adjusted to maximize return subject to a specified aggregate risk level.

TRANSACTIONS COSTS

However, adjusting states' portfolios is not without cost. All activities that managers conduct entail costs. These are termed *transactions costs*. Transactions costs are found in state leasing operations when the productive capacity of the land has to be ascertained and the lease put out to bid; they are present in the sale of land because of appraisals, advertising, and commissions; and the simplest transaction cost is the commission paid to the broker to trade stocks.

Transactions costs need to be incorporated into portfolio decisions because they can affect desired outcomes. In some cases, it may be too expensive to change the existing use. For example, even though agriculture returns much more revenue than grazing, to use a particular parcel of land for agriculture requires drilling wells, fencing, and obtaining good access. This may not be cost effective, because the transactions costs associated with changing the use may be too great to be repaid in the future. A similar situation exists in many of the extensive land uses on trust lands: changing their use incurs more transactions costs than can be recouped from their new use. An alternative is to sell the existing lands and place the money in the permanent fund or buy replacement lands. This strategy also involves transactions costs, however, such as appraising and conducting the sale. Once the money is received, additional transactions costs are associated with deciding how the proceeds should be invested. Transactions costs are an integral part of the overall portfolio strategy and may, in certain instances, become the deciding factor when a manager is choosing among various types of prospective investments.

TIME FRAME OF ANALYSES

The profit maximizing case assumes that, in the long-term, all factors of production—lands, labor, and capital—can be varied so that they are efficiently allocated.[29] The short-term factor composition, however, may differ from the optimal profit maximization composition, for two reasons. First, demand and prices vary considerably from one year to another for many of the resources that the states produced. Thus an optimal allocation of resources in one year most likely will not be optimal in other years. This leads to the second reason a state may be using nonoptimal factor combinations. The "sticky" nature of the adjustment process required to reallocate the land from one type to another, or to reassign personnel from one program to another, means that the states have difficulty reacting promptly to changing conditions. Because of this, a snapshot of their allocations at any moment is inaccurate, since the states' resource allocations likely represent an average of expectations over several years.

Even with the preceding caveats, activity analysis can illuminate areas where changes in management emphasis would produce increases in returns to the trust—especially with regard to resources whose prices do not fluctuate significantly from year to year. Examples of these are grazing and commercial leases (which normally have long lease periods) and some unique minerals on trust land (such as trona[30] in Wyoming) for which long-term demand is steady. For resources that experience cyclical price fluctuations, particularly timber and the hydrocarbons, appropriate time frames for analysis should be longer to reflect these cycles and the ability of the land office to adjust their management staffs. The desired end result should be the optimality condition under which the average factor coefficients over the long-term are approximately equal.

LONG-TERM DEVELOPMENT STRATEGIES

The trust lands were granted to the states to use in support of common schools and other public institutions. Are they worth holding and managing in the twenty-first century, or should the trustees sell the lands and invest the proceeds? Economic development theory provides a framework for analyzing societal choices for sustainable intertemporal resource use.[31] It provides a method for estimating the consequences of (1) holding and managing trust lands, (2) selling them and placing the proceeds in a permanent fund, or (3) consuming the proceeds for current expenditures. The dynamic relationship between maintaining and building the corpus of the trust versus maximizing current annual revenues can be examined as a problem of capital accumulation and management. In this respect, the state lands, their revenues, and permanent funds are a capital asset management system.

Economic development theory provides a number of models suitable for analyzing appropriate management strategies. Each of these theoretical models operates under various assumptions. These are usually based on five elements: whether an ending capital stock is specified; what amount of current annual income is required; the discount or interest rate(s) used; the elasticity of demands for services from the capital assets; and the importance of passing assets to future generations. This last consideration, called *felicity,* has perhaps the biggest effect, since the degree to which future generations are incorporated in current management decisions influences the other assumptions. Current consumption is minimized if future generations are highly valued. The value of future generations' utility is determined by specifying a discount rate, which represents the time preference for current consumption over future consumption.[32] A high discount rate means that current consumption is preferred, while a zero discount rate means that future generations are valued to the same degree as current ones. The amount given up is determined by tradeoffs between consumption and felicity. In Chapter 6 we examine these concepts in the context of intergenerational equity in minerals leasing.

The economic models discussed in this section are intended to highlight various factors that influence the ability of trust lands to fulfill their purpose. We start by discussing discount rates, because of their importance. Next we attack the consumption versus investment problem in terms that are usually applied to state trust lands. Because renewable resource revenues and permanent fund dividends are annually disbursed, while nonrenewable resource and land sales revenues are banked, the common perception is that the underlying value of the trust asset—the corpus—is maintained. In Chapters 6 and 7, we examine why this is not necessarily the case. In the present context, however, we discuss structural models that explicitly consider whether the corpus is being consumed. Our intention in this section is not to attempt to fit a particular state's program to a specific model or, conversely, to specify a "correct" model for states to use. Rather, we hope to highlight tools that permit increasingly specific evaluation of the trust corpus as a resource.

Role of the Interest and Discount Rates

The interest rate or the discount rate represents an individual's or society's preference for current versus future consumption. Basically the interest rate and the discount rate are the same thing viewed from opposite perspectives. The interest rate is viewed from the present to the future; in effect, it answers the question, "If I invest something now, what will I get back in the future?" The interest rate is equivalent to the growth rate expressed as a percentage over a standardized period, generally one or more years. Most of us have experience with interest rates from bank accounts and loans. Discount rates are viewed from the future back to the present. For example, if I knew that I would have to pay X amount N years in the future, by establishing a discount rate I could determine how much I needed to set aside today and invest at that rate so that I would have X amount in N years. Because of the similarity of discount and interest rates, they are commonly used interchangeably.

Interest or discount rates are important in trust management for two reasons: they provide a measure for comparing returns from various management activities; and because their use explicitly indicates a time preference for the present versus the future. In the section on efficient resource management, we discussed ways to calculate the rates of return. These rates of return are equivalent to an interest rate that production of a given resource returns to the trust. The rate of return for each resource can be compared with all others, and with a standard such as the desired return on the permanent fund, to evaluate performance.

Interest rates are also commonly used in benefit:cost analyses to determine whether an investment today will pay off in returns in the future. There is a large literature on benefit:cost analyses in general, and the use of interest rates in particular.[33] We will see how interest rates are linked to time preferences in the next section.

Choices Within Growth Theory

Three different classes of capital management models describe the range of choices states have in managing their trust lands. The first class—extreme choice models—provide the outer maximum limits to either consumption or capital accretion from trust assets. The second class—terminal period models—describe efficient consumption paths over a finite period when the initial assets are given, a termination period is stated, and minimal ending capital stocks are predetermined. The third class of capital management models—infinite horizon models—are applicable to perpetual trusts that require consumption to be discounted by a social rate of time preference that reflects intergenerational equity.

After initially describing each of these classes of economic development models, we discuss each in the context of state trust lands and asset management strategies. Our discussion is based on the state trust lands portfolio model. For this model, income to the trust is the same as production of revenues from products of the trust lands and their permanent funds, after any deductions for state land office management operations. Similarly, consumption is the amount of net production—that is, income—available to the beneficiaries for their current operations. The amount of current consumption determines the capital accumulation and, thus, future consumption levels. The minimum amount of consumption necessary to continue operations is called *subsistence*. The discount rate is differentiated here between the individual's time preference and society's rate based on felicity considerations.

Choices for consumption versus capital accumulation in the aggregate can be described by three equations.[34] The trust's ability to keep up with demands for its services is determined by the growth of beneficiary needs. Using population growth as a proxy for beneficiary demand growth, we can combine the three relationships and express them in per-capita terms to form the fundamental equation for an aggregate growth model.[35]

EXTREME CHOICE MODELS

Given an initial stock of capital (as resources), society can build it up at a maximum rate by consuming only the minimum necessary to sustain its workers;[36] or at the other extreme, society can choose to consume the entire proceeds from its capital, and its productive capacity will slowly wither away as the capital depreciates. This is sometimes called the "golden age" path because no wealth is transferred between generations, the wealth having all been consumed at or before life's end. Society has a range of choices in decisions regarding consumption versus investment.[37] Each combination of beginning capital and consumption choices yields a different path. The key insight that can be derived from this representation is that a direct relationship exists between consumption and maintenance of capital stocks. As a larger proportion of production is consumed, less is available to maintain or build the capital stock. Conversely, as greater amounts of revenues are placed back into the capital stock, less is available for consumption.

Clearly from the point of view of managing the trust assets, a suitable path for beneficiary support should not liquidate the capital of the trust; this in any case is prohibited by the trustee's obligation to preserve the productive capacity of the trust property. On the other hand, accumulating assets without disbursing revenues to the beneficiaries is not an optimal strategy either, since at some point the additional capital or investments in the trust assets will not provide commensurate benefits.[38] Thus, the relevant question becomes how to determine the proper balance of growth of the trust corpus, protection of the trust asset, and consumption.

TERMINAL PERIOD MODELS

One alternative to the extreme choice models is capital growth models that specify an ending capital stock while allowing more than a subsistence level of revenues. This intermediate approach has three guides to use in making growth choices:[39]

- The *Harrod–Domar–Solow (H-D-S) model* is based on the premise that consumption is a constant proportion of income.[40] As income is increased by additional capital, the average propensity to consume yields a proportional savings behavior, which causes the capital stock to increase.[41]
- The *golden rule path* maximizes consumption during all periods, by assuming that capital and consumption levels are both constant over time.[42] The initial level of capital determines available consumption levels, allowable population growth, and the marginal rate of productivity growth required to sustain the economy.[43]
- The *turnpike path* provides the fastest way to achieve growth goals.[44] This is done by first maximizing capital so that it approximates the maximal growth rate under the extreme subsistence path; and then, toward the end of the period, changing the trajectory to converge on an optimal ending capital:consumption ratio.

At this point, whether any of these models provide an exact fit for the trust lands situation is not critical. The question is, what insight can be gained from analyzing management strategies based on these theories?

Harrod–Domar–Solow Model. The H-D-S model is based on the assumption that consumption is a fixed and constant portion of production. By thinking of consumption as consisting of payments to beneficiaries, we can treat the fixed percentage disbursement of income from both surface revenues and interest from the permanent funds as providing for this. However, the situation involving royalty income differs because it is used almost exclusively to build up the permanent fund.[45] Thus in the royalty case, the proportion of income going directly to the beneficiaries is much less than for surface revenues, since it is equivalent to the interest payments from the permanent fund after a lag period. The cumulative effect, however, is that, as income increases (decreases), disbursements to the beneficiaries increase (decrease).

The second part of the H-D-S guide requires that, as income rises with increasing capital stocks, a fixed proportion of this income be put back into the capital stock. Higher incomes then result in greater funds' being returned to the trust corpus. This process is not common among the trust land states, however. Revenues from land sales, easements, and mineral royalties commonly go into the permanent fund; and because of this, these management decisions can be thought of as merely reallocating resources in one form—say, land or minerals—to capital stocks in another form such as bonds. In contrast, in some states, surface rental receipts from grazing, timber, and commercial land leases commonly are disbursed to the beneficiaries after management expenses are deducted. This creates the difference in proportional distribution of income between consumption and capital stock, depending on the source of the revenues; the exact situation varies by state (see Table 2-7). In Idaho, for example, timber revenues go into the permanent fund along with money from land sales, easements, and mineral royalties. Because of this, any increase in timber income from the lands results in an increase in the capital stock in the permanent fund.[46] A more direct example of income distribution effects is offered by Montana, where only 95 percent of surface rental income and permanent fund interest is disbursed to the beneficiaries; the remainder goes back into the permanent fund, a procedure that builds the trust's capital stock.

The third part of the H-D-S model assumes that production of income from the trust lands requires fixed ratios of capital and labor. If capital is the trust corpus, then labor is the management contribution of the state land office. Following this line of reasoning, total aggregate wages represent the revenues provided to the state land office for management of the trust lands, whether these are from legislative appropriation or are based on a percentage of income. The production function for each resource managed by the land office can then be derived by determining how much effort and funds are expended per unit of output. In the short term, at least—and for a given type of resource—the requirement that the proportions of capital and labor be fixed is not unrealistic: a growing economy in and of itself should not require that the proportions of capital and labor change.

Golden Rule Path. The golden rule path model has the characteristic that consumption is maximized during all periods; it differs from the extreme golden age path discussed earlier in that depreciation of the capital stock is mitigated by capital replacement provisions. This can be represented in the trust lands context by the portion of potential income revenue that is placed back into the asset, whether directly from a percentage of receipts or through restocking and/or stewardship requirements on the part of lessees. The concept guiding decisions on this path is that everything beyond what is required to protect the corpus of the trust should be consumed. Because an ending capital stock is specified, consumption during all periods is necessarily based on leaving a residual capital level at the end of the planning period, causing consumption levels to be at all times lower than on the golden age path.[47]

Turnpike Path. The turnpike path model is a composite of the golden rule and subsistence models. In its simplest case, consumption is decreased to the point where maximal growth occurs for a specified length of time.

Once this period is over, consumption is increased until an optimal ending consumption:capital ratio is reached.

These three development models require that an ending point and a time period for achievement be specified. However, the requirement that an ending point be specified does not adequately describe the basis for state trust land management decisions, since they are expected to exist in perpetuity.[48] The ending point can be the current situation for the states in terms of permanent funds, trust land contributions to state education (versus tax rates), and estimates of remaining asset values for historical comparisons. But because no ending period is specified for the future, use of these models for decision-making in a finite time period requires specifying an ending capital asset to pass on to succeeding generations.

INFINITE-HORIZON GROWTH MODELS

Since the trust corpus is expected to produce revenues in perpetuity, infinite-horizon macroeconomic models more realistically represent this situation than the terminal period and capital stock models of the previous section.[49] The Ramsey model[50] provides the basic framework needed to evaluate state trust lands over an infinite planning horizon. This model permits determination of maximum consumption rates subject to the primary constraint that the consumption be continuous in perpetuity. The role of the society (in this case the trust) to save versus consume is modeled in the framework of utility maximization subject to a set of four constraints. These constraints are as follows: the capital asset must provide a steady per-capita level of consumption for the population over time (so that population growth is factored into maximum long-term consumption levels); an initial level of capital must be known; per-capita capital and per-capita consumption must be nonnegative; and the production function must have constant returns to scale.[51] The model also requires that the discount rate be specified explicitly so that any time preference for current over future consumption is included.[52] Elaborations in the Ramsey model include the effects of government borrowing and of taxation on capital stocks.[53]

Breaking down the Ramsey model into its component parts yields valuable insights into the choices available for state management of trust assets. Looking first at the objective function, the utility function of the beneficiaries can take a number of forms, depending on the importance of various concerns such as steady per-capita levels of consumption and reduction in revenue fluctuations. The Ramsey model thus explicitly requires that the beneficiaries' desires be specified.

Since we previously defined risk in terms of the variance in resource prices, a suitable index of the risk associated with retaining versus consuming the resource can be derived this way.[54] This means that resources subject to large fluctuations in prices inherently entail more risk than do resources with smaller price swings. The question then becomes, how much risk is the state willing to assume for increased future benefits compared to present consumption? Two factors are involved in determining a state's willingness to assume risk in production decisions: where the revenues go if the resource is consumed; and what options, at what costs, are available to the states as alternatives to producing the resources. The next section uses a case study of one state's decisions as an example of the choices made in opting to consume rather than to perpetuate the trust corpus.

EMPIRICAL EVIDENCE OF DEVELOPMENT THEORY IMPLICATIONS FOR TRUST MANAGEMENT

The state trust lands and their revenues do not exist in a vacuum; they are tied into general state and local institutional funding mechanisms. This is especially evident when state trust land revenues provide a significant contribution to public school finance. This section takes the economic development models discussed in this chapter and illustrates their use in the context of the trust lands and their resources. We examine the influence of trust funds in public school finance first, with reference to the choices available to the states in management of revenues from trust lands and permanent funds. Next we compare long-term real increases in commodity prices with returns on trust permanent funds, with particular reference to New Mexico's permanent fund returns. Then we derive implicit interest rates and risks in revenue flows, based on the relationships between these comparative returns.

Utah's Permanent Fund: Implications of Diverting Permanent Funds for Operating Expenses

During the period from 1983 through 1987, Utah used its permanent fund as a source of revenues to support public education. The action resulted from a suit by the State Controller against the Division of State Lands.[55] The Controller had sued to resolve the issue of whether lands of a mineral character were granted to the state under the relevant enabling act and original state constitution, or whether these lands came into state ownership by the state only as a result of the Jones Act of 1927.[56] If the 1927 statute was controlling, the constitution's permanent fund provisions were not; accordingly, the mineral revenues could be distributed rather than put into the permanent fund, as required by the state constitution.

The Supreme Court of Utah held that lands of a mineral character did not fall within the provisions of the enabling act and constitution and that, while proceeds for their leases and royalties must be used for the support of

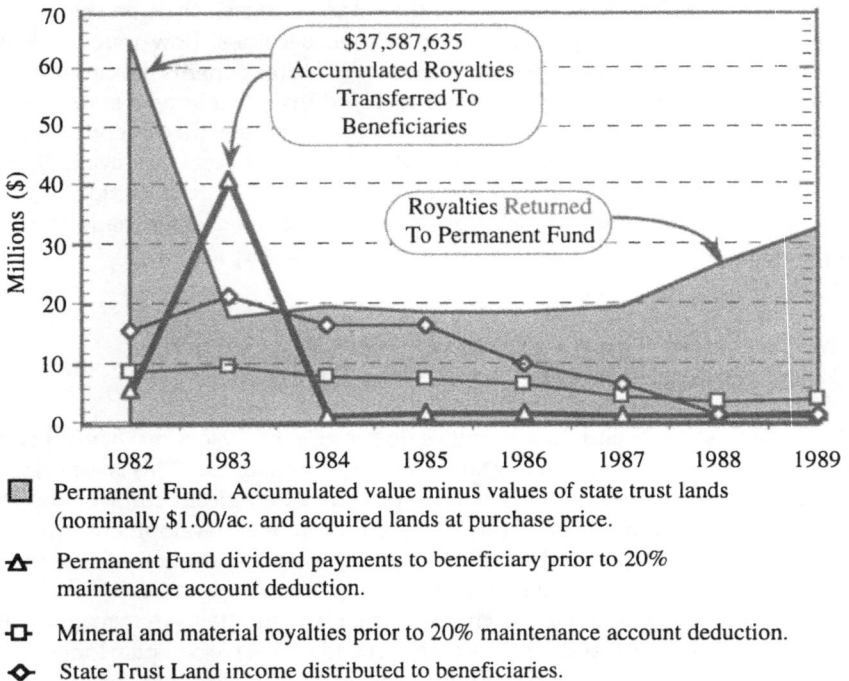

Figure 3-3. Effects of transfer of mineral royalties from Utah's permanent fund on payments to beneficiaries, interest income, and permanent fund levels. *Source:* UTAH DIVISION OF STATE LANDS AND FORESTRY, STATEMENT OF FUND BALANCE.

the designated purposes (public schools and institutions), all net revenues should be distributed directly to the beneficiaries. The court also held that the Jones Act included all mineral rights, whether they were on lands with previously known deposits, or on lands where minerals and hydrocarbons were subsequently found. This provision allowed for the distribution to the beneficiaries of the entire amount of royalties in the permanent fund that had been collected over the 89 years since statehood. Figure 3-3 shows the effects this transfer on the permanent fund, as well as on beneficiary disbursements.

Of particular note in Figure 3-3 is the transfer in 1983 of more than $37 million in accumulated royalties from the trust funds to the beneficiaries. The resulting effect on the Permanent Fund was immediate: it dropped from about $66 million to less than $20 million.[57] The mineral royalties over the period from 1983 to 1987 were disbursed directly to the beneficiaries, providing the majority of their trust disbursements in 1986 and 1987. In contrast, the payments returned to the beneficiaries from the permanent fund were reduced drastically after 1983 as a result of the transfer of the accumulated mineral royalties.

Figure 3-4 shows the effects of these transfers compared to what would have happened if the permanent fund had remained intact. The upper line on Figure 3-4 traces the path of the permanent fund if the royalties had been retained, and if the additional mineral royalties for the period 1983–1987 had been placed in the permanent fund as opposed to being disbursed to the beneficiaries. The net result is that by 1987 the permanent fund would have had an accumulated value of $92 million compared to the $29 million it actually contained.

The cost to the beneficiaries of the approximately $72 million distributed to the beneficiaries instead of placed into their permanent funds is about $4 million per year in perpetuity.[58] Whether this is a good deal for the beneficiaries depends on what the short-term damage to them would have been if they had not received the funds over the period 1983–1987 compared to the long-term costs of $4 million to $6 million per year. The effect is ameliorated to some extent because the Utah Division of State Lands takes a management deduction of 20 percent from both royalties and interest payments on the permanent fund. This double deduction—unique to Utah—tends to shift the weight of the decision in favor of dispersing the funds,

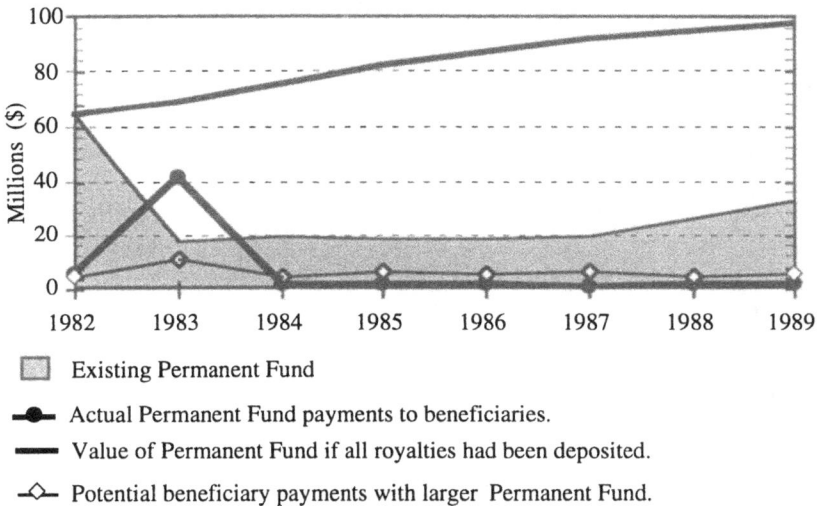

Figure 3-4. Long-term effects of Utah's diversion of permanent fund mineral royalties directly to beneficiaries. *Source:* UTAH DIVISION OF STATE LANDS AND FORESTRY, STATEMENT OF FUND BALANCE.

since it changes the effective nominal interest rate on the permanent fund from 8.5 to 6.375 percent.

The results of this analysis show the effects on the beneficiaries of producing versus retaining resources; and of retaining versus disbursing permanent funds. In the end, the choice about whether to finance the public schools through taxes or bonds or through liquidation of the permanent fund and trust assets is the crux of the intergenerational equity issue, as long as the real price increases of the commodities are outpacing real bond rates and permanent fund yields.

CONCLUSIONS

The preceding study of Utah's management of its permanent fund shows how the tools introduced in this chapter can be used to analyze the management of trust resources. Because the managers are proceeding with clear and specific guidance—to make the trust productive for the beneficiaries—the tools we have presented for evaluating the manager's performance are largely tied to economists' notions of balancing economic risk and achieving high rates of financial returns. We have not discussed techniques for inquiring whether harvest or grazing on a particular site will cause erosion, or a landslide, or will pollute a nearby trout stream. Thus, there are some limits to what can be accomplished with the toolkit presented.

We have demonstrated that, when the goal is clear, we can evaluate with a high degree of precision such basic and apparently politically and emotionally sensitive issues as whether it is better to sell or retain land. We have also seen the centrality of expenditure on labor in evaluating management. Labor is the largest and most flexible category of management expenditure and provides an excellent starting point for assessing the efficiency of a manager's resource allocations. Finally, we have seen clearly that the whole corpus of the trust—the trust portfolio, including the permanent funds—must be analyzed in order to evaluate both the manager's overall performance and the wisdom of specific program components.

We are not deluded that financial returns are the only way, or the best way, or even an acceptable way to analyze public resource management more generally. We do believe, however, that such financial assessments are both possible and ought to be a central part of all public resource management assessments. Because the lease is the ubiquitous tool of virtually all public resource management programs, we believe that it is useful to start there and to recognize that the lease is basically a risk-sharing tool. Even if the federal government is not interested (as the state trustees must be) in returns to the treasury or to the beneficiary, the federal government's lessees are. At the very least, understanding the lease as an economic contract is important, because it permits a realistic inquiry into the incentives that the lease conveys to the lessee and the real priorities of the landowner.

We also believe, however, that focusing on the efficiency of allocations to labor is central to understanding environmentally sensitive management of all public lands. If the manager overinvests in commodity management programs that actually lose money, we believe that the manager—rather than the public or the long-term environmental health of the resource—is likely the primary beneficiary of the investment.

Therefore, while we are realistic about the limits of economic analysis in assessing the full range of resource management outcomes, we are not apologetic. For evaluating trust lands, financial returns are utterly central. On federal lands, efficiency of management is increasingly seen as important. But even if you do not care about financial returns, the tools we have described in this chapter provide an excellent window for assessing overall management effectiveness. In trust program after program, economic efficiency provides sideboards that are essential to environmental as well as fiscal sanity.

CHAPTER FOUR

Cropland and Grazing Leases

This chapter explores the relationship between the trustee and the cropland or grazing lessee and its effects on the trust. We use the detail of these most common of trust land leases to explore the evolving tension faced by the state in dealing with lessees. Traditionally, the leases have been drawn and administered to meet the preferences of the lessees, with little apparent concern for returns to the trust. The more recent trend, however, is toward greater emphasis on the trust and concern for the beneficiary. We look at several levels of cropland and grazing lease decisions in sufficient detail to understand how different provisions benefit one or the other party to the lease. We also briefly explore analytical methods for sorting out who is, in fact, gaining or losing from different lease provisions.

The procedures used by the states for issuing cropland and grazing leases are important for three reasons. First, the leases are the most traditional uses and so provide an appropriate canvas for looking at the evolution of trustee–lessee relationships. Second, agriculture and grazing are the most extensive use of granted lands in terms of surface area. Grazing leases cover more than 90 percent of the surface acreage of trust lands in eighteen of the twenty-two states. Agricultural land leases are smaller in area but produce higher returns. Third, the grazing leases—most especially the grazing fee structure—provide an opportunity for direct federal/state comparison. In many areas in the West, state lands are virtually undifferentiated from surrounding federal lands, yet the states charge anywhere from slightly less to over nine times more than what the federal government charges for grazing. This chapter provides perspective for evaluating those differences.

The effects of cropland and grazing lease policies on the trust and on trust income can be substantial. For example, on the heels of a suit undertaken by beneficiaries, Oklahoma trustees significantly changed their lease program.[1] Revenues from their cropland and grazing program, which had ranged from $3 to $5 million per year prior to the suit (1977–1982), rose to $7 or $8 million per year—an increase of about 67 percent, in the years 1983–1988.[2] This change occurred primarily because the state shifted from a system of preference-right leases to competitively bid leases. This clearly is a crucial element of grazing policy. But most of us—at least those of us who have discussed grazing leases almost exclusively in terms of federal grazing fees—have not given much thought to this and other aspects of leasing. Such neglect, we argue indirectly in this chapter, is costly.

101

The discussion proceeds in four parts. The first tells four quick stories about major decisions that states have made in cropland and grazing leasing. The stories are framed in terms of the ubiquitous question of whether to sell or to retain and manage the resources. A 1970s Idaho decision to sell off the trust's agricultural lands occupies one end of the spectrum. Washington state's opposite decision—to identify agricultural lands for heavy investment and leasing—and Oregon's ambitious program to block in scattered parcels for management lie at the other, more modern end of the scale. Oklahoma's experience, briefly noted above, in shifting from lessee-oriented toward beneficiary-oriented management is the most modern of all. These four stories suggest the broad context in which specific decisions about lease provisions are made.

The next three parts of the chapter look at leasing decisions with a progressively finer and finer lens. First we look briefly at alternative concepts of cropland or grazing lease (including share cropping) and discuss how to define fair market value in that context. Then we examine lease provisions in considerable detail: how a lease is obtained and held, and what kind of qualifications for leaseholding have been used to limit the pool of potential bidders. We also discuss how some provisions, such as preference-right leasing—which have long advantaged the lessee—are now fading from use. The final section of the chapter focuses on how the states set grazing fees. By that point, it should be obvious that fees are but one part of the larger package, not the only relevant issue. We talk in some detail about how low federal fees limit the ability of state trustees to charge higher rates on state lands. An appendix to this chapter provides specific information on how grazing fees are set state-by-state.

The chapter summarizes how states have managed their cropland and grazing lands by drawing together what we believe are promising approaches to an "ideal" grazing and cropland leasing program. Our proposals are built of bits and pieces of all the state programs, suggesting that we have much to learn from the various states, and they highlight the major features of a leasing program. We do not make a point of advocating strongly in behalf of our summary, viewing it rather as a provocative approach to tying together management goals, land capabilities, and leasing procedures that the reader may want to emulate at the conclusion of subsequent chapters.

HISTORY AND CURRENT STATUS OF CROPLAND AND GRAZING PROGRAMS

In Chapter 1, we discussed the historical trend in federal public land management from land disposition to retention to active resource management.

We noted that states followed similar patterns regarding their trust lands. This section uses four case studies of state cropland and grazing programs to show the effects of these patterns on trust land management. The cases focus on state policies pursued in the last twenty to thirty years. Disposition effects on the trust are illustrated with the example of Idaho's selling its agricultural trust lands during the 1970s. In sharp contrast is the example of intensive management of agricultural lands that Washington has practiced during the last twenty years. Shifting to grazing, we describe Oregon's retention policy, emphasizing its success in blocking rangelands through land exchanges with the federal government. Finally, we consider active management in the form of competitive bidding for leases, using Oklahoma's program as an example.

Idaho's Agricultural Lands Disposition

Over the last thirty years, agricultural land prices have increased many times faster than the general rate of inflation. Some of this increase was due to the expectation on the part of purchasers that land prices would continue to increase: many landowners speculated that they could make more money buying and selling land than they could growing crops or grazing livestock. Naturally, farmers who leased state lands—as many had done with the same state parcel for generations—seeing their neighbors realize windfalls from the land market, became intensely interested in purchasing these lands so that they too could participate in the land boom. This happened throughout the trust land states during this period. It reflects a general pattern according to which both state lessees and federal permittees are interested in purchasing their leased property when the future market for property or allotments looks good, while they are satisfied to rent it or pay grazing fees when the market is bad.

Responding to pressure from its lessees in the early 1970s, the Idaho Land Board established a policy of selling the trusts' agricultural lands to the existing lessees at the appraised price. The amount of Idaho's trust land leased for agricultural use thereupon decreased from 55,000 acres in the mid-1970s to 6,000 acres by 1990. Agricultural lease revenues reflected this policy, declining from about $475,000 per year in the mid-1970s to about $100,000 per year by 1990. Figure 4-1 shows the results of the policy on agricultural revenues and acres leased in Idaho. Proceeds from the agricultural land sales were placed in the state's permanent fund. These revenues amounted to about $57 million over the period 1973–1974 to 1990. Sales of $21 million were realized during the 1972–1974 biennium, with another $10 million of annual sales in 1981 and $6 million in 1982. Most of the lands were sold on contract, by the terms of which the purchaser makes an initial down payment and pays the state the remainder of the sale price over a set

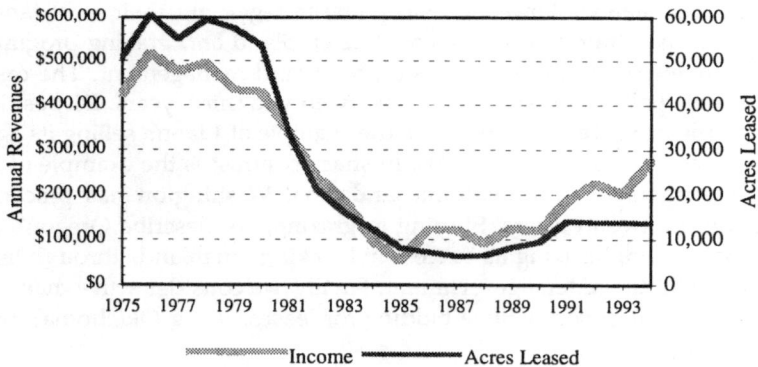

Figure 4-1. Effect of Idaho's land sales on cropland revenues and leased acreage, 1975–1994.

number of years at a set percentage interest. The accumulated interest income from land sales is approximately $1½ to $3 million dollars per year; this money is distributed to the beneficiaries, while principal payments go into the permanent fund.

Idaho's program illustrates how important it is to consider the comparative future returns from the trust asset on the ground compared to the returns from trust assets in the permanent fund. If the combination of annual rentals and increasing future asset values provides a higher return to the beneficiary than selling the land, it is in the best interest of the beneficiary to retain and manage the lands. Conversely, if the permanent fund's purchasing power (offsetting inflationary effects) and annual dividends exceed the expected return from the lands, it is in the best interest of the beneficiary to dispose of the lands. Idaho sold 90 percent of its agricultural lands, lost only 79 percent of its agricultural revenues, and produced three to six times the previous revenues. But this occurred at the same time that farm prices were increasing rapidly and the returns per acre were increasing.

Washington's Intensive Agricultural Land Management

Washington undertook an alternative strategy to managing its agricultural trust lands. Starting in the late 1950s, the state decided to retain its agricultural lands and intensively manage them.[3] As one step, starting in 1969 it initiated aggressive development of irrigated agriculture on suitable lands.[4] The state participated in federal water projects such as the Columbia Basin Project to guarantee adequate irrigation water supplies,[5] and the Washington Department of Natural Resources (WDNR) successfully sued the federal government to obtain an exemption from the historic 160-acre limit on land

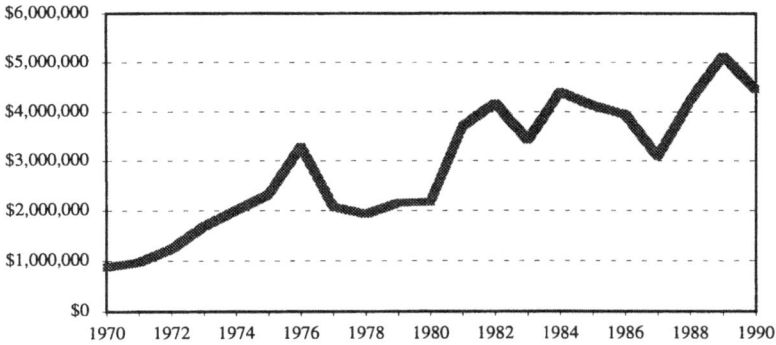

Figure 4-2. Revenues received from agricultural leases on Washington trust lands, 1970–1990.

parcels irrigated with water from federal water projects.[6] The area of irrigated cropland on state trust lands rose from less than 500 acres in 1957 to nearly 34,000 acres today, with WDNR investing $10 million to bring about 16,000 acres into production.[7] Revenues went from about 50 cents per acre per year for grazing and dry cropland, to $50 per acre per year for irrigated row crops, to $500 per acre per year for irrigated orchards and vineyards.[8] The results of the WDNR's intensive agriculture management program can be seen in Figure 4-2, where annual revenues have grown from less than $1 million per year in 1970 to $4½ to $5 million annually by 1990.

The WDNR participates in water projects by paying for the distribution infrastructure (bringing the water to the parcel and maintaining the underground pipelines), while the lessee is responsible for the above-ground costs (pumps and pivots).[9] Prior to making any investment, the department conducts a benefit:cost analysis of the project, using a 7 percent target real rate of return on its prospective investment.[10] As of 1988, the WDNR was receiving a real rate of return of 8.53 percent on its capital investments in irrigation infrastructure.[11] Beyond introducing physical improvements to its lands, the WDNR provides incentives to potential lessees to develop trust lands for high-value uses such as orchards and vineyards. One incentive is that, in exchange for a twenty-five-year lease and phased-in rental payments of $1/acre/year for the first eight years, the lessee agrees to an enforceable plan of development and pays the state 5 percent of the subsequent crop as rental.[12]

Washington's program illustrates that a state can substantially increase its annual cash receipts from agriculture if it is willing to expend reasonable amounts of money to increase the infrastructure on its agricultural lands. The WDNR's strategic planning process provided the key to this monetary participation by identifying areas where investment would increase the long-term return to the trust. Money—in combination with sufficient staff—allowed the WDNR to increase the value of its trust lands. This demonstrates that, under certain conditions, increasing the productivity of agricultural lands pays off in the long term. In the next two case studies, we examine whether this process also works for grazing lands—and if not, how they are different.

Oregon's Rangeland Blocking and Retention

Although this chapter emphasizes trustee/lessee relations, the lessees aren't the only issue; dealing with the federal government and federal land managers clearly affects the states' management. States have traditionally had problems managing their trust lands because of the dispersed, isolated pattern of the original school grants. This difficulty was not terribly important during the disposition era, but it was quickly recognized as a problem when the states decided to retain their trust lands. The problem became particularly acute when the federal government allowed ranchers to organize into grazing districts with the passage of the Taylor Grazing Act in 1934. Passage of the Taylor Grazing Act resulted in the formation of the Western States Land Commissioners Association (WSCLA) which lobbied against the act. A quote from the Montana Land Commissioner's report in 1936 sums up the states' predicament:

> When grazing districts are created under the Taylor Grazing Act, state owned lands will inevitably become included within the boundaries of these districts. It will be next to impossible to obtain a higher rent for school sections within these districts than the rents paid for lands of the United States; and revenues for our schools will thereby be drastically reduced. It will be next to impossible to sell scattered sections of state lands within a grazing district at a fair price. It is so much cheaper to lease the lands at nominal rentals. In this way the operation of the Taylor Grazing Act will seriously impair the value of the lands granted by the United States to the State of Montana for the support of its schools and institutions. It will tend to nullify the grants already made. We believe that this is a great injustice to the state.[13]

Land commissioners recognized the value of consolidating land holdings through exchanges with the federal government.[14] However, not much was accomplished in this regard in any state until the middle to late 1970s and into the 1980s,[15] primarily because of the overwhelming complexity of large-scale land exchanges and because of resistance by ranchers in the grazing districts to such restructuring. The general issue of land exchanges is discussed in Chapter 7.

In spite of these difficulties, Oregon took a different tack just as the "Sagebrush Rebellion" was gaining steam and states' rights to federal lands were being advanced. Oregon's State Land Division had initiated a land exchange program with the federal Bureau of Land Management in the early 1970s. That effort culminated in a memorandum of understanding between the two agencies, from which the state developed a proposal in 1975 to exchange 600,000 acres of its scattered parcels for blocked federal lands.[16] There the matter rested, and little progress was made on the exchange program through the remainder of the 1970s. Then, at a meeting of the Western States Land Commissioners Association attended by then Secretary of the Interior James Watt, the director of the Oregon Division of State Lands vehemently protested the Bureau of Land Management's failure to cooperate in land exchanges.[17] Secretary Watt responded by including in the performance standard for the State Director of the Bureau of Land Management specific goals relating to concluding the land exchanges with the state.

The resulting increased cooperation between the Bureau of Land Management and the Oregon Division of State Lands allowed the state to consolidate its holdings in eastern Oregon into forty-four blocked parcels totaling 543,000 acres.[18] On its blocked units, the state has subsequently invested about $750,000 in improvements, matched by about $675,000 in lessee expenditures. Improvements include almost 130,000 acres of brush control, seeding on 50,000 acres, over 100 new reservoirs and water pits, 16 wells, and more than 300 miles of fence.[19] The blocking and range improvements have increased available forage on the blocked units from 25,000 AUMs to 58,500 AUMs. The cost for each AUM (Animal Unit Month—the amount of forage needed to support an adult steer or cow for one month) generated by state-financed improvements was $38.00. Lessees repay the state's cost through additional grazing fees over a ten-year, interest-free amortization.

But while the division was blocking its lands and rehabilitating its range, it did not revise its grazing fee system or leasing procedures. The basic fee of $2.50 per AUM for blocked lands and $3.50 per AUM for wetlands was established in the 1970s and continued through 1993.[20] The effects of this stability in prices are shown in Figure 4-3: the entire increase in revenues received by the state is attributable to a combination of increases in the carrying capacity of its blocked lands and repayment of state expenditures for these improvements.[21] Thus, while Oregon gained a necessary condition for efficient grazing management—consolidating its holdings—it neglected to meet the sufficient condition by modernizing its grazing fee and leasing procedures.[22] As a result, it was saddled with limited revenues in its grazing program even while having a reasonably manageable land ownership pattern.

Oklahoma's Competitive Leasing System

Oklahoma's emphasis has been on issues not central in Oregon: fees and procedures. Until 1982, Oklahoma's leasing policies and fees followed a tra-

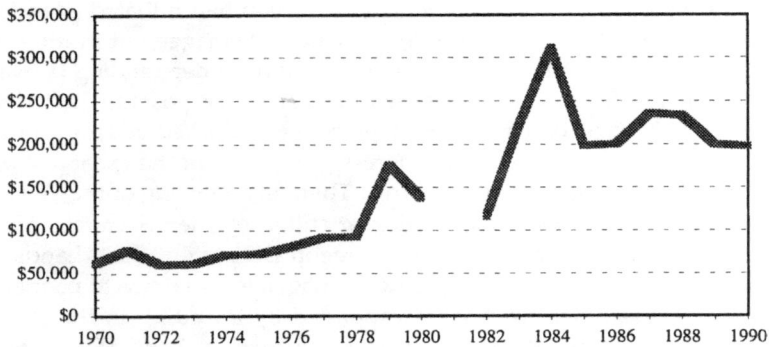

Figure 4-3. Annual grazing revenues on Oregon's trust lands, 1970–1990.

ditional lessee-oriented pattern: fees were low (3 percent of appraised value), existing lessees had virtually absolute preference rights to renew the state leases, and the state even lent money from its permanent fund at subsidized interest rates to farmers and ranchers.[23] Preference-right leases allow the existing lessee to renew the state lease either without competition or by meeting the highest bid. The Oklahoma Education Association, representing the common school beneficiaries, sued the State Land Board over its leasing practices. The State Land Board lost the case and thereupon revised its fee systems and leasing procedures.[24]

Minimum lease fees were set at levels comparable to private cash rates,[25] and all preference rights to lease renewals were abolished.[26] Leases began to be offered at auction.[27] While the original lease fee of 3 percent of appraised price allowed the state to gain revenues during the increase in farm prices during the late 1970s, the introduction of full, fair market appraisal fees and competitive bidding produced an additional 80 percent increase in the revenues the state received. The effect on revenues of the successful court suit and the resulting changes in Oklahoma's leasing program can be seen in Figure 4-4. Fifteen additional personnel were hired to initiate the appraisal program; these numbers have since been reduced to a total of fifteen staff in the entire program.[28] Even assuming that it costs about $50,000 per year to keep an appraiser on staff, the cost of approximately $750,000 per year is compensated for by the revenue gain of at least $2 million per year and by increased effectiveness in monitoring problem leases.

Summary: Policy Changes over Time

While disposition of selected parcels and all sorts of exchanges and repositioning transactions continue, the mass disposition era is over for the state

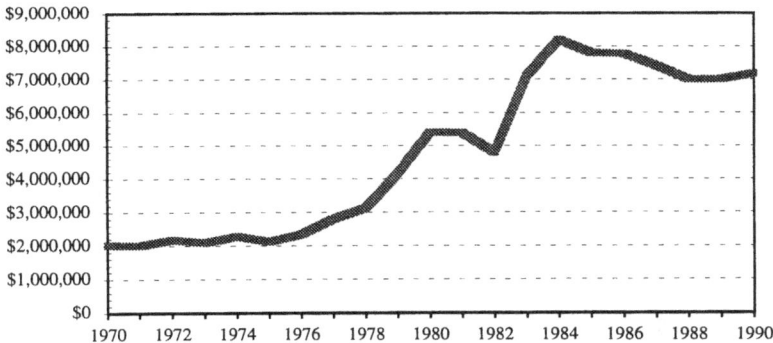

Figure 4-4. Agricultural and grazing revenues in Oklahoma, 1970–1990.

trust lands. States are currently struggling to determine how best to manage their lands, moving from custodial retention in favor of lessees to active management for the benefit of beneficiaries. We have just seen how four states handled major cropland and grazing strategies. In the remaining sections of this chapter, we examine in greater detail how the states determine their agriculture and grazing fee and leasing procedures.

CROPLAND AND GRAZING LEASING THEORY

Leasing procedures define the relationship between the trustee—in this case, the state land managing agency—and users who lease trust lands. Since the states themselves do not produce the commodities whose revenues go to the beneficiaries, but instead lease or rent the lands to private individuals or corporations, the relationship between the state and the lessee ultimately affects the beneficiaries. This section identifies and evaluates specific aspects of this relationship for cropland and grazing leases in the various states.

Appraisal Models for Cropland and Grazing Leases

The most important question in the leasing of cropland and grazing lands is "what is the fair market value of the state land—and associated infrastructure—to a lessee?" This value should in theory become the rental paid by the lessee to the state. Fair market values for state leases are almost always determined by some form of appraisal methods. Appraisals are particularly important because they establish the base value for the leases, which becomes the beginning bid if auctions are held. Since many parcels of trust lands receive only a single bid at auction, the appraised base value often becomes the amount the state receives for the lease. Three approaches are classically used in appraisals to value the lease: comparable sales, income capitalization, and contributory value.[29] These three basic approaches are all variously used in determining the rental value of cropland and grazing lands.[30]

The comparable sales approach is frequently used in developing both grazing fee formulas and agricultural land leases. Theoretically, it takes the fees paid to private landowners, adjusts the value according to differences in the services provided by the landlord, and arrives at a value representing the equivalent private (and presumably fair market) fee. In this way, it does not differ conceptually from the appraisal process that would be conducted for residential real estate: comparable sales prices are adjusted according to differences in the properties to arrive at the appraised value. This comparable sales procedure forms the basis for the PRIA[31] grazing fee system, which is used for federal lands. We examine later in this chapter how the comparable sales approach is used by the states in setting their leasing fees.

The second approach to appraisal of fair market value for leases is the contributory method. Here, the appraisal looks at the value of one input into the production of the commodity. In the case of state lands, the input is the land and (sometimes) some or all of the infrastructure in the form of improvements. The value of this contribution then becomes the rent due from the lessee to the state. In agriculture, this contribution is often based on the percentage of the value that the land provides, versus the value that the labor and inputs of the lessee account for, which leads to a sharecropping system. Equally frequently, the contribution of the land in the form of forage, water access, and water availability is used as the basis for setting fees in grazing leases. Both of these contributory approaches are discussed in the section on fee arrangements.

A third method of determining the contributory value is based on the cost of replacing it in the production of a given commodity. In some respects this is similar to the comparable sales approach, but the difference here is that the replacement often takes the form of a different commodity. Farm and ranch budgets are frequently constructed to determine operational costs. Mathematical programming methods are then applied to model the effect of changing these costs for lease fees to obtain the optimal fee level (the fee just short of where a replacement would be purchased, while still keeping the lessee in business). For grazing, the costs of replacing range forage is usually determined by the price of alternative grazing leases or the cost of hay and feed grain. Replacement costs for crop leases can represent an intensification cost of fertilizer or irrigation water to achieve the same results with less land. The replacement cost approach is frequently used for farm-level decision analysis,[32] and it was used in the 1986 federal grazing fee study commissioned by the Bureau of Land Management and the Forest Service.[33]

The third approach to valuing cropland and grazing leases is based on the capitalized value of the income they generate. The value of the land is amortized over a period of years at a stated discount rate, and the annual amortized value is the rental rate (the income capitalization approach). This approach explicitly acknowledges that the lands should return some percentage of their value every year. The amount that they return can then be used to compare their use for crops and grazing with their returns from another use, or conversely, the returns that might be expected if the lands were sold and the proceeds were placed in the state's permanent fund.

Types of Cropland Leases

Cropland and grazing lease fee systems used today have their origin in the feudal systems of Europe.[34] Agricultural and grazing leases commonly come in three varieties: the state can lease its land and obtain shares of the resulting crops; the state can lease its land on a cash rental basis; or the state can hire labor and produce the crops itself, or use a variant of this approach called "custom farming." Rent shares, commonly called sharecropping, has the longest history in agricultural lease arrangements. Two types of payment are prevalent in sharecropping: the state is paid its part in the commodity produced, which it then markets itself; or the lessee markets all of the crop and pays the state the agreed-upon portion of the proceeds as its share. In cash rents, the lessee pays the state a fixed amount of money for the privilege of the lease. Payments on cash rents are based either on a fixed amount per acre or lease—most prevalent for agricultural leases—or an amount calculated according to the productive capability of the land—most commonly used in grazing leases. Historically, states have not chosen to produce crops themselves on their trust lands. However custom farming is being used increasingly in some parts of the country, so it is worth mentioning.

SHARECROPPING

The first approach to setting rents—that the landowner should be paid rent in proportion to the contribution of land in the final production of commodities—provides the basis for sharecropping arrangements. In this system, a lessee receives use of state trust lands and in return gives the state a portion of the crop as payment for this privilege. While they are most commonly used in agricultural leases, some fee systems in grazing leases are also conceptually based on shares of production.

Considerable controversy has arisen about sharecropping systems in the United States because of the inequities associated with the practice in the Reconstruction South. Another key focus of debate has been whether sharecroppers have sufficient incentive to invest maximum effort on their leased land in comparison to lessees who pay cash rent, or in comparison to owners of their own lands.[35]

While sharecropping almost disappeared after World War II, the rise in land prices and the amount of capital required to work the fields with mechanical equipment in the 1970s encouraged a revival of the practice, particularly in the Midwest. The advantage of sharecropping in present-day agriculture is exactly the disadvantage perceived in earlier times: the tenant does not need to have or spend large amounts of capital to get the land needed to farm.

On the other hand, as the landowner, the state gains advantages but also accepts disadvantages through this cropping system. By accepting some of the risk involved in producing crops, the states allows the lessee more capital to invest in productive improvements such as irrigation systems and high-value, high-input crops. The principal disadvantage of sharecrop leases to the state is in adequately accounting for production. "There is an awful lot of shrinkage on the way to the elevator," said one state land manager.[36] The costs associated with overseeing lessees and auditing their production accounts for the trend toward cash rents. Cash rents also provide a more reliable income stream to the beneficiary.

Several important factors must be considered in sharecropping leases.[37] The first is the split between the tenant and the state, and whether the share is based on the value of the product or on the amount of physical production. This split ultimately determines the *gross* revenues that the state receives. The next question is whether the state contributes for production and/or capital inputs. The degree to which the state invests in both capital and annual production costs changes the relative risk apportionment between the state and the lessee, and it should therefore affect the revenue split between the two parties. The amount of the state's risk is also related to the questions of who markets the resulting crops, and what mechanisms are in place to audit and monitor the leases. Finally, who decides what crops are grown on the leased parcel (which is important, since it determines the resulting values), and does the lease specify how much effort and what level of inputs are required of the lessee? All of these factors determine both the amount of revenues received from sharecropping leases, and the successfulness of this type of leasing procedure in comparison with others. While the state theoretically can receive higher returns from sharecropping, the amount of added effort and risk involved is much greater than in other leasing methods such as cash rentals.

CASH RENTS

In concept, cash rents are much simpler than sharecropping. They are typically calculated as a rental fee per acre. And in contrast to sharecropping, all the production risk is assumed by the lessee, because the state is guaranteed a set amount of rental. Where cash rentals become difficult is in establishing the rent. As we will see in our discussion of fee setting, there are a number of ways to appraise the base value for rental purposes.

CUSTOM FARMING

Custom farming is similar in concept to having the state hire labor to produce crops on its lands. In contrast to the other two leasing arrangements we have discussed, in custom farming most of the risk associated with producing crops resides with the landowner. Typically, absentee owners contract for management with a firm, which then hires others to perform the actual operations required to grow crops. The contract between the owner or manager and the actual operator establishes contractually fixed rates for specific operations, such as plowing, disking, planting, and harvesting. The risks involved in this production arrangement are the highest of the three types. Further, the amount of managerial attention required from the state land office is considered a major drawback. Nevertheless, the returns range around 9 to 10 percent if the owner provides all inputs and the operator provides machinery and labor.[38]

LEASING PROCEDURES

This section presents an overview of how agriculture and grazing leases are administered, particularly with regard to how a lessee obtains a lease and what rights and obligations are attached to the lease. Since these obligations are frequently identified as causal relationships with the fees used to lease the lands, the determination (by state) and an indication of the value (if any) of these rights and obligations are important. How the lease is obtained frequently determines whether the state gets fair market value for it. How the obligations of the lessee are valued determines how much the lease is worth to the lessee. The key to successful leasing procedures consists in striking a balance between attracting industrious lessees and obtaining the highest return from the lands.

Table 4-1 provides a quick comparison of the different leasing procedures that states use for their cropland and grazing lands. Each of these lease provisions is discussed in detail in this section. Our intention is to demonstrate that leasing procedures are important, that they affect the state's ability to obtain fair market value for its resources, and that they indicate the degree to which the state has control over its leases.

How a Lease Is Obtained and Held

Obtaining a grazing lease is the first step in the relationship between the state as landowner and the lessee as developer of the resource. The federal government's procedures for grazing leases, particularly in the intermoun-

TABLE 4-1. Overview of state trust land cropland and grazing lease provisions

Lease Provision	AZ	CA	CO	ID	MT	NB	ND	NM	OK	OR	SD	TX	UT	WA	WY
Fee determination															
Cropshare percent[1]			12½		25					25		25			
Cash rent (fee/acre)			V	V											
Appraised land value (%)	I,D[3]	9%[2]	G,D,I	G,D,I		G,D,I	D,I	G	G,D,I		I,D		I,D	I,D	I,D
Comparable private (%)		I,D,G						I,D					I,D	G	G
Competitive bidding only															I = 4%
Minimum $/AUM (1994)	$1.48	$4.00	$6.42	$4.53	$4.09	$14.50	$4.00	$3.31	$6.25	$2.50	$7.30	$6.25	$2.50	$4.19	$3.00
Lease term															
Years for lease	10	10		10	5,10	5–10	5	5	5		5	10	15	5	10
Renewal possible?	Y			Y	N?	N	N	Y			Y		Y	Y	Y
Preferential right?	Y				Y	N		Y	N		N	N	Y	Y	Y
Absolute	Y												?		
Match highest bid				Y	Y		Y	Y					Y	Y	Y
Base property required?	N			Y	N	N	N	N	N		N	N	Y	Y	Y
Leasing procedures															
Advertising required?	N			N	N	Y	Y	N			Y	Y		Y	
Bidding procedures															
Oral auction				Y		Y	Y				Y				
Sealed bid													Y		
Other					Y			Y							
Are bonus bids used?															
Flat amount				Y	Y	Y	Y					Y	Y	Y	
Percentage of rent				Y	Y	Y	Y					Y	Y	Y	
Rent rate ($/AUM)					Y										
After the lease															
Who owns improvements?[3]	L	S	S	L	L	M	M	L	M	C	L	C	L	M	L
Assignment allowed?	Y		Y	Y	Y	Y	Y	Y	Y	Y	Y		Y	Y	
Subleasing allowed?	Y			Y	Y	Y	N	Y	Y	Y	N		N	Y	Y
Collateral assignment?			Y	Y	Y	N	N	Y	Y	Y	N		Y	Y	Y
Leasehold value?		N		Y	Y			Y	Y	Y			N	Y	Y

Notes:

1. Codes are G = grazing; D = dryland agriculture; I = irrigated agriculture; V = variable.
2. California Code of Regulations. Title 2, Division 3, Chapter 1, Article 2, §2003(a)(7).
3. Codes are L = lessee, all; M = state permanent improvements, lessee movable improvements; C = state cost-shares, costs amortized in rent, state owns resulting improvements; S = state owns all improvements.

Source: WSLCA, Western States Land and Surface Leasing... Summary of Selected Factors, October 1989.

tain and West Coast states, heavily influence how the states handle their leases.[39] Because of this, we compare the provisions used by the federal government to those used by the states. Specific provisions discussed include the bidding procedures (starting with whether competitive bidding is possible) whether a preference right to a lease exists and, if so, whether it depends on owning base property; how the existing lessee can transfer either the lease itself or its value to others; and how the state can recover the lease for other uses or for nonpayment of fees. Each provision is defined (usually in its federal context), and then state practices are discussed. Our hope is to provide a comparison of the diversity of approaches that the states use in determining how to obtain leases and to suggest windows of opportunity through which low-income rental states can increase their revenues.

BIDDING PROCEDURES AND FAIR MARKET VALUE

Identifying who can obtain a state grazing lease goes a long way toward determining whether the state obtains fair market value. As we discussed in Chapter 3, fair market value represents the amount for which the lease would change hands between a willing, knowledgeable buyer and a similarly situated seller on the open market. Three operative criteria must be borne in mind in analyzing the competitive nature of the states' agriculture and grazing leases. First, is either party "under any compulsion to buy or sell"? Second, is the planned agriculture or grazing the "highest and most profitable use"? Third, is the lease "offered for sale in the open market"? We contend that collectively these three traditional appraisal qualifications determine whether the states' leasing procedures allow them to obtain fair market value.

The first criterion—whether the state or the potential lessee is under any compulsion to sell or buy, respectively, a grazing lease—is hotly debated. Two arguments are made, both of which reflect the dispersed pattern in which many of the lands were initially granted and (typically) are still held. First, the state may be compelled to let a lease because its lands are unfenced from surrounding landowners, and as such it would otherwise suffer trespass. Second, because of its land ownership patterns, the state may not have legal public access to its lands (or access to water) except at the sufferance of the adjacent landowner(s). Fencing the lands, obtaining legal access, providing for water, or some combination of these, would be uneconomical in many areas that the states lease for grazing. For these reasons the state may be compelled to lease its lands. Conversely, potential lessees may feel compelled to purchase leases from the state, for various reasons. For example, the lease may have been in the family for generations; the state land may provide the main access to the lessee's deeded land; the lessee may have a major investment in improvements, introduced during prior lease periods; or its forage availability may have been factored into the ranch's overall operating structure and value.

The state may also be compelled to lease if the state imposes qualifications on potential lessees. In the grazing context, this is frequently couched in terms of whether the lessee owns "base property" or can demonstrate that he or she is "in the cattle business." *Base property* is usually defined similarly to how it is in federal requirements.[40] The ostensible intent underlying such conditions is that "base property" will contribute to range conservation by guaranteeing that the lessee has sufficient forage and water to enable his or her stock to move off the public range for a portion of the year. In practice, however, the requirement for base property has been used to limit entry from competing interests, whether they be ranchers outside the immediate area or (in the earlier era of range wars) itinerant sheepherders.[41]

Typically, states have no base property requirements for potential cropland lessees, but they do require that prospective lessees possess sufficient experience to operate the lease. This provision also occurs in grazing leases, where potential lessees are required to "prove" that they are in the cattle business. Washington state, for example, requires that "the applicant must have two years of experience in the grazing or handling of livestock or education in range or livestock management and financial resources to carry out the proposed grazing operation."[42] States typically have other qualifications as well, such as age limitations or the requirement that the lessee be a corporation licensed to do business in the state. Their purposes are twofold: to guarantee that the lessee possesses at least the minimum specified level of competence to handle the requirements of the lease, as a protection to the state; and as an additional barrier to the free entry of potential bidders.[43] As we shall see in Chapter 7, these qualifications have significantly hindered efforts by watershed conservation groups to purchase grazing leases in Idaho in order to "retire" them.

The second appraisal criterion used to determine fair market value is whether the existing use is "highest and best." For example, environmental groups have periodically sought to lease state grazing lands, not to run cattle but to protect other resource values. If these organizations are willing to pay at least as much as the existing lessee, it would seem—based on trust principles—that the beneficiaries would be at least as well off as under the existing lease, since they would have current income as well as protection of the trust corpus. But while states generally have the authority to take back all or portions of grazing leases for other uses, some states also require that land classified for grazing use must be used for grazing. Given the relatively low fees charged for grazing on many dispersed sections of trust land in the West, many potential bidders might willingly pay a premium to obtain the lease to use for hunting or recreational purposes other than grazing. Some states generate both grazing and recreational income from the same parcel; but where regulations limit the potential uses of the parcel, the "highest and best use" criterion for attaining fair market value may be violated.

The third criterion is whether the leases are "offered for sale in the open market." The answer to this question depends on a number of factors: how leases are advertised prior to sale; whether preference rights for renewal of leases are recognized; and how bidding proceeds at auction. Advertising requirements vary from state to state. Some states have no advertising requirement, so a potential lessee must know that a lease is coming due and must request to bid on it.[44] This system obviously favors the existing leaseholder. Other states require that notices of upcoming lease expirations be placed in the newspaper of record in the county where the parcel is located.[45] Oklahoma goes the farthest by running radio spots and billboard advertisements announcing its lease sales.

Lease renewals have the effect of increasing the lease term. Typically, lease fees are updated at the time of renewal, although in some states (such as Nebraska) lessees know that their annual rental is subject to adjustment based on private market charges.[46] Where renewal occurs without open bidding, the process can effectively violate the trustee's responsibility to give the beneficiaries undivided loyalty.[47] Some courts have found that renewals cannot be automatic, that they must be conditioned on the state's not receiving a higher bid.[48] However, a Wyoming court found, to the contrary, that high bids could be overturned if they were out of line with prevailing local conditions.[49]

Whether leases are even opened for competitive bidding varies among states. Historically, preference-right leasing, promising the current leaseholder a right to renew, has been widespread. And whereas the court in *Oklahoma Education Association v. Nigh* found that the preference-right system violated trust principles, many states retain it in some form.[50] The exact form of the preference varies from absolute[51] (in the cases of Arizona, Oregon, Washington, and Wyoming) to a lesser right under which the existing lessee is allowed the opportunity to match the highest bidder in a lease auction.[52] The states of Nebraska, North Dakota, Oklahoma, and Texas give no preference rights for renewal; South Dakota allows the existing lessee one five-year exclusive renewal on the original five-year lease.

Bidding procedures greatly influence whether a state receives fair market value from its leases.[53] If leases are sold on the open market, two basic mechanisms are used: written bids and oral auctions. Written bids, accompanied by a deposit covering the first year's rental, are typically accepted by the state until a specified date.[54] All bids are then opened, and the highest bidder who meets the state's qualifications receives the lease. In contrast, oral auctions are conducted on a given date, usually at the county seat where the property is located.[55] Auctions start with a minimum bid, usually representing the state's AUM fee times the number of AUMs permitted in the lease. Any potential lessees wishing to pay more than this amount place their bids, sequentially competing for the lease by offering the highest total bid, the highest share crop percentage,[56] or the highest amount per AUM.[57]

Whether oral or sealed bids are used in leasing trust lands affects the composition of the bidding and the extent to which bidders are influenced by other bidders. One advantage of sealed bids is that the bidder has sufficient time to analyze potential costs and benefits of a lease, and thus to prepare her/his best bid, without reacting to competitors (or the absence thereof) during the bidding process. There is also a desirable element of confidentiality, since rival bidders need not publicly face their neighbors who presently have the lease. The effects of the confidentiality of written bids may be even more important in increasing the pool of potential bidders when the existing lessee has the financial ability to meet the highest competing bid and retain the lease. In this situation, potential bidders do not have to face the wrath of a leaseholding neighbor who had to pay more than previously to retain the lease.

On the other hand, oral auctions allow a bidder who is intensely interested in obtaining a lease to outbid all other potential lessees. An oral auction thus has the potential to raise the bid price above what might otherwise be offered. There is, indeed, a potential in this system to receive "overbids" as a result of the heat of the process. Although this yields more money for the trust, in the short term, it also increases the likelihood that the lease will be forfeited during its beginning period, or even that the land will be "mined" to cover the lease costs.[58] To prevent this, Montana allows the successful bidder to go back to the department to contest the winning bid if he or she thinks it is too high. This mechanism is frequently used by existing lessees who match competing high bids and then come back to the department to negotiate a lower fee.[59]

Our discussion of the effects of appraisal criteria on efforts to achieve fair market value and competitive bidding are not entirely theoretical. Table 4-2 shows the results of a 1989 survey of the Western States Land Commissioners Association members when asked what percentage of leases involved actual receipt of competitive bids. On first observation, the results of

TABLE 4-2. Competitive bidding for state trust land grazing leases

Question: "If your leases are offered at public auction or some other public bid process, approximately what percentage of tracts receive competition?"

Response	Number	Percent	States
N/A*	10	50	AK, AZ, CA, CO, HI, MN, OR, UT, WI, WY.
0–10%	6	30	ID, LA, MT, NM, TX, WA.
11–20%	4	20	NB, ND, OK, SD.
>20%	0	0	None.

*N/A appears to mean that auction or bid process is not used in the state, with AZ, CO, OR, and WY indicating that they use a preference-right system; and the others, some combination of preference right and competitive bidding.
Source: North Dakota State Land Office, Leasing System Survey (March 31, 1989).

the survey indicate that none of the states have significant competition for their grazing leases. This is probably due, more than anything else, to the dispersed trust land ownership pattern under which the state parcels are scattered, surrounded by other holdings, and too small to form a self-supporting ranch unit. But even given the small amount of competitive leasing, some patterns emerge. The preference right rules have the effect that one would expect. Not surprisingly, states with no preference right had the highest percentage of competitive bids, although even in these states only between 11 and 20 percent of the leases received more than one application. More interesting is the implication that allowing the existing lessee to match the highest bid seems to reduce the number of competitive bids to less than 10 percent.

In looking at the connection between the competitive nature of state grazing leases and the state's ability to obtain fair market value for their cropland and grazing leases, we should consider a series of questions. First, what are the requirements for potential lessees, and do these requirements limit the ability of the state to maximize long-term income from the leases? Second, what measures does the state take to market its leases or to manage its lands so that the highest number of potential bidders is available? And third, when leases are auctioned, is the process set up so that potential bidders are encouraged (1) to bid and (2) to bid the maximum value of the forage to them? If these policies are implemented, the leasing process should be as competitive as possible—given the state's land ownership pattern—and questions of base fees will be of less consequence.

RIGHTS IN THE LEASE

When a lessee obtains a lease from the state, certain rights come with it. These rights are generally described by the legal term *leasehold interest*—the rights and privileges that the lessee of property has by virtue of the nature of the lease.[60] Generally, the lessee is granted use of the property for a certain number of years and has in some cases (as described earlier) a preference right to renew the lease, as well as the right to transfer the lease to others. If all or portions of the leased property are taken by the state for other uses, the lessee has certain rights to compensation, which vary depending on the state. Because the bundle of rights attached to a lease has value[61] to both the lessee and the state, the criteria the various states use to define that bundle are worth examining.

The lease term conveys to the lessee the right to use the property for a set number of years. The length of the lease term is usually fixed by statute,[62] with the legislature and the land board having wide latitude to determine it.[63] Although lease terms vary among the states, terms of five or ten years are the most common.[64] The term of the lease affects how often competition is received; and in some cases, it determines how often lease provisions and lease fees are adjusted. Short-term leases have the benefit of allowing the state to change lessees if a problem is encountered, without going through a lease revocation process. Short-term leases also help keep lease fees at the prevailing market rates, if sufficient competition is available; and they prevent any sort of "squatter's rights" from accumulating as a result of lessees' prolonged holding of a lease. On the other hand, longer-term leases reduce the transactions costs for the state land office, and encourage the lessee to make longer-term commitments to the land, thus (arguably) increasing stewardship.

The conventional wisdom (for which there is no firm empirical support) is that short-term leases encourage "mining" of resources because the lessee has relatively little incentive to protect the land. The increased costs to the agency of monitoring performance of short-term leases, as well as of rebidding them at frequent intervals, may carry with them the added benefit of ensuring that the state land office gets out to the parcel more regularly. The length of the lease term determines to some extent the lessee's management of the land. With a short-term lease, the lessee will be uncertain of his or her future tenure and as a result hesitate to make long-term investments, particularly if they are not compensated at the end of the lease (see the subsequent discussion of improvements). On the other hand, if the lease period is too long, the ability of others to obtain the lease is restricted, and over time the difference between the lessee's rent and the fair market value of the leased land are likely to diverge. Long leases have the added disadvantage (to the state) that the existing lessee may start to view the leased land as his or her property and forget that it belongs to the state.

The fact that cropland and grazing leases have a leasehold value is recognized by local bankers when they accept the lease as collateral for loans.[65] This practice, known as *collateral assignment* of leases,[66] is defined as "a security given in addition to the direct security, and subordinate to it, intended to guaranty its validity or convertibility or insure its performance; so that, if the direct security fails, the creditor may fall back upon the collateral security."[67] Being able to borrow against the value of the lease benefits the lessee; however, it causes problems for the state if the bank forecloses on the loan and ends up owning the lease. Nonetheless, even though some states discourage it, most allow this traditional practice, charging the default assignee only a nominal fee to handle the additional paperwork.[68] Typically, the land board or state land office must approve the assignment, but usually the approval is automatic. Only North Dakota and South Dakota prohibit collateral assignments.[69]

Occasionally, the existing lessee decides not to use the lease for a given year or decides to sell its use to another, either by itself or as a part of a package including the lessee's base property, federal grazing permits, and state leases. Usually, if the ranch is not being sold, the lessee only wants to transfer use of the lease to another temporarily. There are two types of temporary transfers: subleases and pasturage agreements. Subleasing gives the lessee the option to get out from under the burden of his or her lease temporarily, without transferring title to it.[70] In pasturage agreements, the lessee brings in cattle owned by others to graze the leased land, but controls those livestock. In contrast, in subleases, control of the livestock on the property is transferred from the primary lessee to the owner of the cattle.

Considerable controversy surrounds both subleasing as a practice and the distinction between subleasing and pasturage agreements.[71] The controversy arises because the primary lessee frequently receives a substantial additional payment from the sublessee beyond what the lessee pays for the lease. This payment to the primary lessee is called "excess rent." Any surplus in the rental rate paid to the primary lessee above what the state receives that cannot be attributed to the primary lessee's transaction costs constitutes excess rent. Some states explicitly acknowledge the primary lessee's transactions costs by taking a percentage, usually 50 percent, of the additional fees the sublessee pays; other states ignore the difference between their fee and what the primary lessee receives, charging only a small transfer fee to approve the sublease. Excess rent from subleasing is, in effect, a transfer of trust benefits from the beneficiary to the lessee. Hence, the trust is violated because it is not receiving full fair market value.

Lease assignments are different from subleasing agreements, but they raise many of the same issues. Transferring title to the lease is called *assignment*, and is defined as "transfer by a party of all of its rights to some kind of property, usually intangible property such as rights in a lease, mortgage, agreement of sale or a partnership."[72] All states allow this practice, pending board approval, and charge only nominal fees to execute the paperwork. The right of assignment gives the lessee flexibility at little or no cost to the trust. Where significant consideration is paid to the prior lessee by the new one, however, this consideration again indicates that the state is receiving less than fair market rentals, and the difference represents a loss to the trust.

How the state handles subleasing and lease assignments provides important indicators about whether its agents are acting with undivided loyalty to the beneficiaries or with the traditional orientation toward the lessees. If the state does not adequately control either subleases or assignments, and if it allows the original lessee to receive substantial amounts of money to transfer use of the lease, the state evidently is not receiving full and fair market value and is not acting with undivided loyalty to the beneficiary. If the lease is let at fair market value, any lessee should be indifferent between holding it and transferring it, with the only added value being the cost of finding alternative croplands or forage. The amount of the payment by another to the original lessee and the amount that a bank will lend on collateral for the lease are indications of the difference between the amount the state is receiving and fair market value.

IMPROVEMENTS

A final area of interest in relation to state cropland and grazing leasing procedures is how improvements to the leased lands are handled. An improvement is, generally, what it sounds like: "A valuable addition made to property (usually real estate) or an amelioration in its condition, amounting to more than mere repairs or replacement, costing labor or capital, and intended to enhance its value, beauty or utility or to adapt it for new or further purposes. . . ."[73] Who pays for improvements, and how these are dealt with at lease termination are important considerations for both the lessee and the trustee. Important issues include how various types of improvements are distinguished, what cost-share mechanisms are in place, who approves improvements, and how improvements affect competition for leases.

Improvements come in basically two types: fixed ("permanent") and movable ("nonpermanent"). Examples of fixed improvements are fences, wells, stock ponds, land terracing, and some types of brush control (above and beyond maintenance). Movable improvements commonly include tanks, pumps, stock gathering facilities, and sometimes fences.

Some states encourage lessee investments and may cost-share for approved fixed improvements. Five states have programs under which they contribute money or adjust the lessee's rent payments to pay for fixed improvements. North Dakota and Texas give lessees rent credits for introducing approved permanent improvements.[74] Oregon cost-shares but requires that the lessee repay the state's cost over ten years with no interest.[75] Utah cost-shares rangeland improvements to the extent of providing materials, with the lessee contributing equipment and labor.[76] For agricultural leases, Washington usually pays for wells and underground main pipelines (the fixed part), while the lessee pays for the movable pump and pivot.[77] In the remaining states, both fixed and movable improvements are constructed at the lessee's cost; the lessee is then reimbursed when the lease terminates or changes hands.

How improvements are handled at the end of the lease term or if the land is sold differs among the states. Table 4-3 shows a categorization of these policies. Two general patterns exist: in some states the lessee is required to remove the improvements unless he or she can reach agreement with the subsequent lessee; in others, the new lessee is required to compensate the previous lessee for the value of the improvements, with different measures of values among the different states. Generally, prior lessees always have the option to remove their improvements if this can be accomplished without harm to the land.[78] Oklahoma requires removal of movable improvements.[79] Only in Colorado do all improvements, except fences, be-

TABLE 4-3. Compensation methods for cropland and
grazing lease improvements

Compensation Method	States Using
Appraised fair market value	AZ, MS, MT, NB, SD, WY.
Replacement cost – depreciation	ID, NM.
Undepreciated cost or value	ND, OR.
No compensation	OK.
Unknown	CA, LA, TX, UT, WA.

long to the state.[80] When the previous lessee is compensated for his or her improvements, their value is appraised and the state or the subsequent lessee pays this value to the prior lessee.[81]

Who owns the improvements and how they are appraised and transferred at lease termination significantly influences the state's ability to achieve fair market return. On the one hand, the state clearly has an interest in encouraging its lessees to make improvements to the lease that will increase its productivity and stewardship—especially if the lessee is paying fair market fees. On the other hand, if the existing lessee is paying substantially less than fair market fees, while at the same time placing expensive improvements on the lease that have no value to anyone else, requiring future lessees to pay the existing one for the improvements could reduce the likelihood of receiving competitive bids. The state has two options for overcoming this problem. First, it can finance all the permanent improvements and require the lessee to remove the others at the end of the lease. To deal with existing lessee improvements, the state can adopt an accelerated depreciation schedule so that, at the end of ten to twenty years, no value remains that requires transfer. This technique works well with older improvements that are approaching the end of their useful life. Second, the state can be particularly vigilant in the future about the types of improvements that it approves, endorsing only improvements that are fixed, contribute value to the property that can be recovered by fees, and are useful to other potential lessees.

REVERSION AND LEASEHOLD INTERESTS

The combination of the lessee's rights in the lease and the compensable improvements affect how the state handles the lease when it decides to change the use of the leased land. A number of different situations may lead the state to use its lands for some other purpose than the existing agricultural or grazing use. Perhaps the parcel is part of a land sale or exchange. Where development of oil and gas or other mineral rights entails extraction of subsurface resources, production may require that portions of the surface be occupied by the subsurface lessee.[82] Finally, another, higher-valued surface use, such as commercial development, communications sites, roads, or pipelines, may supersede agriculture or grazing. When the state initiates a land use change, the typical lessee is interested in two kinds of compensation: the value of the improvements, and the value of the "leasehold interest" above and beyond the value of the improvements. The first item is easily dealt with: the existing lessee is generally compensated for improvements in the manner discussed in the previous section. States also refund any prepaid rent.

The second area is much more controversial. *Leasehold interest* means the "rights to the use and occupancy of the property subject to various obligations, [and] . . . is said to have value when contract rent is less than market rent, which is the amount a property could earn in a competitive real estate market."[83] States generally do not concede that the lessee has a leasehold interest beyond the value of approved improvements and prepaid rent. Some states explicitly specify in their statues, rules, or lease forms that no leasehold value is allowed.[84] Other states remain silent on this question, following the federal practice of not acknowledging the interest but accommodating it when it is pressed. A few states even specify that their lessees are responsible for any leasehold taxes on their interests in the lease.[85] The primary reason states are unwilling to acknowledge a leasehold value is because it indicates that rental rates are below market value, which is prohibited. Nonetheless, there is considerable evidence that leasehold values exist. Whether the states acknowledge these values or not, bankers finance loans based on their existence.

Our analysis suggests that most of the rights inure to the lessee, and not necessarily to the benefit of the trust. Specifically, the state relinquishes control over the leased property when it allows for preference rights, collateral assignments, subleasing, and compensation to the lessee for the undepreciated replacement value of improvements. The state—and the trust—gains control of leases when it opens the bidding process through competitive leases whose availability is broadly advertised; when it disallows collateral lease assignments (since there should be no value left if fees reflect full market value); and when it either requires the existing lessee to remove improvements at the end of the lease term or requires the future lessee to pay only the appraised fair market value for improvements that are useful to future lessees.

FEES AND FEE SYSTEMS FOR CROPLAND AND GRAZING LEASES

Much of what we discussed in the previous section goes on in private, to the great advantage of lessees; fees are the *only* aspect of cropland and grazing leasing that have received public airing. We now investigate how the appraisal methods just described are applied in practice in the various states. First we examine how agricultural fees are determined. Then we look at how grazing fees are established. There are clear differences here between agriculture and grazing, so we discuss them separately and then ask, why they are handled differently. We also spend some time analyzing the federal government's grazing fee system, and again ask why some states have chosen to adopt it. Fees are only one item in the bundle of rights and obligations in cropland and grazing lease programs, but they are an important indicator of how close the state is to achieving fair market value for its resources. Fees, and how they are determined, provide a data point on the continuum between traditional and modern leasing practices.

Cropland Lease Fees

Unlike grazing fees based on the Animal Unit Month (AUM), which is a relatively standard measure, the fees charged by the states for their agricultural leases cannot easily be generalized. Two aspects of the leases are crucial: how each state appraises its lands; and how prospective lessees bid on the leases. The appraised value is important because it sets the base bid price for a lease. How leases are bid is important because it determines whether any competition exists to boost the winning bid above the minimum appraised price. In the previous section, we discussed bidding and lease procedures; this section focuses on how the states set their base agricultural lease fees.

Each state uses one of the three appraisal methods described in the second section of this chapter for its agricultural leases: comparable appraisals, contributory value, or income capitalization. Comparable appraisals are used to set base agricultural bid values in Arizona, California, Nebraska, North Dakota, Oklahoma, and Texas. Nebraska, North Dakota, and Oklahoma base their appraisals on county or regional comparables and then, in the cases of Nebraska and North Dakota, make adjustments for productivity and services provided. California and Texas make individual farm- or ranch-specific appraisals to determine the minimum bid.

The contributory value appraisal approach is seen in the states that use sharecropping systems: Montana and Washington. In Montana, the usual state share is 25 percent, but this is reduced to 15 percent for certain high-valued crops such as potatoes. Montana is unique in having potential lessees bid on the percentage share they will give to the state when leases are auctioned.[86] In Washington, the share depends on the crop, as does the method of payment. For orchard and vineyard crops, the state takes 5 percent of the value of the crop after production starts, requiring only a nominal rental payment before the plants start bearing. The state markets its share of cereal crops and dry beans, taking payment from the elevator or warehouse.[87] The share that the state takes for these crops is between 5 per-

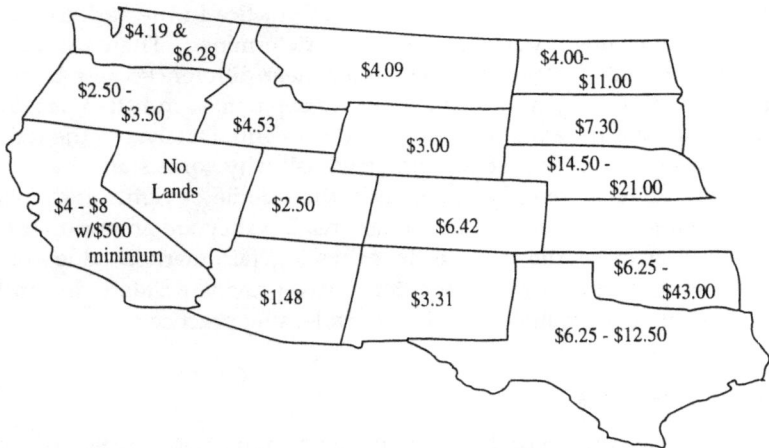

Figure 4-5. Minimum AUM grazing fees on state trust lands in 1994. NOTES: In Oregon, the $2.50/AUM is for blocked lands, $3.50/AUM on meadow lands. Most ranchers pay a higher fee to reimburse the state for improvements. PRIA fee is used in California on lands within BLM grazing allotments. Other lands are leased on the basis of individual comparable private lease rate appraisals. Washington grazing fees are differentiated into Permit Range and Leased Range. See text for details. Idaho fees vary according to whether cattle or sheep are grazing.

cent and 40 percent, depending on region and crop.[88] For other crops grown on irrigated farmland (with the exception of orchards and vineyards), the lessee markets the crop and the state takes an annual cash rent determined by comparable private agricultural leases in the county.

Grazing Fees

States establish a minimum fee, usually based on the Animal Unit Month (AUM), that provides a base value for their grazing receipts prior to any bonuses received from competitive bidding. Figure 4-5 shows the minimum fees for fiscal year 1994 on state trust lands. Depending on the state, fees are adjusted either annually or at lease renewal. The amount of competitive bidding varies radically among the states. Generally, the easternmost states have significant competition, while those in the intermountain region have relatively little competition (see Table 4-1). The minimum fee in an area without significant competitive bidding frequently becomes the standard lease fee.

The same three appraisal approaches discussed in relation to cropland leases—comparable sales, contributory value, and income capitalization—can also be used to characterize the grazing fee systems the states use. The contributory valuation approach can be further subdivided in two divisions:

PRIA-based formulations that use indexes to adjust fees; and revenue divisions similar to sharecropping, called *cattle price shares*. Which states use which of these four basic approaches to determining the fair market value for their grazing is shown in Figure 4-6. The states' grazing fee determination procedures are discussed in general terms using the four divisions. Additional information on how grazing fees are determined is provided in the appendix to this chapter, which includes state-by-state specific grazing fee formulas. Because the federal government's system dominates most discussion of grazing fees, we start our investigation there, and then take up (in turn) cattle price shares, comparable sales, and the income capitalization approach.

PRIA-BASED PRICE- AND COST-INDEXED FORMULAS

In the Public Rangelands Improvement Act (PRIA) of 1984, Congress established a grazing fee system for federal lands based on the contributory valuation approach, which focuses on the lands' value in the production of

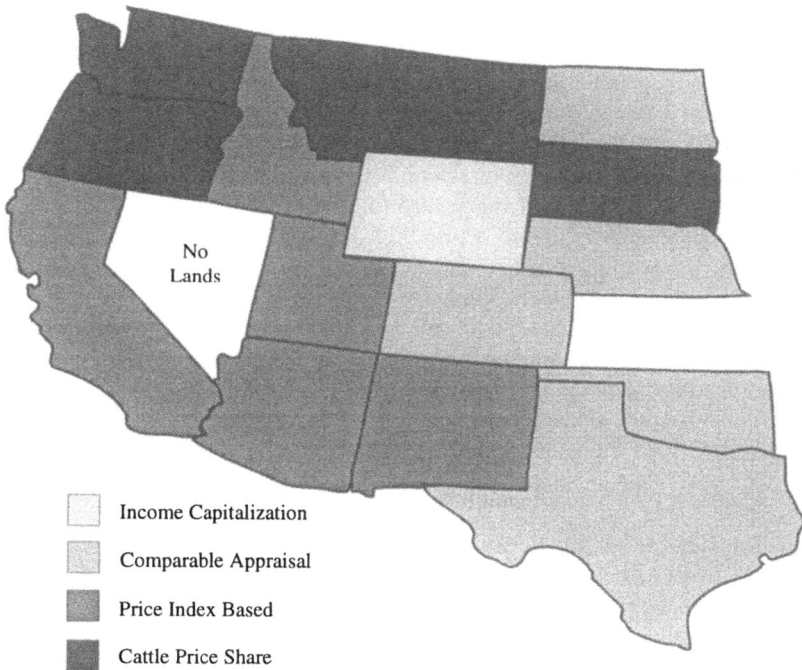

Figure 4-6. Various approaches to establishing trust land grazing fees. NOTE: As of 1995, Oregon has shifted from using an income capitalization approach to using a cattle price share approach.

cattle. The derivation of the federal fee system under PRIA is important since it provides the basis for many of the state fees formulas.[89] The PRIA formula and its state derivatives differ from the strict contributory valuation: rather than determining each year the relative value of the various inputs to produce cattle, the PRIA formula uses a base value that is then changed by the behavior of various price indexes. These indexes generally include movements in beef prices, private pasture leasing rates, and the cost of materials such as fencing, gasoline, and trucks that are used by ranchers.

In establishing grazing fees on their lands, the states have been influenced by the federal PRIA formula, particularly where federal land lies adjacent to the trust land. Five states (Arizona, California, Idaho, New Mexico, and Utah) currently use fee systems either identical to or derived from the federal system.[90] Of these five states, three use the PRIA formula to establish a base rate, and then modify it to account for local differences. Arizona takes the PRIA fee and discounts it 22.5 percent to account for lessee improvements and leasehold taxes. California uses the PRIA formula on state lands within BLM grazing allotments but charges a minimum fee of $500 per year per lease. Utah adds 35 cents to the PRIA fee, plus 5 cents more for weed control. The two other states, Idaho and New Mexico, use a PRIA-like system of price indexes to adjust their grazing fees. Unlike the PRIA formula, however, the statistical methods applied in these two states use a different base value (adjusted annually), as well as different weights for the importance of the various cost and price indexes. Moreover, Idaho's base fee depends on whether cattle or sheep are grazing the leased lands (sheep get a discount because of bad market conditions).

The problems with the states' use of index formulas to obtain fair market value are similar to those identified in criticisms of the federal PRIA formula. First, there is controversy over whether the base value established in previous years is accurate. Second, when a fee is based on several composite price indexes that tend to vary together, the fees tend to swing wildly—and typically downward—because some factors are double- or triple-counted. Moreover, the data included in the composites are not always relevant to the range livestock industry.

CATTLE PRICE SHARE APPROACH

In contrast to the price- and cost-indexed approaches to determining the contributory value of the states' land in the production of cattle, the price share approach explicitly divides the value of the commodity produced between the state and the lessee. This division is based on the conversion of forage to beef. An AUM represents the amount of forage needed to support a steer or cow for one month. Because the steer or cow is putting on weight (or maintaining its weight) by eating this forage, the gain resulting from the state's forage can be estimated; 50 pounds per AUM is typically assumed, although this depends on the season of use and on whether steers or calves are the ultimate product. The value of the weight gain is then determined by the price of beef.[91] But since forage is not the only input required in producing beef, the rancher's contribution to the forage gain is also factored into the split between the state and the lessee. Ranchers contribute the original mother cow (in the case of cow–calf operations) or the calf itself (if steers are being raised), along with production inputs in the form of veterinary services, water, salt, fencing, and management. The essence of the cattle price share approach thus involves assigning equitable shares based on the relative contributions of the two parties.

Four states (Montana, Oregon, South Dakota and Washington) currently base their grazing fees on the cattle price share model. In the past, Idaho and Arizona also determined their fees by this method. Montana and Washington want 12 percent of the assumed weight gain per AUM; Oregon currently charges 12.5 percent, with an annual 2.5 percent escalation to 20 percent; while South Dakota wants 21 percent. The base assumptions of the method, using Washington's formula as an example, are that a 50-pound growth gain is achieved each month, that 40 percent of the end value is contributed by the land (recall the production function of land, labor, and capital from Chapter 3), and that of land's proportion the state's contribution to forage production in the form of raw land is worth 30 percent. This means that, of the 50 pounds of beef produced, the state wants 12 percent, (or 6 pounds of the 50) as its share [that is, $50 \times .4 \times .3 = 6$]. Multiplying the 6 pounds by the weighted average price for cattle gives the base AUM fee.[92] Each state's exact procedures are shown in the chapter appendix.

Each of the states has (or had) its own modifications of this basic formula. Washington decreases the formula to account for the leasehold tax on the lessee's improvements, and it increases the base rate by 50 percent on some leases where the lessee exercises control over turn-in and turn-out dates and animal numbers. Montana used to modify its fee up or down by 10 cents per AUM if the parcel's carrying capacity was above or below the normal bound. South Dakota uses the price of calves to determine the fee, while Washington and Montana use steer prices. Oregon uses a more complex procedure that subtracts the birth weight of the calf, subtracts another 20 percent for death loss, and then adjusts the formula for a per-AUM gain.

The cattle price share approach has the intuitive appeal of sharecropping in general: the production of commodities is a partnership between the landowner and the tenant, and each shares in the risks and rewards of the enterprise. There appears to be considerable room for discussion between the states and the lessees over the proportion that each should receive, but at least with this method the calculation and the division are explicit. The ranchers may not know with certainty what the grazing fee will be in the future, but they at least know what part of the end value of the product is theirs and what part of it they must pay the state. The state is relieved of uncertainty, too, because, whereas price-indexed methods such as the PRIA formula are unpredictable in many ways, the price used in the share ap- proach is directly related to the value of the product.

COMPARABLE APPRAISALS

An alternative to contributory value approaches uses the prices charged by private parties, adjusted for differences based on the services provided, to set the base grazing fee. The comparable appraisal approach assumes that all services provided by the state are comparable to those of private landowners. Of the five states that use this approach, only one (Colorado) applies a single fee (75 percent of the private grazing fee determined by the USDA June Enumerative Survey) statewide; the other four (Nebraska, North Dakota, Oklahoma, and Texas) conduct site-specific or regional ap- praisals. In Nebraska, the state is divided into production capability zones based on soil type, rainfall, and productive capability. A similar process oc- curs in North Dakota, where the lands are appraised according to produc- tivity indexes (measuring the amount of forage produced per land area [AUMs per acre]) determined for each county. Oklahoma's process is sim- pler in that the state collects county-level appraisal information, which forms the basis for opening bids. No adjustments for services are made in Oklahoma. Texas uses a site-specific appraisal approach in which each indi- vidual parcel is appraised on its productive capacity.

The comparable appraisal approach is appealing because it theoretically allows the private market to establish the fair market value for the grazing leases. However, some—but not all—states have found two problems in its application. The first is that, in many states in the West, there are few pri- vate grazing leases, which raises the possibility that those used in the ap- praisals may not be truly representative of the state's leases. This contrib- utes to the second problem: adjustments for differences in services, both site-specific and across the board, between the state and private leases are not accurate. Examples of the types of adjustments at issue are for fencing, water, inaccurate area surveys, noxious weed control, construction of per- manent improvements, and high administrative costs (see the appendix for state-by-state details). Any of these problems can be overcome if the compa- rable appraisal sets the base fee, which is then bid up on the basis of any specific parcel's usefulness to potential bidders. This is generally the case in states that currently use the practice. The method would likely fail in areas where few private grazing leases exist, such as in most of the intermountain region of the West, where the major landowner is the federal government.

INCOME CAPITALIZATION APPROACH

The final approach to setting grazing fees assumes that a lessee should pay a specified percentage of the land value as the annual grazing fee. This means that the amortized land value is the lease fee. Two primary questions attend its application: what is the underlying value of the lands, and what percentage of the value is an equitable fee? Only Wyoming now uses this approach. By statute, Wyoming can charge from 2 percent to 5½ percent of the appraised land value as a grazing fee; it currently charges 2 percent.

This capitalization approach has appeal to the beneficiaries and, sometimes, to the state because the percentage paid as fees is directly comparable to other methods of trust performance such as return on the permanent fund. Until recently, there was little pressure by the lessees to modify the system, since the base percentages and land values are low. In application, the problems with the system result from issues raised by the primary questions posed above: the land values used to set the base fees are low and/or unrepresentative of the leased areas; and the percentage capitalization is also low, especially when compared to the potential returns on even a conservatively invested permanent fund. As with the other approaches, if the leases are competitive, the exact base fee becomes less important because the difference will be made up at the auction.

It should be clear that the fees charged are only part of the overall package that constitutes a lease. A state's procedures and its land ownership pattern control to a large extent how competitive the leases are. In the absence of competition, the method used to establish the base fee acquires paramount importance. Any of the fee-setting systems that we've described here can be an adequate starting point for establishing the fair market value for grazing leases. The issue, however, is how well the different parts of the fee system—and the overall leasing procedures—work in practice now and in the future. Two of the fee systems we have described possess the attributes of being equitable, being simple to administer, and encouraging good stewardship: the comparable sales approach, and the cattle price share approach. The comparable sales approach works well in areas where sufficient private leases exist to provide an adequate number of examples to use in setting the state fees. Where adequate private leases are not available for comparison, the cattle price share method seems preferable because of its simplicity and clarity.

CONCLUSIONS

What Have We Learned About Cropland and Grazing Leases?

We started this chapter by telling four stories about how state trustees have evolved in their management of cropland and grazing lands. Through these examples, we saw that state strategies for management of trust lands have ranged from disposing of them (in the case of Idaho) to what we would call enlightened retention (in the case of Oregon's blocked range land) to active management of cropland and grazing lands (in the cases of Washington and Oklahoma, respectively). Even in active management, however, different approaches are apparent. Washington has increased the capital value of its agricultural lands through participation in federal irrigation projects. Oklahoma, under pressure from its courts, has increased its revenue flows from its cropland and grazing lands by adopting bidding policies that shift advantages away from the lessee and toward the trust. Other states align themselves along the continuum from retention to management, with calls for disposal periodically emanating from state legislatures. Precisely where each state exists along this continuum can be deduced from its overall package of leasing procedures and fee systems.

One way to establish where an individual state lies on this continuum of leasing procedures and fee systems is to place it relative to the fair market value theories discussed earlier. The primary fair market valuation question is what constitutes an equitable return to the trustee for use of its lands? Three different theoretical approaches to appraising this value were introduced: comparable sales, contributory value, and income capitalization. There is nothing new or innovative about these approaches; they are the stuff of traditional real estate appraisals. But what is new—or new to most people looking at management of public lands—is applying these appraisals to the valuation of public resources, whether they be state or federal. We saw in the theoretical discussion that the valuation of leases reflects both the fee and the package of rights and obligations called the *leasehold*.

The rights and obligations of the leasehold, and particularly, their effect on the competition for leases were discussed in the third section of this chapter. The primary theme of the discussion was the tension between the trustee and the lessee over control of the lease, and how this tension affects the state's ability to obtain fair market value for its resources. The tension is embodied in various leasing procedures. Using three determinants of fair market value from appraisal theory, we asked questions about whether provisions incorporated in the various states' leasing procedures contributed to, or undercut, attainment of fair market value. The effects of preference rights to lease renewal, of subleasing, and of collateral assignments were all mentioned as impediments to true competitive leasing, the first determinant of fair market value. We discussed briefly how states' bidder qualifications limit the competition for leases, especially when agriculture and grazing might not be the "highest and best" use of the leased parcel. The third criterion, whether either party is under compulsion to buy or sell, relates more specifically not only to bidder qualifications and preference rights, but to the existing dispersed land ownership patterns in which the states find themselves. The remedies we suggest to overcome this problem are more structural than leasing procedures, but acknowledging the problem focuses the state's energies on overcoming it.

What Would an Ideal Leasing System Look Like?

We have talked about lessee/trustee tension and who benefits from which arrangements. A fruitful way to summarize all this detail is to offer a hypothetical "ideal" leasing system. We do not recommend that you adopt our program, but it does offer a place to start asking questions about the fit of the leasing systems with the goals and objectives of specific parcels. We start by specifying the objective of the leasing program: to return to the trust the fair market value of the resource, while protecting and enhancing the productive capabilities of the trust corpus. With this objective in mind, and recognizing the limits imposed by the existing geographical pattern of the lands and the existing lessees, our first strategy would be to classify the cropland and rangelands according to their potential to meet the state's management objective. Once the lands have been properly classified, strategies specific to each type of land can be developed.

The land classification process can mirror the historical disposal, retention, and management theme. States appear to be using three types of lands for cropland and grazing purposes. First are blocked, fenced lands with legal access that occupy large enough parcels to make them economical for someone besides the adjacent landowners to use. These lands would seem to be most suitable for intensive management for their existing uses. The second type of land may have potential for other uses in the short or long term, such as parcels located on the fringes of urbanizing areas, near major highways, close to developing recreational areas, or with topographic features that make them suitable for communication sites or other special uses. The state may do well to retain lands in this second category until the anticipated future uses can be arranged. The third land category consists of isolated, dispersed, small parcels that have no legal access and only one or a few surrounding landowners, and that are prohibitively expensive to manage (such as in terms of fencing and water) compared to their potential revenue returns. Lands in this last category are clearly uneconomical for the state to manage, and thus should be disposed of either by sale or by exchange.

Different management strategies and different leasing procedures are called for with the different categories of land uses. Intensive management strategies can be cost-effective for blocked lands of good quality. In this case, the state should be willing to make investments that improve the productivity of the lands: water developments, cross-fencing, brush control, and access. However, the state should retain ownership of these improvements to reduce impediments to competitive bidding for the leases. If true competitive bidding prevails, then theoretically the rental fee system that the state uses becomes less important in determining whether the state obtains fair market value, since bonus bids will make up the difference between the base fee and the value of the lease to the lessee. For blocked parcels designated for intensive management, a competitive bidding system involving advertising, written or oral bids, and a lease term of five to ten years with no right of renewal would appear to be optimal.

State parcels identified for retention, but not for intensive management, should be managed under different lease procedures. Management efforts should be made to facilitate the conversion of use from agriculture and grazing to the highest and best potential use. This might involve, for example, obtaining legal access to the parcels, working with county or local agencies to rezone the lands, and in some cases going so far as to plat the lands to increase their future sale value. Leasing procedures should emphasize the changing nature of the tenure by restricting the current lessees from making capital-intensive improvements; neither should the state make investments that are not beneficial for the expected future use. Any existing approved lessee improvements should be placed on an accelerated depreciation schedule. Fees charged for agriculture and grazing use should reflect the fact that this is an interim land use, pending ultimate conversion to other uses or sale. Fees could be established either by using a revenue share system or by adopting a base fee adjusted by price indexes. Competition for leases should not be emphasized unnecessarily, but neither should any preference rights be granted that allow the existing lessee to purchase the lands if the state decides to sell them.

Parcels identified for disposition due to their small, isolated, and/or uneconomical nature should be placed under strictly custodial management. Lease terms should be short, perhaps only annual. No improvements should be permitted, and existing ones should be depreciated. If no legal access exists to the property, and if the state believes that the costs of obtaining access would be justified by higher selling prices, then the state should attempt to obtain access. The existing lessees may be given rights to renew, but they should be given no preference right to purchase the property, subject to the following condition: if the benefits of obtaining access do not outweigh its costs, the state should attempt to sell the lands to the adjacent landowner at an appraised fair market price. Revenues received from these land sales could go either into the permanent fund (as is traditional) or, perhaps better, into a "land bank fund"[93] to purchase other cost-effective replacement properties.

This chapter has emphasized how the states' agriculture and grazing programs are beginning to emerge from a long period of domination by their lessees. Frequently driven or empowered by court decisions, trustees are developing programs for efficiently managing widely dispersed resources. Key aspects of this evolution include establishing fee systems and leasing procedures that provide incentives for good management, while at the same time allowing a competitive process to set the fair market value for the resources produced from these trust lands. Although the balance between the state and the lessee continues to shift in favor of the trust beneficiary, the important variable in determining the pace of this reconfiguration continues in many states to be the lessees' political power.

APPENDIX: DETAILS OF STATE GRAZING FEE FORMULAS

This appendix provides specific background material to aid readers in understanding each state's grazing fee system. The material on the states' grazing fee formulas is presented alphabetically by state within each category.

Federal PRIA Fee Formula

For federal lands administered by the Bureau of Land Management and the Forest Service, the Public Rangelands Improvement Act (PRIA) of 1984 determines the calculation of grazing fees.[94] The federal fee structure used on Bureau of Land Management and Forest Service lands (with the exception of the National Grasslands and lands owned by other departments of the federal government) is:[95]

$$\$/AUM = 1.23 \times [FVI + (BCPI - PPI)]/100$$

where:

FVI = Forage Value Index
BCPI = Beef Cattle Price Index
PPI = Producer Price Index
BV = Base value (= 1.23)

provided that the annual increase or decrease in such fee for any given year shall be limited to not more than plus or minus 25 percent of the previous year's fee.

The starting point for setting the federal fee is the base value of $1.23 per AUM set by the 1966 Western Livestock Grazing Survey (WLGS).[96] The WLGS used information on private grazing lease fees and services provided, and then compared costs of private leases, including fees, to the costs of grazing federal lands excluding the fee. This difference between the two then equals the fee for the federal lands. The difference between the two rates started at $1.78 per AUM for cattle. After adjusting the private leases for differences in season of use, landowner services and size of lease, and then weighted 80 percent for cattle and 20 percent for sheep, authorities determined that the average difference was $1.23. This $1.23 per AUM became the base fee that was to be attained over a ten-year period, starting in 1969, by the Forest Service and Bureau of Land Management. Only half of the fee increases required under the 1969 Fair Market Value Formula ever occurred because of legislative and executive moratoriums.[97] In 1978, PRIA established a new process to determine grazing fees.

The PRIA formula used the $1.23 base rate from the 1966 WLGS, then adjusted it to current conditions by using three prices and costs indexes: the Forage Value Index (FVI); the Beef Cattle Price Index (BCPI); and the Prices Paid Index (PPI). The FVI tracks prices of private forage leases; the BCPI tracks changes in beef prices at the stockyard; and the PPI tracks the costs of doing business for ranchers in the West. The (BCPI − PPI) determines whether beef prices are rising faster than production costs. The difference is then added or subtracted to the index of changes in private forage lease costs reflected in the FVI. Figure 4-7 shows the behavior of these indexes over the period 1970–1995, contrasted with the actual and formula federal grazing fees (PRIA after 1979). Notice that the Private Grazing Land Lease Rate (PGLLR) tracks closely with the price indexes.

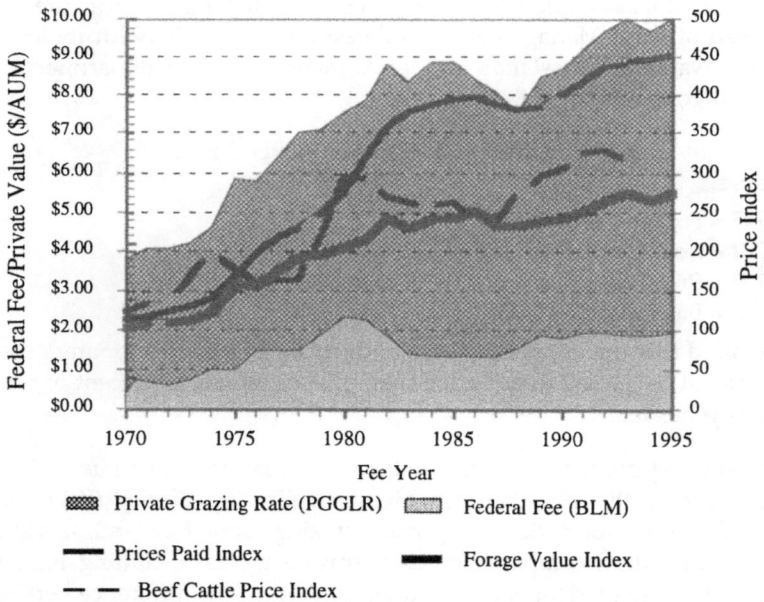

Figure 4-7. Comparison of beef cattle price (BCPI) and price paid (PPI) indexes, private grazing rates (PGLLR), and federal grazing fees, 1970–1995.

Because the FVI is determined from the PGLLR data, they follow exactly the same path. On the other hand, the relative paths of the BCPI and PPI are of interest, since they theoretically should influence what private landowners can charge for their forage. Because of this potential relationship, how the price indexes are constructed becomes important.

The FVI uses information in the U.S. Department of Agriculture's June Enumerative Survey (now conducted in the spring), which asks landowners how much is being charged for private grazing leases in their area. The resulting figure, the PGLLR, is reported by the USDA in the December issue of *Agricultural Prices* on a state-by-state basis and in averages for eleven western states, sixteen western states, and nine plains states. The FVI uses the eleven western states' average as its data source. The index is calculated by taking the average PGLLR value for 1964–1968, which was $3.65, and setting this equal to 100. Annual FVI values are then determined by dividing that year's PGLLR value for the eleven western states by the $3.65 base, and multiplying the resulting quotient by 100 to convert it into an index number.[98] The BCPI is constructed similarly to the FVI, except that it uses the price per hundredweight (cwt) of beef.[99] Again, the eleven western states' average is used, as well as the 1964–1968 average of $22.04, as a starting point for the index value of 100.

The PPI adjusts the fee based on the costs that ranchers pay for the various inputs required to raise cattle. The PPI is a composite index, that is it reflects different price changes that a rancher would typically use. Table 4-4 shows the different price indexes that comprise the PPI and their weights and for comparison purposes, also the components and weights of the national index of livestock production costs.

Notice the differences between the national and PRIA weights and components. One difference is that one-third more weight is given to production inputs in the PRIA PPI, while no weight is given to general consumer prices in it. A second difference is that the weights assigned to index components corresponding to users of public lands—particularly fuel, building and fencing materials, farm and motor supplies, and other machinery—have three to four times the emphasis in the PRIA index that they have in the national index, while components in the national index associated with penned production of livestock are not present in the PRIA PPI.

State PRIA-based Price- and Cost-indexed Formulas

In the Public Rangelands Improvement Act (PRIA) of 1984, Congress established a grazing fee system for federal lands based on the contributory valuation approach—that is, on the lands' value in the production of cattle. The derivation of the federal fee system under PRIA provides the basis for many of the state fees.[100] The PRIA formula and its state derivatives vary from the strict contribu-

TABLE 4-4. Producer price weights in the national index compared to PRIA formula index

Index Component	National Index of Prices Paid	PRIA PPI Formula
Consumer price index	30.4%	
Production commodities	57.6	80.0%
Feed	11.8	
Feeder livestock	11.7	
Seed	1.8	
Fertilizer and agricultural chemicals	5.9	
Fuels and energy	3.5	14.5
Farm and motor supplies	2.2	12.0
Autos and trucks	2.5	4.5
Tractors and self-propelled machinery	4.5	4.5
Other machinery	2.7	12.0
Building and fencing material	3.6	14.5
Farm services	7.4	18.0
Interest	4.0	6.0
Taxes and insurance	2.8	
Farm wage rates	5.2	14.0
Total	100	100

Source: Secretaries of Agriculture and Interior, Grazing Fee Review and Evaluation (1986) at 28, Figure 3.10.

tory valuation in that, rather than determining each year the relative value of the various inputs to produce cattle, they use a base value that is changed to reflect the behavior of various price indexes. These indexes generally include movements in beef prices, private pasture leasing rates, and the cost of materials (such as fencing, gasoline, and trucks) that are used by ranchers.

In establishing grazing fees on their lands, the states have been influenced by the Federal PRIA formula, particularly where federal lands are their predominant neighbor. Five states currently use fee systems that are either identical to or derived from the federal system. The subsections that follow identify the exact method used by each state. Of the five PRIA-formula states, three use the federal formula to establish a base rate, and then modify it to account for local differences: Arizona takes the PRIA fee and discounts it 22.5 percent to account for lessee improvements and leasehold taxes; California uses the PRIA formula on state lands that fall within BLM grazing allotments, but it charges a minimum fee of $500 per year per lease; Utah adds 35 cents to the PRIA fee, plus an additional 5 cents for weed control. The other two states, Idaho and New Mexico, use a PRIA-like system of price indexes to adjust their grazing fees, but they relied on statistical methods to establish their base values.[101] Idaho's base fee depends on whether cattle or sheep are grazing the leased lands (sheep get a discount due to bad market conditions). The price indexes that Idaho uses are the same as those used in the PRIA system, except that the current fee is also factored into the formula. However, the price index weights used by Idaho vary from the PRIA formula's equal weights.[102] New Mexico's grazing fee system uses the same price indexes as the PRIA formula, but it weights them differently and uses a different base value. The state then takes the ratio of the annual value over the average of the previous five years to smooth out yearly fluctuations. New Mexico further limits increases or decreases to 33⅓ percent in any given year.

ARIZONA

Arizona's fee is based on the PRIA formula discounted 22.5 percent for lease-owned improvements.[103]

$$\text{Fee/AUM} = (\text{Base} - 0.28) \times [(\text{BCPI} + \text{FVI} - \text{PPI})/100]$$

where:

Base Fee = $1.23
The $0.28 represents the range improvement investment and taxes paid on improvements by grazing lessees on state lands.
The BCPI, FVI and PPI are defined as per PRIA on an 11 western states basis.

CALIFORNIA

California's fee is "An annual rental based on appraised value for the intended use."[104] The State Lands Commission bases fair market value on appraisals for lands outside BLM allotments; PRIA is used for lands intermixed with BLM grazing allotments. Intermixed lands form the majority of the state's ownership. All leases require a minimum $500 per year payment.

IDAHO

Idaho's fee structure was adopted by the Land Board in 1990 and then modified in 1992 and 1993. It uses a PRIA-like set of price indexes and then multiplies the result by a base value that differs according to whether cattle or sheep graze the leased land. The price index formula is:

$$\text{IDFVI}_{(t+2)} = -6.92 + (0.13)(\text{FVI}_t) + (0.60)(\text{BCPI}_t) + (0.33)(\text{PPI}_t) + (0.74)(\text{IDFVI}_t)$$

where:

$\text{IDFVI}_{(t+2)}$ = Predicted value of the Idaho Forage Value Index for the year the grazing fee is to be set (namely, two years hence)
FVI_t = Most recent published Forage Value Index for the 11 western states
BCPI_t = Most recent published Beef Cattle Price Index for the 11 western states
PPI_t = Most recent published Prices Paid Index for the 11 western states
IDFVI_t = Most recent published value for the Forage Value Index for Idaho

Base value by which the preceding formula is multiplied is $2.20. For 1992, the formula equals 2.72, resulting in a fee of $4.99 per AUM for cattle and

$3.74 for sheep. In 1993, the Idaho Land Board lowered the base value, which had the effect of lowering the 1994 fee 25 percent from its 1993 level. The 1994 fee is $4.53/AUM for cattle and $3.40/AUM for sheep.

NEW MEXICO

New Mexico's formula is similar to the PRIA formulation in its use of a base value adjusted by weighted price indexes. In New Mexico, however, the base changes from year to year, and the weights of the price indexes differ from the PRIA formula.

The annual rental for a lease is calculated as:

$$\text{Annual Rental} = \text{Base Rate} \times \text{Economic Variable Index} \times \text{Carrying Capacity} \times \text{Acres of Lease}$$

Economic Variable Index (EVI) is calculated using the State Land Office Adjustment Factor (SLOAF), which is a weighted price index formula, with variation limited by a five-year average value:

$$EVI_t = SLOAF_{t-1}/SLOAF_{5\text{-year}}$$

where:

EVI_t = Index used in making annual adjustments for changes in forage market prices

$SLOAF_{t-1}$ = FVI reported the year prior to the current fee period

$SLOAF_{5\text{-year}}$ = Moving 5-year average of the FVI.

The succeeding years SLOAF is calculated as:

$$SLOAF_{t+1} = -14.92 + (1.57 \times FVI_t) + (0.26 \times BCPI_t) - (0.67 \times PPI_t)$$

The USDA indexes used are for the 11 western states.[105] The Forage Value Index (FVI) is the JES for the 11 western states. The BCPI and the PPI are the same ones used in the PRIA federal grazing fee calculation, again using the 11 western state average.

New Mexico limits increases or decreases in the fee to 33 1/3 percent per year. Beginning in 1993, the NMSLO will reduce fees 25 percent on grazing lands appraised in good or excellent condition.[106]

UTAH

Utah bases its fee on the Federal PRIA schedule because of intermixed land ownership.[107] A 35 cent per AUM fee is added on top of the PRIA formula. A 5 cent per AUM. fee for noxious weed control is additional.[108]

State Cattle Price Share Approaches

Each of the four states that currently base their grazing fees on the traditional sharecropping model, where the land owner and the lessee divide the crop or the proceeds from the crop, is discussed individually in the subsections that follow. In each case, the lessee markets the crop—in this case cattle—and subsequently sends the state its share. However in practice the method is not quite this simple.

Critical to an understanding of how crop-sharing works is the concept of an Animal Unit Month (AUM) of forage. An AUM is the amount of forage needed to support a steer for one month. But that steer is putting on weight during each month of eating the state's forage—on average about 50 pounds of weight per AUM of forage. Consequently, the states want a share of the value of this increased steer weight. South Dakota takes the highest share: 20 percent of the gross value of production. Montana and Washington each take 12 percent. Oregon's system is currently in transition.

To calculate their share, they use the value per hundred weight (cwt) of cattle—a common metric—reported by the state livestock bureau to the USDA as the market price. However, reported prices vary according to whether the sale is for steers, weaned calves, or an average of all cattle marketed. In addition, the price per hundred weight varies among the western states, by as much as $10/cwt (10 cents per pound). Recall that the PRIA federal grazing fee formula uses the eleven western states' average. In contrast, Montana, Washington, and South Dakota each use their own states' beef prices—in Montana and Washington, for 500-pound steers; while in South Dakota, for 425-pound weaned calves. Translating these figures into a split in the physical production, South Dakota wants 10 pounds of every 50 gained, while Montana and Washington settle for 6.

The states then introduce further variations on the straight share formulas. Montana once charged an additional fee (10 cents per AUM) if the leased parcel had a capacity to graze twenty or more animal units per section, while reducing the fee 10 cents per AUM if the land could carry fewer than fifteen animal units per section. South Dakota uses an average of the last five years of weaned calf prices. Washington first reduces the fee by the amount of the leasehold tax to the state that the lessee pays (17.5 percent) but then charges an additional 50 percent fee to holders of leased range, because the state allows them greater flexibility in managing these lands.

Oregon recently adopted the cattle price share approach to setting grazing fees, using a base rate from which to calculate the weight gain attained from an AUM of forage. Weaner calves are used as the basis for determining value, since the majority of state grazing leases are cow–calf operations. The weight of the weaned calf, assumed to be 405 pounds as marketed in the three counties where the grazing land is located, is used as a starting point. From this, the birth weight of the calf (assumed to be 85 pounds) is deducted, and the resulting 320 pounds is divided by the nine months the calf is assumed to be consuming the state's forage, yielding the weight gain from an AUM of forage. The precise resulting figure, 35.6 pounds/AUM, is then truncated to 30 pounds/AUM, based on the rancher's "rule of thumb." This 30 pounds/AUM weight gain is then adjusted to represent the marketable calf crop by assuming a 20 percent death loss (displayed as a multiplier of 0.8). The resulting 24 pounds of weight gain per AUM is multiplied by the average calf price per pound reported for the three counties to establish the total value from an AUM of forage. This total value is then distributed between the state and the lessee. Oregon will start with the state receiving a 12.5 percent share in 1995, and then incrementally increase the state's share by 2.5 percent per year until a 20 percent share is reached.

MONTANA

The base rate in Montana which establishes a minimum fee per land area, is computed as the average price per pound of beef cattle on the farm in Montana for the previous year times 6.0 times the AUM carrying capacity of the land. Translated into an AUM formula this is the average price per pound of beef × 6.[109]

The state can charge an additional 10 cents per AUM if the land has a capacity to graze twenty or more animal units per section, but can reduce the fee if the capacity is less than 15 animal units per section. The average price per pound of beef cattle on the farm in Montana is based on statistics published by the USDA.[110]

OREGON

Oregon takes 12.5 percent (1995) of the value of an AUM as its grazing fee. The value of an AUM is calculated as:

$$\text{AUM Fee} = (W - B)/9 \times D \times S \times V$$

where:

W = Weight of average marketed weaner calf (assumed to be 405 lb)
B = Birth weight of calf (assumed to be 85 lb)
D = Death loss during birth and growth (assumed to be 20%), which gives a 0.8 multiplier
S = State share of resulting 24 lb/AUM weight gain
V = Average price per pound for weaner calves in three counties

The monthly weight gain (36 lb) is arbitrarily reduced to 30 lb, based on recommendations of a Grazing Advisory Committee. State share starts at 12.5 percent for 1995 and increases by 2.5 percent annually to a maximum of 20 percent.

SOUTH DAKOTA

South Dakota takes 20 percent of the value of the beef produced on its land as rent. The fee is calculated by using the nonweighted five-year average price per pound for 425-lb calf × 425 divided by 12 × 20 percent.[111]

The price per pound is determined by the price of a 425-lb calf at weaning time, using statistics published by the South Dakota Crop and Livestock Reporting Service of the USDA.[112]

Rates are based on a formula that was established 13 years ago. The Commissioner determines the percentage of price that is rent.[113] On state lands, lessees do their own fencing, weed control, and water.[114]

WASHINGTON

Washington uses a two-tier fee structure, depending on the control exercised by the lessee. The different types are called "permit range" and "lease range."[115] A share formula is used for permit ranges. For leased range (called "dry land grazing") the WDNR uses the average of the last five years' permit range fees determined by the formula above, then multiplies them by 1.5 to account for differences in the flexibility given to the lessee. On leased range, the lessee determines cattle numbers, season of use, put on and take out dates, etc. Lease fees are adjusted every five years at lease renewal. Grazing fee formula is:[116]

$$\text{AUM Fee} = \frac{L \times S \times G \times P + A}{(1 + \text{LHT})}$$

where:

L = Proportion of average stockman's investment assigned to land

S = Landlord's fair share of land income

G = Average pound gain in livestock weight for permitted grazing season, cattle and sheep to be separately computed

P = Average past year's selling price of livestock per pound, from the reports of the Agricultural Marketing Service of the USDA

LHT = Leasehold tax as established by law and administered by the state department of revenue

M = Number of months in permitted grazing season

A = Permittee's share of assessments on permit rangelands

The formula is based on the following production assumptions: 50 lb growth gain per month, of which 40 percent is the permittee's investment assigned to the land, and 30 percent is the landlord's share [that is, 50 × 0.4 × 0.3 = 6].[117]

State Comparable Appraisal Approaches

The comparable appraisal approaches used by five states on their trust lands grazing leases are based on prices charged by private parties, and then adjusted to account for differences in services provided by the state as compared to those of private landowners. Of the five states using this approach, only one (Colorado) applies a single fee state-wide; the other four use site-specific or intrastate regional appraisals. All five states display a similar pattern in adjusting their rates in connection with comparable private grazing rates. Colorado simply takes 50 percent of the private grazing fee determined by the USDA June Enumerative Survey (JES) fee. The other four states use more detailed adjustment methods. After examining how these four states conduct appraisals, we will discuss the various adjustment mechanisms they use. Detailed fee formulas are presented in a table following these discussions.

The four states that conduct site-specific or regional appraisals are Nebraska, North Dakota, Oklahoma, and Texas. In Nebraska, the state is divided into production capability zones based on soil type, rainfall, and crop patterns. Private grazing lease appraisals for each of these zones are conducted under contract by the University of Nebraska–Lincoln. The results of these appraisals, after adjustments for services provided, form the opening bids for Nebraska's leases. A similar process occurs in North Dakota, where the lands are appraised according to productivity indexes determined on a county-wide basis. The productivity index measures the amount of forage produced per land area (in AUMs/acre). Private grazing lease fees are gathered county by county, including a measure of the average productivity of leases within each county. The fee for each state parcel is then adjusted based on its own specific productivity in relation to the county's average, with additional adjustments made for services and other factors. Oklahoma's process is simpler: the state collects county-level appraisal information that forms the basis for opening bids, and no adjustments for services are made. Texas uses a site-specific appraisal approach in which each individual parcel is appraised on its productive capacity.

Adjustments for services provided by the state in comparison to private landowners are factored into the fee formulas in Nebraska and North Dakota. Nebraska credits the lessee for fences and range land water at a rate of fifty cents per AUM in western Nebraska and one dollar per AUM in eastern Nebraska. North Dakota adjusts its fees in two ways: first, there are adjustments that are applied to all leases, and then there are another set applied on a parcel-specific basis. Across-the-board adjustments are $1.50/AUM for fencing, and a fee reduction of 20 percent to account for average survey error—i.e., that the state's parcels are smaller than the acreage listed. Parcel-specific adjustments are primarily for water and improvements. Water allowances are given in the Badlands area ($0.50 per acre), or if water is not present on a given parcel, then the fee is reduced 40 percent. North Dakota also reduces fees where the state cost-shares improvements with the lessee. Examples of cost-share fee reductions are noxious weed control, construction of permanent improvements, and high administrative costs.

COLORADO

Colorado uses the simplest method to determine its grazing fees. Until recently, it took 50 percent of the average private grazing rate over the most recent 5 years in Colorado, as determined by USDA,[118] with the limitation of a maximum increase of one-third at any one time during the lease period.[119] In 1994, the fee was increased to 65 percent, and it was raised again in 1995 to 75 percent. A single fee is used statewide, changing in October for the following year. The state is currently considering a regional appraisal-based fee system.

NEBRASKA

The grazing fee structure in Nebraska is based on statewide comparable appraisal surveys of private rangeland conducted by the University of Nebraska. The state is divided into various production capability zones, and private rental values are determined for each zone, soil type, and crop pattern. The state then makes adjustments based on differences between the services that the state—compared to a private landlord—provides. The resulting rate is adjusted annually, and lessees are billed semiannually for this amount. Leased lands are resurveyed for capability at least every three years. Lessees bid on bonuses above the current rental rate at auction.

Credit for fences and wells for rangeland vary from $0.50/acre in western Nebraska to $1.00/acre in eastern Nebraska. Cash rent rates in 1992 for sandy grassland vary from $4.05/AUM in southwestern Nebraska to $14.00/AUM in eastern Nebraska after fencing and well credits are applied. For silty grassland, the cash rents vary from $4.45/AUM to $20.00/AUM after fencing and well credits.[120]

NORTH DAKOTA

"The board of university and school lands shall set the minimum rental for uncultivated and cultivated lands, which shall be subject to review and change when deemed necessary by said board."[121] The fee structure that North Dakota currently uses is:[122]

$$\text{Rent} = (\{[(\text{Grass PI/Regional PI}) \times [(\text{Co. Price} - \$1.50) \times 0.80]] - \text{AB}\} \times \text{Grass Acres}) - \text{C,D,E}$$

where:

PI = Productivity Index calculated by site-specific and county forage production.

Across-the-board adjustments are:
  Fencing = $1.50
  Survey Error = 20% (i.e., × .80)

Tract-specific adjustments are used for:
  (A) Badlands Area Water = −50¢ per acre (only applied to designated tracts)
  (B) Administrative Allowance = 10¢ Per Acre (only applied to designated tracts)
  (C) Noxious Weeds = −(Acres of Weeds × Dollar Per Acre Cost Share)
  (D) Permanent Improvements = −Lessee's Out of Pocket Costs
  (E) Lack of Water = −40% (i.e., × 0.60)

OKLAHOMA

Oklahoma's fee structure is determined by county private grazing rate appraisals.

TEXAS

Minimum lease amount is 5 cents/acre.[123] "A lease shall be awarded to the highest responsible bidder."[124] The fee structure is then a "fixed fee per animal unit . . . assessed according to the maximum carrying capacity of the land under lease. Current rate was increased in 1983 by $10.00 and is now $50 per animal unit, or about $4.17 per AUM."[125]

State Income Capitalization Approach

Wyoming statutes require that the minimum rental fee for grazing be between 2 percent and 5½ percent of the appraised land value, which varies by land classification, as a grazing fee.[126] In 1981 $600 was set as the land value to support 1 AU for 12 months. The appraised rental value was 3.33 percent.[127] In practice, the land board seems to establish the rental rate without reappraising lands. "The minimum annual rental shall be: (i) For grazing land, $1.65 per AUM of carrying capacity leased for 1989; $2.05 per AUM of carrying capacity leased for 1990; and $2.50 per AUM of carrying capacity leased for 1991."[128]

How this works out in practice is that the lands are classified by production potential, as range, hayland, or dry agriculture. The per-acre forage production on these lands is converted to AUMs. The appraised value of land to produce an AUM of forage is then determined on the basis of appraisals done for the farm loan section of the department. The board then determines what percentage of this appraised value in the range of 2 to 5½ percent to set as the grazing fee. More realistically, a subjective notion of what is an acceptable grazing fee drives the process of back-calculation so that the fee calculated falls in the range of 2 to 5½ percent of the appraised land value.

For 1994 the Wyoming State Land Board, as a result of an advisory committee's inability to reach consensus, set the grazing fee at $3.00 per AUM. In addition, the board established a $3.50 per AUM fee for the 1995 grazing season; however, the board subsequently froze this increase, ostensibly due to drought. The Wyoming board's intention is to go back to a capitalization approach to setting grazing fees after 1996.[129]

CHAPTER FIVE

Trust Land Forestry

Forestry provides an important perspective on trust lands management because, in contrast to all of the other trust programs, timber management is visible to the general public. Although forest management is a major revenue producer in only four states, timber production as a land use and government activity is sufficiently controversial on federal lands that the advocacy and debate spill over onto the trust lands. Trust land forestry therefore presents an opportunity to discuss trust management in the context of a sometimes heated conflict between management for general public benefit and management to meet the priorities of the specified beneficiaries. This tension revolves around protecting existing stands of old-growth timber,[1] silvicultural practices in production forests, and cumulative effects of state timber harvests in combination with harvests on federal and private industry lands. The trustees are under considerable pressure as well to allow public hunting and recreation access to the forested state trust lands.[2] These familiar debates over timber management are in general less intense on trust lands than on federal lands. However, the trust mandate gives us an opportunity to explore public expectations of what should be subsidized and what should be sold at full market value, in a public resource context.

The unavoidable visibility of timber harvests is enhanced by the landholding pattern that predominates on the major trust timberlands. These lands are unusual among trust resources in that they frequently are held as consolidated areas instead of in dispersed sections.[3] With aggregated parcels comes increased public awareness of management activities and noncommodity values associated with these lands. Simultaneously, of course, the large blocks of timberland are of relatively high value to the trust, both in standing inventory and productive capacity. Therefore, in addition to the general public and the environmentalists, the beneficiaries may be more observant of their management. The tensions that can arise between management for timber production and management for environmental protection and multiple uses provides the context for this chapter.

A third aspect of timber management visibility results from the fact that management of the trust forest resources may not be the only highly visible timber program undertaken by state agencies acting as trustees. Frequently the trustee has statewide forest fire protection responsibilities. In Oregon, that assignment actually predated the management of forested trust lands.[4] In all four states that have major trust land timber programs, forest practices are regulated by the same agency that manages the trust forest lands. Extension forestry is also an administrative function of these offices. Thus, whereas the grazing program may be primarily of concern to the lessees and whereas most minerals programs may be small and largely invisible, forestry tends to attract a great deal of attention irrespective of its extent or revenue-producing capabilities.

The first part of this chapter describes the management context of state timber programs. Because of the peculiar county lands in Oregon and forest board lands in Washington, our discussion of the land base for trust land timber management and the revenues produced contains a particularly detailed examination of the origins of these forest trust lands. We talk about overinvestment in timber management and some management regimes that are characteristic of timber programs, including mixed authorities and contracting out among government agencies. Most of the discussion focuses on the four major state programs: in Washington, Idaho, Oregon, and Montana.

The second section introduces the issue of conflict between beneficiary and general public benefits by discussing two recently litigated issues that clarify the legal definition of the matter. Those cases identify seemingly hard lines about undivided loyalty and maximum profit that appear to leave little room for discussing general public benefit. When we shift to the definition of the beneficiary in state constitutions and law, however, we find the hard lines beginning to soften a bit, leaving room for a broader definition of management criteria.

In the third section, we turn to the nuts and bolts of decision making—choices that underlie the touchstone criteria of sustained yield, fair market value, and maximum or full return to the beneficiary. Again, we find considerable room for ambiguity and for approaching both goals—general benefit and beneficiary benefit—simultaneously. We show that, at a minimum, the two are not necessarily incompatible. The trustee has much discretion, and this needs to be understood. For example, even if a state chooses to manage its timberlands solely to produce revenues, selecting the time frame for management is a crucial decision that affects the beneficiary, the community, and the environment. Similarly, in states and counties that have a high dependency on timber for jobs and public finance, the trustee can define the revenue-maximizing strategy so as to provide for long-term sustained yield. The trustee may also decide to manage in order to even out changing harvest levels that would produce undesirable fluctuations in revenues received by beneficiaries. Finally, the state can attempt to meet some multiple-use objectives in addition to simply providing revenues for the beneficiary.

We do not want to be Pollyannas about this. The conflicts between timber production and general public benefit are real and are likely to continue. It is important for all parties to understand, however, that even the clear lines drawn in the sand seem to disappear as we get closer to them.

MANAGEMENT CONTEXT OF STATE TIMBER PROGRAMS

This first section covers the context within which the trust forests are managed. We first discuss the land base and revenues produced in all states, to justify our decision to reserve our detailed analysis for Idaho, Montana, Oregon, and Washington. Furthermore, forest lands in two of the four states (Oregon and Washington) require a supplemental introduction: the data and analyses include not only the (by now) familiar common school and public institution grant lands, but also lands that have become state property through tax defaults. These lands are managed by the state with the counties[5] as the beneficiary of the income produced.

State Trust Land Forest Base

Forested lands and timber revenues form a significant part of state trust lands management in some states.[6] Figure 5-1 shows these areas for the trust land states. Three states in the upper Midwest—Michigan, Wisconsin, and Minnesota—have forested state lands as a result of tax foreclosures. Although Minnesota and Michigan have enormous holdings, none of these three states manages its state forest lands under the trust doctrine. A number of states have no commercial forest trust lands, including Arkansas and Nevada (which have no surface lands) and North Dakota, South Dakota, Nebraska, and Oklahoma (which own only grazing and agricultural lands). We exclude all of these states from further discussion in this chapter.

Three major clusters based on timberland ownership can be observed in the states that remain in the discussion. The largest holder is the state of Alaska, with slightly over 4.6 million acres. Medium-size owners include Washington, with slightly more than 2 million acres; Idaho, with over 1 million acres; Montana, with 638,000 acres; and Oregon, with 827,000 acres. Finally, small timberland-holding states include Arizona, with 12,000 acres; California, with 95,000 acres; Colorado, with 274,000 acres; New Mexico, with 112,000 acres; Utah, with 150,000 acres; and Wyoming, with 203,000 acres.

The pattern of revenues received from forest resources on state trust lands is affected both by the amount of trust lands and by their relative productivity—which mostly relates to their location. Figure 5-2 shows the revenues received from timber on state trust lands for 1992. Reliance on a single year's revenue data is hazardous, particularly in the case of timber, where significant price increases were realized as a result of supply constraints in the Pacific Northwest. However, the data do show the comparative importance of timber revenues among the various states.[7]

Two things emerge from the basic data in Figures 5-1 and 5-2. First, one

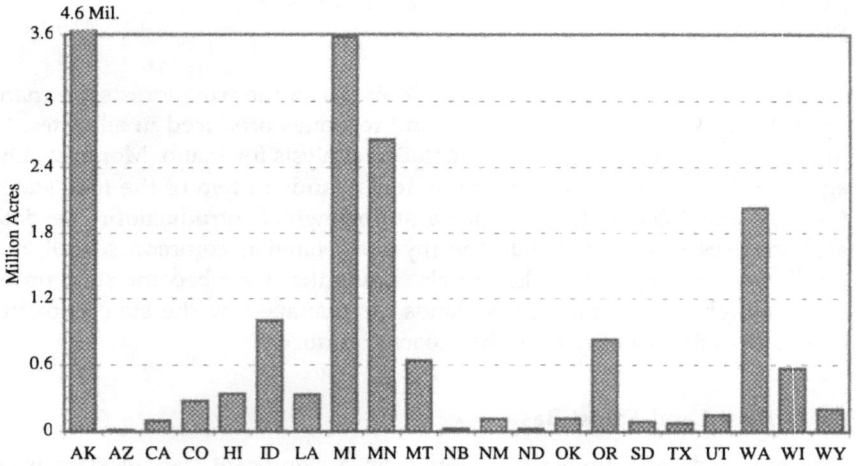

Figure 5-1. State-owned or managed timberlands in the western United States.
Source: Waddell et al., Forest Statistics of the United States, 1987 (Resource Bulletin PNW-RB-168, Pacific Northwest Research Station, U.S. Forest Service, Portland, Oregon); and Western States Survey Responses.

might wonder whether there ought to be any timber management at all in some of these states. Dividing the revenues received from timber (Table 2-6 and Figure 5-2) by the state land office staff assigned to timber management (Table 2-1) gives the monetary return per employee (FTE). Figure 5-3 shows these returns for the states. The revenues received per employee range from a high of $625,000 in Colorado to a low of about $7,000 in Wyoming. States

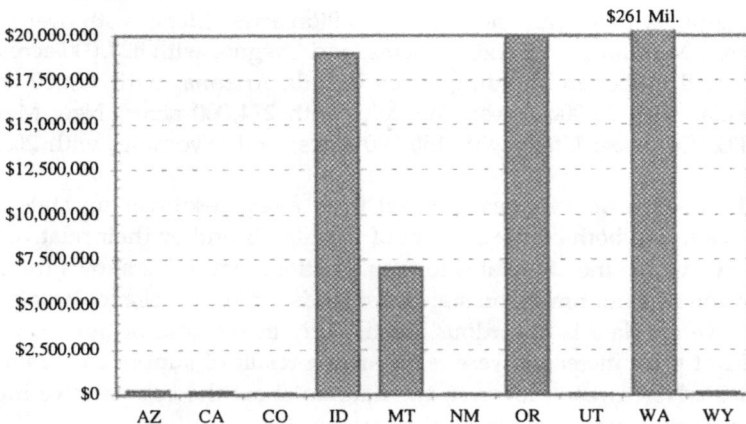

Figure 5-2. Timber revenues from trust land forests, 1992.

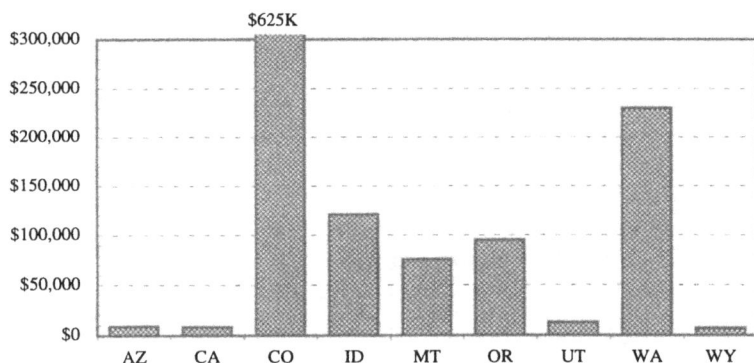

Figure 5-3. Revenues per employee in the states' timber management programs.

where the revenues per FTE are $50,000 or less include Arizona, California, Utah, and Wyoming. These states' programs are clearly marginal at best as sources of revenue production for the trust.

The comparative return per employee across the resource management programs—detailed in Table 3-1—provides another index of the comparative efficacy of timber management, in this case across resource programs within a specific state. This comparison shows what the state gives up in management of other resources by overemphasizing its timber program. Using these tools, we can see that personnel are overallocated—based on efficiency criteria determined by revenues per employee—in Arizona, Utah, Wyoming, and California. With the exception of the four major producer states, these other timber programs are overallocating personnel, even in comparison to their cropland and grazing programs—which, as we saw in Chapter 4, generally receive comparatively more staff than is efficient compared to subsurface management programs.

In the four minor producer states, the proceeds from timber management are not sufficient to justify the extent of their programs. Three possible explanations for the existing overallocation of personnel resources to the states' timber programs come to mind. First, depending on how trust management activities are funded, it may be that appropriated funds rather than trust receipts are spent on forest management. If that is so, an apparent overinvestment still benefits the trust. Second, the traditional forestry ethic asserts that if land is forested, it should be managed. Third, there is a distinct possibility that the excess personnel are "leaking" out to other forest management programs, such as fire protection (especially in Utah and Wyoming). Thus, according to portfolio theory, forested state lands in states where the revenues they generate are nominal should be evaluated for exchange or conversion to other uses, since their management for timber is unproductive for the trust. We say more about this in our discussion of Washington's Transition Lands Program later in this chapter and in Chapter 7.

The acreage revenues data show that four states invite further analysis of their timber programs because they provide significant revenues to the trust: Idaho, Montana, Oregon, and Washington.[8] Figure 5-4 shows the production from these four largest state trust land managers. Two areas of production data are important in any analysis of their programs: first, the level of harvest from one state compared to that from the others (the scale phenomena); and second, the amount of fluctuation in harvests, which affects the annual revenues received by the state. With regard to the first area, it is true that the states with the most land (see Figure 5-1) harvest the most timber; but a closer look at harvest per acre reveals the relative productivity (in terms of yield) of the states' timberlands.[9] The states differ in the amount of timber harvested per acre from these lands due to differences in site quality, stocking levels, and markets. Over the ten-year period from 1978 to 1987, average harvests per acre of *total* forest lands owned by the state trust were 47,000 board feet (47 MBF) per acre in Montana, 148 MBF per acre in Idaho, 285 MBF per acre in Oregon, and 359 MBF per acre in Washington. The differences among the four states affect both forest management and the value of the resources involved in forest management.

The levels of fluctuation in the annual amount harvested and in the revenues received are also of interest because they relate to our portfolio view of the trust assets. Figure 5-4 graphically demonstrates these fluctuations. Over the ten-year period shown, harvests in Washington show substantial annual differences (in fact, Washington's annual fluctuations often exceed the total harvests in Idaho and Montana). Fluctuations in harvest rates are generally the result of factors beyond the state's control, such as macroeconomic cycles affecting housing construction and changing environmental constraints, such as rules protecting the northern spotted owl.

These fluctuations indicate the relative riskiness of timber production; they also provide an indication of the amount of variance in revenues received by the state, which is important for states where timber receipts are directly distributed to the beneficiaries instead of being placed in the permanent fund (Table 2-7): Oregon's receipts go into the states' permanent funds; Idaho's, Montana's, and Washington's receipts are disbursed to the beneficiary.

This basic production information sets the stage for examining how the various states manage their timber resources. We will continue to emphasize where tensions exist among the state managing agency, the users of the commodity, the beneficiary, and the public at large. Before continuing with this analysis, however, we must distinguish the revested lands.

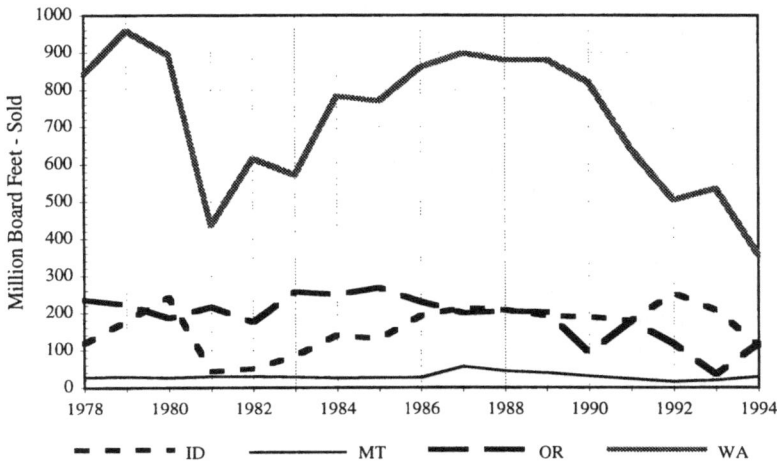

Figure 5-4. Production from the largest state trust timberland owners. *Source:* Western States Survey Responses.

Origins of the County and Forest Board Lands

Almost without exception, the lands we have been discussing were granted to the states with the expectation that the proceeds from their sale would be used to support the public schools. A salient exception is the large acreage in Oregon and Washington managed by the trustee for the benefit of the counties.

During the late nineteenth century, speculators in Oregon bent or ignored land disposition statutes in order to assemble large holdings of granted school land that were valuable for timber.[10] Land purchasers provided the state land office with descriptions of the tracts they wanted, and the state in turn requested those lands from the U.S. General Land Office. Since the state lands were frequently cheaper to purchase than the federal lands, had a higher acreage limitation, and could be obtained in blocks, the institutional grant lands were in high demand. Speculators also acquired the rights to previously claimed state sections and to state sections within the forest reserves, which gave them the right to select federal lands elsewhere in lieu of the state lands.

Thus, the state trust lands that passed into private ownership in Oregon were frequently consolidated into large holdings by timber companies. The timber on these lands, and on the federal lands privately obtained under the various land disposal acts, was then harvested as demand justified. Many timber companies allowed huge parcels to revert to the counties for back taxes during the depression or after harvesting and forest fires wiped out any short-term value the lands might have had for timber production.[11] In Oregon these reverted lands comprise significant resources: a total of 652,000 acres.[12] Revenues from these lands, after management expenses are deducted, are returned to the county of origin. These reverted lands are held under different terms from those governing the lands granted to the state in its enabling act. As noted in Chapter 1, the trust responsibility operative on the school land grants is defined in the state's enabling act and state constitution. In contrast, the Oregon trustee's responsibility for county forest lands is defined by state legislation.

A third form of trusteeship governs Washington state's management of 622,500 acres of Forest Board lands. Although the counties receive 75 percent of the revenues from their management, these are not county lands. They were deeded to the state by counties in return for cancellation of delinquent general taxes or were purchased by the state. The lands are "principally suited to the growing and harvesting of timber," and are held by the state to promote reforestation.[13] The state was to manage the lands to protect its interest in a continuing supply of timber for mills. Much of the land at issue was, as in Oregon, cut over by its original owners and then abandoned in lieu of paying property taxes. Much of it was also burned repeatedly during huge turn-of-the-century fires. Finally, large tracts of Forest Board lands in the five northern counties (Clallam, Jefferson, Skagit, Whatcom, and Snohomish) were physically and economically inaccessible and therefore were never logged. Currently they hold about half of the old-growth timber in state ownership. And although the Forest Board lands are not held in trust for the counties, the manager's responsibility to the counties in connection with them has been interpreted similarly to the responsibility that exists with regard to other trust lands. In *County of Skamania et al. v. State of Washington*[14] the state supreme court held that a beneficial trust existed with regard to the Forest Board lands. However, a different set of facts—perhaps one focusing on the purpose of the lands, rather than on a raid on the receipts—would likely yield a different result.[15]

Timber Management Organization

The greater visibility of forest resources probably accounts for the unusual organizational structure that surrounds the four major timber programs. Each program exists in an institutional matrix that includes ancillary programs such as forest practices regulation and forestry extension that do not have institutional correlatives in state grazing, mineral, and other resource management systems. In this section, we discuss three components of management for timber production: how the agency is structured; where the revenues go; and how the agency is funded.

AGENCY ORGANIZATIONAL STRUCTURE

Three different institutional structures for the management of state forested trust lands are found in the four states. In Oregon, the Division of State Lands does not, in fact, manage the state's trust forest lands. The Oregon Department of Forestry manages all the county forest lands, and it manages the state common school and institutional trust forested lands under contract with the Division of State Lands.[16] The Oregon Board of Forestry is composed of seven public members, with the state forester serving as secretary of the board. In contrast, the Oregon State Land Board is composed of three elected officials: the governor, the secretary of state, and the state treasurer. Even though about 20 percent of the lands managed by the Department of Forestry are entrusted to the Oregon State Land Board, the Land Board does not have representation on the Board of Forestry. This separation of management responsibilities is not found in the other three states. In Washington, the Department of Natural Resources manages both the Forest Board lands and the state school and institutional trust lands (with the exception of the University of Washington lands).[17] A similar situation is found in Idaho and Montana: although these states do not have county forest lands, the department of state lands in each of these states manages both forested and nonforested trust lands.

In addition to managing the trust's timber resources, in many states the same agency manages other timber-related programs. These programs generally fall into three types: forest fire protection; timber harvest regulation on private lands; and forestry extension services for private and industrial forest lands. Many states combine other forestry-related programs with their trust timber management.[18] Combining trust forest management with other forestry-related programs has two possible effects. First, the trust may receive benefits from the knowledge and expertise gained as a result of coordination with other forestland owners. The amount of this benefit—which could be called a *positive externality*—is difficult to quantify. Second, a certain amount of trust resources may "leak" into these other programs—generally as a result of poor employee time accounting, but also in some cases due to other management priorities' impinging on the management of the trust. The latter diversion is particularly noticeable when the trust's forest managers are part of the state's forest fire-fighting force. In this case, even if the personnel time spent fighting forest fires is compensated, there may be an uncompensated opportunity cost to the foresters' trust management responsibilities, particualarly if the trust's forest management responsibilities are confused with the agency's other forest-related activities. This situation gives rise to potential and—based on the return per employee data shown in Figure 5-3—probably actual diversion of trust resources.

WHERE THE REVENUES GO: TIMBER REVENUES DISTRIBUTION

Distribution of timber revenues differs slightly from state to state and is complicated by the fact that the trust programs have state beneficiaries defined by the constitution and county beneficiaries defined by statute. Although this topic was covered generally in Chapter 2, the picture is sufficiently complex in the timber resources area to justify a brief recitation of prevailing terms and conditions.

Timber receipts and the interest from the permanent funds etablished for public school trust lands go into the common school construction fund in Washington state. On the average, the Common School Construction Account provides about 50 percent of school construction costs.[19] In Montana, revenues from timber sales go into the income fund of the institution owning the land.[20] Montana differs from the other states in disbursing only 95 percent of the renewable resource revenues and only 95 percent of the interest on the permanent fund to the public schools; the remaining 5 percent of each of these sources of income is placed in the permanent fund.[21] Idaho places receipts from the sale of timber—along with land sales, easements, and mineral royalties—into its permanent endowment fund, with the interest distributed to the beneficiaries.[22] Receipts from state school and institutional trust land revenues in Oregon are distributed to county school accounts after deduction of management expenses.[23]

In Washington, 75 percent of all Forest Board lands receipts go to the county where the land is located; the other 25 percent is retained to cover management costs. The Oregon county trust lands receipts go directly to the beneficiaries after management costs are deducted. Small amounts of revenue from land sales and rights-of-way are produced in Oregon on the county forest lands. Those receipts are distributed directly to the county of origin.[24]

HOW THE AGENCY IS FUNDED

State timber management expenses are funded by a number of different processes. The most common approach is to deduct a percentage of revenues from renewable resource receipts prior to distributing the remainder to the beneficiaries. In Oregon, only renewable resource revenues are used to fund the operations of the Department of Forestry (and the Oregon Department of Lands, for nonforested state trust lands). There is a difference in the division of revenue between county trust lands and state school and institution trust lands in Oregon. The Oregon Department of Forestry receives 36¼ percent of the revenues from the county forestland, but recovers only administrative costs for forestry management on the common school lands.[25] In the case of county forest lands, receipts from land sales and rights-of-way are used to purchase other lands or are returned to the county of origin. In Washington, 25 percent of the revenues from renewable and nonrenewable resources, including land sales, on both granted and board lands are deposited into management cost accounts. Expenditure of monies from those accounts must be authorized by legislative appropriation.

Finally, in some cases agency management costs are funded directly from the state general fund, as (with small exceptions) in Idaho and Montana. Management cost recovery in Idaho includes a forest improvement program to maximize the revenue production from state-owned forest lands by levying a 10 percent fee on gross revenues from timber sales.[26] The remaining funds are deposited into the endowment fund; timber management operations of the Idaho Department of Lands are funded by direct legislative appropriation.[27] Montana has a resource development program funded by an amount not to exceed 2½ percent of the income received from trust lands, although this program's resources are primarily used in range and agricultural development projects.[28] The remainder of Montana's forestry management activities are funded through direct legislative special appropriations.[29]

Tracing the revenues and management programs is more difficult with regard to the state's trust forestry than with regard to some of the state's other programs. But because the lands are more consolidated and more visible to the general public, the recreating public, and the environmental community, these lands get a great deal of scrutiny. We discuss that scrutiny—specifically the tension between benefit for the beneficiary and benefit for the general public—in the next section.

TRUSTEES' OBLIGATIONS TO THE BENEFICIARY VERSUS THE GENERAL PUBLIC

The greater visibility of forestry programs has led to conflict between the trustee's obligation to the beneficiary and public perception that the trustee should manage the forested lands for general benefits, including environmental protection and recreational access. In this section, we use a brief recital of two recent and very important court cases to reiterate two crucial points about school trusts: first, undivided loyalty to the beneficiary is defined in state (not federal) documents and obligations; second, undivided loyalty is defined in terms of fair market value and maximized returns to the trust. Having identified those apparently hard-edged rules, we must interpret them into the context of specific language in state constitutions and statutes. Our discussion of this matter will demonstrate that state constitutions are not as unambiguous or inflexible as one might imagine. Indeed, state constitutions and statutes in timber country show a real commitment to general public benefits.

Two Interesting Cases Addressing Trust Benefit versus General Benefit

The tension between benefit to the trust and benefit to the general public has come up in two recent cases, both involving the timber sales program in the state of Washington. Both offer sharp reminders of the legal obligations of the trustee, which we first discussed in the Introduction. Beyond that, the cases make three other crucial points: first, together they plumb the basic legal arguments involved in reconciling general benefit versus undivided loyalty; second, they underscore the importance of state constitutions and statutes, as opposed to federal documents, in defining the trustee's obligations; third, they appear to reach different conclusions. These points and the disputes in which they are embedded provide a wonderful starting place for appreciating the ambiguities of the beneficiary versus general benefit tension that underlies trust land timber management.

In the first dispute—*County of Skamania v. State of Washington* (a 1984 case)—the Washington State Board of Education and other plaintiffs had challenged the constitutionality of a state statute that allowed timber purchasers to default on timber purchase contracts and eased the purchasers' burden of extending or modifying them.[30] The issue arose out of a putative crisis in the timber industry. Timber purchasers paid extraordinarily high prices for timber harvest contracts during the late 1970s, basing their bids on the assumption that timber prices would continue to rise.[31] When prices fell instead, purchasers were left holding contracts requiring them to pay $300 to $800 per thousand board feet (MBF), while the market value of the timber during the early 1980s was around $175 per MBF.[32] The timber industry petitioned the state legislature for relief, and the state legislature obliged[33] over the explicit objections of the state Department of Natural Resources, which manages the trust lands.

After losing at the trial level, Skamania county and the other appellants appealed to the state supreme court, challenging the statute as an unconstitutional diversion of trust property to the timber industry and (arguably) the general benefit: $90 million in contract rights were let go with very little in return to the trust.[34] The timber industry responded by releasing a consultant's report predicting that the trust would be negatively affected if purchasers were forced carry out the terms of their contracts. The consultant alleged that forcing purchasers to perform on their contracts would produce no short-term benefit to the trust but would cost jobs and force some firms into bankruptcy. In the long term, bankruptcies would lessen competition in the industry, causing a decline in both future sales and future revenues.[35]

In reversing the trial court and finding for the appellants in *Skamania,* the state supreme court cited three points of conflict between the relief legislation and basic trust principles. First and foremost, the act violated the trustee's duty of undivided loyalty. "To our knowledge," the Court stated, "every case that has considered similar issues has held that the state as trustee may not use trust assets to pursue other state goals."[36] It cited with approval the trial court's finding that "the primary purpose in enacting the Act was to benefit the timber industry and the State as a whole, at the expense of the trust beneficiaries."[37] And it cited an Arizona case that concluded similarly that "the Enabling Act does not allow trust lands to be used for the purpose of subsidizing public programs no matter how meritorious the programs."[38]

Second, the court noted that "a trustee has a duty to manage trust assets prudently."[39] The court concluded that "the testimony of a forestry consultant is simply too speculative and conjectural to justify the Act's provisions. We hold that no prudent trustee could conclude that the unilateral termination of these contracts was in the best interests of the trusts."[40]

Finally, the court concluded that the act "falls far short of the state's constitutionally imposed duty to seek 'full value' for trust assets." Cases have disagreed about whether the trustee must in all circumstances adhere strictly to specified procedures—such as public auctions—to ensure that fair market value has been received. Some courts, including the U.S. Supreme Court in the crucial *Lassen* case,[41] have been willing to forgo procedural dotted i's and crossed t's so long as the basic principle of fair market value was protected. The *Skamania* court hinted (without explicitly saying so) that, at least in this instance, it would have been a stickler for process.[42]

On a related point, the *Skamania* court also dealt, in dicta, with the issue of "enhancement." The question involved here is simple: is it a violation of the trustee's duty of undivided loyalty to use trust resources in a way that benefits others but *also* benefits the trust? The *Skamania* court cited early U.S. Supreme Court decisions to suggest that, if an action benefits both the trust *and* the general public, it is not allowed:

> In *Ervien v. United States* . . . the state of New Mexico used funds obtained from trust assets to advertise and promote the state of New Mexico. The state argued that this advertising had the effect of "enhancing the prospective prices to be derived" from later sales of trust assets, and that the program therefore benefited the trusts. The Supreme Court held that this arrangement violated the state's fiduciary duty to the trusts, since the funds benefited *both* trust lands and non-trust lands.[43]

This is an extreme and avoidable formulation of the standard response. The *Skamania* court was obviously irked by the legislature's interference with the discretion of the Department in behalf of the timber industry. Nevertheless, it is difficult to envision a trust-enhancing activity that would not benefit something or somebody else. The more usual conclusion is that maximum returns and fair market value are the standard. If those are achieved, then enhancing others in addition to the beneficiary is not likely to be a stumbling block.[44] However, if full return and fair market value are not achieved, and the trust is merely enhanced or left in a break-even situation, the action may be problematic.[45] The rhetoric of the *Skamania* court emphasizes full and fair returns to the trust somewhat more than those who advocate protecting the productivity of the corpus might prefer.[46] It would be difficult, however, to fault the emphasis on returns in the context of such an ill-disguised raid on the trust as provided the basis for *Skamania*. All issues of this type, however, are not so easily resolved.

A more recent case, *Board of Natural Resources of the State of Washington v. Brown*,[47] appears to reach a different conclusion. Therefore, we will discuss it briefly even though it is of most interest to aficionados of the tenth amendment.[48] *Brown* involves a federal statute, the Forest Resources Conservation and Shortage Relief Act,[49] that restricts the export of all unprocessed timber harvested on public (but not private) lands. The act continued a long-standing outright prohibition against exporting logs harvested on federal lands west of the 100th meridian and established new restrictions on two categories of state lands. In states whose annual sales were under 400 million board feet, exports were prohibited outright. In states whose volume exceeded 400 million board feet, the act banned 75 percent of the harvest outright and allowed for an increase in that percentage if the U.S. Secretary of Commerce found that conditions so warranted. As we have seen (Figure 5-4), only one state—Washington—harvests more than 400 million board feet annually on state lands.[50]

The state of Washington, which at that time exported about 80 percent of its harvest, sued. The state claim of greatest interest to us here was its assertion that the federal government, having granted the lands in order to provide support for common schools, "has a continuing obligation to act in the best interest of the federal land-grant trusts."[51] Clearly, the goal of the federal statute was a general public benefit—to support the wood-processing industry by ensuring that domestic raw materials would be processed in domestic mills.[52] And there was certainly no ambiguity about this benefit's being achieved at the expense of the trust. The federal district court found that the counties involved would suffer an "immediate economic injury from the ban" which could cost the state as much as $500 million in the next decade alone.[53]

Nevertheless, the trust-based part of the state's argument did not win at either the district court level or in the court of appeals. Without discussing trust principles or general benefit as opposed to undivided loyalty, fair market value, or enhancement, the appellate court simply rejected the state's claim. Citing a 1946 U.S. Supreme Court decision, the court observed that "no part of all the history concerning these grants . . . indicates a purpose on the part of Congress to enter into a permanent agreement with the States under which States would be free to use the lands in a manner which would conflict with valid legislation enacted by Congress in the national interest."[54] Valid legislation "trumps the Boards' ability to use the trust lands in whatever way they wish," concluded the Court.[55] The states hold their trust lands subject to all valid federal regulations.

The state did enjoy a brief victory when the export ban was found unconstitutional on nontrust grounds. Part of the federal statute had directed the state governors to adopt specific regulations and to consult formally with state officials prior to adopting these regulations; this provision the Court found offensive to the tenth amendment.[56] However, Congress rapidly amended the offending sections of the legislation, and the ban is now in full effect.

We may safely conclude that the federal government has more latitude to injure the trust than does the state. This is because, as the federal court of appeals in *Brown* made quite clear, the federal government is not an ongoing party to the trust nor is it bound by the trust's terms. Any trust is defined in state law and by the state constitution. But that is the easy question. The harder issue involves what the *state* can do that might impede returns to the trust. *Skamania* suggests that the state, being bound by the trust, is not allowed to enact legislation or pursue policies that would impair the trustee's ability to maximize returns to the trust. But this is not a reasonable conclusion: the trustee of state lands is as much bound by state air and water pollution control, mine reclamation requirements, and similar regulations as are private operators. How then do we distinguish between divided loyalty, (which is impermissible) and reasonable state regulation?

The question—when phrased to include "reasonable" state regulation—almost answers itself: *reasonable* is a good enough wiggle word to permit practically anything. Clarifying guidance can, however, be found in a third aspect of the *Brown* case. Among the other arguments that the court of appeals rejected was Washington's assertion that the export ban violated the equal protection clause of the U.S. Constitution—that banning exports from public but not private lands impermissibly discriminated against public lands. The court found, to the contrary, that the "differential treatment of public and private lands is rationally related" to the federal government's purpose in adopting the ban. While Washington's argument failed, the issue of discrimination or disparate treatment has general relevance. State law cannot single out the trust lands. The trusts cannot be obligated to donate resources to highway construction or parks programs. Nor can the state regulate (or abrogate) state trust contracts in a unique way. However, state laws of general applicability, such as a water quality regulation or historic preservation statute, can be applied to trust lands even if significant losses are imposed on the trust. Occasionally, state courts have held that the state trust lands are obligated to comply substantively but cannot be bound by the procedural requirements of another state program.[57] Hence, the general principle of nondiscrimination raised in the *Brown* case seems to provide useful guidance in this confusing area.

For our discussion of the general public's versus the beneficiary's benefit, these cases tell us several important things. First, although the trust is real and binding, it is a state matter, not a federal one. Therefore, we must look for the definition of the goals and obligations of the trust in state law. Second, the obligation to the beneficiary is to achieve full value, maximum returns, and fair market value for trust resources. But where do general public benefits fit into this discussion? The answer is that the lessons from the court cases are not as clear as they seem at first blush.

Defining Benefit to the Beneficiary in Constitutions and Land Management Statutes

Having used the *Skamania* case to draw some rather hard lines about general public benefit, we now begin the process of eroding them. First, we look at state constitutional language regarding the beneficiary. Both the language and the interpretation of key documents has evolved. Second, we show that, within the statutory language defining trust land forestry programs, there is room in discussions of multiple use and management priorities to raise important questions about the fit between beneficiary benefit and general benefit.

Skamania notwithstanding, it is not a matter of settled fact that the trust documents preclude management of forested lands for the general benefit. The state constitutions to which *Brown* points on definitional issues are not so unambiguous as the obviously irritated *Skamania* court would suggest. As was repeatedly pointed out in Chapter 1, the exact language in the key state documents varied depending on when the state was admitted to the Union.[58] Some states have also petitioned Congress to modify their enabling acts and have amended their constitutions to change the trust language. And as also noted in Chapter 1, interpretation of the documents has varied over time. As a result, the concept of the states' trust role has evolved over the years.

The language in Article X of the Montana Constitution regarding state trust lands is explicit regarding the trust duties and requiring the attainment of fair market value:

> (1) All lands of the state that have been . . . granted by congress . . . shall be public lands of the state. They shall be held in trust for the people . . . for the respective purposes for which they have been or may be granted.   (2) No such land . . . shall ever be disposed of except in pursuance of general laws providing for such disposition, or until the full market value of the estate or interest disposed of, to be ascertained in such manner as may be provided by law, has been paid or safely secured to the state. . . .[59]

The language in the Washington Constitution is practically identical.[60] In contrast, the language in the Idaho Constitution requires securing the maximum possible gain for the beneficiary, stating; "It shall be the duty of state board of land commissions to provide for the location, protection, sale or rental of all lands heretofore . . . granted to the state by the general government, under such regulations as may be prescribed by law, and in such manner as will secure the maximum possible amount therefore."[61] These federal grants of lands to Idaho were found by the state supreme court in *Barber Lumber Co. v. Gifford*[62] to constitute a trust fund, with the Board of Land Commissioners as the instrument to administer this trust. The principle that the board must act to secure the greatest measure of advantage to the beneficiary was also found to hold in *Barber.*

Recent modifications of the Oregon state constitution and enabling legislation have broadened the concept of trust from its narrow interpretation as being solely for the benefit of the trust institution and solely for maximum revenue generation. For example, the constitution now states that; "The board shall manage lands under its jurisdiction with the object of obtaining the greatest benefit for the people of this state, consistent with the conservation of this resource under sound techniques of land management."[63] This provision is codified to provide for management of the lands administered by the Oregon State Forester "so as to secure the greatest permanent value of the lands to the whole people of the State of Oregon, particularly for the dedicated purposes of the lands and the common schools which the resources of the lands are devoted."[64] The thrust of this change is to broaden the definition of the trust to include the entire populace of the state, not just the interest of the beneficiaries, while giving preferential treatment to the original purposes of the grants. The criterion of securing the greatest permanent value of the lands differs from the criterion of securing maximum benefit, especially if maximum benefit is thought of in present-value terms.[65]

Constitutional language is confounded, moreover, by requirements in a few states that state lands be managed for multiple use. Where they exist, state multiple-use mandates do not necessarily carry the same meaning as the more familiar federal language. The federal Multiple Use Sustained Yield Act of 1940—the basis for all subsequent multiple-use management in federal legislation and regulations—defines "multiple use" as "the management of all the various renewable surface resources of the national forests so that they are utilized in the combination that will best meet the needs of the American people . . . and not necessarily the combination of uses that will give the greatest dollar return or the greatest unit output."[66] Contrast that definition with the mandate of the Washington Multiple Use Act:

> The legislature hereby directs that a multiple use concept be utilized by the department of natural resources in the management and administration of state-owned lands under the jurisdiction of the department where such a concept is in the best interests of the state and the general

welfare of the citizens thereof, *and is consistent with the applicable trust provisions of the various lands involved."*[67] [Emphasis added.]

In comparison to federal legislation, "multiple use" in Washington state is based much more on revenue production, being defined as: "The management and administration of state-owned lands under jurisdiction of the department of natural resources to provide for several uses simultaneously on a single tract and/or planned rotation of one or more uses on and between specific portions of the total ownership consistent with the provisions of RCW 79.68.010."[68] Similar language is found in the corresponding Oregon statutes, where fish and wildlife environment, landscape expanse, protection against flood and erosion, recreation, and production and protection of water supplies are permitted to be supported, again as long as these uses are not detrimental to the trust purposes.[69]

As we have previously concluded[70] the state constitutions are not as hidebound as conventional wisdom might suggest. Notably, the revenue maximization/full market value notion itself possesses significant porosity. We discuss this as part of our coverage of revenue generation and sustained yield.

We begin, however with a simple yet crucial observation: Managing to attain fair market value for the products sold from the trust lands is operationally different from managing those lands to produce maximum revenues from them. The first requirement is reactive: if products such as timber are sold, they may not be sold for less than the fair market value. In contrast, revenue maximization may require managing lands in a specific manner before attempting to sell the resources.[71] In forestry this type of management may have negative impacts on local communities and may cause revenue fluctuations, due to variations in the amount of timber being harvested from state trust lands, or in the type of product being grown, or in environmental consequences. Nevertheless, managers have enormous leeway to consider general benefits in choosing how and on what terms to maximize revenues.

Long-term Sustained Yield

Further erosion of the hard line announced in *Skamania* results from contemplation of statutes requiring managers to achieve long-term sustained yield. In defining that concept, trustees must address two areas of local concern: the continuing supply of logs from forests into the future, and periodic fluctuations in log supplies.[72] The first area involves the long-term yield of forest products from the state trust forests. The second area requires sustaining an even flow of timber from the trust forests. These concerns, in turn, have two sources: perpetuating revenues for the trust beneficiaries (and for the state land office management accounts), and avoiding rollercoster fluctuations in annual revenues to the beneficiaries[73]

Not all sustained yield directives are madated by statute. In Montana, the state supreme court found in *Jerke v. Department of State Lands* that the notion of sustained yield is *implicitly* contained in the constitutional direction to achieve full market value for trust resources.[74] In Montana, sustained yield is recognized as playing an important role in educational finance, in resource stability, and in the state's economy.[75] Discretion to receive less than maximum income is allowed in the management of the state lands if the action serves to maintain the long-term productivity of the land and to guarantee income to the beneficiaries in the long run.[76]

The state of Washington defines sustained yield as "management of the forest to provide harvesting on a continuing basis without prolonged curtailment or cessation of harvest."[77] This is expressed on a volume basis, without specifying grade, size, or species of timber. Washington's allowable cut is assigned by decade, and policy allows for annual variations of up to 25 percent to take advantage of market situations, so long as the decade harvest level is achieved.

Sustained yield is not legislated in the Idaho statutes or constitution. The constitution states that the endowment trust lands will be managed "in such a manner as will secure the maximum long term financial return to the institution to which granted."[78] The state's forest management plan mentions sustained yield, however, when discussing achievement of harvest potential.[79] Oregon's trust forests are managed on a sustained yield basis according to department policy, although without direct statutory approval.[80] Beyond this, management of the timber harvest must proceed in such a way as to prevent significant declines in future harvest levels when the maximum sustained yield from the trust forests is being determined.[81]

The forestry profession's ideological commitment to sustained yield has become an important component of timber trust management, with or without statutory direction. It constitutes a significant addendum to the commitment to maximize revenues on trust lands.

In this section we have discussed two things: hard-edged rules from court cases that seem to indicate that the trustee has little discretion to manage for general public benefits; and statutory and constitutional language in the four key states suggesting, at the very least, that the hard edges are starting to get a little soft. At a minimum, ample room exists in the available language to identify a clear tension between the state's duty of undivided loyalty to the beneficiary and its obligations to the general public of the state.

ISSUES IN STATE TIMBER MANAGEMENT PROGRAMS

In this section, we attempt to muddy the water further. Even if revenue maximization is the controlling notion, numerous choices that managers confront can be used to create room for diverse additional general benefits. For example, while emphasizing revenue generation, the manager must still decide what type and quality of product to sustain. Moreover, one must ask what revenue maximization entails in forestry programs. Different decisions on that issue can lead to different results with regard to revenue fluctuations and the timing flows of timber from the trust forests. Within the broad context of forestry oriented toward timber production, there are diverse opportunities for assessing and achieving general public benefits.

Revenue Generation and Its Effects

In the previous section we discussed how sustained yield has been identified as a management goal for the forested state trust lands. In Chapter 3, in discussing revenue generation, we clearly distinguished among revenue maximization, profit maximization, and cost-constrained management. We now examine how sustained yield and revenue generation become issues in the management of forested trust lands. These issues are discussed in the context of the trustee's making choices that all fit within some reasonable definition of "undivided loyalty" but that have different impacts on the beneficiary and the general public benefit.

WHAT IS BEING SUSTAINED?

Typically, sustained yield policies focus on the continuing output of a specified volume of timber, without regard to its quality or type. Thus, harvesting wood chips or pulp instead of high-quality lumber would be considered maintaining a sustained yield, as long as the volume harvested remained the same over time.[82] Because of the high opportunity costs that result from the slowdown in physical volume growth as trees age, commercial forestry has tended toward cutting trees at younger ages. This changes the product harvested from what are called "sawlogs"—trees to be made into lumber and plywood—to chips and wood pulp that can be economically and efficiently obtained from younger, faster-growing trees.

An alternative approach to sustained yield focuses on sustaining the economic value of the production over time.[83] To do this requires some foresight or estimation of what future prices of the potential forest products will be—that is, the prices for high-quality lumber and veneer, for construction-grade lumber, and for chips and pulp. If the prices for the higher-quality products are expected to rise rapidly as the trees that grow these products become in short supply, the prudent forest manager should allocate part or all of the available forest lands to producing these products.

Other alternative approaches to sustained yield focus on sustaining jobs in local communities or on sustaining forest ecosystems. Because mechanization and changes in production technology tend to reduce the number of jobs per unit processed, maintaining jobs in timber-dependent industries ultimately requires either increasing amounts of raw materials or increasing processing (remanufacturing) of the materials (or both). The long-term trend is for fewer jobs per million board feet of timber harvested, particularly in the sawmilling sector of the industry. In contrast, jobs per unit harvested in the logging sector have remained relatively stable; and jobs in the secondary manufacturing sector have increased. Regarding the second, alternative approach, efforts to sustain forest ecosystems have sought to replicate pre-European forest patterns, often by reducing timber harvest levels, using selective harvesting techniques, and increasing the frequency of fires. Sustaining the ecosystem, as we shall discuss in Chapter 7, is not far removed from the trustee's obligation to protect the productive capacity of the trust. Efforts in that direction would be difficult to exclude from the realm of permissible activities.

We are not making up eco-definitions here or speculating that trustees *might* at some future time select program goals from among these "alternative" interpretations of the standard volume- and value-based sustained yield formulation. Existing trust lands forestry programs already embrace many of these nontraditional definitions. Specifically, the Oregon Division of Forestry manages the county trust forests to produce high-quality saw logs. In this case, both the beneficiary and the manager believe that these products will increase in price in the future and provide a stable source of jobs in the county. Washington, too, broke with strict volume/value sustained yield dogma by designating about 200,000 acres of trust forests on the Olympic Peninsula into an experimental program to manage for sustained forest ecosystems, both biological and social.

MAXIMIZING PRESENT NET WORTH?

Revenue maximization, as distinct from profit maximization, was discussed in Chapter 3. In the forestry context, revenue maximization implies producing the highest level of monetary returns from production of timber—irrespective of cost—from the present time to infinity. Profit maximization, in contrast, focuses on net revenues after costs are deducted to determine how to achieve the highest return to the trust. Maximizing present net worth is the long-term analog to maximizing profits. In it, future receipts and costs are discounted to the present by using a discount rate, as discussed in Chapter 3.

For states where present net value maximization is an objective, the choice of a discount rate reflects how the trustee values future returns and costs in comparison to current ones. Simply, the discount rate reflects the trustees' desire for the future return on their investment. A low discount rate means that future effects are valued relatively similarly to current ones, whereas a high discount rate means that events (either returns or costs) are more highly valued today than in the future. Inflation also needs to be factored into the determination of discount rates, since it effectively adds its rate to the discount rate (because inflation decreases the value of future returns in relation to current ones). Thus, the effective discount rate is a combination of the inflation rate and the nominal (return on investment) discount rate.

The choice of a discount rate is particularly critical in forestry, since investments made today will not mature until decades have passed. In a 1988 survey of state trust managers, nominal discount rates used for forestry planning ranged from 3.75 percent (Montana and Oregon) to 7 percent (Washington).[84] Oregon is unique in establishing different discount rates between the common school beneficiaries and the county forest beneficiaries for evaluating forestry programs on their lands. The nominal discount rate for the common school lands is set at 3.75 percent, reflecting the willingness of the school beneficiaries to make forestry investments with smaller short-term payoffs.[85] The nominal discount rate used for planning on lands that Oregon manages where the counties are the beneficiaries is set at 4.5 percent. This reflects the counties' desire for present returns, and it means that potential investments in forest improvements must yield a higher degree of benefits on their lands in order to be approved. Montana uses 3.75 percent as a discount rate, representing the return on triple-A corporate bonds plus an adjustment for risk associated with future stumpage prices and treatment costs. Arizona uses 5 percent as a discount rate. Washington uses the highest discount rate, 7 percent, which represents the target return that the Department of Natural Resources attempts to earn not only for forestry but on its other investments as well.

FLUCTUATIONS IN HARVESTS AND REVENUES

It has long been the policy of the U.S. Forest Service to maintain approximately equal harvest volumes over time (averaged over ten years). This policy, called "even flow," in concert with long-term sustained yield, has the effect of limiting current harvests to the amount that could be harvested in perpetuity in the future.[86] While even flow may be the policy of the U.S. Forest Service, less than half the states with timber trust programs use it.[87] The common trustee response is that "the state [California, in this case] tries to take advantage of high timber prices." The even flow policy, in concept, requires that the state sell timber at the same level (averaged out over a number of years), regardless of market conditions. This means that some timber would be sold when the market was bringing low prices, while limits would be placed on timber sales during periods of high demand, thus forfeiting the opportunity to sell more at higher prices during this time. Whether an even flow policy is the best for the beneficiary depends on two ancillary factors: the timber sale arrangements, and how timber sale revenues are disbursed.

Timber Harvest Timing

Timber is typically sold from state lands either by sealed bids or by oral auction. Oral auctions are used exclusively in Idaho, and in the majority of sales in Oregon and Wyoming. Sealed bids are used exclusively in Arizona, California, and Montana, and in the majority of sales in Colorado and Utah. The purchaser then has the amount of time specified in the contract—usually three to five years, but sometimes extended—to harvest the timber. However, the purchasers, recognizing that there are cycles of demand and timber prices, attempt to buy timber sales when demand and prices are low and to harvest and sell the timber when prices are high.[88] This practice effectively defeats even flow policies, and shifts any advantage (risk premium) for future prices entirely to the purchaser at the expense to the state. Meanwhile, the state as seller retains the risk that the timber will be burned in a forest fire or that increasing environmental constraints will prevent harvests in the future.[89]

States have responded to problems in their traditional timber harvest procedures in three ways. First, the time period during which the purchaser is required to harvest timber has been shortened, from five to ten years down to three to five years in many states. Second, the price that the state receives for the value of the timber it harvests is now indexed in some states. Indexing takes into account price changes between the date of the sale and the date the timber is harvested by the purchaser. Third, to reduce potential environmental risks, trust land managers in Oregon have proposed dividing the harvest and sales into parts, with the state maintaining contract crews that would harvest the sales at the discretion of the state and then sell logs either at the site in the woods or at a central log yard. Oregon officials believe that this procedure would retain more control in the state's hands, while at the same time reducing its exposure to environmental and theft risks.

All of this again raises the question of whether the trust is best served by maintaining a forestland base. As we saw in the first section of this chapter, timber management in many states is not productive for the trust. States that do have productive timber programs are under steadily increasing scrutiny from the general public over their forest management practices. Given this tension between the public and the trustee, we now look at conscious decisions by states regarding the retention or disposition of their trust timberlands.

Maintenance of Trust Land Base

Perhaps the most elementary question in trust land management is whether the trust lands should be retained or sold. In contrast to the U.S. Forest Service, the states' forest managers do not view their responsibilities as being tied to specific acres within specific boundaries. The trustees are generally willing to reposition their holdings, although states usually attempt to maintain a consistent total acreage. States use three strategies (singly or in combination) to maintain their timberland base. First, they may use a "land bank" process under which the proceeds of trust timberland sales are used to purchase replacement lands instead of going into the permanent fund. Specific legislation in Washington allows the state to bank desirable lands, exchange the banked lands for common school lands, and then sell the newly banked lands.[90] Second, states have decided to stop selling their forested trust lands, at least for consolidated tracts. Oregon maintains its county forestland base;[91] and in 1969 the Oregon Land Board decided to stop selling common school trust lands, with the exception of scattered and isolated parcels, and instead to manage them for long-term income production.[92] The Montana State Land Board currently has a policy of not selling state lands unless they are isolated parcels and or in federal special-management areas.[93] A third strategy is to limit the amount of trust lands sold in any one year, while at the same time using land exchanges to maintain the trust land base. Idaho does not sell more than 100 sections (64,000 acres) per year of all types of lands, and it sells only to eliminate management and administrative problem areas.[94] On the other hand, Idaho exchanged more than 50,000 acres of trust lands during 1985–1987. Exchanges are also the preferred method for maintaining the timberland base in Montana, targeting lands with high revenue-generating potential, good access, and site productivity.

Thus, while early state policies encouraged the sale of trust lands, both for their revenues and as an inducement to settlement, current emphasis is clearly on retention of forested trust lands. Existing state policies in Washington,[95] Oregon, Idaho, and Montana mandate the maintenance of the forestland base on the state school and institutional trust lands, while allowing for sales and exchanges to rationalize the pattern of ownership. Isolated and fragmentary sections of state lands in Oregon that are not suitable for management may be sold, with the proceeds designated for purchase of replacement lands.[96] The policy with respect to Oregon county forest trust lands is to replace them within the same county, or otherwise to return the proceeds from the original sale to the county of origin. In Idaho, "all state-owned lands classified as chiefly valuable for forestry, reforestation, recreation, and watershed protection are hereby reserved from sale and set aside as state forests."[97] Proceeds from land sales in Idaho go into the permanent fund; however, forest lands may be acquired by the department, with the acquisition cost being repaid by timber sales revenues.[98] Lands classified as timberlands in Montana are restricted from sale.[99] Land exchanges may be conducted, with the approval of the county commissioners.[100]

Washington goes farther than the other states by identifying what it calls "transition lands" where the future use is expected to be other than intensive forestry. *Transition lands* are defined as "land currently being managed for natural resource production that has characteristics indicating an opportunity for more efficient management or to obtain a higher economic return by the conversion of the land to another use."[101] The concept of identifying and managing lands as resources—rather than as specific parcels—returns to portfolio theory as an organizing principle. But portfolio theory revolves around protecting the value and productivity of the trust corpus, whether it is lands, personnel, or permanent funds.

Protection of Corpus of Trust

We next examine three areas in which protection of the corpus is important to a state's timber management program: forest practices on trust lands; the relationship among standing timber, disbursements, and the state's permanent fund; and access to trust lands by the general public. The issues revolving around these three topics are so complex that we will only be able to outline the contours, rather than provide elaborate discussion or solutions.

FOREST PRACTICES

From a strict forestry viewpoint, the most important consideration in evaluating forest practices is how they affect the future productivity of the site for growing timber. From a broader ecological perspective, forestry practices affect the ability of the forest to perpetuate biological systems that depend on a range of features within and without the individual parcel, such as watersheds, anadromous fish, and biological diversity. Past practice has focused almost entirely on maintaining the physical productivity of the lands for timber production. Current and future policies will increasingly emphasize protection of a broader range of forest resources.

Two generally interrelated forestry practice concerns have aroused public concern about the management of trust lands. The first is the practice of even-age management, which usually results in or from clear-cutting. In clear-cutting, all the trees within a particular piece of forest are removed during harvesting. After preparing the site subsequent to harvest (often by burning the slash left over from the harvest), young trees are planted to replace those harvested. This results in a stand of even-age trees. Frequently, it also results in thick growths of brush and deciduous trees that grow in the high light after the overstory of large trees has been harvested. Brush and deciduous trees are considered undesirable because they suppress the growth of the planted seedlings.

The presence of brush and deciduous trees after clear-cutting leads to the second forestry practice issue: whether and how to use herbicides to control the undesirable vegetation. The difference in growth rates, at least in the early years, between tree plantations that have been sprayed with herbicides to suppress competing vegetation and those that have not is significant, usually representing roughly a five-year head start. On the other hand, herbicide spraying in combination with even-age management tends to create biological deserts similar to agricultural crop fields. Spraying can also have negative effects on water quality, which is especially important along the borders of the trust land parcels.

STANDING TREES AS A COMPONENT OF THE CORPUS

A final issue in forestry practices relates to management of old-growth forests on trust lands. From a strictly financial perspective, some would argue that the best thing the trustee can do with old growth is to harvest it and replant the area with faster-growing seedlings. This is especially true where the discount rate is relatively high, since this implies that the trustee cares more about current income than future income. However, things are not quite this simple: the general public is increasingly interested in protecting old growth for its existence value; and the value of the standing timber in the old growth is just as much a part of the corpus of the trust as if it were cut and the proceeds placed in a bank. The existence value that the public (or portions of it) places on old growth is because it is effectively a nonrenewable resource, at least in the lives of currently living people. The perception of one state timber manager, Washington, is that, if its practices (including harvesting old growth) become too controversial, the public through its elected representatives will pass legislation that limit the state's timber management options. Thus Washington has removed the bulk of its remaining old growth from near-term harvest until better management alternatives are available.

An alternative view is to consider the standing old-growth trees as part of the trust corpus. At first blush, this may seem to contradict the trust principle to make the corpus productive. However, given the uncertainty involving nonmonetary values of old-growth forests, and the expected premium that the market will place in the future on high-quality timber from these trees, it may make sense for the trustee, at least in the near term, to preserve some or all of these stands. Considerations that come into play when old growth is considered part of the corpus include the risk inherent in retaining an asset that could burn, be killed by disease, or placed off-limits for harvest in the future. This risk is then weighed against the likelihood of increased value (whether harvested or not) of the old growth in the future, due to its scarcity. Conversion of the value of old growth into revenues for the trust does not even have to involve harvest. Washington transferred the value of the standing timber when the state legislature appropriated funds to buy the harvest rights to the timber, thus making the trust whole while preserving the old growth.

PUBLIC ACCESS TO TRUST LANDS

Public access strategies are discussed in greater detail in Chapter 7. At this point, we are interested in how public access is incorporated into the states' forest management programs. In most states, access to trust lands is defined by state law regarding access to all other lands. If the state is an open-access state, the trust lands are open for hunting and fishing unless posted to the contrary. Washington, for example, is an open-access state; and for a lessee to post trust lands requires the approval of the department.[102] Eleven other uses are also identified as being compatible with the obligations of the department to fulfill its trusteeship obligations; uses, including those listed, must be conducted without having a financial impact unless compensation is provided.[103] Oregon is also an open-access state; the trustee is required to give consideration to multiple values in the sale, exchange, and leasing of state trust lands.[104] However, lands cannot be dedicated to uses that preclude income generation.[105] Multiple-use management is allowed in Montana.[106] Montana includes grizzly bear habitat in its multiple-use management.[107]

Idaho, of the four states, is the only one without a multiple-use statute.[108] It has, however, reserved from sale "all state-owned lands chiefly valuable for forestry, reforestation, recreation, and watershed protection" as state forests.[109] Within the Department of Lands' policies, the objectives for state forested lands "shall be . . . to improve timber productive capacity and assure maximum long-term financial returns to the endowment trusts without permanently diminishing other uses such as watershed, forage, recreation, wildlife habitat and enjoyment of the aesthetic quality."[110]

CONCLUSIONS

There is undeniable tension between maximizing returns for the beneficiary and achieving general public benefits—particularly if general public benefits are defined exclusively in terms of wilderness preservation or other more or less rigid notions of nonuse. But more broadly defined, general public benefit need not be incompatible with meeting the trustee's obligation of undivided loyalty to the beneficiary. Although that notion appears engraved in stone in cases such as *Skamania,* a closer look at the state statutes and constitutions yields a significantly different perspective on the concept of the beneficiary. More room for approaching both goals simultaneously is, perhaps, to be found in the fundamentals of timber management—in answers to such questions as what is the product to be sustained, what is the discount rate, and what is the desired periodicity in revenue flows. This does not eliminate the potential for conflicts between trust land managers and environmentalists: those conflicts are real, important, and likely to be intense at times. It is important, however, to understand both the clear priorities of trust land timber management and the room for flexibility that exists underneath the seemingly rigid dictates of the trust.

CHAPTER SIX

Mineral Resources

Minerals management in state trust lands invites—and indeed makes possible—discussion of two crucial issues: the interplay of federal and state management programs, especially with regard to how federal policies affect the state; and intergenerational equity. We will raise these two issues in connection with a description of state mineral leasing programs, a summary of the resources and revenues produced, a description of standard leasing procedures at the state level and of interesting variants on these, and a case study analyzing key aspects of the program.

Minerals provide the largest source of trust revenues in seven states, and all states have at least a small minerals program. In this chapter we focus on two broad categories: hardrock minerals and energy minerals. Hardrock minerals include ones that glitter (such as copper, iron, gold, and silver) and ones used in construction and chemical processes (such as potash, potassium, sulfur, gemstones and industrial clays and sands). Hardrock minerals are major revenue producers only in Arizona, Montana, Utah, and Wyoming. However states have—or have had—about forty different minerals specified in either prospecting or production leases. The second type of minerals are energy resources, including the hydrocarbons (coal, oil, and gas) and geothermal steam. California, New Mexico, Oklahoma, Texas, and Wyoming derive the vast majority of their state trust lands' revenues from the production of energy minerals, far surpassing any other resource in their receipts.

This chapter's first theme is the differentiation between hardrock and energy minerals. The states generally do not draw the enormous distinction between energy and hardrock minerals as is found on federal lands. Both state energy and hardrock mineral leasing resemble federal energy minerals programs defined by the 1920 Minerals Leasing Act and subsequent statutes. We juxtapose the federal and state government's minerals programs, and we explore the wealth of insight and specific suggestions for thinking about leasing programs in general that the state programs provide.

The second theme of the chapter is a more fundamental issue: whether to develop the mineral resources and use the proceeds to meet the needs of current citizens, or to leave them in the ground for future generations. The debate over intergenerational equity turns significantly on the question of how the corpus of the trust is conceived: what is the relationship between the land resources and the permanent fund? We use tools developed in

Chapter 3 to explore this issue, observing the growth in mineral commodity prices and comparing this growth to what has been received (and distributed) from the states' permanent funds.

We begin with two essential reference points for those unfamiliar with minerals issues. First, we describe the Darth Vader of all public lands policy—the General Mining Act of 1872. This is useful because the 1872 act so colors our thinking about minerals that we need to present state programs as distinguished from the federal hardrock program. Then we describe three standard phases of minerals development: preproduction, production, and postproduction. The preproduction phase includes exploration activities, and we pay special attention to the difference in programs as between areas known to be valuable for minerals and those whose mineral potential is more speculative. The discussion of production focuses on incentives to encourage the lessee to produce, the matter of how royalty rates are used, and the question of how prices are determined and audited. A brief examination of the lease termination phase focuses on reclamation. With that background established, we return to our normal format and focus on mineral leasing revenues in the second section, including types of minerals recovered and the revenues they produce in each state.

We then return to our first major theme—the influence and effect of federal mineral laws on the states' hardrock minerals program—in a discussion of hardrock minerals. Although the federal government's approach to hardrock minerals is unlike that of any state program, both state and federal governments use many standard procedures—prospecting permits, leases (land) held by production, and so on. But state programs differ in three crucial ways: all states charge rental for both prospecting and surface leases; many states have provisions for competitive bidding for mineral leases in known mineral areas; and all states require the lessee to pay a royalty on the value of the minerals produced from state trust lands.

The fourth section focuses on state oil and gas programs and the hows and whys of timing development decisions. We examine long-term growth in the prices of the energy minerals. Then we discuss this growth in the context of the returns on the states' permanent funds, as a basis for comparing the "produce versus retain" quandary. The states' energy minerals programs provide an excellent basis for studying the tension between generating present revenues and deferring exploitation to the future. The notion of the trust corpus as the repository of asset values is central to our discussion of whether the minerals should stay in the ground or should be converted into money to be placed in the permanent fund. For states lucky enough to have considerable amounts of energy minerals, those resources' development—and its timing—profoundly affects the beneficiaries in both present and future generations. But because even this decision is not simple, its various ramifications are examined.

The chapter concludes by revisiting the two themes and demonstrating how they fit with trust principles, showing how the trust notion can be useful in setting up an "ideal" minerals leasing program. We ignore the artificial difference between the two categories of minerals, picking and choosing the features amenable to effective development of all minerals. We then proceed to the second theme and ask how and when to make the decision to retain or to develop. Our goal is to provide a substantial broadening of the narrow federal horizon for achieving minerals management goals.

GENERAL MINERAL LEASING PROCEDURES

Overview of the General Mining Act of 1872

The 1872 General Mining Act established a federal mineral location system. Although this discussion focuses on hardrock and energy minerals, common parlance frequently recognizes three categories, not just two. The influence of the federal rules for minerals on public lands is so pervasive that the minerals on state lands are often categorized by the standard means of accessing them on federal lands: (1) locatables, (2) leasables, and (3) salables:[1]

THREE GENERAL CATEGORIES OF MINERALS

The three general categories of minerals under federal law can be characterized as follows:

- *Locatables* is another term for hardrock minerals. On federal public lands, locatables are accessed under the 1872 General Mining Act. The desired ore can be "native" (or in pure form) but it is more commonly associated with various other ore minerals.[2] The term *locatable* refers to the process used to establish ownership over the minerals: specifically, a prospector (or more commonly today, a large corporation) stakes out a claim to the minerals that she/he/it has located. As we discuss later, the federal government receives no revenues from the production of minerals under the 1872 General Mining Act.
- *Leasables* include the energy minerals such as oil, natural gas, coal, and oil shale, and the "fertilizer" minerals such as phosphate, potash, and sulfur. Also included are nonfuel—but hydrocarbon-based—minerals such as native asphalt and bitumen rock. The term *leasable* refers to the fact that the federal government leases lands for exploration and production of these resources under the 1920 Mineral Leasing Act and similar statutes. The government takes a fee for the land rented in the lease, a bonus payment

at the lease auction, and a royalty from the value of the any resulting production.

- *Salables* are minerals regulated by the Common Varieties of Minerals Act of
  1947[3] and subsequent laws.[4] Frequently called *construction-grade minerals*,
  they can be thought of as resources used in raw form as "materials," such
  as sand and gravel, pumice, stone, and clay. They are generally sold at a
  set price per cubic yard. Salables are not as distinctive in state programs
  as they are on federal lands. States treat some varieties similarly to hardrock minerals (and hence they are discussed in the same section as these),
  but other varieties are considered bulk commodities and are sold by the
  cubic yard; these are an increasingly important source of revenues.

The preceding three categories form the broad framework for conversations
about government mineral leasing programs. However, the states have broken down the conceptual boundaries that prevail on federal lands. It is interesting to consider where and to what extent the states have been influenced by the federal programs.

EVOLUTION SINCE THE 1872 GENERAL MINING ACT

The General Mining Act of 1872 was intended to encourage exploration
and development of the public domain.[5] Under the "location system" established by the act, prospectors are given free access to the public domain to
explore for minerals; those who succeed in locating a valuable deposit are
granted a claim to the deposit that is good against all rivals, access to the
claim rent-free, and the right to extract the mineral without paying the government a royalty. In addition, the miner can take title to the claim in a "patenting" process that requires "proving up" the location of the valuable deposit.

This basic scheme remains in place today. Its core is the doctrine of *pe-
dis possessio* ("toe hold"). In order to have a valid mining claim, a prospector
must do four things: discover a valuable deposit of a mineral covered by the
act; locate the claim on the ground with stakes or boundary markers; record
the claim in the appropriate local jurisdiction; and annually perform at least
$100 worth of "assessment work" to make the claim productive.[6]

In addition, the locator—as the prospector is frequently called—is given
the right to patent (or take fee title to) an unlimited number of 20-acre
claims, plus a 5-acre mill site for each claim. This patenting process requires
the locator to prove up the claim—that is, demonstrate that a "valuable deposit" has been located and meet certain other requirements. Originally,
mining on the public domain was almost totally under the control of the developer. No license, bond, plan, or permission was required prior to either
exploration or development. Only at the stage of the patenting process did
the federal government become involved.[7]

Complaints that the law has not been changed in almost 125 years are untrue.[8] Both the Forest Service and the Bureau of Land Management now require advance submission of mining plans aimed at protection and reclamation of surface resources.[9] Moreover, all mining operations are subject to environmental laws and regulations such as the Clean Air Act, the Federal Water Pollution Control Act, the Safe Drinking Water Act, and the Endangered Species Act.[10]

The provisions and applicability of the 1872 act have also been altered by other forms of subsequent administrative, legislative, and judicial action. Beginning in the early twentieth century, Presidents Roosevelt and Taft sharply reduced the extent of the act's coverage by withdrawing enormous areas of the public domain from "mineral entry."[11] For its part, Congress, beginning with the passage of the 1920 Mineral Lands Leasing Act, has excluded whole categories of minerals from the coverage of the 1872 act. Coal, oil, gas, phosphate, and numerous energy and construction minerals are no longer covered by the 1872 statute. The 1872 act was not appropriate to the development requirements of oil, coal, and other sedimentary deposits. And because many dubious "gravel mines" emerged as hotels and second homes in scenic spots throughout the federal lands, construction minerals are now accessed under a leasing system or sold by the cubic yard.[12] This process of excluding minerals from coverage under the 1872 act now effectively defines the hardrock category: at the federal level, they are the only ones that remain under the 1872 act.

The most important administrative action in this area redefined the notion of "valuable deposit" for purposes of identifying or patenting a claim. Originally a valuable deposit was defined as one that an ordinary "prudent person" would invest time and capital to develop. The historic standard of prudence, developed and applied by the U.S. Geological Survey, focused on the workability of the deposit: was it technically or physically possible to extract an ore? In the years immediately following the passage of the 1970 National Environmental Policy Act, however, the Department of the Interior redefined *prudence* to include a profit: a valuable deposit was one that the developer could extract *at a profit*.[13] This new rule required that the cost of complying with all applicable environmental regulations be included in calculating the potential profit. Critics have charged that the new rule makes the system too unpredictable and difficult to apply: a deposit that is valuable when mineral prices are high will not be if prices fall; and the determination of prudence turns as much on an individual firm's financial situation as it does on the deposit itself. Nevertheless, the new policy has been approved by the courts and has remained in place for several decades, serving as a valuable authority in land management agency efforts to challenge problematic claims and prevent the patenting of bogus and marginal operations.

The 1872 act was again altered significantly with the 1976 passage of the Federal Land Policy and Management Act (FLPMA). First, FLPMA established "recordation requirements." Three years after the passage of the act, all claimants were required to record their claims to federal land with the Bureau of Land Management. Any claim that went unrecorded was thenceforth void.[14] This was of inestimable value in clearing title to thousands of acres where confused and forgotten claims clouded title and confounded management. Further, claimants were (and are) required by the 1976 amendments to give notice annually of their assessment work. Failure to do so in a timely fashion constitutes abandonment of the claim.

Most of the reform efforts of the 1970s era were aimed at two goals: including hardrock mining in the land use planning and environmental protection and reclamation programs that were beginning to dominate federal land management agency programs; and preventing the patenting and fraudulent use of nonproductive mining claims.[15] The locator's right to patent the claim, which remains in force, continues to be a target of environmental advocates, but recent efforts are aimed at securing a fair return to the government for both the mineral extracted and the land used during operations. Proposals for leasing systems with royalties and rents, imposition of a tonnage tax, elimination of the patent system, and changes in the assessment fee circulate annually. Early Clinton-era proposals envisioned creating jobs by using increased federal minerals revenues to clean up abandoned mines.[16]

Mineral Development Phases

The difficulty in achieving basic reforms of the 1872 act appears tied, in part, to the mystique of the prospector, with his tin pan and floppy-eared mule. Yet mineral resources rarely come flowing to the surface or lie about on the surface in their native form anymore. Prospectors wishing to develop the resources must first locate them, then set up systems to produce the minerals, and finally (at some point) decide that production is no longer economical and terminate the operation. Each of these three phases has unique requirements with regard to the actions of the developers and in relation to the states' regulatory mechanisms. Here, we will discuss these in general terms, saving specifics for the next two major sections.

The extent and value of mineral resources on state trust lands depend on a number of factors, known and unknown.[17] The existence of mineral resources is frequently not known prior to exploration activities. Even when mineralization is known to be present, the recoverable amount is determined by economics, which is affected by market conditions and the price received for the commodity, as well as by the costs of extracting it. Figure

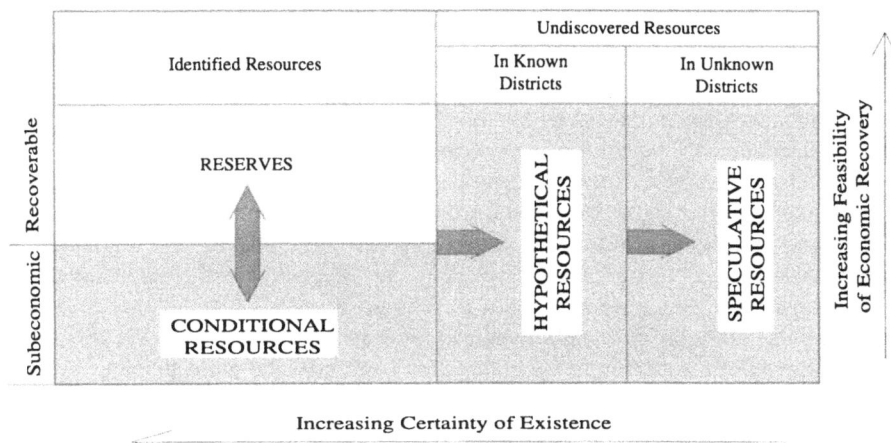

Figure 6-1. "McKelvey Box" diagram of mineral resources and their development potential. *Source:* Redrawn from JENSEN & BATEMAN, ECONOMIC MINERAL DEPOSITS (3d ed. 1981), at 4.

6-1 provides a diagram depicting this relationship between the certainty that a resource is present and the economic viability of recovering it.

The box diagram in Figure 6-1 represents the entire universe of minerals existing in the earth's crust. Within this universe, there exist known and unknown mineral deposits, some of them economic and others uneconomic to recover. The interior lines of the box contain arrows representing the fact that boundaries between the categories change based on knowledge, technology, and economics. The first major division in the box (running vertically) is between identified and undiscovered mineral resources. The left-hand side represents discovered resources, where the existence and relative quality of the mineral deposits is known. When the presence of deposits is known, they are called "proven." In contrast, the right-hand side represents presently undiscovered mineral deposits—called either "hypothetical" or "speculative," depending on whether they exist in areas of known mineralization. The arrow facing to the right, perpendicular to both vertical lines, indicates that discovered and hypothetical mineral resource categories increase over time as a result of additional knowledge and prospecting.

However, knowing that deposits exist does not ensure that they are economically feasible to recover, nor that they are available even if economically feasible due to political considerations. Economic feasibility is distinguished by the horizontal line dividing the recoverable and subeconomic categories of identified resources. Identified resources that are economic to recover are called *reserves*. Identified resources that are not economically recoverable—at present—are called *conditional resources*. The term *conditional* is important: changes in commodity prices, recovery technologies, and costs cause the boundary between economic and subeconomic categories to shift up and down, as indicated by the double-headed arrow in Figure 6-1.

Similarly, as exploration activities occur, the boundary between the amount of identified resources and the remaining amount of undiscovered ones shifts to the right. Even for undiscovered resources, there is a division between potential resources in areas that are generally known to contain minerals (called "hypothetical resources" in Figure 6-1) and those that may occur in areas that are not known to contain minerals (called "speculative resources"). The difference between known and unknown districts is based on information available to both the developer and the state prior to initiation of exploration activities.

The differentiation among identified resources, hypothetical resources, and speculative resources is important because the amount of risk faced by the prospective developer changes. This is similar to what we observed in our discussion of risk and return in Chapter 3. At the extreme, there is no knowledge of the potential for mineral development at a particular site, and the developer accepts the entire risk that any exploration activity entails. By taking on this high level of risk, the successful developer is generally rewarded by receiving a greater return on investment. At the other extreme, if the extent and value of an identified resource are known at a specific site, the risks faced by the developer are much reduced, while the value to the state is fairly well known. In this case, the returns to the developer are less generous, since the amount of risk is also less.

The balance of risk between the developer and the state is also affected by the political climate surrounding the project—that is, by whether the development is generally supported by the state's population or is controversial. The past performance of the state land office in fulfilling commitments to project approval will also indicate to the developer its relative risk. In addition, the availability and type of financing for the mineral development affects the risk to both the developer and the state. For the developer, financing depends on the likelihood of project approval, expected prices for the resources produced, and (sometimes) competition for funds in the larger economy. The state incurs risk (both political and economic) in commencing a relationship with a developer who may or may not have sufficient resources to develop a resource that may or may not have a market by the time production starts.

Any mineral development, whether hardrock or energy, involves a standard sequence of operations to produce the commodity. The general contours of the development process for hardrock minerals are shown in Figure 6-2. Energy mineral development goes through an analogous process. The length of time required to initiate production varies depending on

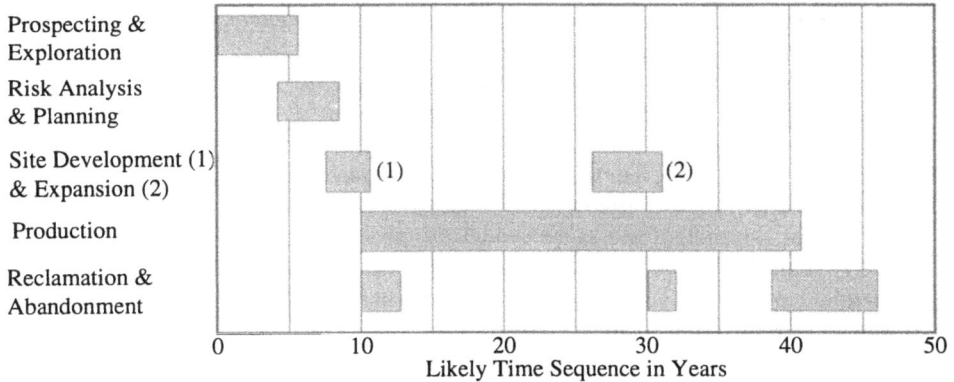

Figure 6-2. Stages of mining operations. *Source:* L. N. Wenner, Minerals, People, and Dollars: Social, Economic, and Technological Aspects of Mineral Resource Development. U.S. Forest Service, Northern Region, R2-84-08 (August 1984).

the type of deposit and on the amount of time required to conduct marketing studies, negotiate marketing agreements, and conduct any required environmental studies. As Figure 6-2 illustrates, this period can easily consume ten years after exploration rights are first obtained. Another two to three years may be spent conducting additional exploratory drilling, performing metallurgical testing, and constructing infrastructure for the mine, mill, and waste disposal facilities.

PREPRODUCTION PHASE

Before minerals can be produced, they must be discovered. In some cases, discoveries on adjacent areas or prior geological mapping suggest a high likelihood that minerals are present on a given tract.[18] In some cases, "known" is defined as proven, rather than potential, occurrence of the resource. States have different policies for distinguishing between known and unknown geological areas (as differentiated in Figure 6-1). For example, some states allow prospecting or exploration permits in both types of areas, others only in areas of unknown potential. Because returns to the state are much higher under known conditions, identifying the tract as one or the other has enormous ramifications.

Historically, ore deposits were discovered only if they were exposed at the surface. As more and more of the easily recognized deposits were found, other methods had to be developed to locate "hidden" deposits. Among the methods now used are geophysics, geochemistry, geobotany, core sampling, trenching, and even remote sensing by high-altitude aircraft and satellites. The age of the individual pick-and-shovel prospector is past, but many federal and state mineral exploration procedures have not kept pace. Both tend to be primarily concerned with exploration activities that require a physical presence on their lands.

In the conventional location system, exploration starts when the grizzled prospector "stakes" out a claim. These days, at least in most states, staking is done at the state land office, where a mining company or geologist obtains an exploration (or prospecting) permit for a specific tract of land. This permit gives the holder the exclusive right to explore for a specific mineral or minerals, for a given length of time by payment of a permit fee and (usually) an annual rental based on the number of acres covered by the permit. Exploration activities allowed under the permit vary by state: some states limit exploration to nonmechanical means (which in Utah does not even require a permit); other states require an approved plan for mechanical exploration, which usually consists of digging trenches or hillslope cuts, or drilling cores or wells.

The second (and less intrusive) type of prospecting—commonly used for oil and gas—is called *geophysical exploration;* its target may not even be the specific state tract but rather characterization of larger areas. Seismic surveys are one type of geophysical exploration. In these, long lines are laid out where at intervals explosives (or sometimes just large physical "thumpers") are set off to bounce shock waves off the various subsurface layers. The pattern of the waves reflected back to the surface provides an indication of the subsurface geology; of particular interest are indications of any formations, traps, or other features favorable to the occurrence of deposits of oil and/or gas pools. When the states issue geophysical exploration permits, they usually charge by the hole or by the mile of survey. These permits are usually available even when the specific state tract is already leased for mineral production.

PRODUCTION PHASE

Once the resource is discovered, fully explored, and determined to be economically exploitable, it may be brought into production if favorable marketing, political, environmental, and financial factors prevail. Three conceptual areas are important in the production phase: what property is owned by the state and leased to the producer; what incentives are given to the developer to maximize recovery and (hence) the state's return; and how leases are audited to guarantee that the state is receiving its fair share.

Resource Ownership. The concept of what is owned in the lease becomes important at this point and has been the subject of considerable case law in the United States, especially since the Gold Rush days. There are two important concepts in ownership of mineral resources: "ad coelum," and the "rule of capture." *Ad coelum* ownership is treated as taking the form of a vertical column extending beneath the surface boundary of the claim to the center of the earth.[19] The rule of capture applies principally to liquid or "fugitive" resources, such as oil and gas, which occur in pools or basins. It gives the surface owner overlying the pool the right to as much of the pool as can be captured. Because these resources are extracted by pumping, they flow toward the well regardless of surface ownership boundaries. States overcome the fugitive nature of the resources problem in two ways, both of which have application primarily in oil and gas leases—and to a lesser extent in geothermal leases. The first approach involves "unitizing" leases among ownerships overlying a single pool to give all surface owners a share of the production from a single well. The second approach involves requiring the lessee to drill "offset" wells to capture oil and gas that would otherwise flow outside the lease area to others' wells.

Unitization rules follow state law and apply to all ownerships.[20] Unitization can be either voluntary or involuntary, and it is almost exclusively limited to oil and gas resources. With respect to a single underground pool, involuntary unitization can be required of individual owners generally only if a majority of the mineral owners—the percentage varies by state—elect to form a unit.[21] On the other hand, voluntary unitization is common during secondary or tertiary recovery, where costs are higher. The purpose of the voluntary unitization is to extract minerals whose recovery would otherwise be uneconomical by spreading the cost over a number of different owners, while guaranteeing that any resulting benefits will also be shared.

The requirement for offsetting wells is found in virtually all oil and gas leases, whether private or public. Offset wells are typically required to be drilled on a lease within a specified time after wells on adjacent tracts within the same pool start producing. Originally intended to prevent drainage of a shared underlying pool by adjacent wells, the provision for offset wells also ensures that the state receives its fair royalty share. This is because it is possible for a single company either to own or to have other leases within a single pool. If these other leases have lower royalty rates than the state's lease, the production company has an incentive to drain the oil and gas through the wells that carry the lowest production costs and/or royalty. By requiring offset wells, the state has a stronger basis for obtaining royalties.

The classic *ad coelum* ownership doctrine is modified by some states in their leasing procedures. The general term for these covenants is *stratigraphic leasing*. It involves, both in hardrock and in energy minerals leasing, specifying depth boundaries for the leases. For example, in hardrock mining, leases specify that the lessee is entitled to develop down to a certain depth (usually, 1,000 feet). Similar provisions in energy minerals leasing are called "Pugh clauses." Pugh clauses are generally used in pooling agreements, but they can also be used stratigraphically for a single lease. In stratigraphic Pugh clauses, the lessee—generally after the initial lease term—is required to designate the productive zones desired under lease extension by production. The remaining zones are then available for subsequent production leases. The net result is that the state as resource owner has another tool to provide incentives for production from state lands.

Incentives for Production. The state also has other mechanisms to induce the lessee to produce minerals. Some apply during the prospecting period, but others reflect the changing relationship between the lessee and the developer after the reserves are proven. The two procedures used in prospecting permits—escalating rentals and diligent development requirements—are commonly used during the production process. Escalating rents work the same way in production as they do in exploration leases. Rentals for the first years of the lease, called the *primary term*, tend to be nominal (generally about $1.00 per acre). These increase when the lease is renewed, commonly doubling or more. As in prospecting, the escalating rent rates are intended to provide an incentive for early and diligent production.

Diligent development must be demonstrated by the lessee in order to retain leases past the primary period. In almost all cases, a mineral lease can be continued indefinitely or as long as it is actively producing, or "held by production." The criteria used to define diligent development vary among the states. Generally, the lessee is required to demonstrate to the state's satisfaction that exploration is continuing, that the amount of royalties produced are at some minimum level, or that a specified amount of money is being spent to develop the lease. Alternatively, the lessee may pay the state a penalty if expenditures are not made.

Two factors unique to the production phase are used to induce the lessee to produce: up-front payments to obtain the lease, and variable royalty rates. As we discussed in Chapter 3, three types of payments are commonly received for natural resource leases: surface land rentals, bonus payments to obtain the lease, and royalties on the value of the commodities produced. Each of these payments has a different impact on the developer's incentive to produce. The surface rental fee can be considered an annual holding payment. The size of this payment, if it is large, induces the lessee to produce, particularly if the rental payment is credited to royalty payments, as is frequently the case.

The effectiveness of bonus payments as an incentive to produce is hotly debated.[22] The general parameters of the argument go as follows. Bonus payments represent a transfer of risk from the resource owner to the producer, rather than a sharing of risk. The amount of risk that an individual lessee incurs depends in part on the number of leases the lessee holds. Any single company in the oil and gas industry is likely to hold a significant number of leases, thus distributing the risk involved in being saddled with any single bonus payment. On the other hand, since hardrock mineral deposits tend to be concentrated, a specific lessee is much more likely to incur a risk that is not distributed across a larger portfolio. Because of this difference between the two types of resources, the provision for and amounts of bonus payments—and their effects—differ.

A second and related incentive effect of bonus payments is their effect on the production decision—that is, when to produce and for how long. Bonus payments are frequently large (especially in oil and gas leases) and are paid at the time the lease is obtained. Because this payment is made before any proceeds from the lease are obtained, it provides an incentive for the lessee to accelerate development in order to obtain revenues to repay the original expense. Opponents of bonus payments say that lessees treat them as fixed (rather than marginal) expenses, and consequently the payments do not enter into production decisions.[23] They do however transfer money, or economic "rent," from the producers to the owners of the resource.

The third component of leasing payments that affects the lessee's incentive to produce minerals from the lease is the amount of royalty charged by the state. The conventional economic wisdom asserts that the lessee will produce up to the point where the marginal revenue from production equals the marginal cost to produce, with the royalty payment considered as part of the production cost.[24] Because the royalty is treated like any other cost, production will last longer—all other things being equal—if a low royalty rate is imposed.[25] In general, however, royalties are a very small cost component in the overall mining operation, and consequently are not a major determinant in production decisions.

Production Costs. Cost in minerals processing tend to be directly related to the quality of the deposit. Efficient exploitation technologies also vary according to deposit quality. Table 6-1 identifies three different processing stages—primary, secondary, and tertiary—and provides examples of different extraction technologies used for each. The exact production processes depend heavily on the mineral involved and the manner in which it is found. For example, many industrial minerals, whose recovery typically involves moving large amounts of raw materials, use other production procedures than those illustrated in Table 6-1. The costs of mineral development

TABLE 6-1. Examples of mineral processing development stages

Processing Stage	DEVELOPMENT METHOD	
	Hardrock Minerals	Energy Minerals
Primary	Classical grinding and milling	Wells
Secondary	Heap leach	Stripper wells
Tertiary	In situ extraction	CO_2, Steam injection

and production are commonly related to the size, grade, mineralogy, configuration, and location of a deposit.

The relative costs of production at primary, secondary, and tertiary stages depend on the specific technologies used and the configuration of the resource. Some modern technologies, such as heap or pressure leaching, are very inexpensive compared to traditional grinding and milling. In some cases, the metallurgy of the ore requires these chemical processes; in other cases, expense—as in heap-leaching low-grade gold deposits—justifies the procedure. In oil and gas, the costs associated with secondary and tertiary production are almost entirely related to whether needed materials to inject into wells to increase pressure are locally available.

Secondary production processes for hardrock minerals are based almost entirely on chemical extraction. Chemical extraction works on low ore concentrations—either virgin rock material or tailings piles that result from primary processing. For energy minerals, secondary processing usually takes place when production drops to "stripper" levels that produce only a few barrels of oil per day. Secondary processing, usually involving injection of waste saltwater from other wells, is used to increase field pressure. This procedure can result in large increases in production at relatively low cost, depending on the cost of the injection materials.[26] Usually, however, the relatively low volume of oil produced, given the fixed costs of pumping and transportation, mean that the profit from these wells is lower than during primary production.

Costs typically increase even more rapidly in comparison to revenues for tertiary production processes. Examples of tertiary production in hardrock minerals involve cases where it is not economically feasible—given extremely low ore concentrations—to mine the base material physically. In these cases, "in situ" mining is used: fluids are injected into the ore-bearing strata (which are sometimes fractured by explosions or injection), and the resulting slurry of mineral-bearing solutions is pumped to the surface, where the different fractions are separated. Similar processes are used in tertiary recovery processes for oil and gas. In this case, carbon dioxide (CO_2) or steam is injected into previously bearing strata to dissolve oil adhered to rock, and/or to pressurize the pool to push the remaining oil to the surface.

The royalty is the state's share of the "economic rent" or profit received from production of its minerals. But the amount of royalty the state receives depends on the relative risks of production, the costs of production, and the resulting value of the products. Generally, the relative value of a deposit declines over time as the resource is depleted, whether it consists of oil and gas or hardrock minerals. Because of this depletion in value (or quality), extraction costs tend to rise over the course of the production period.

Figure 6-3 shows a graphic representation of the relationship between resource quality (concentration) and production costs. Meanwhile, the price re-

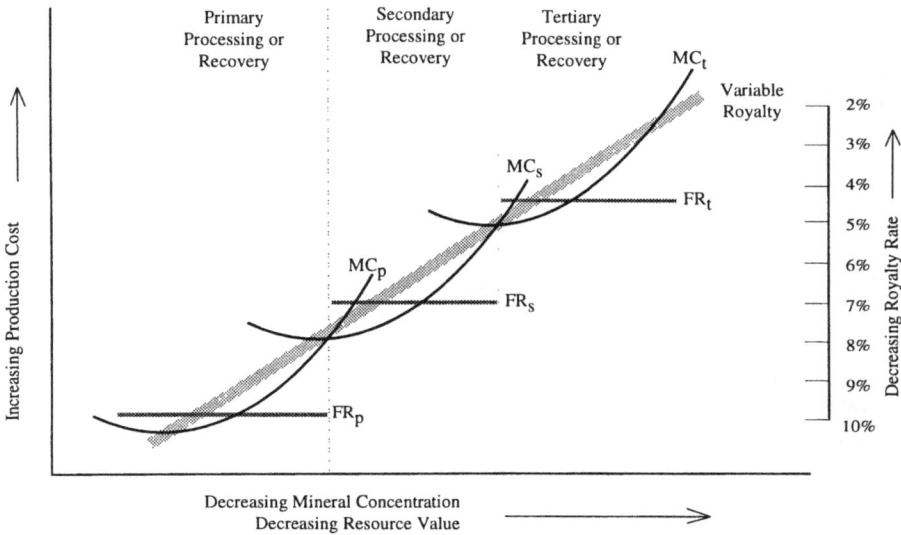

Figure 6-3. Stylized representation of the relationship among mineral concentration, production costs, production technology, and royalty rates. NOTE: MC = marginal cost; FR = fixed royalty; subscripts denote primary (p), secondary (s), or tertiary (t) production.

ceived for the resource after processing—although it fluctuates based on macroeconomic effects—stays essentially the same regardless of the extraction cost. Figure 6-3 also shows the relationship between extraction costs and royalty payments by the lessee to the resource owners.[27] Recall from Figure 6-1 that the line between subeconomic and economic resources depends on both the market price as well as the cost of extraction. Extraction costs are related to the technology used to recover the mineral and to the concentration of the mineral in the deposit, whether it be oil and gas in a pool or hardrock minerals in a vein or dispersed as low-grade ore, as the examples in Table 6-1 showed.

The choice faced by the resource owner is whether or not to establish a royalty procedure that motivates the lessee to produce the resource and to continue producing it as long as it is economically feasible. Three types of royalty systems are possible: first, the royalty may be set at a fixed percentage of the value of production; second, the royalty percentage may vary according to the concentration or value of the deposit, but remain within fixed upper and lower bounds; third, the royalty percentage may vary continuously, depending on ore concentration or production value. Figure 6-3 displays the relationship among these three types of royalty procedures in relation to the marginal costs of producing the resource. Fixed royalty percentages (at least when they are based on gross value) have the disadvantage that, over a large proportion of the production region, they are either too high or too low; thus they do not provide incentives to produce (if too high) or do not adequately compensate the resource owner (if too low).

Royalty procedures are fine-tuned to different production technologies when different rates are fixed for primary, secondary, and tertiary stages of production. This type of royalty-setting is common in oil and gas production, with royalty reductions for stripper and injection wells. It is used less commonly in hardrock minerals leasing. Royalties for hardrock minerals, if they vary, tend to be continuous depending on ore concentration or value. This type of procedure is used by the states (as we will see in the next section) for copper, gold, silver, and uranium leases. Leases are usually structured so that the grade of ore (concentration) is specified within fairly narrow bounds for each royalty percentage class. Royalty percentage classes are usually based on an interval width of 1 percentage point each within a range of 2 percent to 10 percent of the gross value.

Valuing the Resources. Establishing the production value that is used to determine royalties is not as straightforward as it might seem. There are two possibilities: the state can use the gross price received for the ore at the mine mouth or for oil and gas at the well; or the state can take its royalty as a share of the net proceeds after smelting, refining, or other processing. Occasionally the state has provisions for determining value based on both; that is, there is a minimum of the net value, but this minimum royalty must equal a minimum of the gross value. Setting the price from which royalties are calculated is a problem because "arm's-length transactions" between the lessee and the processor in many cases do not exist. Frequently the miner, the processor, and the wholesaler/retailer are the same, which means that prices are not determined at fair market value, but instead are based on some form of internal corporate accounting that can easily be shifted to the detriment of the state's interest. Determining the fair market price in these instances requires back-calculating—what economists call "derived"—prices from the point of first sale and then deducting reasonable processing costs to arrive at an appropriate wellhead or mine-mouth price.

Alternatives to using prices reported by the lessee overcome the problem of determining fair market value. For some resources, local prices are reported by third parties. This is common in oil and gas, where they are called "field prices." Another mechanism, used frequently in hardrock minerals, involves adjusting the prices based on reported price indexes. This process is used for copper leases in Arizona, gold leases in Colorado, and uranium leases in Idaho. In these states, a base price per unit of output (pound of processed material or ton of ore) is established at the outset of the lease. At the same time, the contemporary price index value is identified for use as the base index value. In subsequent periods, the price is calculated as the original price per unit times the ratio of the current price index divided by the base price index.

Royalty auditing provides another source of mineral income to the states. The most common approach is to use the various reports of the states' oil and gas conservation divisions (on volumes extracted), compare these with the state department of revenue's severance tax reports, and then cross-walk these to the royalty reports submitted by the lessees. States have made some good money by conducting audit operations. Typically, it takes a few years for the money to start coming in (because the companies contest the audits); then money starts rolling in from current and look-back audits; and then, after a while, the amount received from audits drops as back settlements are resolved and companies increase their contemporaneous compliance.

POSTPRODUCTION PHASE

How a lessee terminates production depends on whether it plans to return or not. States have established procedures in both cases. If mineral production is anticipated to resume at some time in the future, the termination process is called "shut-in," and one set of holding procedures applies. In contrast, if the lease is being abandoned, another set of procedures is used to begin reclamation of the site.

A special situation is involved when the state's subsurface lessee negotiates with the surface lessee for compensation for "surface damages." An oil and gas lease generally gives the subsurface lessee the implied right to reasonable use of the surface to locate, develop, and produce the minerals.[28] Oil companies customarily pay the surface owner a fee for any damages to the productive capability of the lands and improvements. Typically, surface damages equal the reasonable value of growing and immature crops and the appraised value of damages to the surface lessee's interest in any improvements.[29] Generally damages are limited to the amount of rent that the surface lessee would pay for use of the land.[30]

One interesting issue here is how these damages are split between the state and the surface lessee. South Dakota lets the lessee negotiate for the damages; then it splits the fees fifty–fifty with the lessee, and the state's share goes into its permanent fund (since it represents a reduction in the value of the corpus).[31] North Dakota negotiates a surface damage fee from the subsurface lessee (generally about $1 per acre), and then it splits this fee with the surface lessee according to how much time is left on the lease.[32]

MINERAL REVENUES FROM STATE TRUST LANDS

In this section, we focus on the revenues received from mineral production on state trust lands. Four general categories of revenues are received. First, payments are received for prospecting or exploration permits prior to actual production. Second, once production leases are awarded through conversion of prospecting permits or through competitive bidding, surface rental payments (sometimes called "delay rentals") are received. Third, if the lease is competitively bid, revenues in the form of bonus payments are received by the state. Fourth, once mineral production commences, royalties based on the value of minerals produced are paid to the state by the lessee.

Table 6-2 provides a comparative summary of mineral revenues received for a single year in the various states. The table is divided by resource category: hardrock minerals, oil and gas, coal, and geothermal. Within each of these four categories, payments for surface rentals and royalties are separated. In addition, for hardrock minerals, prospecting permit payments are reported where used; and for energy minerals, bonus payments are reported where available. A single year's data does not provide the type of comprehensive picture that would be available from a longer time series, but it does permit comparisons among states that we can use to identify major minerals producers.

Hardrock Mineral Revenues from State Trust Lands

While Table 6-2 provides information on the gross revenues received by the states for their hardrock mineral programs, it does not reveal the diversity in the various minerals leased under either prospecting or production permits. Table 6-3 lists which states lease for prospecting or production of various mineral resources. Approximately forty different minerals are leased or produced on state trust lands, as shown in Table 6-3.

Despite the large number of minerals leased or prospected for on state trust lands, only a handful actually produce significant revenues for the states. Arizona receives approximately $300,000 per month, primarily from a single operating copper mine that produces silver and gold as by-products. Wyoming receives about $8 million per year from trona leases (trona is a mineral compound that yields soda ash, which is used in producing glass and other substances). Utah receives $100,000 per year from a tar sand called gilsonite (also known as uintaite) that contains pure black bitumen asphalt. New Mexico receives almost $1 million annually in potash rentals and royalties. Texas receives about $15 million per year from hardrock minerals royalties, primarily from sulfur production.

As with all mineral royalties, those from hardrock sources tend to follow the boom-and-bust cycles prevalent in the industry. Large acreages of land can be leased for nominal amounts—at least during the initial prospecting and lease phases—as we discuss in detail in the next section. These rental payments then form a floor to which royalties are added based on the discovery of economically viable ore resources combined with good market

TABLE 6-2. Mineral revenues from state trust lands

State	Data Year	HARDROCK MINERALS Prospect Permits			OIL AND GAS			COAL		CONSTRUCTION MATERIALS		GEOTHERMAL		Total
		Prospect Permits	Surface Rentals	Production Royalties	Surface Rentals	Production Royalties	Bonus Bids	Surface Rentals	Production Royalties	Surface Rentals	Production Royalties	Surface Rentals	Production Royalties	
Alaska														
Arizona	1990		$147,083	$3,065,426	$44,313					$121,408	$1,743,644			$5,121,874
California	CY'90	$10,415	$8,920	$8,769		$37,667				$0	$310,725	$100,070	$4,679,623	$5,156,189
Colorado	1989		$58,425	$79,704	$2,031,531	$4,819,571	$1,214,367	$33,665	$2,620,008	$5,826	$152,573			$11,015,670
Idaho	1990		$55,389	$42,315	$32,243	$0	$0	$0	$0	$27,243	$427,776	$2,110	$10,447	$597,523
Montana	1990	$19,087	$30,657		$2,274,254	$3,712,716	$225,303		$2,302,504		$108,725			$8,673,246
Nebraska	1990				$210,707	$886,877	$35,486							$1,133,070
New Mexico	1990		$81,887	$1,121,947	$3,317,889	$101,933,322	$10,216,494	$379,965	$91,558	$11,925	$624,618	$1,000		$117,780,605
North Dakota	1990		-0-	-0-	$316,467	$3,948,956	$4,916,793		$778,723		$8,607			$9,969,546
Oklahoma	1990	-0-	$104,260	-0-	$101,510	$17,362,668	$2,832,142	-0-	-0-		$64,098			$20,360,418
Oregon	1990				$69,349	$36,834					$5,146			$111,329
South Dakota	1990	$1,425	$0	$0	$22,824	$839,328	$73,707			$45	$22,121			$959,781
Texas	1990		$273,006	$15,945,340	$2,089,291	$122,183,524	$19,519,035	$5,638	$543,366	$539,139	$8,157			$161,106,496
Utah	1990				$2,392,875	$6,283,392	$284,468			$20,989	$29,845			$9,011,569
Washington	1990		$79,414		$66,837			$1,800			$647,060			$795,111
Wyoming	1990		$199,905	$7,641,686	$1,342,796	$21,044,338	$3,157,439	$384,971	$3,979,647	$38,919	$591,876			$38,381,577

Note: Shading indicates aggregated entry.

TABLE 6-3. Minerals leased or produced on state trust lands since 1970

Mineral	AK	AZ	CA	CO	ID	MT	NB	ND	NM	OK	OR	SD	TX	UT	WA	WY
Bauxite																
Beryllium													L			
Copper		P		L	P				L						L	L
Gold		P	L	L	P	P					L				L	L
Iron ore															L	
Lead				L											L	
Mercury																
Molybdenum		P		L		L							L		L	
Nickel															L	
Platinum															L	
Polymetallic sulfides	P			L											L	
Silver		P	L	L	L	P					L		L		L	L
Zinc				L	P										L	
Coal	P			P	P		P	P	P				P	P	L	P
Geothermal			P		P				L				L			
Helium									P							P
Oil and gas	P	L	P	P	L	P	P	P	P	P	P	P	P	P	P	P
Oil shale and sands				L												L
Other fissionable				L	L											
Uranium		L		P	L								L		L	P
Gilsonite														P		
Iodine										P						
Phosphate					P	L										L
Potash									P							P
Salt									P						L	
Soda ash and trona																P
Sulfur													P			P
Asbestos																
Barite						P										
Bentonite				L	L										L	P
Borate		P														
Diatmoaceous earth					L						P					L
Dolomite				P											P	L
Feldspar			L													
Fluorspar				L									L			
Gem stones				P	P	P										L
Gypsum				L												
Industrial garnet					L											
Industrial gems				L	L											
Mica																
Perlite																
Talc and soapstone						L							L			
Zeolite													L			
Basalt				P											P	
Caliche								P				P				
Clay				P	P	P									P	
Granite												P				
Limestone				P	L	L	P								P	P
Marble and travertine						P										
Peat				P		P										L
Pumice and volcanic		P		P	P											
Quarry Rock			P	P							P					
Sand and gravel	P	P	P	P	P	P	P	P	P	P	P	P			P	P
Sandstone				P	P											
Scoria				P	L			P								P
Shale						P										
Slate																

Codes: L = leased; P = produced

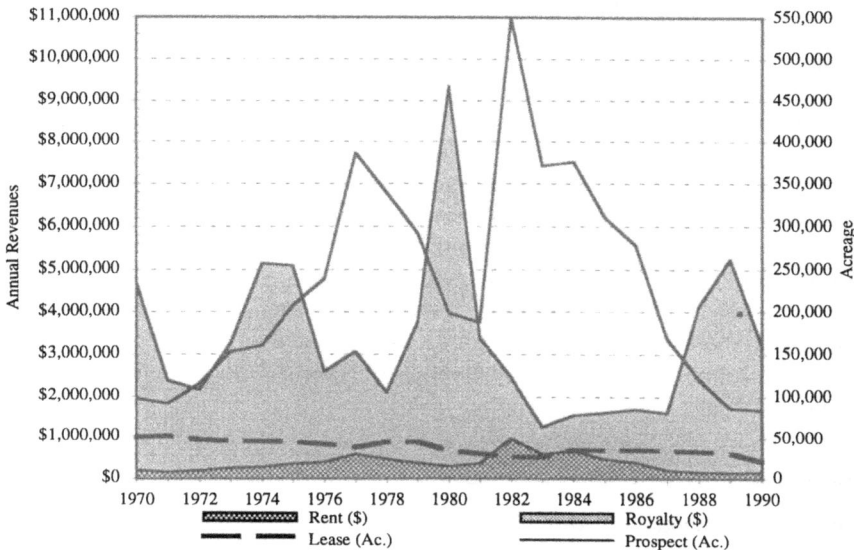

Figure 6-4. Mineral revenues, leased acreage, and prospecting permit acreage in Arizona, 1970–1990.

conditions. The relationship among the various components and their effect on revenues are shown for Arizona in Figure 6-4.

Notice the relationship in Figure 6-4 among prospecting permits, leased acreage, surface rentals, and production royalties. The principal mineral produced in Arizona is copper, but quantities of gold and silver are intermixed with the copper ore in disseminated, low-grade concentrations (called *porphyry deposits*). While the number of acres leased for hardrock mineral production has stayed relatively flat (with a declining trend) between 25,000 and 50,000 acres, the acreage covered by prospecting permits has fluctuated greatly, with peaks in 1977 and 1982 and troughs in 1981 and 1989. Rental payments show a direct relationship with the acreage leased—especially in Arizona, where payments do not vary during the lease term (see Appendix Table 6A-1). Royalty payments, on the other hand, correspond to a combination of factors: market demand (as demonstrated in ore values, which can be derived from metal prices); whether the ore concentration on the state lease is economically viable to produce; and when, if the state lease is part of a larger mining operation, production reaches the state tract. Arizona's hardrock royalties peaked in 1979 at almost $9 million per year. They reached another high in 1989 due to increased royalties as a result of the Supreme Court decision in *ASARCO v. Kadish* (490 U.S. 650), which held that a fixed royalty rate was contrary to enabling act and state constitutional appraisal and true value requirements. They have now stabilized at about $4 million per year because only one of the two large copper leases is producing.

Similar relationships among prospecting acreage, leased acreage, rental payments and royalty payments can be seen in other states. The vagaries of external markets drive the amount of exploration and production of hardrock minerals. Where states have unique mineral deposits (such as trona in Wyoming and gilsonite in Utah), production and royalties are tied to specific uses and demands. Where states have hardrock minerals of more general use and marketability, such as gold and copper, production is driven almost exclusively by metal prices, which are influenced by larger market forces (inflation in the case of gold), by the overall level of production (as in the case of copper), or by the availability of substitutes (such as fiber optic cable for copper wire).

Industrial Minerals and Materials

We have emphasized in our discussion the production and leasing of state hardrock minerals, but another class of resources—called industrial minerals and materials—bears comment. These resources are commonly known in the federal minerals lexicon as *salables*, and they are sold on a per unit basis rather than being "located" under provisions of the 1872 Mining Law or leased under the 1920 Minerals Leasing Act. Industrial minerals play an important role in some states, as the revenues figures in Table 6-2 and their number in the bottom half of Table 6-3 indicate. Every state has leases for sand and gravel, the most common industrial mineral. But some states also have significant localized production of other industrial minerals, such as borates in California or scoria in Wyoming.

While the federal government sells its industrial materials by the cubic measure under the Common Varieties Act of 1955 (30 U.S.C. § 611), states more typically lease their materials under a royalty system based, like the one for hardrock minerals, on a percentage of market value. Appendix Table 6A-2 shows the royalties collected on industrial minerals and materials; the notes to that table elaborate on specific state practices. For example, Idaho determines its materials royalties by one of three methods: the cubic yardage in place; an adjusted volume after removal; or a percentage royalty. Idaho specifies as its due the highest payment calculated according to the three methods.

Because sand and gravel leasing is common among the states, and because demand is frequently high in specific locations close to urban areas, examples of innovative strategies to maximize the benefit to the trust have arisen. Perhaps the most creative is a lease that Nebraska let for sand and gravel mining on a parcel of trust land located between Omaha and Lincoln.

Due to the high water table in the parcel, the sand and gravel mine will eventually create a lake. Instead of allowing the lessee to remove the materials and conduct minimal restoration, Nebraska has specified in the lease that the lessee must, as a part of the mining operation, design and contour the area so that at the end of the lease period it can be developed for residential lots, each with waterfront access.

Energy Mineral Revenues from State Trust Lands

Energy mineral production on state lands is an entirely different matter from hardrock mineral production. States that are well-endowed with energy minerals (principally oil and gas, and to a lesser extent coal) have received and continue to receive large amounts of revenues in the form of royalties and bonus payments. As in the case of hardrock minerals, exploration and production rates are influenced by market forces beyond the states' control. We look at the effects of these in the case study in the next major section; here we concentrate on which states produce which energy minerals and how much revenue they receive.

OIL AND GAS

Cursory examination of statistics regarding state energy mineral production often confuses students of trust lands. This is because some of the major oil and gas producer states, including Alaska, California, and Texas, receive major portions of their revenues from sovereign lands production, primarily along the coasts. Sovereign lands differ significantly from trust lands,[33] but they are frequently managed by the same agency. Hence, the offshore revenues are difficult to distinguish from trust lands. While Texas receives considerable revenues from onshore oil and gas production sited on school trust lands, Alaska and California do not. As a result, the major state trust land oil and gas producers are Texas and New Mexico; and minor—but still significant—producer states are Wyoming, South Dakota, Colorado, Utah, Montana, North Dakota, Nebraska, and Oklahoma. Figures 6-5 and 6-6 show production in these states.

The pattern of production from oil and gas mirrors in many ways that described for hardrock minerals: as market prices—or the expectation thereof—rise, the increased demand for oil and gas leases is reflected in higher competitive bonus bids. Royalties react similarly: first, royalty payments increase from existing leases when oil and gas prices increase; then, after the burst of development that results from the increased demand (which was reflected in the bonus bids), the royalty payments for the new leases start flowing to the states. On the other hand, rental payments remain stable, increasing only when the amount of leased land increases, and

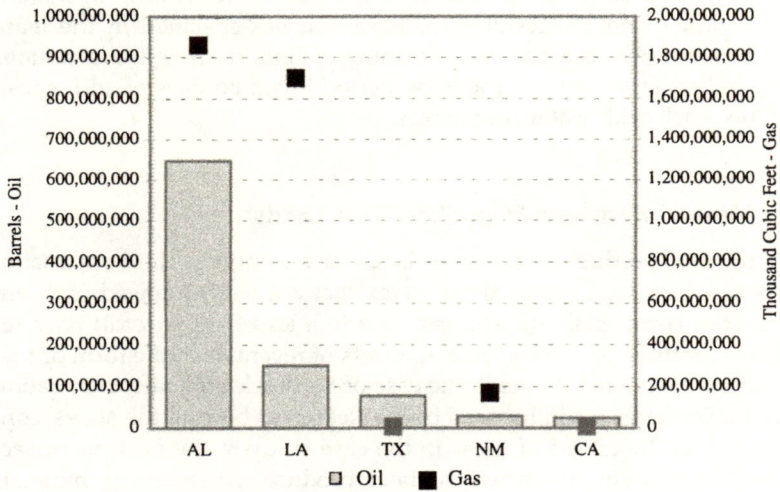

Figure 6-5. Major state oil and gas producers.

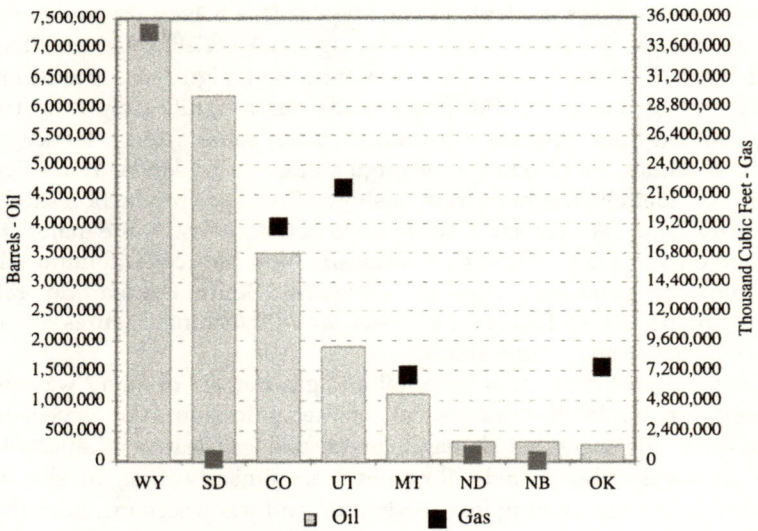

Figure 6-6. Minor state oil and gas producers.

200

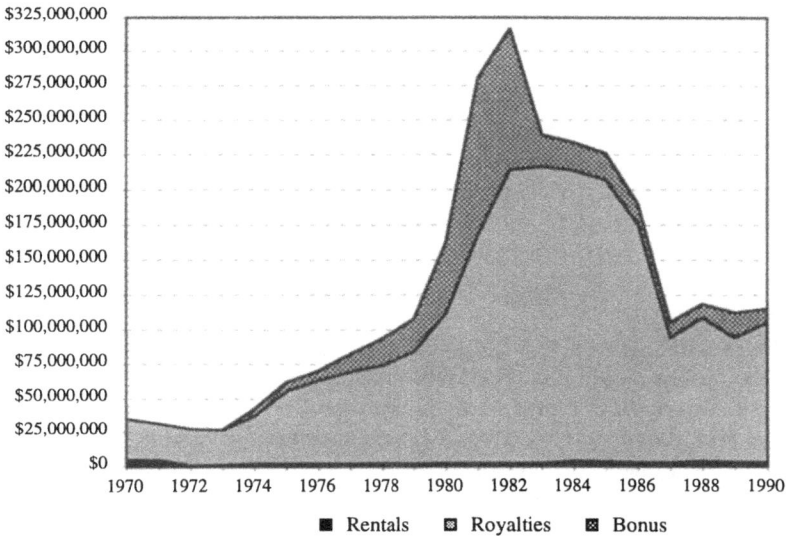

Figure 6-7. Relationship among rentals, royalties, and bonus payments in New Mexico, 1970–1990.

frequently decreasing if rentals are offset with royalty payments. Figure 6-7 shows this pattern for New Mexico over the period 1970–1990.

Macroeconomic cycle effects—specifically, the first and second OPEC oil embargos—are evident in the behavior of the Producer Price Index (PPI) for crude petroleum, which went from 15.5 in 1972 to 33.5 in 1975 (the first embargo), then rose from 37.4 in 1977 to 75.9 in 1980 (the second embargo), and finally peaked at 109.9 in 1981. Prices plunged over the next six years due to conservation, increased supplies, and the breakdown of the OPEC cartel. The PPI for crude petroleum dropped to the 46 to 50 range in the late 1980s and has stabilized at that level since.

Macroeconomic cycles affected all the producer states. Figure 6-7 shows an example of these effects on New Mexico's trust land revenues from oil and gas production. The first OPEC embargo, in 1973, just about doubled prices, which is reflected in the increased royalty payments to New Mexico between 1973 and 1975. In response to higher prices, production also increased from existing leases over the same period; and higher prices caused more competition for leases, which is shown in the slightly increasing amounts of bonus payments (represented by the dark shaded wedge) from 1973 to 1977. The second OPEC oil embargo came in 1978, again doubling prices. Increased prices and increased demand for leases are reflected in the extremely high amount of bonus payments received during the period from 1978 to 1981. Royalty payments kept pace with the increased oil prices during this period. The price bust that accompanied the Reagan recession in 1982 caused bonus payments to evaporate (although they would tend to fall anyway, because of the paucity of available unleased acreage), and royalty payments for most of the remainder of the 1980s fell as prices fell. In the late 1980s, the cycle bottomed out because economic recovery increased the demand for oil and gas, but prices remained stable. With the increased demand— and the re-leasing of parcels previously leased during the boom years—bonus payments again increased, but this time at a level much reduced from their previous amounts.

COAL

There are three basic types of coal and two different ways to mine them. The types are anthracite (hard coal), bituminous and subbituminous (soft coal), and lignite (brown coal). In North America, hard coal is found almost exclusively in the East and Midwest. In the West, with the exception of certain places in Utah, coal is usually mined—or "stripped"— from the surface. Major state producers of bituminous coal are Wyoming, New Mexico, Montana, and South Dakota. Lignite coal is found in western North Dakota, northwestern South Dakota, eastern Montana, and Texas. Lignite has a comparatively low heating value, and as such does not have a demand beyond the locality where it is mined. Another way to classify coal is by its use: either as thermal coal or as coking coal. Coke, used in producing steel from raw iron ore, is made when bituminous-grade coal is heated in the absence of oxygen. Some coal mined on state lands in Utah and Colorado is used to produce coke. Bituminous, subbituminous, and lignite thermal coal goes primarily to generate electric power. The demand for thermal coal was initially responsive to prices for substitutes (generally oil and gas), which created demand for construction of coal-fired power plants. Because of this substitution effect, a resurgence of interest in coal production occurred during the Carter years; and many federal coal leases were let during the first years of the Reagan administration, when oil and gas prices and demand were high. Present-day demand for coal reflects the large installed base requirements of these existing power plants.

Coal production, while related in many ways to the cycles described earlier for oil and gas, differs because of how it is mined and how it is marketed. When coal is surface mined, the state's section(s) are conjoined with other private or federal lands in a larger area called a *logical mining unit (LMU).* The state's sections are mined when they are reached by the large shovels and excavators. Because of this process, the state's tracts may be leased for years before being actually mined; but when they are reached, the state receives a large amount of revenues as the operation passes through. In many cases, surface-mined coal is marketed to "captive" coal-powered electric generating plants, often located at the "mine mouth." Because of the integral role that the surrounding coal plays in the operation of these plants, the amount of coal mined in a given time interval tends to be stable,

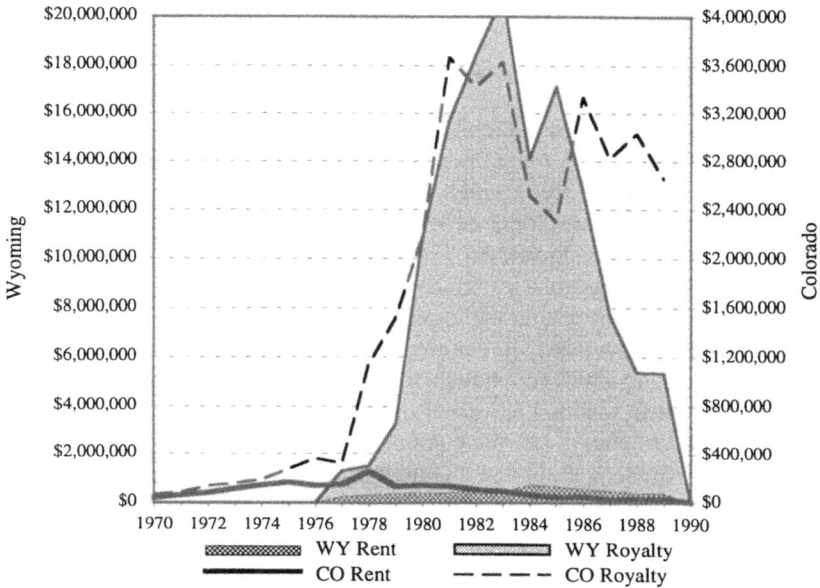

Figure 6-8. Coal revenues in Colorado and Wyoming, 1970–1990. NOTE: The scale difference of Wyoming data to Colorado data is 5 to 1. Revenues are cumulative by state.

even if the amount mined from state tracts is not. Prices are largely determined outside the captive market, however, since coal is also priced as a substitute for other energy forms such as oil and gas. Consequently, coal prices are linked to the other energy minerals' prices, rising and falling in approximately the same cycles.

Figure 6-8 shows the effect of price and demand cycles on coal production rents and royalties on state trust lands in Colorado and Wyoming, two of the six state producers (the others are Montana, North Dakota, Texas, and Utah). In both states, coal revenues increased rapidly after the mid-1970s. In Wyoming, the increase was the result of large coal-fired power plants' coming on-line in response to OPEC-induced shifts in federal energy policies.

GEOTHERMAL AND URANIUM

Geothermal and uranium are the two other energy minerals that states have traditionally leased. From the late 1940s through the 1970s uranium exploration was conducted in most of the western trust land states, and production occurred in Idaho and New Mexico. During this period, the federal government—first through the Atomic Energy Commission, and subsequently through the Energy Research and Development Administration and the Department of Energy—was the only domestic purchaser of uranium ore, most often in the form of "yellowcake" (U308). This "sole source" market gave rise to unique royalty procedures that we discuss in the next section. The slowdown in construction of nuclear power plants, along with the development of alternative sources of uranium overseas, reduced the price and demand for uranium ore to the point where no exploration or production currently occurs on trust lands.

Geothermal is another minor energy source that once showed great promise of becoming a significant producer of revenues for the states. During the late 1970s (because of government encouragement and high oil prices) significant geothermal exploration was undertaken in the trust land states. Production revenues were received in two states (California and New Mexico), but only in California has geothermal provided significant continuing revenues; these reached a high of approximately $12 million per year in the mid-1980s, but they have since dropped to about $5 million per year at present. The reduction is due to a combination of low energy prices (royalties are linked to alternative energy prices) and to technological problems with reducing steam pressure in the geothermal fields. Idaho also receives a small amount of geothermal royalties, and interest has resurged in Oregon as a result of a recent agreement by the Bonneville Power Administration to construct a geothermal power plant southwest of Bend for the City of Eugene's utility company. Exploration and development of geothermal resources in other states are currently at a standstill.

In the next two sections we return to the theoretical concepts discussed in the first section of this chapter, to see how the states have incorporated these models into their leasing procedures. First we look at the states' hardrock mineral programs, examining their leasing procedures and then comparing these procedures to the federal government's approach under the 1872 General Mining Law. Next we focus on energy minerals, again first examining the states' leasing procedures but then looking at the development versus retention decision.

STATE LEASING PROGRAMS FOR HARDROCK MINERALS

This section examines the states' hardrock mineral leasing programs in greater detail in two areas. First, state hardrock mineral programs provide a number of different strategies for resource development and valuation. Second, state hardrock mineral programs absolutely demonstrate that the states can do what the federal government does not: lease the mineral rights to their lands and receive royalties for the minerals recovered. The information in Appendix Table 6A-1 shows that, while the states do not receive enormous revenues from their hardrock mineral programs, neither do they give this resource away for free. In this section, we first provide information on the various ways that the states lease their hardrock minerals resources. Then we look at the effect that requiring fair market value has on one state's royalty payments, and we analyze the differences between state and federal procedures.

Leasing Procedures for Hardrock Minerals

Our discussion of state leasing programs follows the same three-stage format we used in the first section. The processes the states use to determine the commercial potential for hardrock mineral leases prior to actual production are covered first. Then we look at how the states lease their minerals during the production phase, focusing primarily on rental and royalty payments and how leases are continued past their initial fixed term. The final part inquires into which states require reclamation for their mined land and how this is done.

Comparisons among the various procedures that states use are summarized in Appendix Tables 6A-1 and 6A-2. Both tables are divided into the production stages. The top parts deal with whether prospecting or exploration permits are used, how long the permits are valid, and how much the state receives for the permit. The middle part of Table 6A-1 covers the production phase, again emphasizing the length of the leases and how they are renewed. Table 6A-2 shows the fees and royalties earned by the various states. The last section of Table 6A-1 indicates whether a state requires reclamation as a condition for production leases.

PREPRODUCTION

State programs vary considerably on the specific terms and conditions of hardrock leasing, but most programs follow the distinction between known and unknown areas discussed earlier. In areas of known geologic activity, access to explore is usually offered competitively. If the lease is not taken up at auction, exploration access to the property is generally available for a nominal fee "over the counter." In areas of unknown mineralization, leasing normally begins with a permit for prospecting or exploration. The initial prospecting permit is of limited duration—at least in the states' case. To renew or extend the permit, the permit holder usually must conduct a specified amount of assessment work, or show evidence of "diligent development."

The fees and the rental charged for the permit are designed to encourage the permit holder to determine whether minerals can be produced economically on the parcel, rather than to hold the area for speculative purposes. States accomplish this in three ways. First, they limit the number of years an exploration permit can be held. Initial permits commonly have a duration of only one to three years, renewable for total terms of up to six years. Second, states vary the amount of the rental charged over the period of the exploration permit. For example, Arizona charges $2.00 per acre as its rental fee for the first year of the exploration permit; it charges none for the second year, but then charges $1.00 per acre per year for years three through five, at which time the permit terminates. Oregon starts off with a fee of 50¢ per acre per year for the first three years, but then increases the fee tenfold to $5.00 per acre per year, for the last three years the permit can be renewed.

The third mechanism states use to encourage exploration activity is to require a certain level of expenditure for assessment—that is, exploration—activities on the lands covered by the permit. Some states specify exactly how much expenditure is required. Thus Arizona requires that $10.00 per acre per year be spent during each of the first two years, and then doubles that amount to $20 per acre per year for the third through fifth years. In other states—for instance, Oregon—assessment expenditures for each year of the renewed lease must be nine times the rental rate, or $45.00 per acre per year. Montana requires that $250 per year per lease in labor and materials be expended. Other states allow the definition of diligent exploration to be negotiated between the permit holder and the state land office. Table 6A-2 provides details on the various state requirements.

PRODUCTION

Leasing procedures vary depending on the resource and how it was discovered. If a deposit is found in an unknown area under a prospecting permit, the discoverer has the right—and indeed is required—to convert the permit into a lease prior to removing minerals in quantities larger than are required for assay purposes. As shown in Table 6A-1, the exploration permit holder is given a preference for the production lease in almost all cases; and except in New Mexico, the exploration permit holder does not have to bid competitively, or match the highest bid to obtain the lease.

Surface Rental Payments. Surface rental fees for the various states are shown in the top portion of the production part of Table 6A-2. All states charge fees—essentially holding fees—based on the acreage of the leased tract. Two important items are involved with surface rental fees and their incentive effects: first, whether the fee increases over the period of the lease and, if so, by how much; and second, whether the fee is offset by production royalties (what we called "delay rental" in the first section of this chapter). Surface rental fees stay the same, at reasonably low rates, in Arizona ($0.75), California ($1.00), Colorado ($1.00), Idaho ($1.00), Oklahoma ($1.00), Oregon ($1.00), Texas ($2.00), and Utah ($1.00). Montana, New Mexico, and Wyoming increase their fees after the primary period, of three to five years. Montana's surface rental fee goes from $1.00 per acre per year in the first three years to $2.00 per acre per year for years four and five, and then tops out at $3.00 per acre per year for year six and for each year of any subsequent leasing period. Wyoming's fee doubles from $1.00 per acre per year for the first five years to $2.00 per acre per year for years six through ten. New Mexico's fee increases by the highest multiple (10), but since it starts at only 5¢ per acre for the first three years, the increase is only to 50¢ per acre thereafter.

However, New Mexico and South Dakota go even further with escalating rents by including delay royalty payments after the first two lease periods:[34] in South Dakota, rental is $1.00 for the first three years, $2.00 per acre for the next two years, $5.00 per acre for years six through ten, and $10.00 per acre for years eleven through fifteen, with an additional advance royalty of $10.00 per acre for the eleventh year, rising in increments of $10.00 per acre for each year through the fifteenth year. By the end of the fifteen-year term, a lessee in New Mexico or South Dakota pays $60.00 per acre in surface rental and advance royalty fees.

Escalating rental and delay royalties are set up to provide an incentive for permit holders to develop mineral leases. Their effect varies according to the lessee's perception of the potential worth of the lease, either to develop at once or to hold for speculative purposes. In New Mexico's case, the 5¢ per acre rental fee for the primary term of three years encourages many lessees to hold permits purely for speculative purposes. This is demonstrated by the fact that most of the leases are dropped when the surface rental fees go up to 50¢ per acre, even though this is still lower than any other state rate.[35] It is in the state's interest to have a surface rental fee policy that encourages development while discouraging speculation. Escalating fees is one way to accomplish this.

Hardrock Royalties. Minimum royalty rates for hardrock minerals are displayed in the lower half of Table 6A-2. Three possible royalty-setting policies are observable among the states: royalties may be set at a fixed percentage, usually of gross value; royalties may vary depending on the ore concentration or value; or royalty rates may be negotiable between the lessee and the state. Some states adopt one type of policy for all their nonenergy minerals, while other states mix-and-match among the three. For example, minimum fixed royalty rates of 10 percent in California and 5 percent in Montana are charged irrespective of the specific mineral involved. In contrast, the other states vary the percentage royalty depending on which mineral is produced, generally within the range of 2 percent to 12½ percent of gross value. Table 6A-2 provides the specifics for each state. The other possibility—variable royalties depending on the ore concentration or value—is used by Arizona for copper, gold, and silver (2 percent to 8 percent based on a combination of ore concentration [copper] or ore value [gold and silver]); by Idaho for metalliferous and nonmetalliferous minerals (ranging from 2¾ percent to 10 percent of value) and for uranium (2½ percent to 10 percent, based on ore concentration); and by Utah for gemstones (3 to 12½ percent of value).

Lease Extensions. Another important policy consideration in the states' hardrock mineral leasing programs is how production leases are renewed. All states separate their leases into initial fixed terms, and secondary (renewal) terms. Initial terms generally last for three to twenty years, as itemized in Table 6A-1. New Mexico and South Dakota have the shortest primary terms at three years, while California has the longest at twenty years. Most states are in the five- to ten-year range. There are generally two different ways to extend a production lease once the initial term of the lease expires. First, all leases can be extended automatically if minerals are being produced and royalties are being paid to the state. This extension is called "held by production," and it carries only one caveat: in some states royalty payments must be equal to twice the annual surface rental payment to qualify. The second way to extend leases past the initial term is to renew them, by paying additional rental fees as described earlier, or by proving to the state that the lessee is undertaking "diligent development" (that is, is expending a specified level of money to determine whether minerals are present and economically extractable). In some states, the requirement for expenditures can be met by paying the state essentially a fee equal to the development expenditure requirement as a penalty. Diligent development requirements vary considerably by state, as shown in Table 6A-2 and as previously discussed. California and Utah do not require proof of development expenditures as a condition for renewing leases.

POSTPRODUCTION

At some point in every production lease, continuing to produce from the deposit becomes economically infeasible. This point is reached when the deposit is "played out" in mining terms; and the precise time at which it occurs depends on technology and economics. States need to know when active and potential mining is terminated, for two reasons. First, once a lessee terminates operations (and the lease), the parcel becomes available for leasing to others. Second, most states (as listed in the bottom of Table 6-4) require the lessee to reclaim the mined area and mill site prior to lease termination. Since it may be in the lessee's interest to avoid paying the cost required for reclamation, the state needs to set a point at which it can objectively conclude that production has been terminated and that the reclamation provisions of the lease are henceforth enforceable.

States usually base their determination of when a lease has stopped producing on the leasehold's royalty payment history. If royalties are not paid for six months after having been paid for an established previous period, the lease is deemed terminated and reclamation is required. Lessees can avoid this termination by paying a "shut-in" royalty fee based on a percentage of the previous royalty payments.

Reclamation requirements vary considerably by state. They usually are determined by other state statutes and often are administered by another state agency. For example, even though New Mexico has long required reclamation as one term of its hardrock mineral leases, until recently the state did not have a mining reclamation statute, so there were no standards. Other states (for example, Oregon) simply require reclamation without specifying the necessary extent, other than insisting that it be completed within one year.[36] In contrast, Idaho has very specific requirements for reclamation that specify best management practices for each of the various mine facilities (roads, adits, tailings ponds, and so on) that must be reclaimed.[37]

STATE LEASING POLICIES FOR ENERGY MINERALS: RETAIN OR DEVELOP?

Although state programs are generally similar to each other and are not significantly different from federal or private management practices, numerous variations in management tools exist among the states. The first part of this section compares the different state leasing policies for energy minerals. Then we examine one of the most important decisions a state can make: whether to exploit these nonrenewable resources and place the resulting revenues in its permanent fund or to retain the minerals in the ground and await higher prices. Because we tie this decision to the states' permanent fund returns, our discussion in many ways mirrors the sell versus retain decision discussed in Chapter 4. However, in a close reading of the very tedious and apparently standard details of New Mexico's lease terms and conditions, we find implicit policy decisions that have enormous implications for intergenerational equity.

Energy Mineral Leasing Procedures by State

The discussion in this part follows the production sequence structure laid out in the first section of this chapter. The discussion of the preproduction phase focuses on the bidding procedure whereby a lessee obtains the right to produce energy minerals. In connection with the production phase, our discussion is oriented toward rental and royalty procedures. States' use of special lease provisions—such as Pugh clauses and unitization agreements—are also examined. Appendix Tables 6A-3 and 6A-4 provide detailed compilations of state leasing and fee procedures.

PREPRODUCTION

The preproduction phase of energy mineral development resembles that of hardrock minerals. The need to determine whether the resource is available in commercial qualities and quantities and the need to obtain state authorization to develop the discovered deposit are both present. In contrast to the hardrock situation, however, the known versus unknown distinction does not generally play a crucial role in energy mineral development. In oil and gas leasing, the more important distinction is between old and new leases. In most cases, leases for energy minerals in new areas are let first on competitive bids. If no bids are received, access to the parcel may be obtained "over-the-counter" at the state land office, for the minimum rental and/or bonus price. Thus, energy mineral leasing is driven by two factors: industry demand for new production areas, and the turnover in areas held under existing leases. As shown in Table 6A-3, mineral leases are initially held for a limited term, generally between five and ten years. They may be renewed, or held by production, if significant deposits are found and produced. Otherwise the leased tract reverts to the state. At this time, depending on demand and the likelihood of economic production, the tract may be reoffered by auction for exploration and development.

Sales of new leases are typically conducted at periodic intervals, either quarterly or annually, depending on interest. The state may use either of two methods to decide which new tracts to offer. One approach is to allow the public—in this case, exploration and development companies—to "nominate" certain tracts for sale. Nominations generally must be submitted by a specified date and must be accompanied by a deposit covering the first year's rental and/or a minimum bonus payment. A lease sale is then held, and the nominator may or may not obtain the lease. Alternatively, the state may place new and expired leases for sale periodically based on its own assessment of demand. After determining which of its available parcels are likely to receive bids, the state publishes a notice of their availability and then holds an auction.

Lease sales procedures vary slightly among the states. A lease auction is usually held. If there is a nominating entity, and if this entity is the only party interested in the lease, the lease is obtained for the minimum rental and bonus as provided by statute. If more than one potential bidder is present, bids are accepted, either in written form, or as oral bids in an auction. The winning party usually receives the lease based on the highest bonus offered, although in the past bidding by royalty percentage has been used by some states. If parcels are placed up for lease sale and there are no bidders, the state usually has provisions to sell these tracts over-the-counter for the minimum rental and/or bonus price. In either case—auction or over-the-counter—states have the right to (and do) reject bids if they are deemed unjustifiably low.[38]

Once the initial lease is obtained, the lessee has a period (usually on the order of three to ten years—see Table 6A-3) within which to commence production. Prior to production, the lessee pays a nominal rental fee of $0.75 to $3.00 per acre per year. Depending on the state (see Table 6A-4), this fee may be fixed for the duration of the lease or may increase during the lease term. Development expenditures are also required, but these vary by state over the primary term of the lease. Montana requires none during the first five years, $1.25 per acre per year for the sixth year, and $2.50 per acre per year for the seventh through tenth years. Arizona and Oregon charge more (see Table 6A-4), but neither state has any operating leases.

PRODUCTION

Three facets of fee and leasing procedures are of major interest in the production phase: surface rental fees; royalty rates; and how fair market value is determined. Surface rentals are fairly straightforward. The lessee pays rental until production begins. Thereafter, the lessee makes royalty payments to the state. Determining what the royalty will be is anything but straightforward.

Surface Rental Fees. Surface rental fees are handled in basically the same way in hardrock and energy mineral programs, except that fees in the initial period are commonly higher for energy minerals, whereas fees in secondary and subsequent terms do not escalate to the same degree as for hardrock. The pattern is that surface rentals are generally $1.00 per acre per year for the primary term, and then either stay the same or escalate moderately at lease renewal. In Idaho, for example, the surface rental for oil and gas leases is $1.00 per acre per year for the primary term of the first ten years, but increases from the eleventh year onward to either $3.00 per acre per year (if there is no production) or $1.50 per acre per year (if there is production). Wyoming simply doubles the fee for years six through ten. Fees stay the same or are reduced if the lease is "held by production"—that is, if royalty payments are being made. Appendix Table 6A-3 shows the length of the primary and secondary terms for the various states, while Table 6A-4 shows the surface rental payments required for these periods.

Royalty Rates. Royalty rates are based on the market demand for the leases in combination with the likelihood of economically viable production from a specific lease or area. When energy minerals prices are high in combination with low-cost production, royalty rates tend to creep up (however, unless provisions are included to vary the rate at renewal, they are constant for a specific lease during the lifetime of production). Conversely, if resource markets are bad, states are pressured to reduce royalty rates (as well as severance tax rates) as an incentive for leasing and production. This has occurred primarily in the coal region of Montana, North Dakota, and Wyoming.

Royalty rates used by the states for oil and gas production are generally in the one-eighth to one-sixth range—that is, from 12½ percent to 16⅔ percent. South Dakota uses statutory minimum rate of one-sixteenth (6¼ percent) for oil. Oklahoma uses a standared three-sixteenths (18¾ percent) share for both oil and gas. Both Texas and New Mexico received higher royalties for oil during the boom years of the late 1970s: New Mexico used a one-fifth (20 percent) share on some of its leases, while Texas received one-fourth (25 percent). At one point Texas even allowed bidding for royalties instead of bonus payments. Royalty rates for natural gas are typically equivalent to the ones used for oil, but they occasionally vary, as in Montana.

Royalty rates for coal track those used for oil and gas, but they are commonly somewhat lower because of the higher extraction costs. Royalty rate distinctions are also common between surface-mined and subsurface-mined coal. Royalty shares for surface-mined coal are typically one-eighth, although Utah uses 8 percent and Texas takes one-sixteenth. Underground-mined coal royalties are usually less, most frequently being 8 percent of the value of production. Both Utah and Texas have the same royalty rate for both surface- and underground-mined coal.

The royalty rate for geothermal steam is usually 10 percent. This rate is applied by New Mexico, Oregon, and Utah. California uses a sliding royalty scale of from 10 percent to 16⅔ percent. Royalty rates for uranium (see Table 6A-2) range from 2½ to 10 percent in Idaho, 8 percent in Utah, to 5 percent in New Mexico, Oregon, and Wyoming.

Determination of Fair Market Value. In determining the fair market value of its resources, the state has the same difficulty that other royalty owners have: deciding how to value the production. Frequently, one subsidiary of a power company extracts the mineral and another uses it to generate electricity. Under such circumstances the sale from extracter to user is not an "arm's-length transaction" and therefore cannot be used to determine the fair market price on which the state's royalty is supposed to be based. There are two alternative procedures for making this determination. The first is to use published prices, similar to the price index method that is used for hardrock minerals. Where significant oil and gas production exists, a reported "Posted Field Price" commonly sets the base for determining the value of the production from a specific lease. Posted field prices are essentially offers to buy crude petroleum (and gas) by a specific production or marketing entity (such as Shell or Amoco). Because they are offers to purchase for a specific price at a specified quality, they can be used to determine value royalty payments. But because minerals produced are not all of the same quality, adjustments have to be made between the posted field price and the mineral's specific lease price. Adjustments are usually made based on the mineral's specific gravity (that is, density), and then—depending on the specific lease terms—further altered for transportation and processing costs.

Where posted field prices and arm's-length transactions are not available as a mechanism to value the production at the wellhead or mine mouth, prices need to be "worked back" from the point of first market sale. At its simplest, the method takes the product at its point of sale—for example, electricity sold from the generating plant into the transmission grid, or gasoline sold at the pump or to wholesalers, or natural gas sold to pipeline companies—and then backtracks through the stages of processing, subtracting costs (both capital and operating) at each stage until the source point (well or mine) is reached. The remaining value "derived" from this process becomes the price of the raw material from which the royalty is calculated. States with high levels of production have found that they can obtain significant additional revenues by employing economists and chemical and petroleum engineers to calculate derived prices accurately instead of relying on the lessees' determination.

Allowance for Taking Royalties "in Kind." In almost all cases, the state's lease form or lease rules provide for it to take its royalty "in kind"—that is, as a percentage of the physical product. Because of the difficulties and costs of processing the raw materials, states are usually hesitant to do this. The only resource that the states have taken in kind is natural gas. Texas has a large program to provide natural gas from its trust lands for state institutions. During the 1970s energy crises, New Mexico sold to cities natural gas that it had taken as a portion of its royalty payments. Proceeds from these sales were then deposited in the beneficiaries' permanent funds.

POSTPRODUCTION

All leases have a finite lifetime as the resource is depleted. This lifetime is based on a combination of two possibilities: the quality of the energy mineral may decrease as higher-value, more easily extracted resources are developed; and the market price of the mineral may change, affecting the economic viability of exploitation. Once a producing energy mineral lease reaches its point of economic nonviability, the lessee can pursue one of two alternatives: suspend production until the market improves, or relinquish the lease to the state. The first possibility—temporarily suspending (or "shutting in") the well—is commonly provided for in oil and gas leases that are held by production. If the lessee suspends production, the state usually allows the lessee to pay a shut-in royalty fee for a specified period to retain the lease. With the second possibility, the lessee simply returns the lease to the state and proceeds to do the required reclamation work on the well sites.

All states require reclamation bonds—either at the time the lease is obtained or prior to production, depending on the state—so that the state can pay for protecting and restoring the leased tract if the lessee fails to do so. Reclamation requirements allow return of the bond when, at a minimum, the well is capped. Capping involves pouring concrete down the well pipe to block it so that fluids, such as brine or low concentrations of oil and gas, cannot pass through the pipe to contaminate aquifers. Reclamation also requires the removal of all surface equipment and the subsequent grading and reseeding of the area.

Intergenerational Equity: Produce or Retain?

The most important decision states make in their mineral programs is whether and when to commit themselves to developing their resources. A state makes a long-term commitment to development at the time a minerals lease is issued, since provisions in state mineral leases allow the lessee to continue the lease as long as minerals are being produced. Lessees thus usually continue production as long as it is economically viable: in some individual oil and gas leases, state minerals have been in continuous production since the 1920s.

It seems reasonable to ask, first, whether mineral production is appropriate at a given site, and second, whether the present is the best time to make such a commitment. The timing of the lease commitment raises the equity issue between generations, commonly called *intergenerational equity*. Intergenerational equity deals with effects on future generations of present-day decisions. Effects on future generations fall into three distinct, but interrelated classes: economic effects, environmental effects, and social effects.

The basic economic equity question is whether the *value* of the resource should be *consumed* by current generations instead of being left for future ones. Underlying this question is the issue of whether present generations appropriately value the resource. For example, a production–consumption decision for oil and gas involves whether or not to consume the resource for its heating value. But alternative known and unknown uses exist for these resources: petrochemical companies are constantly developing new products—including medicines and plastics—that use hydrocarbons as basic building blocks. So one intergenerational issue is whether it is better (and for whom) to consume resources today when their future value is uncertain.

A second economic equity issue arises in the unique circumstance of the state trust lands. Because royalty payments from mineral production are placed in permanent funds, the value of the resource arguably continues to be maintained for future generations. Thus, the original production versus retention question (minus consideration of present-day compared to unknown future values) mutates into the question of whether the underlying value of the resource retained in the ground would increase at a rate less than, greater than, or equal to the permanent fund. Comparing these two values is more complex than this, however, because states typically distribute the annual dividends from their permanent funds to the beneficiaries, whereas resources retained in the ground provide no proceeds to current generations, but pass all of their increased value on to future ones. Finally, one key economic criterion for comparing retaining versus producing minerals is how well states' permanent funds retain their underlying value for passage to future generations.

Environmental intergenerational equity revolves around the present and future effects of mineral production. These environmental effects have spatial and temporal components, both of which affect current and future generations. Local, current, environmental effects from mineral production weigh heavily in initial production suitability considerations. And there are longer-term local environmental consequences such as potential groundwater pollution and tailings piles that may result from production decisions. Thus local environmental effects from a production decision directly affect both current generations and future generations in health and aesthetic terms, and indirectly affect them in relation to the underlying value of the trust parcel for other uses.

Larger-scale intergenerational environmental equity issues also arise in connection with states' production decisions. For example, acid rain is a predictable consequence of various types of mineral production by the states: copper refining, and oil and gas and coal consumption. Acid rain effects are typically regional, affecting the localities downwind from the producers/consumers. Global intergenerational environmental equity issues also result from hydrocarbon production decisions. Global climatic warming is hypothesized to be caused by the high levels of hydrocarbon burning that have occurred in the last thirty years. While the states' contribution to widespread environmental effects of mineral production is arguably minor, localized environmental effects are not necessarily so.

The third intergenerational equity issue revolves around present and future social effects of a state's mineral production decision. Here again, the effects may be both positive and negative. Beneficial social effects include those that typically result from high employment levels during minerals development and production, an advantage heightened by the comparatively high wages paid by mineral industries. These wages pump money into local economies, contributing to an overall higher quality of community life.

On the other hand, the very nature of mineralization means that at some point economic production ends. And at this ending, dependent local communities suffer adverse social effects: unemployment; bankruptcies; spousal, alcohol, and drug abuse; and a decreasing tax base that can cause communities to wither away. The underlying social equity question is whether it is appropriate to increase the social well-being of generations existing during mineral production when that choice contributes to the lack of social well-being in future generations.

Other important factors pertain to the comparative political costs of pursuing development (which are increasingly seen in terms of adverse environmental impacts) and of deferring development (which find expression in the need—rhetorical or actual—to find alternative sources of school funding if income from resource exploitation is delayed or forgone). The basic issue with respect to the state trust lands involves what a trustee's precise duties are, given the complicated nature of intergenerational equity issues. In two important cases (discussed in Chapters 4 and 5), both the *Nigh* and *Skamania* courts said that, by the terms of its creation, a state lands trust was not allowed to provide larger social benefits, such as subsidized loans to farmers and ranchers or protection for logging companies. And certainly, trustees have an obligation to be prudent in their management of permanent funds. But on the other hand, the permanent fund is not normally managed by the state trust lands' managers.

Recognizing that intergenerational equity arises in virtually all development decisions, we will use oil and gas management in New Mexico to illustrate the kinds of management decisions that present intergenerational equity issues. Oil and gas leasing is a peculiarly useful area to focus on because—in contrast to other resources—the timing decision here is crucial. If the trustee delays a timber harvest, the beneficiaries may not like waiting for the receipts; but in the absence of fire or similar catastrophe, the resource remains and even perhaps gains in value. Similarly, coal or hardrock minerals do not rot or evaporate simply because the state decides not to develop them at any given time. Oil and gas, however, are fugitive resources. Because they can migrate across ownerships, development timing is crucial. The state may be forced or induced to produce to maintain efficient pool pressure or to participate in forced unitization. New Mexico's experiences over the last twenty years provide various intergenerational effect examples resulting from production decisions that can be studied profitably.

The case of New Mexico provides a good example of the long-term factors involved in development decisions. Figure 6-9 shows twenty-five years of data on the growth of New Mexico's permanent fund in relation to royalty payments, annual disbursements to beneficiaries from the trust lands, and annual payments to beneficiaries from the permanent fund.[39] Permanent fund growth over this period is almost entirely the result of growth in oil and gas royalties, which began rising rapidly as production and prices increased after the two OPEC oil embargos in the mid- and late-1970s. New Mexico—like most other states—responded to increased interest in oil and gas production by leasing large trust land tracts for exploration. There was no strategic plan and no overall policy document to guide the leasing process. New Mexico simply responded to market forces indicating that it was good (at that time) to make a long-term commitment to producing oil and gas from its trust lands. And it certainly has been good to the trust, at least for current generations.

Present New Mexicans have benefited greatly from oil and gas production from trust lands. The state's permanent fund has grown rapidly and re-

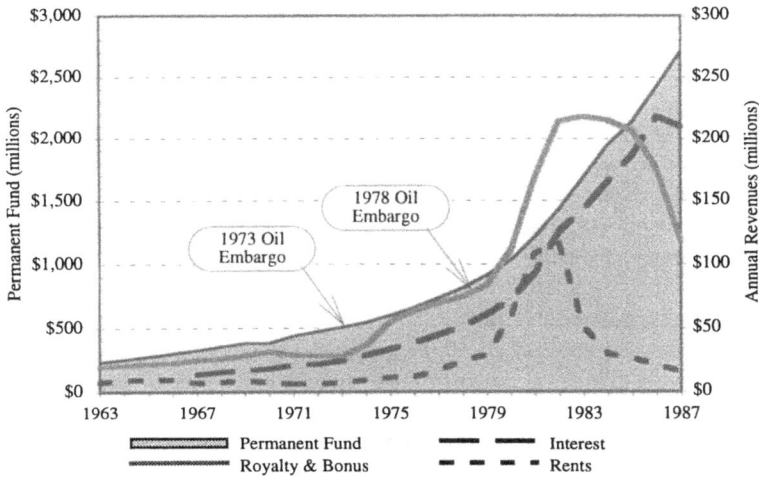

Figure 6-9. Revenue flows (in $ millions) in relation to the permanent funds in New Mexico 1963–1987. *Source:* NEW MEXICO STATE INVESTMENT COUNCIL, ANNUAL REPORT.

sulting dividends have quadrupled from approximately $50 million per year in 1980 to about $220 million per year by 1986.

The case can also be made that future generations benefit from this development as well, since the permanent fund has increased its value sevenfold from about $500 million dollars in 1973 (the first OPEC embargo) to about $3.4 billion by 1994. So at least from an economic intergenerational equity perspective, the oil and gas leasing and development that occurred in the 1970s and 1980s appears to have benefited both present and future generations.

However, proper analysis of economic equity considerations is not so simple. While New Mexico made long-term commitments to oil and gas production during this period, the economic returns it received from this leasing activity were less beneficial than first meets the eye in Figure 6-9. Many of the complexities arise from the lease terms and conditions discussed earlier. Although the state did not have an explicit leasing program or strategy, a clear commitment emerges from its lease terms: respond to market demands for leases and then allow them to be held by production. This unstated policy has enormous impacts on returns and on intergenerational equity.

First, the state receives a portion of the *value* of production, and not a specified amount of money per barrel of oil or thousand cubic feet of gas. Thus, the state receives more money in royalties when oil and gas prices are high, and less when prices are low. (And prices have been stable and low since the mid-1980s.) But the state's leases allow the lessees to make the production decisions, and lessees have to produce—as long as they cover their pumping and refining costs—in order to hold their leases (absent shut-in royalty). Thus the state, through its "held by production" lease provision, forces lessees to pursue oil and gas extraction during periods when prices are low, instead of waiting and letting rising prices encourage production (and higher royalties). The existing strategy benefits present generations (albeit inefficiently) through increased dividends, to the detriment of future generations.

Future generations are affected by this implicit production strategy, because it is questionable whether the present generation is actually passing resources on to future generations by placing royalties in the Permanent Fund. In the past and likely in the foreseeable future, high oil and gas prices typically coincide with periods of high inflation; indeed, high oil and gas prices are frequently a major contributing factor to high inflation. Inflation causes the values both of minerals and of the permanent fund—particularly dividends—to appear greater than they actually are. This illusion is particularly impressive in connection with the nominal value of the permanent fund in Figure 6-9, which is continually increased by royalty deposits. Equally illusory are the impressive beneficiary dividends paid out of high permanent fund interest rates during the late 1970s and early 1980s that resulted from inflation. From appearances, everything looks rosy for both current and future generations due to oil and gas production.

But the true story offers less reason for optimism with regard to current and future generations. Figure 6-10 shows evidence of this in the real rate of return received by New Mexico's permanent fund. While the nominal interest rate received on the permanent fund grows over the period from about 1 percent in 1963 to 9 percent by 1985, after inflation is removed (represented by the GNP deflator), the real rate of interest received by the permanent fund is revealed to have been frequently negative and provided only an actual rate of return on the order of 5 percent when it was positive. This negative or marginally positive interest rate in the real value of dividends is camouflaged by the ever-increasing distributions resulting from high royalty deposits. But even these dividends purchased less each year due to inflation. Even worse for future generations' equity, the real value of the permanent fund was decreased every year by inflation (albeit, again somewhat offset by increased royalty deposits).

Through its investment and dividend distribution policies, each state makes an implicit statement about how it values future generations. The amount of revenue that future generations are deprived of through inflationary effects on the permanent fund depends on two things: the fund's investment strategy [bonds and other fixed investments are particularly vul-

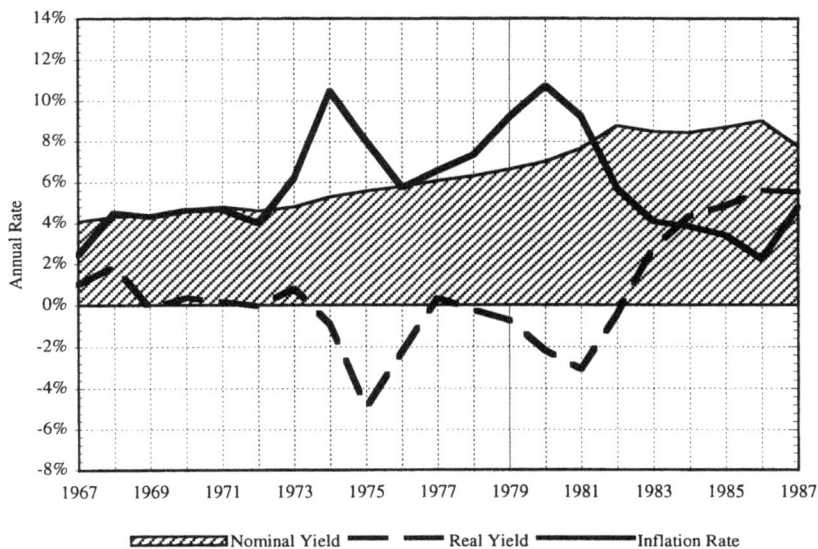

Figure 6-10. Nominal and real interest returns on New Mexico's permanent trust fund, 1964–1987.

nerable compared to stocks]; and whether a portion of the permanent fund is retained to offset inflation [so far only Montana does this]. If the fund invests in equity stocks, in comparison to bonds, it takes about half the present dividends from stocks compared to interest from bonds in exchange for future growth in the equity value of the permanent fund. And if the state retains interest and dividends to offset inflation, it explicitly acknowledges that permanent fund payments made to future generations are as important as those made to present ones. Permanent funds as a trust resource are discussed in greater detail in Chapter 7.

Moreover, while the political implications of producing a resource are sometimes great, as we discussed in Chapter 5, the ramifications of not producing may also be important. If commodity resources are not produced because their value is rising faster than the yields from the permanent fund, it may be necessary to obtain alternative funds to support the public schools. Alternative funding mechanisms include increasing local property taxes or state general taxes, or reallocating funds from other programs. These options are not necessarily easy for policymakers to contemplate. Their quandary is mitigated somewhat by the fact that, as discussed in Chapter 2, in most states, the school lands provide only a small percentage of the school resources; thus, the receipts from the trust simply provide the first drops in the school funding bucket, which become invisible when the state legislature appropriates the remainder of the state's share of school funds for the year. Nevertheless, the issue of the timing of the flow of revenues to the beneficiaries is an important component of the decision about the timing of development.

Conclusions

This chapter has emphasized two issues: intergenerational equity and the interplay of federal and state lands programs in mineral production. We conclude, as we did in Chapter 4, by discussing an ideal leasing scheme. States have moved beyond the federal models for mineral leasing in a number of significant ways. At bottom, however, the systems are similar and, we find, poorly thought out in terms of their appropriateness to trust goals.

FEDERAL STATE INTERPLAY AND AN IDEAL LEASING SYSTEM

As with grazing and timber, the federal government's minerals management programs dominate the discussion of all publicly held minerals. Unfortunately, the least evolved of the federal programs—the 1872 Mining Act—receives the greatest attention. As a result, most people remain unfamiliar with the general contours of the process used for accessing all minerals on state lands and energy minerals on federal lands. Unlike the 1872 act, that system gives the government enormous control over the timing, location, and intensity of development—control that is almost totally lacking in the location system the federal government employs for hardrock mining.

Observing the interplay between the federal and state systems enables astute critics to cut through the numerous misrepresentations that pervade this field of public debate. Despite advocacy to the contrary from both mining concerns and state officials, state hardrock leasing prospers where the deposits justify investment. State officials who complain that they cannot sell what the federal government is giving away are not vindicated by the facts. Their lot is undoubtedly adversely affected by federal hardrock giveaways, but where mineral value exists, they can and do sell leases. State mineral programs produce enormous revenues in five states: Colorado, New Mexico, Oklahoma, Texas, and Wyoming. At the federal level, mining concerns appear to be crying wolf when they argue that they could not operate effectively without the federal location system. They do just fine at the state level in the absence of the privileged access that "discovery" has traditionally entailed. The states offer more than twenty different models that the federal government could choose to emulate.

The interplay of state and federal programs also offers enormous perspective on making improvements. Most obvious minor improvements could be made in the area of access. For example, continuing the system of prospecting permits seems to have scant justification. The primary purpose of these permits is to give the prospector a right to lease if minerals are discovered in the area covered by the permit. However, permits are just as frequently used for speculative purposes as for exploration purposes. This is because, if the permit holder has an exclusive right to a lease, and especially if the permit can be held for a long period, it may be in the prospector's best interest to wait for surrounding mineral owners to determine whether economic deposits exist, and then develop or sell development rights to the state parcel. Some states have discovered that they can eliminate prospecting permits and go directly to leases that are constructed to provide incentives for the lessee to explore and, if warranted, produce minerals. Another area in which improvements could be made is in lease periods. Original lease periods should be established on the basis of the expected length of time reasonably needed to initiate mineral production. This time period could be expected to vary by resource and geographic area (as a result of prior exploration and/or development). Lease length can be reasonably negotiated so that the state's interest in development is protected.

But the central element of an ideal leasing system is for each state to have a plan. Rather than just picking up the general contours of the federal format, and elaborating it with a laudably diversified array of lease terms and conditions, the states ought to review their programs with a clear notion of what they are trying to accomplish. Recognizing that a mineral lease held by production makes a long-term commitment of trust resources, and observing that few states have an explicit mineral development strategy, our first recommendation is that states develop a sound strategic plan for their minerals program. Such a plan would do the following:

• Assess mineral availability on trust lands.
• Analyze potential extraction costs, both financially and environmentally.
• Schedule development plans for suitable minerals and parcels.
• Target uses for the resulting royalties.

Suitability for mineral development would be linked explicitly with the benefits to be derived from mineral royalties in a strategic land. This linkage should allow states to anticipate development opportunities, where these exist, while reducing the likelihood of entering into long-term leases in areas and under terms that are not in the beneficiaries' best interest.

Once a decision has been made to lease a tract or an area for mineral development, lease provisions protect the state's interests and provide incentives for the lessee to produce the minerals in a manner beneficial to the trust. Specifically, lease provisions should do the following:

• Encourage development when it is in the state's best interest, and discourage it otherwise.

- Make holding the lease for speculative purposes costly; that is, the provisions should motivate the lessee either to develop or to drop.
- Allow both the state and the lessee flexibility to reduce production during times of low prices. Typically this is handled through shut-in royalties, which could be reduced or credited to future rentals or royalties when in the state's best interest.

Much public discussion of royalties focuses on whether net or gross royalties are used. Our analysis shows that this does not much matter—that royalty rates are functionally equivalent, depending on adjustments made in the royalty formula prior to taking the state's percentage. This situation is not unlike the discussion in Chapter 4 of how grazing fees are calculated. In this case, cost deductions, far more than the base royalty rate, drive the benefit that the state receives. More interesting is the possibility that the state may obtain higher benefits through variable royalties than through fixed royalties. While most hardrock royalty rates are low enough to have only a minimal effect on production decisions, the state can benefit at the margin through variable royalties. Such a scheme might have the following components:

- The price used for the royalty calculation is indexed to market prices.
- The royalty percentage varies according to the concentration of the mineral, with a lower rate charged for lean concentrations and a higher rate for richer ones.
- The royalty calculation may be adjusted according to production costs.

INTERGENERATIONAL EQUITY

Ultimately, both the state's strategic plan and its standard lease provisions need to be analyzed in light of when and if the state's best interest is served by developing its mineral resources. The strategic plan can be used to identify areas suitable for development—areas where the likely benefits from production exceed the environmental and other opportunity costs incurred. Well-conceived lease provisions will provide incentives for development of these suitable areas. However, the development decision, the lease provisions, and intergenerational equity are linked by the fact that the initial production decision is only in the long-term interest of the trust if the proceeds are protected in the permanent fund. And this linkage between the permanent fund and development decisions has been absent in the past. It makes no sense, for example, to allow production of oil at a royalty value of $16.00 per barrel if the royalty proceeds are placed in a permanent fund where, due to inflationary effects, their value is reduced an equivalent of $8.00 per barrel after ten years, or to $4.00 a barrel after twenty years. And it especially does not benefit the trust if, as a result of mineral production, long-term commitments are made that preclude use of the area in the future, given that future uses and values are unknown.

Potential but currently underemphasized uses of trust resources are the subject of the next chapter. We explicitly discuss states' permanent funds as an underutilized trust resource. We emphasize the need to link the permanent fund with state land management strategies, as we have done here. Then we examine other potential trust assets—some that are extensive land uses (such as recreation), and others that are locally intensive (such as commercial developments and water resources). The point is to look through the portfolio lens at trust lands, their resources, and the resulting revenues.

APPENDIX: DETAILS OF STATE MINERAL LEASING PROCEDURES

This appendix provides specific state-by-state information on leasing procedures. The purpose of providing this information is to establish a basis for making comparisons of how the federal government and different states handle their mineral programs. General sources of information for these tables are state land office annual reports, state statutes, state administrative rules, and state lease forms.

The following tables are included in this appendix:

Table 6A-1. Comparative state hardrock mineral management policies.
Table 6A-2. Comparative state hardrock mineral fee and royalty policies.
Table 6A-3. Comparative state energy mineral management policies.
Table 6A-4. Comparative state energy mineral fee and royalty policies.

The notes that accompany these four tables are integral to understanding them. Since many minerals policies vary by resource and have changed through time, the notes accompanying the tables provide explanatory information. Sources for specific table information are identified. For coastal states, the oil and gas revenues listed represent only receipts from on-shore leases. Revenues produced from state sovereign lands (beds and banks of navigable waterways, as well as bays, inlets, and the inner coastal zone) are excluded where possible.

Because coal is managed similarly to hardrock minerals in some states, but similarly to oil and gas in others, the top lines in Tables 6A-1 and 6A-3 indicate where, for a specific state, coal leasing information is contained.

TABLE 6A-1. Comparative state hardrock mineral management policies

Phase and Policy	AK	AZ	CA	CO	ID	MT	NB	NM	ND	OK	OR	SD	TX	UT	WA	WY	US
Coverage																	
Metalliferous	Y	Y	Y	Y	Y	Y	Y	Y	Y		Y	Y	Y	Y	Y	Y	Y
Coal	N	Y	N	N	N	Y	Y	N	Y		Y	Y	Y	N	N	Y	N
Preproduction																	
Exploration Permits																	
Exclusive?	NU	Y	Y	NU	Y	Y	Y	NU	Y	Y	Y	Y	Y	NU	Y	NU	NU
Acreage limitation		20	960		20	640	N		N	160	N	640	640		640	N	¼–20
Initial term (years)	1	1	2		2	10	3		1	5	3	3	1		7		N/A
Max. renewal (years)		4	1		2	N	N		N	N	3	12	4		N		N/A
Preference to lease?	Y	Y	Y		Y	Y	Y	Y	Y	N	Y	Y	Y	Y	Y	Y	N/A
"Delay" Rental Lease?				N	Y	Coal	Y	Y	Y	NU		Y	N, Y	Y	NU	N	NU
Auction?	N	N	N	N	N		N	N	N	Y	N	N	N	N		N	
Max. initial term (years)		1	20	10	10	10	3	3	10	5	10	3	20	10	10	10	
Renewal term (years)		1	10	HBP	HBP	HBP	HBP	2	HBP	HBP	HBP	12	HBP	2	2	10	
Acreage limitation	N	20	960	N	640	640	HBP	640	160	160	640	640	N	2,560	2,560	1,280	
Competitive Leases in																	
Known Mineral Areas?	N	N	Y	Y	Y	N	N/A	Y	Y	N/A	Y	N	N	N	N	N	NU
Lease Only if in State's Best Interest?	N	N	Y	Y	Y	Y	Y	Y	Y	Y	Y	Y	Y	Y	Y	N/A	
Production																	
Max. initial term (years)		20	20	10	10	10	3	3	5	5	10	5	20	10	20	10	NU
Renewal term (years)		20	10	HBP	HBP	HBP	HBP	20	HBP	HBP	10	12	HBP	HBP	20	10	
Allowable length (years)	55	40	HBP	HBP	HBP	HBP	HBP	HBP	HBP	HBP	50	HBP	HBP	HBP	HBP	N/A	
Acreage limitation	N	20	960	N	640	640	N	640	160	160	640	640	N	2,560	640	1,280	
Postproduction																	
Reclamation required?	Y	Y	Y	Y	Y	Y	Y	Y	Y	Y	Y	Y	Y	Y	Y	Y	N

Codes: N/A = not applicable; NU = not used; HBP = held by production; Y = yes; N = no.

Notes:

General reference: GENERAL ACCOUNTING OFFICE, MINERAL ROYALTIES: ROYALTIES IN THE WESTERN STATES AND IN MAJOR MINERAL-PRODUCING COUNTRIES. GAO/RCED-93-109 (March 1993).

Alaska: Alaska has both claim and lease systems. Information here is for leases. See GAO report for details.

Arizona: 9 ARIZONA REVISED STATUTES ANNOTATED, title 27, Minerals, Oil and Gas; 11B ARIZONA REVISED STATUTES ANNOTATED, title 37, Public Lands (West 1993, 4/1994 Suppl.); ARIZONA ADMINISTRATIVE CODE, title 12. Natural Resources, ch. 5, Land Department, arts. 18, 19 (Mineral Leases, Prospecting Permits) (June 30, 1994). Arizona has exploration permits, but also allows location claims similar to the 1872 Mining Act. Mineral leases require prior discovery; therefore, no "delay rental" is used, although $100 per claim per year development is required.

California: CALIFORNIA CODE OF REGULATIONS, title 2, Administration, Division 3, State Property Operations, ch. 1; State Lands Commission. (Barclays 4-1-90). Also PUBLIC RESOURCES CODE, div. 6 (Rev 1-1-83). See also GAO Report, note 1.

Colorado: Colorado State Board of Land Commissioners, "Guidelines, Colorado Mining Leases" (1987).

Idaho: IDAHO CODE, title 47, ch. 7. State Board of Land Commissioners, "Rules and Regulations Governing Exploration and Surface Mining Operations in Idaho" (IDAPA 20:09, November 1, 1989).

Montana: MONTANA CODE ANNOTATED § 77-3-100 et seq.

Nebraska: NEBRASKA STATUTES §§ 72-301 et seq. No statutory limit on holdings, but 640 acres is generally the largest-size lease. The state has the option to issue prospecting permits or leases; it usually chooses to lease. All leases are offered publicly. No statute requires reclamation, but the state conditions the lease.

New Mexico: New Mexico State Land Office, SLO Rule 2 (January 10, 1984).

North Dakota: North Dakota Century Code § 38-11-02 (West 1964 & 1992 Supp.). Also, "Mining Lease." North Dakota Land Board has not established leasing rules for hardrock minerals. Only materials (sand, gravel, scoria) are presently produced.

Oklahoma: OKLAHOMA STATUTES ANNOTATED, ch. 64, § 451.

Oregon: OREGON ADMINISTRATIVE RULES, ch. 141, div. 71, §§ 400-660 (September 1982). Leaseholder has the right of first refusal to request that the division renew the lease for an additional period of time past the original 50-year limit.

South Dakota: SOUTH DAKOTA CODIFIED LAWS §§ 5-7-18 to 5-7-33 (including laws that went into effect 7/1/93). SOUTH DAKOTA ADMINISTRATIVE RULES, title 4.

Texas: TEXAS GENERAL LAND OFFICE, NATURAL RESOURCES CODE, ch. 53; and TEXAS ADMINISTRATIVE CODE, ch. 10. Exploration and development of coal, lignite, sulfur, salt, and potash are handled by sealed-bid lease sale; exploration of all other minerals, and shell, sand, and gravel are under prospect permits and preference right leases (T.A.C. § 10.1(b)(1)). For "Relinquishment" Act lands, sold between 1895 and 1931, the state retains the mineral interest, but the surface land owner is generally allowed to act as the state's agent for mineral leasing and receives a 20 percent share of the bonus, rental, and royalties as payment (T.A.C. § 10.5). Exploration permit acreage limits are plus or minus 10 percent of 640 acres, to accommodate survey errors. Initial terms range from 1 to 20 years.

Utah: Utah Natural Resources—State Lands and Forestry, "Rules Governing the Management and Use of State Lands in Utah" (43d ed., August 1993).

Washington: WASHINGTON REVISED CODE, 79.14.070. Washington issues a "Mining Contract." A conversion period includes the time leading up to commercial production after discovery is made. During this time, a plan of development is submitted to the Washington Department of Natural Resources.

Wyoming: Wyoming Board of Land Commissioners and Wyoming Farm Loan Board, "Rules and Regulations Governing Leasing of Sub-surface Resources" (effective March 1, 1982). WYOMING STATUTES, title 36, ch. 6. Mineral Leases. Board of Land Commissioners, "Rules and Regulations," ch. 16—Surface and Subsurface Survey Activities (May 1990). Subsurface lease activities are authorized (§ 16-3) after notice to surface lessee and state, and agreement to pay surface damages to lessee and state.

United States: 43 C.F.R. Part 3840 (hardrock mining claims under the 1872 Mining Act); Part 3500 (solid minerals other than coal and oil shale, including phosphate, sodium, potassium, sulfur, and gilsonite). Under the 1872 act, there are two types of location claims: lode and placer. Lode claims allow up to 1500' by 600' along a vein; placer claims allow an individual 20 acres, with a total claim of 160 acres allowed for an association (43 C.F.R. 3844, 3842.1-2). Five-acre patents are available for mill sites (43 C.F.R. 3844). The assessment work requirement of $100 per claim per year (43 C.F.R. 3851.1) has been replaced by payment to the Bureau of Land Management of this amount to continue possessory interest in a location claim.

225

TABLE 6A-2. Comparative state hardrock mineral fee and royalty policies

Phase and Policy	AK	AZ	CA	CO	ID	MT	NB	NM	ND	OK	OR	SD	TX	UT	WA	WY	US
Preproduction																	
Exploration Permit	NU	Y	Y	NU	Y	Y		NU	N/A	Y	Y	Y	Y	NU	Y	NU	NU
Initial (years - to -)		1-1	1-2		1-2	1-3				0-5	1-3	1-3	1-1		1-3	1-5	N/A
($/acre/year)		$2.00	$1.00		$50.00	$1.00				N/A	$0.50	$1.00	$0.50		$2.00	$1.00	
Renewal (years - to -)		3-5	3-3		N/A						4-6		2-5		4-7	6-10	N/A
($/acre/year)		$1.00	$1.00		N/A	$2.50-$3.00					$5.00	$2.00-$10.00	$0.50		$3.00	$2.00	
Required Development			NU							NU		NU		N/A		NU	
Initial (years - to -)	1-2	1-2			1-2										1-7		
($/acre/year)	$5.00	$10.00			$100/yr	$2.50/ lease					$1.00-$3.00				$3.00		$100/yr
Subsequent (years - to -)	3-	3-5									4-6						
($/acre/year)	$10.00	$20.00			N/A	$2.50/ lease					$45.00				N/A		N/A
Production																	
Surface Rental																	
Initial period (- to -)	0-5		1-20	1-10	1-10	1-3	See Notes	1-3	1-5		1-10	1-3	1-1	1-10	1-5	1-5	
($/acre/year)	$0.50	$15.00/ claim	$1.00	$2.00	$1.00	$1.00		$0.05	$1.00		$1.00	$1.00	$2.00	$1.00	$5.00	$2.00	$0
Subsequent (- to -)	6-10		21-30	11-	11-20	6-	N	4-5	6-		11-	4-5	2-		6-10	6-10	
($/acre/year)	$1.00	$15.00/ claim	$1.00	$2.00	$1.00	$3.00		$0.50	$1.00		$1.00	$2.00	$1.00	$1.00	$10.00	$2.00	$0
Royalty Calculation																	
Rent credit to royalty?	N	Y	N	N	Y	N	N	N	N/A	N	Y	Y	N	Y	Y	Y	N
Constant or variable?	C	R,V,C	R,V	V	C,R,V	R,V	V	R,V	N/A	C	R	C	R	R,C	C	R,V	R
Net (N) or gross (G)?	N	N	N,G	N,G	G	G	G	G	N/A	G	G	G	G	R,N,G	G	G	G
Minimum Royalty (%)																	
Metalliferous	3	5	10	4-7	2¾-10	5	5		1½-5		5	2	6¼		5	5	0
Copper		2-8		4-7	2¾-10			2						4		5	0
Gold/silver		2-8		4-7	2¾-10			2		5	5			4		5	0
Uranium			10	6-10	2½-10			5	5-15	5	5			8 (G)	5,R		0
Nonmetalliferous	3	5	10		2¾-10					Neg.	Neg.	2	6¼				0
Bentonite/zeolite																10	0
Diatomite																5	0
Gemstone				7		5		5						10 (G)		5	Case
Gilsonite														10 (N)			5
Phosphate					5%									5 (N)			Case
Potash								5					6¼	2 (N)		5	5
Sulfur								2½					12½	12½		5	5
Trona														5		8	0
Other minerals	3	5	10	4-7	5-10	V	5	2-8	N/A	Neg.	Neg.	2	6¼	5	5	5-10	0, 2

Codes: N/A = not applicable; NU = not used; G = gross; N = net; R = by resource; C = constant, V = variable; Y = yes; N = no; Neg. = negotiable.

Notes:
General reference: GENERAL ACCOUNTING OFFICE, MINERAL ROYALTIES: ROYALTIES IN THE WESTERN STATES AND IN MAJOR MINERAL-PRODUCING COUNTRIES. GAO/RCED-93-109 (March 1993).

Alaska: Alaska has both claim and lease systems. Information here is for leases. See GAO report for details.

Arizona: 9 ARIZONA REVISED STATUTES ANNOTATED, title 27, Minerals, Oil and Gas; 11B ARIZONA REVISED STATUTES ANNOTATED, title 37, Public Lands (West 1993, 4/1994 Suppl.); ARIZONA ADMINISTRATIVE CODE, title 12, Natural Resources, ch. 5, Land Department, arts. 18, 19 (Mineral Leases, Prospecting Permits) (June 30, 1994). Leases require $100/claim/year worth of development. The net royalty equals gross proceeds minus processing, transport, and taxes (R-12-5-1805(E)(1)). Differences in requirements between Type A claims (vein, lode, or ledge re. 1872 Mining Act) or Type B claim (any mineral deposit using public lands survey boundary).

California: CALIFORNIA CODE OF REGULATIONS, title 2. Administration, div. 3, State Property Operations, ch. 1, State Lands Commission. (Barclays 4-1-90). Also PUBLIC RESOURCES CODE, div. 6. (Rev. 1-1-83). California requires an advance deposit of $3,000 (CEQA-exempt) to $5,000 (CEQA surface disturbance review) for processing costs, environmental reviews, and mitigation monitoring prior to issuing a prospecting permit or a lease. The royalty calculation allows commission-approved transport or processing deductions in determining the state's royalty share of gross value (P.R.C. § 6895). The state will negotiate for the net smelter returns royalty calculation.

Colorado: Colorado State Board of Land Commissioners, "Guidelines, Colorado Mining Leases." 1987. Rent is not credited to royalty after production starts.

Idaho: IDAHO CODE title 47, ch. 7. State Board of Land Commissioners, "Rules and Regulations Governing Exploration and Surface Mining Operations in Idaho" (IDAPA 20:09, November 1, 1989). Idaho has a comprehensive set of royalty schedules for industrial minerals and construction materials. Generally, the royalty is 5 percent of gross value minus any transportation charges to the point of sale. However, for each commodity, a royalty rate per ton is also allowed, based on whichever is the greater amount, either 5 percent of gross or: 1¢/lb. for garnet or staurolite; 50¢/bank cu. yd. or 38¢/short ton for sand and gravel; 75¢/bank cu. yd. or $1.00/short ton for diatomaceous earth; 75¢/bank cu. yd. or 50¢/short ton for clay, silica, feldspar sands and mica; $2.65/bank cu. yd., $1.50/loose cu. yd., or $1.15/short ton for pumice and volcanic minerals; 10 percent of net sales value of the finished product for gem quality stones and 12 percent (but not less than $12.50/ton) for raw industrial-grade stones; and a royalty of between 2.5 percent and 10 percent for uranium and other fissionable products depending on their assay percentage (concentration). "Bank" cubic yard is defined as the volume in place prior to removal; for sand and gravel, a conversion factor of 15 percent shrinkage (25 percent in Ada County) is allowed for measurement after removal and a conversion of 1 bank cu. yd. equals 1.5 short tons is assumed. In addition, for gemstones, a prepaid royalty is assessed for renewal leases of $500.00 per year per lease for years one through five and $1,000 per year per lease for lease years six through ten. This prepaid royalty will be credited against production royalties on a lease year basis.

Montana: MONTANA CODE ANNOTATED § 77-3-100 et seq.

Nebraska: NEBRASKA STATUTES §§ 72-301 et seq, for statutory minimum rent. Sand and gravel leases are the state's second highest mineral use. Statutory minimum royalty of 5 percent. Rent for sand and gravel is $50 per acre per year plus 5 percent royalty.

New Mexico: New Mexico State Land Office, SLO Rule 2 (January 10, 1984).

North Dakota: NORTH DAKOTA CENTURY CODE § 38-11-02 (West 1964 & 1992 Supp.). Also, "Mining Lease." See notes for Table 7A-3.

Oklahoma: OKLAHOMA STATUTES ANNOTATED, ch. 64, § 451.

Oregon: OREGON ADMINISTRATIVE RULES, ch. 141, div. 71, §§ 400-660 (September 1982).

South Dakota: SOUTH DAKOTA CODIFIED LAWS §§ 5-7-18 to 5-7-33 (including laws that went into effect 7/1/93). SOUTH DAKOTA ADMINISTRATIVE RULES, title 4. Royalty of 2 percent of gross returns minus transport and smelting or reduction costs.

Texas: TEXAS GENERAL LAND OFFICE, NATURAL RESOURCES CODE, ch. 53 and TEXAS ADMINISTRATIVE CODE, ch. 10. Royalties are calculated at the mine mouth, with some exceptions for post-"mine" costs. Royalty and rental amounts are statutory minimums; higher rates can be negotiated.

Utah: Utah Natural Resources—State Lands and Forestry, "Rules Governing the Management and Use of State Lands in Utah" (43d ed., August 1993).

Washington: WASHINGTON REVISED CODE, 79.14.070. Surface rentals for years 11 through 20 is $20.00/acre/year.

Wyoming: Wyoming Board of Land Commissioners and Wyoming Farm Loan Board, "Rules and Regulations Governing Leasing of Sub-surface Resources" (effective March 1, 1982). WYOMING STATUTES, title 36, ch. 6. Mineral Leases. Board of Land Commissioners, "Rules and Regulations," ch. 16–Surface and Subsurface Survey Activities (May 1990).

United States: 43 C.F.R. Part 3840 (hardrock mining claims under the 1872 Mining Act); Part 3500 (solid minerals other than coal and oil shale, including phosphate, sodium, potassium, sulfur, and gilsonite). Royalties for gilsonite (a hard asphalt compound) and potash are determined on a site-specific case-by-case basis. Royalties for sodium and potassium are 2 percent of gross value.

TABLE 6A-3. Comparative state energy mineral management policies

Phase and Policy	AK	AZ	CA	CO	ID	MT	NB	NM	ND	OK	OR	SD	TX	UT	WA	WY	US
Coverage																	
Oil and gas		Y	Y	Y	Y	Y	Y	Y	Y	Y	Y	Y	Y	Y	Y	Y	Y
Coal		N	N	N		Y	N	N	Y	N	N	N	N	Y	N	Y	Y
Geothermal		Y	Y	N		N	N	Y	N	N	Y	Y	N	Y	N	N	N
Preproduction																	
Geophysical Permits																	
Auction?		NU	Y	Y	Y	Y	Y	Y	Y	Y	Y	Y	Y	NU	NU	NU	N
Acreage limitation										160		640					
Term (years)			3	1	3 mo.	1			1		Neg.	5	1 mo.				
Max. renewal (years)				NU	3 mo.	N/A	1–2 mo.	3 mo.		6 mo.	Neg.	HBP	1 mo.				
Preference to lease?			N	N	N	N	N	N	N	N	N	Y	N				
"Delay" Rental Lease?																	
Auction?	Y	S	NU	Y	Y	Y	Y	Y	Y	Y	Y	Y	Y	S	Y	Y	Y
Max. primary term (years)		5		5	5	10	5, 10	5	5	3	10	5	5	10	5–10	5	5, 10
Secondary term (years)		HBP		1	5	HBP	HBP	5	HBP	3	HBP	HBP	GF		HBP	HBP	
Acreage limitation		2,560			640	640	N	1,280	160	160	Neg.	640	2,560	2,560	640	720	2,560
Production																	
Max. primary term (years)		5	20		10	10	5, 10	5	5	3	10	5	5	10	5–10	5	5, 10
Secondary term (years)		HBP	HBP		HBP	HBP	HBP	HBP	HBP	HBP	HBP	HBP	HBP		HBP	HBP	HBP
Acreage limitation		2,560	960		640	640	N	1,280	160	640	N	640	2,560	2,560	640	720	2,560
"Pugh" Clauses?																	
Areal	Y		Y		Y	N		Y	Y	Y	N	Y	N	N	Y	Y	
Depth	Y		Y		Y	Y		N	N	Y	N	N	Y	N	Y	N	
Pooling / Unitization?																	
Voluntary		Y	Y	Y	Y	Y	Y	Y	Y	Y	Y	Y	Y	Y	Y	Y	Y
Forced		N	N	N	Y	Y	Unclear	Y	Y	Y	Y	N	Y		Y	Y	N
Postproduction																	
Shut-in royalty ($/ac)	$1.00	None	$2.00	$2.00	N	$100–400 lease/year	Rent	Twice Rent	$10.00	$1–3	$1.00	$1.00	$1,200	$1.00	$5.00	$2.00	NU
Reclamation required?		Y	Y	Y	Y	Y	Y	Y	Y	Y	Y	Y	Y	Y	Y	Y	Y

Codes: N/A = not applicable; NU = not used; S = some minerals; GF = good faith, HBP = held by production; Y = yes; N = no; Neg. = negotiable.

Notes:

General: Montana Department of State Lands, "Questionnaire Results: Oil and Gas Lease/Rules Terms As of May, 1991" [hereinafter cited as 1991 Questionnaire].

Alaska: *Source:* 1991 Montana Questionnaire.

Arizona: 9 ARIZONA REVISED STATUTES ANNOTATED, title 27, Minerals, Oil and Gas; 11B ARIZONA REVISED STATUTES ANNOTATED, title 37, Public Lands (West 1993, 4/1994 Suppl.); ARIZONA ADMINISTRATIVE CODE, title 12. Natural Resources, ch. 5, Land Department, arts. 21, 22 (Oil and Gas Leases, Geothermal Leases) (June 30, 1994). Competitive leases in known geological areas; otherwise, noncompetitive. Competitive parcel size limitation is 1,280 acres. Geothermal leases have a term of ten years.

California: CALIFORNIA CODE OF REGULATIONS, title 2. Administration, div. 3, State Property Operations, ch. 1, State Lands Commission. (Barclays 4-1-90). Also, PUBLIC RESOURCES CODE, div. 6 (Rev 1-1-83). For geothermal, leases or prospecting permits may be given. Geothermal prospecting leases are sold by sealed bids.

Colorado: Colorado State Board of Land Commissioners, "Guidelines, Colorado Oil and Gas Leases" (1987). Prior to 1986, Colorado leases had a five-year extension period. Minimum lease size is 40 acres.

Idaho: IDAHO CODE title 47, ch. 7. State Board of Land Commissioners, "Rules and Regulations Governing Exploration and Surface Mining Operations in Idaho" (IDAPA 20.09, November 1, 1989).

Montana: MONTANA CODE ANNOTATED §§ 77-3-100 et seq.

Nebraska: NEBRASKA STATUTES §§ 72-901 et seq. No statute on geophysical permits; state issues for 30-60 days. For existing oil and gas lease, lessee approval is required for others' geophysical exploration. Auctions are oral. No Pugh clauses are used at present. Pre-1990 production only from Jay Sands (4,500'–5,000'); post-1990 some production from Permian layer (8,500'–9,000'). Shut-in royalty requires payment of rent and state approval.

New Mexico: New Mexico State Land Office, SLO Rule 2 (January 10, 1984).

North Dakota: NORTH DAKOTA CENTURY CODE § 38-11-02 (West 1964 & 1992 Supp.); Board of University and School Lands, "Coal Rules and Regulations" and "Geothermal Lease Rules."

Oklahoma: OKLAHOMA STATUTES ANNOTATED, ch. 64, § 451.

Oregon: OREGON ADMINISTRATIVE RULES §§ 141-70-000 through 141-70-170. State of Oregon, Division of State Lands, "Oil and Gas Lease." The term and maximum renewal for geophysical permits are subject to negotiation with the Division of State Lands. The size of delay rental leases issues subject to negotiation with the division, but no lease may be issued for greater than 40 acres without auction.

South Dakota: SOUTH DAKOTA CODIFIED LAWS §§ 5-7-18 to 5-7-33 (including laws that went into effect 7/1/93). SOUTH DAKOTA ADMINISTRATIVE RULES, title 4.

Texas: TEXAS ADMINISTRATIVE CODE, title 31, §§ 9.1–9.9 found in 14 TEXAS REGISTER 2775 et seq. (June 9, 1989). Shut-in payment is double the annual rental or $1,200 for each well. Primary terms run from one to five years.

Utah: Utah Natural Resources—State Lands and Forestry, "Rules Governing the Management and Use of State Lands in Utah" (43d ed., August 1993).

Washington: Washington Department of Natural Resources, "Oil and Gas Leasing Program" (July 1985). WASHINGTON REVISED CODE § 79.14.070. Washington issues five- to ten-year leases for exploration and production. Continuation of lease past the initial period is by production, drilling, or work leading to production.

Wyoming: Wyoming Board of Land Commissioners and Wyoming Farm Loan Board, "Rules and Regulations Governing Leasing of Sub-surface Resources" (effective March 1, 1982). Board of Land Commissioners, "Rules and Regulations," ch. 16–Surface and Subsurface Survey Activities (May 1990). Subsurface lease activities are authorized (§ 16-3) after notice to surface lessee and state, and agreement to pay surface damages to lessee and state.

United States: 43 C.F.R., Parts 3100 (Oil and Gas), 3200 (Geothermal), and 3400 (Coal). Geophysical permits for oil and gas exploration are not required except in Alaska; a notice of intent to conduct the operations is sufficient. The term of delay rentals for oil and gas differs: five years for competitive leases; ten years for noncompetitive (that is, over-the-counter, if no competitive bids are offered). The maximum leased area also differs: 2,560 acres for competitive leases and 10,240 for noncompetitive. Maximum lease sizes and many other leasing procedures differ for Alaska and offshore areas.

TABLE 6A-4. Comparative state energy mineral fee and royalty policies

Phase and Policy	AK	AZ	CA	CO	ID	MT	NB	NM	ND	OK	OR	SD	TX	UT	WA	WY	US
Preproduction																	
Geophysical Permit																	
Initial (years - to -) ($/acre/year)	1-1 $1.00	1-5 $1.00	1-3 $0	1-1	$100/mile			$100-200	1-1 $1.00	0-5 V	$50/permit	NU	$850-900/mi		NU	NU	NU
Renewal (years - to -) ($/acre/year)			NU	NU		N/A		N/A	N/A	N/A	$50/permit		$850-900/mi				
Required Development																	
Primary (years - to -) ($/acre/year)			NU	1-5 $1.00	1-5 GF	6-6 $1.25		1-5 $0.25		NU	NU	NU	NU		$1.25		
Secondary (years - to -) ($/acre/year)				6- $10.00	6-10 $1.00	7-10 $2.50		6-10 $0.50							$1.25		
Production																	
Oil and Gas Rental																	
Initial period (- to -) ($/acre/year)	1-1 $1.00	1-5 $1.00	1-20 $1.00	1-5 $1.00	1-10 $1.00	1-10 $1.50	$1.00-2.00	$0.25-1.00	1-5 $1.00	1-2 $1.00	1-5 $1.00	1-3 $1.00	1-5 $0	1-10 $1.00	1-10 $1.25	1- $1.00	1-5 $1.50
Subsequent (- to -) ($/acre/year)	$1.50-3.00	6- $1.00	HBP $1.00	6- $10.00	11- $1.50-3	11- $1.50	$1.00-2.00	$0.25-1.00	6- $0	2-3 $2.00	6-10 $1.00	4-5 $2.00	$0	11- $1.00		Prod. $2.00	6- $2.00
Coal Rental																	
Initial period (- to -) ($/acre/year)		$15.00/claim	N/A	1-5 $1.00	N/A	1-10 $3.00		1-5 $5.00	1-5 $3.00	V	N/A	N/A	1-1 $2.00	1- $1.00	1-20 $10.00	1-5 $1.00	1-20 $3.00
Subsequent (- to -) ($/acre/year)		$15.00/claim		6-10 $11.00		11- $3.00		6-10 $5.00	6-8 $5.00				2- $1.00			6-10 $2.00	

TABLE 6A-4 *(Continued)*

Phase and Policy	AK	AZ	CA	CO	ID	MT	NB	NM	ND	OK	OR	SD	TX	UT	WA	WY	US
Geothermal Rental																	
Initial period (- to -)		1–10	1–10	1–	1–5	N/A		1–5	N/A	N/A	1–3	N/A			1–5	1–5	1–10
($/acre/year)		$1.00	$1.00	$1.00	$1.00			$1.00			$1.00			$1.00	$1.25	$1.00	$1.00
Subsequent (- to -)		11–	HBP	N/A	6–10			6–10			5–10				6–10	6–10	11–80
($/acre/year)		$1.00	$1.00		$2.00			$5.00			$5.00			$1.00	$2.50	$2.00	$1.00
Royalty Calculation																	
Rent credit to royalty?	N	Y	N	N,Y	N	Y,N	Y	N	N	N	N	N	Y	Y	Y	Y	Y, N
Constant or variable?		R	R	V	R	R	V	C	V	C	R	R	R	R	V	R,V	
Net (*N*) or gross (*G*)?	*N*	*G*	*G*	*N,G*	*G*	*G*	*G*	*G*	*N,G*	*N*	*G*	*G*	*G*	*G*	*G*	*G*	
Minimum Royalty (%)																	
Oil–primary	12½–16⅔	12½	16⅔	12½	12½	13	12½–16⅔	12½–20	12½–16⅔	18¾	12½	12½	12½–25	12½	12½	16⅔	12½
Oil–secondary			16⅔	12½	12½	13		12½–20	12½–16⅔	18¾					12½	16⅔	
Gas	12½–16⅔	12½	16⅔	12½	12½	12½	12½–16⅔	12½–20	12½–16⅔	18¾	12½	12½	12½–25	12½	12½	16⅔	12½
Coal–surface		5	N/A	12½	N/A	12½	5	12½	6–8	V	N/A	N/A	6¼	8	V	12½	12½
Coal–underground		5	N/A	8	N/A	10	5	8	N/A	V	N/A	N/A	6¼	8	V	8	8
Geothermal		12½	10–16⅔	N/A	10	N/A	5	10	N/A	N/A	10	10		10	10	N/A	10–15

Codes: N/A = not applicable; NU = not used; GF = good faith; R = by resource, V = variable; HBP = held by production; *N* = net; *G* = gross; Y = yes; N = no.

Notes to Table 6A-4:

General: Montana Department of State Lands, "Questionnaire Results: Oil and Gas Lease/Rules Terms As of May, 1991" [hereinafter cited as 1991 Montana Questionnaire].

Alaska: *Source:* 1991 Montana Questionnaire.

Arizona: 9 ARIZONA REVISED STATUTES ANNOTATED, title 27, Minerals, Oil and Gas; 11B ARIZONA REVISED STATUTES ANNOTATED, title 37, Public Lands (West 1993, 4/1994 Suppl.); ARIZONA ADMINISTRATIVE CODE, title 12. Natural Resources, ch. 5, Land Department, arts. 21, 22 (Oil and Gas Leases, Geothermal Leases) (June 30, 1994). Coal leases and royalty provisions handled under hard rock regulations (see Tables 6-4 and 6-5).

California: CALIFORNIA CODE OF REGULATIONS, title 2. Administration, div. 3, State Property Operations, ch. 1, State Lands Commission (Barclays 4-1-90). Also, PUBLIC RESOURCES CODE, div. 6 (Rev. 1-1-83). California can use a net profits lease for oil and gas (P.R.C. § 6827). Geothermal rental rates increase substantially: first year rental is $1.00/acre; second is not more than $5.00/acre; and for the third year and every year thereafter, rent is not more than $25.00/acre until a well is drilled (P.R.C. § 6910). After production is initiated, rent is renegotiated to not less than $1.00 per acre per year, with a minimum royalty of $2.00 per acre per year (P.R.C. § 6913). Minimum geothermal lease is 640 acres, with maximum 5,760 acres (P.R.C. § 6922).

Colorado: Colorado State Board of Land Commissioners, "Guidelines, Colorado Oil and Gas Leases" (1987). Geophysical permits are not required prior to leasing, and are not required on land leased by the permittee. However, they are required on land not leased by the permittee. Coal leases require a $10.00 per acre per year recoupable advance royalty for extensions beyond the initial five-year term. If production does not occur after the tenth year, the lessee gives up the lease or renegotiates a new lease. There has been no competition for coal leases in the last several years, so auctions have not been necessary. Oil and gas rights are leased after public auction for a five-year term. Lessee can apply for a one-year extension for a five-year term. Colorado has no existing geothermal production; rent would be $1.00 per acre per year, but royalty is to be set by the board as a percentage of market value. *Source:* Letter from Mark Davis, Minerals Manager, Colorado Board of Land Commissioners, November 28, 1994.

Idaho: IDAHO CODE, title 47, ch. 7. State Board of Land Commissioners, "Rules and Regulations Governing Exploration and Surface Mining Operations in Idaho" (IDAPA 20.09, November 1, 1989). The surface rental rate for geothermal leases increases to $3.00 per acre per year for lease years 11 and onward.

Montana: Montana geophysical permits are $50.00 per shothole and $100.00 per mile for vibroseis. Royalty payments are credited to rent for oil and gas, but not for coal.

Nebraska: NEBRASKA STATUTES §§ 72-901 et seq. Geophysical exploration fees are $500 per mile for grassland (state owns grass) and the maximum of either $50 per mile or the amount of the surface damage payment to the cropland lessee. Damages must be paid to state and lessee. Oil and gas rental and royalty rates depend on location. There are three different possibilities: in areas with significant production history (generally, southwestern Nebraska) rental is $2.00 per acre per year with a royalty of 1/6 (16.67 percent) and a term of five years; in counties bordering these areas, rent is $2.00 per acre per year with a royalty of 1/8 (12.5 percent) and a term of five years; and in all other counties, rental fee is $1.00 per acre per year with a royalty of 1/8 (12.5 percent) and a term of ten years.

New Mexico: New Mexico State Land Office, "SLO Rule 1 Relating to Oil and Gas Lease" (6/19/85); "SLO Rule 6 Relating to Coal Leases on State Land" (8/23/89), "SLO Rule 7 Relating to Geothermal Resources Leases" (1/20/84), and "SLO Rule 17 Relating to Seismic Exploration on Unleased State Lands" (8/3/88).

North Dakota: NORTH DAKOTA CENTURY CODE § 38-11-02 (West 1964 & 1992 Suppl.). Also, "Mining Lease." Net royalties are used for coal leases based on the cost of mining. Coal leases have a minimum royalty of 6 percent or 15¢ per ton, recent leases have been 8 percent or 25¢ per ton. Gross royalties at wellhead are used for oil and gas, based on posted field prices.

Oklahoma: Commissioners of the Land Office, "Rules and Regulations Governing Sale and Operation of Oil and Gas Leases" (November, 1990). OKLAHOMA ADMINISTRATIVE RULES §§ 3-101 through 3-161. Oklahoma requires that exploration companies pay surface damages as well as obtain a lease or approval of the working interest owner.

Oregon: OREGON ADMINISTRATIVE RULES, §§ 141-75-010 through 141-75-200 and §§ 141-70-000 through 141-70-170. State of Oregon, Division of State Lands, "Oil and Gas Lease." Rental for years six through ten includes a $1.00 per acre per year delay penalty until a well is drilled. Geothermal fees are $50.00 for each exploration application and $100 for each exploration permit issuance. Geothermal rentals for year four of the lease are $3.00 per acre. Geothermal renewals past year 10 are $5.00 per acre. If lessee discovers geothermal resources on leased premises, the division and lessee may negotiate a rental of less than $5.00 per acre, but not less than $1.00 per acre until commercial production.

South Dakota: South Dakota Codified Laws §§ 5-7-18 to 5-7-33 (including laws that went into effect 7/1/93). South Dakota Administrative Rules, title 4. Oil and gas leases classified in "incremental" status qualify for one-half standard royalty rate. South Dakota has a steeply escalating rent schedule. (S.D.A.R. 5-7-22) where the rent for the fourth and fifth years is $2.00 per acre per year; rent for years six through ten is $3.00 per acre per year; rent for years eleven through fifteen is $10.00 per acre per year, with an additional advance royalty that increases $10.00 per acre per year starting with $10.00 per acre per year in the eleventh year and ending at $50.00 per acre per year in the fifteenth year (for a total rent + advance royalty of $60.00 per acre per year.

Texas: Texas Administrative Code, title 31, §§ 9.1–9.9, found in 14 Texas Register 2775 et seq. (June 9, 1989). No royalty deductions are allowed for transport or taxes (§ 9.7(b)(1)(A)). Fees for geophysical exploration are $850/mile if vibroseis is used; $900/mile if dynamite is used. No rentals are paid on any resource once production has started. No rentals are charged for oil and gas leases; however, advance royalties equaling one to two months of expected royalty payments are required.

Utah: Utah Natural Resources—State Lands and Forestry, "Rules Governing the Management and Use of State Lands in Utah" (43d ed., August 1993).

Washington: Washington Department of Natural Resources, "Oil and Gas Leasing Program" (July 1985). Washington Revised Code § 79.14.070. Washington can reappraise minimum annual royalties after year 20 of a lease, and thereafter at ten-year intervals. Geothermal leases are for up to 55 years; held by payment of rental and compliance with five-year plans of development. Minimum rental fees for years 11–55 of geothermal leases are $10.00 per acre per year.

Wyoming: Wyoming Board of Land Commissioners and Wyoming Farm Loan Board, "Rules and Regulations Governing Leasing of Sub-surface Resources" (effective March 1, 1982). Board of Land Commissioners, "Rules and Regulations," ch. 16–Surface and Subsurface Survey Activities (May 1990).

United States: 43 C.F.R., Parts 3100 (Oil and Gas), 3200 (Geothermal), and 3400 (Coal). 53 Fed. Reg. 22,813-22,848 (6/17/88) amendments. Rent payments are credited to royalties for oil and gas leases issued prior to August 1976.

233

CHAPTER SEVEN

Emerging Strategies and Issues

This chapter focuses on emerging topics in trust land management. Shifts in public taste, politics, and state and national economies have created interesting new contexts for discussing such management. We discuss these trends and emerging strategies under two headings: more aggressive trust land management; and new controversies that this approach has produced, particularly among environmentalists. We conclude with a brief discussion of sustainability—a broad and ill-defined topic that we believe is peculiarly relevant to the trust lands.

At least three factors seem to have contributed significantly to intensifying trust land management and sharpening the debate over it. First, litigation, changing state and national economies, and a number of "tax revolts" have focused unusual attention on the trust revenues. For many decades, trust land programs were a rather cozy undertaking directed primarily at meeting the needs of lessees. During the 1960s and early 1970s, pivotal litigation at both the federal and the state levels abruptly refocused managers' attention on their trust obligations to the beneficiary. Tax revolts of the same period—and the subsequent bust in the national economy—have led beneficiaries and trust officials to explore new management strategies and income sources (some of them marginal) for additional revenue production opportunities.

Second, in part because of this increasingly aggressive management, there is increased controversy surrounding trust lands. Aggressive public resource management emphasizing profit eventually attracted the attention of environmentalists, especially in the context of timber. And to the dismay of historic or potential lessees, some trust managers are exploring ways to involve the trust in resource protection and recreation programs that are revenue-neutral or actually reduce trust income in a specific or short-term context. The result is a noticeable intensification of controversy and public discussion over the management of state trust resources.

Third, changing technology, tastes, and political priorities have created "new" resources and focused increased attention on some long-familiar but unmanaged older ones. Water, for example, is not a new resource, but it has only recently been included by some trustees in their portfolio. Several states are now aggressively managing water as a trust resource. Other resources, more legitimately regarded as new, include commercial real estate development. The economic boom of the late 1970s and early 1980s encouraged trustees to seek profits for the trust in hot real estate development markets. This has created new constituencies and new controversies for trust land managers.

One interesting indicator of the increased debate is the number of reconsiderations of trust land management that occur in the same time frame. Oregon recently completed a major reassessment of its trust obligations and issued, after much study and debate, a new attorney general opinion.[1] Meanwhile, after legislation calling for wholesale restructuring of the State Lands office failed to pass,[2] Utah conducted a major review by a committee appointed by the governor pursuant to legislation, and made major changes in its trust land organization and priorities.[3] Several other states are pursuing major readjustments in specific programs: in Washington and Oregon regarding the sale of timber; in Oregon regarding grazing; in New Mexico regarding investment of permanent funds; and in Arizona, under threat of a lawsuit from the Center for Law in the Public Interest, regarding its grazing program.

The future of trust lands management will include new resources and new management strategies and controversies, but also intensified scrutiny surrounding these oldest of public resources. We look in this chapter at a selection of current programs and debates, beginning with ones that involve a clearly more aggressive stance—and frequently, new strategies—from managers.

MORE AGGRESSIVE MANAGEMENT OF TRUST RESOURCES

As discussed in Chapter 1, the U.S. Supreme Court's decision in the case of *Lassen v. Arizona Highway Department*, 385 U.S. 458 (1967), is a watershed in trust land management. *Lassen* and a host of state-level decisions relying on its conclusions[4] seem to have reinvigorated trust principles in school land management and turned trustees' attention away from traditional renewable resource management concepts toward a more businesslike and beneficiary-oriented style of management. Trust managers are motivated to view the resources in their care as a portfolio and actively to seek out and develop new and profitable strategies, locations, and resources, as well as new opportunities to serve (and be seen as serving) the beneficiary. This general impulse has only been heightened by the economic constraints of the early 1990s.

An Aggressive Approach to Old Resources: Permanent Fund Management

From the perspective of aficionados of federal land management, the most peculiar aspect of state trust management is probably the permanent fund.

Although permanent funds have been attached to the program for more than a century and a half, they are just now being treated as part of the portfolio. The permanent funds serve as a repository to maintain the asset value from nonrenewable resources. The states invest the proceeds of the permanent funds and only disburse to the beneficiaries the annual dividends. States are becoming increasingly attentive to the permanent funds, and several have developed creative ways to use them to support the beneficiaries. Oklahoma, for example, is currently pursuing a state constitutional amendment that would allow it to offer the permanent fund as collateral for local school bond offerings. Such backup typically allows a school board to improve its bond rating from A to AA or AAA, achieving significant benefits for the trust beneficiaries.[5]

Although creative uses of permanent funds are important, most recent attention has focused on management of the funds. Two factors tend to offset the original commitment to maintain the value of the permanent fund: first, inflation eats away at the "purchasing power" of the fund, particularly when all the dividends are disbursed annually. Second, because in many states the types of investments allowed for the fund are restricted, the value of the permanent fund only increases as a result of additions from the conversion of land-based resources. The investment restrictions limit growth resulting from management of the assets contained within the fund itself.

Nevertheless, because the permanent fund is the repository of revenues received by the trust from generally nonrenewable resources such as oil and gas, coal, and land sales and easements, the fund is itself one item in the states' larger portfolio. Its use can be evaluated in the same manner as the other resources—that is, by assessing the tradeoffs between risk and return—to determine the percentage of the states' portfolio that should be held as the permanent fund as opposed to being reinvested in oil, timber, or other revenue-producing properties.

Equally important, the permanent funds provide a benchmark to use in assessing the comparative performance of other assets. Absent transactions costs, the state can always examine its various resources and their management programs to determine whether they are meeting a target rate of return. If investments in timber production, for example, do not make as much as returns on the permanent fund, the trustee ought to consider selling the timberland and putting the receipts into the more lucrative permanent fund. The permanent funds, therefore, help resource managers sharpen their inquiry into what the target rate of return for resource management investments should be. Under this careful analysis, as we have repeatedly suggested, managers may reject some programs as simply not being worth the investment.

This section proceeds in three parts. First, we describe and discuss the amounts of the various states' permanent funds. Then we use the information on permanent fund levels and payments to beneficiaries to determine their rates of return, both in nominal dollars and as inflation-free real dollars. Third, we examine how the states manage their permanent funds—in particular, which state agency manages the fund and what criteria it uses to determine the fund's investments.

STATES' EXISTING PERMANENT FUNDS AND THEIR HOLDINGS

The states' permanent fund levels in 1990 are shown in Table 2-5. Items displayed in Table 2-5 include the fund levels for total and common schools, the amount of annual contributions from trust lands into these funds, and the amount of dividends flowing from the permanent fund back to the beneficiaries for these two categories. Also included is the percentage rate of return from the funds, calculated as the amount of the dividends divided by the amount of the fund.

The flow of revenues into the states' permanent funds is generated by land sales and sales of nonrenewable resources, although the exact determination of which revenues go into the permanent fund and which are distributed to the beneficiary varies from state to state (see Table 2-7). States that have sold or are selling significant amounts of valuable trust land (for example, Arizona) continually increase their permanent funds as the sales are conducted and as the mortgages (if any) are paid off. States lucky enough to have significant energy mineral resources on their lands receive large amounts of royalty revenues, as we saw in Chapter 6. These states doubled or tripled the value of their permanent funds during the late 1970s and early 1980s during the oil boom. Similarly, as we saw in Chapter 5, states that developed large timber programs and placed the revenues from these—their "green oil"—into their permanent funds increased their permanent funds during periods of high demand and high prices for timber.

These trust resources are transformed from their natural state into trust assets in the permanent funds. However, their flow into the permanent fund varies according to market demand and prices, and according to the amount converted and sold. As a result, when prices and demand are high—as was the case in the late 1970s and early 1980s with regard to land sales, energy minerals, and timber—revenues flow rapidly into the states' permanent funds. But at the same time that prices were high for these trust resources, inflation was also comparatively high. Consequently, the real value of the states' permanent funds, as expressed in constant-dollar purchasing power, did not rise as much as their "nominal" accounting value would lead one to believe.[6]

The effect of inflation on the "real" value of the states' permanent funds is dramatically illustrated in Figure 7-1, which shows the growth of two states' permanent funds during the period 1970–1992. The permanent fund of the first state—New Mexico—multiplied approximately eight times,

New Mexico

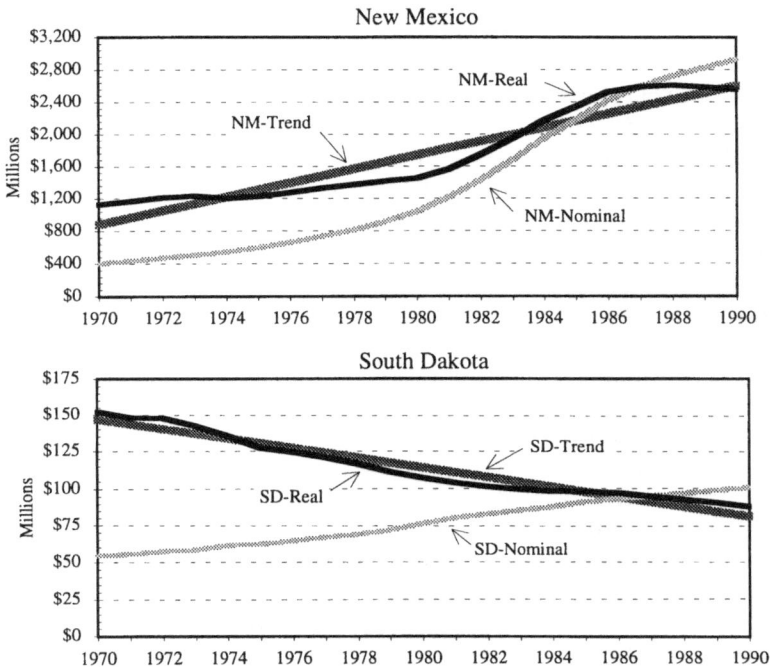

South Dakota

Figure 7-1. Examples of state permanent fund trajectories, 1970–1990.

from $400 million to $3.2 billion in nominal terms, in twenty years as a result of high production of oil and gas. Its value in "real" dollars corrected for inflation, however, merely doubled over this same period. As a result, the addition of $2.8 billion in oil and gas revenues, after adjustment for inflation, resulted in an increased value addition of only $1.2 billion for New Mexico's permanent fund.

In New Mexico's case, the permanent fund withstood the effects of inflation due to large infusions of additional capital from oil and gas royalties. South Dakota's permanent fund, as shown in the lower half of Figure 7-1, did not. While South Dakota's fund increased in nominal terms from $50 million in 1980 to about $100 million by 1990, inflationary effects ate up all the increased capital additions and half the original value. In 1987 constant dollars, the value of South Dakota's permanent fund decreased from slightly more than $150 million in 1970 to about $85 million by 1990. Comparing nominal and real returns for states' permanent funds demonstrates the effects of inflation on the value of the fund and emphasizes the importance of developing investment policies that recognize and ameliorate inflationary effects.

RATES OF RETURN ON STATE PERMANENT FUND INVESTMENTS

The first way to recognize inflationary effects is to track the nominal and real rates of return on states' permanent funds. In this case, nominal returns are defined as the beneficiary sees them: as the amount of dividends distributed to the beneficiary as a percentage of its permanent fund value. (The nominal rate is really the net return, because permanent fund management costs are deducted.) The real rate of return to the beneficiary is determined by subtracting the inflation rate from the nominal rate of return. Inflationary effects on permanent fund yields can clearly be seen by viewing the difference between nominal and real rates of return for three states over a 21-year period, in Figure 7-2. The graph demonstrates that, at least until the 1980s, states were totally unprepared to counteract inflationary effects in their investment policies. This is illustrated by the negative "effective" or real rates of return many states earned on their permanent funds after inflation is deducted.

The top portion of Figure 7-2 tracks three states—Idaho, New Mexico, and Texas—that appear to have received moderate rates of return on their permanent funds over the last twenty plus years. These rates of return have varied from about 4 percent to 10 percent, depending on the state and the year. Nominal rates of return were generally lower in the early 1970s, but have averaged between 8 percent and 9 percent since 1985. However, when the effects of inflation are subtracted from the rates of return to calculate the real (postinflation) rate of return, the states' experience is revealed as mixed at best. State permanent funds have received only moderate real rates of return, in the range of 2 percent to 6 percent, and then only during periods of low inflation (such as pre-1973 and post-1985). The high inflation of the mid-to late-1970s and early 1980s effectively stripped the permanent funds of their ability to provide real dividends for their beneficiaries.

In the early 1980s, state permanent fund managers began to recognize the attendant problems of high inflation and the need to maintain the real value of the permanent fund. The trust land manager—as portfolio manager—should examine the relative rates of return of the various trust assets to determine an optimal proportion of holdings. In the preceding example, the portfolio manager might decide to retain the oil and gas in the ground as an alternative to allowing production (through leasing) when the royalties to be placed in the permanent fund have a negative real rate of return. Alternatively, the permanent fund manager might seek out investments whose value outpaced inflation, such as stock in oil and gas companies.[7]

However, portfolio (and trust) managers are faced with two problems in managing resources and permanent funds under these strategies. First, in most states there is no linkage between the trust land manager and the permanent fund manager, which results in little communication and no coordi-

Nominal Rates of Return

Real Rates of Return

Inflation · · · · · · New Mexico — — — — Texas Idaho

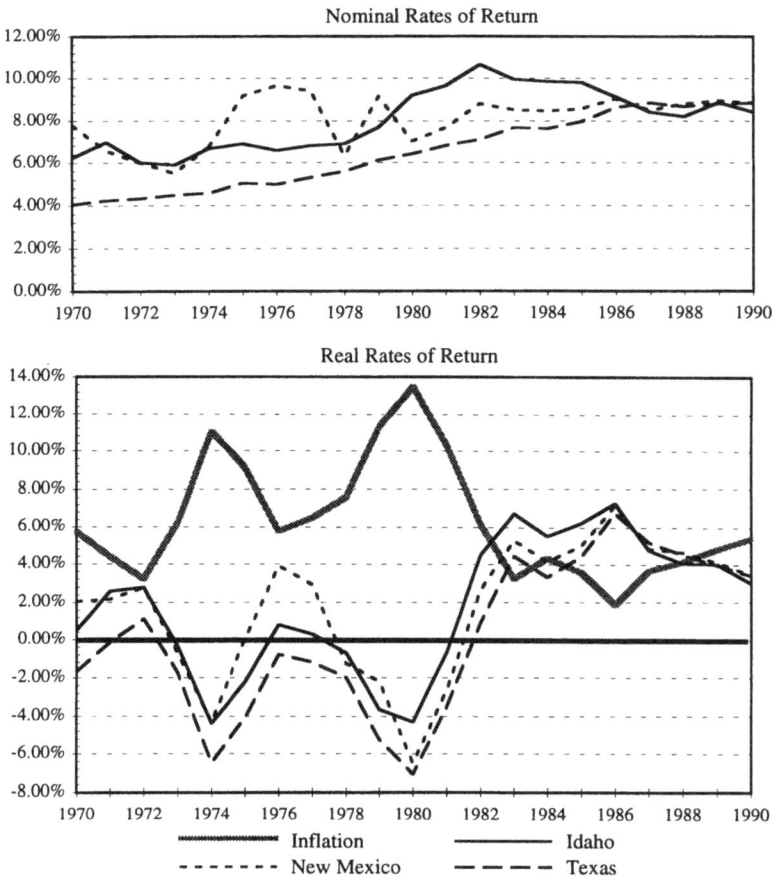

Figure 7-2. Examples of state permanent fund rates of return, 1970–1990.

nated production decisions. Second, many state constitutions and statutes limit the ability of the permanent fund manager to purchase equity stocks and corporate bonds, which greatly impedes any effort to implement a portfolio theory such as by purchasing stocks that are expected to outpace inflation and generate capital growth. These topics—administration of the permanent funds and investment criteria—link the permanent funds to the larger trust asset portfolio.

PERMANENT FUND MANAGEMENT

The importance of who manages the permanent fund, and the linkage and communication between permanent fund management and trust land

TABLE 7-1. Administration of state trust permanent funds

Administration	States Using
Managed by agency other than land office.	AZ, CA, CO, ID, MT, NM, TX, UT, WA, WY
Beneficiaries manage fund directly.	CA, CO, TX
Land office represented on investment board.	NM, SD
State land office manages permanent fund.	NB, ND, OK, OR

management, is little discussed. Four organizational arrangements are used by the states: in some, all management is done by an agency other than the state land office, the revenue generator; in the third type, permanent fund management is done by another state agency, but the state land office (or commissioner) is represented on the oversight board; in the fourth, the state land office also manages the permanent fund. Table 7-1 tells which states use which arrangements.

In the vast majority of states, the permanent fund manager is administratively separated from the state lands manager. In a few cases, such as New Mexico, the state land commissioner has a seat on the permanent fund investment board. In three states (California, Colorado, and Texas), the beneficiaries administer the permanent fund directly. In only four states is the permanent fund managed by the same agency that manages the trust lands.

The benefits of integrating permanent fund management and trust lands management into a single portfolio management scheme are numerous, including, in particular, communication and linkage between land and fund management. But there are also drawbacks to this integration. Many states' managers of trust lands permanent funds also manage either other state permanent funds (for example, the mineral severance tax funds) or short-term general fund revenues. There is certainly the possibility of returns to scale in management of permanent funds if specialized investment expertise is obtained. Whether these benefits outweigh the lack of linkage between the lands and the permanent fund should be analyzed on a state-by-state basis.[8] Whichever way the state decides to administer its permanent funds, more crucial to fund management are the criteria that guide and constrain the manager.

STATE INVESTMENT CRITERIA

State permanent fund administrators of all orientations are typically constrained in the types of investments that they can make. In many cases, investment criteria are found in state constitutions and statutes that were first enacted as a result of scandals in the early days of the permanent funds. Examples of bad investments (in hindsight) were legion, such as silver mines in Nevada and railroads in the south prior to the Civil War. As a result, newer states (and some older states) incorporated into their constitutions or enabling legislation provisions that the permanent fund could only be invested in government bonds and securities, or that required the permanent fund to support local development by purchasing first farm mortgages.

Many states restrict the types of investments that can be made with permanent fund moneys. There are three broad categories of restrictions. First, some states (Arizona, Oregon, and Washington) are prohibited from making equity investments. Second, some states (such as New Mexico) are allowed to invest only a specified or maximum percentage of the permanent fund in equity stocks and bonds. Third, some states (including Texas) may freely choose the types of investments that, in the permanent fund trustee's judgement, serve the best interest of the beneficiaries.

The lesson learned by permanent fund managers by the mid-1980s is that restricting the types of investments available for permanent funds contributes to their decline in real value during periods of high inflation. From the 1980s onward, permanent fund managers have attempted to free themselves from state constitutional limitations and legislative mandates so that they can aggressively seek the best mix of investments.

The graph in Figure 7-3 shows the effects of different interest criteria on long-term dividend trends in five states.[9] While the trend among all five states in this example is toward increased dividends over time, the graph demonstrates that the states differ among themselves both as to absolute dividend return rate (the comparative elevation of each state's trend line) and as to the rate at which each increases its permanent fund dividend yield (the slope of the trend lines). As we saw in Figure 7-2, the types of investments that state permanent fund managers made after the period of high inflation in the late-1970s protected dividend yields to some extent, and this is reflected in the in-

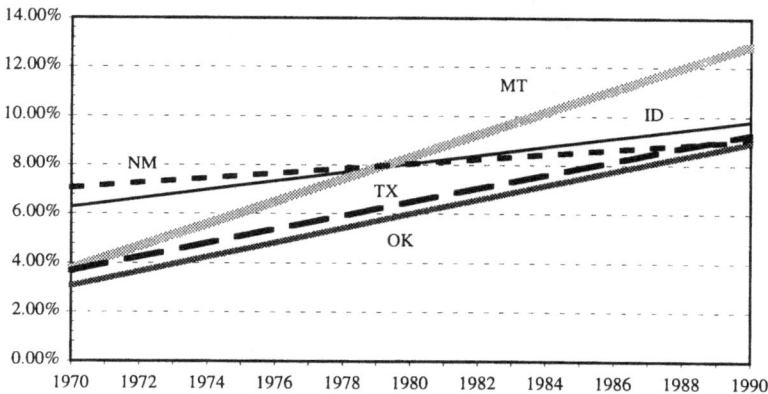

Figure 7-3. Difference in nominal interest rate trends among five states, 1970–1990.

creasing slope of the trend lines in Figure 7-3. In addition, four of the states tracked in Figure 7-3 ended the twenty-year period with approximately the same 9 percent to 10 percent net nominal yield on their permanent funds. Thus the results of these states' permanent fund investment policies are fairly consistent, even while the mix of their investments differs.

The key goal in managing a permanent fund is to maintain the purchasing power of the stream of dividends flowing to the beneficiaries. There are basically two ways to do this: by pursuing an aggressive policy of fund investment, or by retaining a portion of the dividends. One way to maintain the fund's purchasing power is through equity investments. However, restrictive investment policies combined with inflation make maintaining purchasing power quite a challenge. Most of the late-joining (phase-four) states placed severe constitutional restrictions on their investments of permanent funds. Some (such as North Dakota) have successfully altered those restrictions, and others (such as South Dakota and Oklahoma) are currently trying to do so by statute or constitutional amendment. Still other states have been able to diversify their portfolios to include stocks and bonds as well as the traditional safer—and less remunerative—investments in government securities and mortgages. For example, New Mexico allows up to 20 percent of its permanent fund to be invested in stocks.[10]

A second strategy for maintaining the purchasing power of the permanent fund in the face of inflation is to have the fund retain a portion of the dividends. For example, Montana distributes only 95 percent of its renewable revenues to beneficiaries, with 5 percent going into the permanent fund; similarly, it distributes only 95 percent of the dividends of the permanent fund, retaining the other 5 percent.[11] This automatically offsets inflation of up to 5 percent, thereby maintaining the "purchasing power" of the permanent fund. Other states are working toward this strategy.[12]

We argued in Chapter 3 that the permanent fund ought to be viewed as constituting an integral part of the trust portfolio. Effective management of the funds themselves is an important issue, although in only five states do the trustees play a role in that undertaking. The financial market has drastically changed since constitutional and statutory directions on investment types were first enacted; and throughout the West, state land commissions are working aggressively to allow permanent fund managers to choose their portfolio of investments solely on the basis of the trust mandate to exercise undivided loyalty to the beneficiary under the prudent person standard. Of more direct concern here is the continuing issue of whether shifting assets between the land resources and the permanent fund are in the beneficiaries' best interest. Trustees have been increasingly aggressive in ensuring that consideration of permanent fund management and trust land management are linked. The pressure on the trustees to produce revenues for the schools has caused them to take a more active role in the management of the funds.

Liquid Assets: Trust Water and Water Rights

Unlike the permanent funds, which have not always been viewed as part of trust lands management, water has always been recognized as a valuable resource in the western United States. But managers of public lands, both federal and state, have rarely paid close attention to water in connection with their activities.[13] This is most apparent and least explicable, perhaps, when it involves federal land managers. The U.S. Forest Service has only recently begun seriously addressing the water component of its 1891 mandate.[14]

State school land managers have come to the water party even more belatedly. We offer three possible explanations for this peculiar state of affairs. The first applies to public resource managers generally: the emphasis of these professions in the field has been biological. Because its efforts were focused on trees, the Forest Service did not regard water as important until quite recently. Other state and federal agencies, drawing on the same professions and modeling their behavior on the dominant Forest Service paradigm, followed suit. The second explanation is relevant primarily to trust land managers: within their state political systems, they have generally lacked clout. Their attempts to claim water on state trust lands have been thwarted by politically powerful commodity interests and their representatives in state government. Few politicians in the country match the traditional power of the State Engineer in most arid jurisdictions, and the state lands trustees have not always been able to assert their rights in the face of opposition from such entrenched authorities. Finally, there is a perception (explicitly stated in some, but not all, state constitutions) that the water of the state belongs to the citizens of the state to be appropriated by private individuals for "beneficial uses." In the West, such appropriation has traditionally constituted a property right not tied to the specific parcel of land where the water is diverted or developed. Thus, in some states, the trustee has permitted municipal and private claimants to appropriate the rights to water on trust lands. This interpretation of the constitution perhaps reflects the power differential addressed earlier. In any event, legislatures that acceded in this process have been reluctant to overturn these practices, and trust land mangers, in turn, have been hesitant to claim water for trust purposes.

Several factors appear to be breaking down this reticence about participating in water politics. One is the water rights adjudication process now underway in many states: trustees increasingly recognize that, if they do not claim water now, they may lose the right ever to do so. Another relates to the urban sprawl currently encroaching on state trust lands. This circumstance changes how both water and the land are viewed: several states have adopted aggressive urban/commercial lands development programs that focus attention on water requirements.

These nascent steps are confounded by several ubiquitous factors. First, throughout the western states, trust water resources have not been inventoried, and uses have not been quantified. What data have been collected on state trust lands are generally not organized around water. Second, it is common for most water rights on state trust lands to be established in the name of the lessee; and thus many states have lost title to much of their potential water. In the two case studies that follow, state trustees appear to be moving aggressively into water management. In Montana, the land office is deeply involved in a statewide adjudication process. This involvement resulted in an important court decision—*Department of State Lands v. Pettibone*, 702 P. 2d 948 (1985), enhancing the trustee's control of water on state trust lands. The *Pettibone* court ruled that title to waters developed on trust lands vest in the state, not in the lessee. The language of the ruling is an important first step among the states toward a legal definition of water as a trust resource. This case also opened the issue of federal reserved water rights' attaching to state trust lands. Meanwhile, in Colorado, the State Land Board is aggressively pursuing control over its water and attempting to develop and market it through a royalty rate system.

WATER MANAGEMENT ON MONTANA STATE TRUST LANDS

In Montana, the Department of State Lands (DSL) by statute[15] and by regulation[16] allows lessees to divert waters on the leasehold, develop them, and put the water to use on or off trust lands. Surface and groundwater rights have been filed on grazing and cropland tracts.[17] Water is used for stock watering on most of the sections, but no established water rights are associated with it. Little groundwater is used on state trust land because pumping water for irrigation is an economically marginal proposition, given the short growing season and low-value forage crops in Montana. There is usually an abundance of surface water from headwater sources.

Selling and leasing water is not allowed in Montana. Recently, however, the DSL has required easements or land-use licenses for new water diversions located on trust land. For the licenses, the DSL receives $100/year; but because this is a land-use fee it is not considered a water sale. This fee is, however, charged only on new diversions, not on existing ones. Hence, the DSL does not receive direct compensation for most water use on state trust lands. The state indirectly receives compensation for water use through grazing and cropland lease fees. On irrigated tracts, the DSL receives a minimum one-quarter crop share unless the DSL has a cash lease arrangement with the lessee (see Chapter 4). Compensation is not received for diversions on state land that convey water to private property.[18] The DSL reports that hundreds of stream diversions on state lands have been set up to supply water to private lands with no benefit to the state. In some cases, private owners have established water rights and then diverted entire streams from trust lands, leaving the state lands high and dry.[19] To reclaim state water rights, the DSL believes that its only realistic alternative is to pursue federal reserved water rights.

Control of Water Rights. The major vector of the Montana DSL's newly aggressive posture in water management is the statewide adjudication. Still, legal recognition of the DSL as holder of water rights perfected on state trust land came very late in the adjudicative process. The DSL began filing for water rights when a test basin was established for the Powder River. The twenty-three water rights for which the state filed in that basin[20] were also claimed by the state's lessees. In a 1978 preliminary decree, the chief water judge held that the lessee, not the state, owned water rights perfected on state trust lands. The DSL's appeal of that decision could not go forward until a final decree was issued.[21]

The 1983 Powder River final decree also held in favor of the lessees, and the DSL appealed this ruling to the Montana Supreme Court. In 1985, the court's decision in *Department of State Lands v. Pettibone*[22] overturned the decree and ruled that the state is the owner of a water right diverted or developed on state school trust land. The court based its conclusion on trust principles, arguing that "an interest in school lands cannot be alienated unless the trust receives adequate compensation for that interest. Water that is appurtenant to the school lands is an interest for which the trust must receive compensation." The court also stated that "any law or policy that infringes on the state's managerial prerogatives over the school lands cannot be tolerated if it reduces the value of the land." It concluded that the lessee, in making appropriations on and for school trust sections, acted in behalf of the state.

Unfortunately, prior to the DSL's 1985 victory in *Pettibone,* the Montana legislature had acted to accelerate the statewide adjudications: it set a filing deadline of April 30, 1982, for all pre-July 1, 1973 water rights, and announced that failure to file prior to that deadline constituted abandonment of such rights. Until 1985, however, the DSL could not legally hold water rights. Faced with that quandary, and correctly anticipating its victory in *Pettibone,* the DSL decided to file for water rights anyway.

In fact, the DSL filed approximately 8,500 claims by the 1982 deadline in the statewide adjudication. In its filings, the DSL focused only on situations that met the same criteria as did the claims involved in the pending appeal: claims in which both the point of diversion and the place of use occurred on state trust lands. This policy rested on the idea that, if the appeal was won, the similarly situated claims filed would certainly be secure. In making this strategic decision, the DSL relinquished an enormous number of claims; however, its filing strategy was necessitated by the fact that it lacked the administrative resources to file all potential claims before the statutory deadline. The DSL's consultants relied on information provided by lessees when researching historical and existing water use on state trust lands and did not field-inspect information from aerial photographs. Approximately 2,000 additional stock water rights fitting the *Pettibone* criteria were not filed before the deadline because they were identified too late. The DSL also estimates that more than 1,000 claims for water with a point of diversion on state trust lands but a place of use off state trust lands were not filed by the state because of the lack of sound information. The DSL did not file for irrigation rights in cases where the diversion occurred off trust land. Overall, the state estimates that between 20,000 and 40,000 acres of irrigated lands could be lost.[23]

The DSL's efforts to reclaim these lost water rights were not successful. First, the DSL filed an *amicus curiae* brief to an appeal to the Montana Supreme Court to determine whether water rights claimed after the 1982 deadline remained valid or were legally abandoned. The DSL argued that its nonfiling of certain claims was due to factors beyond its immediate control. Such factors included "shortage of staff and funds for the S.B. 76 adjudication; the logistical problems of thoroughly evaluating water rights on the thousands of parcels that comprise more than 5,000,000 acres of trust lands sprinkled across the state, and completing accurate claims thereon within the allowed filing period; and the coolness (at times, hostility) of the Water Court toward the State as a water rights claimant during the early years of the adjudication program, a situation that was not rectified until 1985 (more than three years after the close of the filing period). . . ."[24] Second, the DSL argued that conclusive abandonment of a valuable property right of water conflicts with the peculiar trust principles governing the administration of the school lands.[25] Finally, the DSL threatened to claim water rights for school trust lands under the implied reservation doctrine.

Trust Land Reserved Water Rights? In its decision, the Montana Supreme Court ruled that late-filed claims were conclusively forfeited as a result of owner negligence, not as a result of excessive and unreasonable court action.[26] However, the DSL argument that a federally reserved water right, as originally recognized in *Winters v. United States,*[27] exists for trust lands is worth noting.[28] An *amicus* brief in *Pettibone* outlined a theory of a reserved rights doctrine applicable to state trust lands.[29] The brief points to the federal withdrawal of state trust land from settlement, reserving it for a specific purpose (as provided in the Organic Act of the Territory of Montana), and argues that this purpose is as specific as a reservation of federal lands for Native American Indian Reservations, National Monuments, or National Forests, all of which have received federal reserved water rights. The brief further asserts that water must contribute to accomplishing the purpose of the reservation, which is to raise money for the support of common schools.

Accordingly, a water user on state school lands is not an appropriator, but rather a person participating in the purpose for which these lands were reserved and under this rationale, exercising the state's federally reserved water right.

The court refused to address this argument, stating that "it is perhaps best to keep the reserved rights doctrine confined to situations where it arose and is most appropriate; as an accommodation between federal and state interests." Nevertheless, the notion is an interesting one. Because school lands were frequently reserved from the public domain long before statehood, the possibility of truly ancient priority dates for school lands water may eventually elicit more thorough judicial attention.

Conclusions Regarding Montana's Water Program. The Montana story is typical in three important particulars. First, it evinces the cost of starting late in the water game. State trust land managers probably never will achieve for the beneficiaries more than a small percentage of the value of the water arising on trust lands. Second, it suggests some reasons for this seeming neglect by the trustees: parties involved in state water politics have not welcomed DSL efforts to protect trust resources. We saw in Chapter 1 that the trust doctrine did not effectively bar state raids on school trust lands for highways and water diversions until the mid-1960s *Lassen* decision. It is hardly surprising that another several decades elapsed before trustees began to make headway in the even more intense competition that characterizes western water wars. Finally, the Montana case correctly suggests the importance of statewide adjudications in focusing trust manager's attention on water issues. The increasing importance of trust principles and the growing attention of trust beneficiaries have prompted states to invest considerable effort in claiming and managing trust water. Montana's Herculean efforts in the Powder River adjudication are atypical, but they may soon be regarded as an early prototype in a first and crucial wave of aggressive trustee action.

WATER MANAGEMENT ON COLORADO STATE TRUST LANDS

Although Colorado has met with more success than Montana in its initial sorties into water management, the same historic losses of water will continue to confound its trustees' efforts to get full value for trust water assets. In this case study, we discuss three specific efforts that the Colorado Board of Land Commissioners (BLC) has made in water management: seeking control over trust water; gaining compensation for water used on state trust lands; and developing water for trust purposes. Because Colorado water law is unusually idosyncratic, however, we begin by briefly reviewing the context and terms of the situation.

Overview of State Water Law in Colorado. The Colorado Constitution provides that "the rights to divert the unappropriated waters of any natural stream to beneficial uses shall never be denied." It also states that water belongs to the citizens of the state[30]—a declaration that is frequently cited to explain the BLC's past reluctance to claim state trust land water rights. Colorado uses the prior appropriation doctrine to apportion rights to surface water, which includes waters in streams and waters directly tributary to those streams (tributary groundwater). Nontributary groundwater[31] and tributary groundwater whose withdrawal has remote effects on natural streams are administered separately from surface water. Some groundwater is further classified as designated groundwater—water entirely separate from surface water—which is neither tributary to any stream nor available for the fulfillment of decreed surface water rights. Applications for appropriation of designated groundwater are made to the Colorado Ground Water Commission. The priority of claims for designated groundwater is determined by the doctrine of prior appropriation. Applications for permits to construct wells outside designated groundwater basins are made to the State Engineer, and a copy of the application must be filed with the appropriate water court.

Populated areas of Colorado lie outside designated groundwater basins. As a result, most applications for well permits go to the State Engineer. Because underground water is presumed to be tributary to a stream, and because most streams in Colorado are overappropriated, the State Engineer usually denies permits for wells outside designated groundwater basins unless there is a Water Court–approved augmentation plan.[32] To make matters more complicated, another category of groundwater, called "not nontributary," is also designated. This is water that does not meet the statutory definition given above for nontributary groundwater, although it lies outside a designated groundwater basin.

Water rights in Colorado are not recognized by state water officials unless they have been confirmed by adjudication.[33] Except for permits to authorize the construction of wells, no permitting system exists in Colorado's water law system. Instead, the legislature has delegated these administrative duties to water judges. Seven water divisions corresponding to the drainage basins of major rivers were established by the Water Right Determination and Administration Act of 1969 (Water Right Act). For each division, a water judge presides over all water controversies raised in the district courts of the counties situated within the division.

Water rights in Colorado are not generally appurtenant to the land. Once a water right is perfected by appropriation, it may be conveyed separately from the land on which it was first applied.[34] Restrictions on out-of-basin export are imposed on the sale and lease of water and water rights in Colorado. The owner must put the water to beneficial use in order to maintain the right to it. Colorado beneficial uses include impoundment of water for recreational purposes (including fishery and wildlife and such traditional uses such as domestic, agricultural, and manufacturing purposes). Sustaining minimum instream flows to preserve the environment is also considered a beneficial use, but the rights to water for this purpose can only be claimed by the Colorado Water Conservation Board.

A priority date is assigned to surface water rights based on the date of first beneficial use or, if this date cannot be supported, from current application date or filing date. Priority dates for nontributary groundwater rights are driven by the specifics of a given filing. Surface water rights and groundwater rights are quantified by using tests that include the purpose of the appropriation, the amount of practicably irrigable acreage, and various commercial requirements. The owner of a water right may also exercise the power of eminent domain for access, reservoirs, pipelines, and rights-of-way.

Control over Water. Approximately 120,000 acres of Colorado trust lands are irrigated, roughly half by groundwater and half by surface water. But like Montana's DSL, Colorado's BLC faces intense political pressure not to file for water rights. Because of this pressure, surface water put to use on state trust lands has historically been claimed in the name of the lessee. When trust land is leased, the surface water rights held by the lessee are considered an improvement. Those that originate from a ditch or irrigation company (ditch rights) are called "collateral water stock." When the lease is transferred or terminated, the lessee must be compensated for this improvement; otherwise, the lessee can sell the water right.[35]

In recent years, in an effort to gain control of water resources on or under state trust lands, the BLC has added a lease stipulation that any water developed on the lease must be filed in the state's name.[36] Under this arrangement, the lessee is compensated for improvements such as wells, but not for the water right itself, at the termination of the lease. Most trust land groundwater rights are of recent origin, so most are registered in the BLC's name because of this recent change in lease stipulations. The BLC reports that some 6,000 to 7,000 wells have been drilled on trust lands.

In spite of the BLC's efforts to establish title, water rights established on state trust lands have not been quantified, nor is there available information on the amount of surface water used on these lands. Initial surveys of groundwater resources on trust lands have been conducted, however. Of the irrigated state trust land in Colorado, lessees hold title to 65 percent of the water rights (collateral water stock) and the BLC holds title to the remaining 35 percent (closed water stock).[37] Collateral water stock rights not affected by the new lease provisions are potentially transferable from state trust land at lease termination.[38]

In many cases, land owners adjacent to state trust lands (and therefore not subject to the changed lease provisions) have filed for surface water that originates on state trust lands and applied it for use on their own lands.[39] The amount of water lost as a result of these filings by nonlessees is unknown, and the BLC has not been able to reclaim these past surface water rights. To safeguard against future claims by nonlessees, the BLC reviews monthly water court resumes and cross-files for any water claimed on state trust lands. The BLC is usually successful in water rights adjudications if the point of diversion and the place of use are both on state trust lands.

On a larger scale, the BLC has lost control over water rights on state trust lands vis-a-vis other state and federal interests. The San Luis Valley Closed Basin Project offers one example of this. In 1938, Colorado, New Mexico, and Texas signed a compact to apportion waters in the Rio Grande.[40] By 1965, Colorado was more than 900,000 acre-feet behind its delivery commitments under the compact. To meet this commitment, the State—as part of a Bureau of Reclamation project—began pumping groundwater from wells along the east side of the valley (the Closed Basin) into a channel and thence to the Rio Grande. Since 70 percent of the well-field supplying water to the Rio Grande is on state trust lands, the BLC feels that this project has robbed them of a significant resource.[41] It is unclear what entity will have control over this developed water once the indebtedness has been paid off, but the BLC has aspirations in that regard.

Compensation for Water Use. The trust often receives no compensation for water use from state lands. In the past, when a successful claim for a water right was made by a nonlessee, the trust was at most compensated through the resulting right-of-way transaction—an arrangement that generates considerably less income than the water would command in a normal lease/sale market. In three such cases, the state has had little choice but to allow municipalities to pump groundwater from state trust lands under a right-of-way arrangement with little or no compensation to the trust. In contrast, when water is applied on state trust lands, the trust is indirectly compensated through grazing or cropland fees[42] paid by the lessee. When groundwater rights are leased apart from the land leases, the state is directly compensated for water use.

In a new strategy, however, the BLC is applying procedures similar to those used in oil and gas leasing to groundwater development: it leases water as an undeveloped resource but charges a royalty from the lessee as compensation. This strategy has been used in one much-discussed lease with the president of a metropolitan water district, Rangeview Metropolitan District.[43] The lessee plans to develop and market 30,000 acre-feet of nontributary groundwater from state trust lands east of Denver, using water rights adjudicated in the state's name. Of the 30,000 acre-feet, 16,000 acre-feet will be used on state trust lands, and the remainder will be sold to a municipality. The BLC will receive a 12.5 percent royalty on water sales for nonutility use and 10 percent royalty for water sales that go to public utility uses.

Water Development Projects. Following a recent hydrological study of its resources, the BLC has developed eleven irrigation wells on state trust lands; four of these wells were drilled in the San Luis Valley, and the other seven in the High Plains of eastern Colorado.[44] In connection with one of those wells, the Black Squirrel Creek project, the board is in the process of developing water rights primarily for Colorado Springs' municipal use. The state trust lands in the basin (approximately 200,000 acres) are currently leased for grazing. Black Squirrel Creek is a designated groundwater basin (not part of an active flow of a major drainage) with a tributary groundwater supply reportedly lost to evaporation and phreatophytes. The BLC plans to install wells with a 1,000-gpm capacity. Approval of this plan hinges on the BLC's ability to prove that the water from this basin is nontributary to the already completely appropriated Arkansas River.

CONCLUSIONS

After decades of neglecting water resources, states are starting to move to protect these valuable trust assets. However, participation in water programs is expensive and somewhat risky for the trustees. Gathering the data to make and defend claims, committing the resources to monitor and counter competing claims, and raising the funds to develop water that has successfully been claimed are all costly endeavors; and the return to the trust is not guaranteed. Nevertheless, states are becoming increasingly active in water management. We do not expect that a "typical" state water program analogous to the fairly standardized approaches to grazing, cropland, and mineral leases will emerge. Because there is no equivalent federal program to define the public's and lessee's expectations in water, states are more likely to define their own unique initiatives. As the Colorado situation suggests, each state program will have to adapt itself to the rigorously defined and firmly established parameters of existing law and regulation that are peculiar to each state. Further, the lands and their water resources vary tremendously, as do the aspirations of the trustees. Each state must take advantage of the openings that nature, politics, and fiscal realities allow. Water is now firmly on the agenda as a trust resource; and although they are likely to encounter continuing pressure to abandon this understanding, it is increasingly clear that trustees are not allowed to do so.

New Resources: Commercial Development of State Trust Lands

Permanent funds and water resources are obvious items that are appropriately attracting increased attention of state trustees. Other resources such as commercial land development have the opposite emotional valence. For instance, it is difficult for observers accustomed to thinking about Forest Service and Bureau of Land Management programs to adjust to the idea of trust lands administration that includes condos and warehouses in its public resource management. We attempt to ease the shock with a few lines about kelp and mushrooms, but the heart of this section is undeniably on commercial lands. This area, like water policy, has elicited enormously different institutional responses at the state level. And again, standard format for state involvement is unlikely to evolve. This may be due in part to the fact that we are not dealing here with a traditional commodity: commercial development emphasizes the resource value of the *location* of the lands. In this section, we emphasize real estate development and communication sites, with a brief digression into land exchanges. Given the complexity of even that limited subject, we can only survey existing state programs and identify the parameters we consider important when considering commercial uses of state trust lands.

In their quest for new sources of revenue for trust beneficiaries, trustees have become increasingly sensitive to the economic value of products that historically were not thought worthy of mention. In the last several years, numerous panels at the Western States Land Commissioners Association meetings have addressed the profit potential of minor resources. Coastal states frequently present information on the growing market for kelp and seaweed, and drier states have discussed land conversions to support the burgeoning salsa market by growing chili peppers; but minor forest products are the most frequent and widespread entry in this field. Many states have begun to lease access to trust forest lands for the purpose of collecting decorative ferns, boughs, and edible mushrooms. This emphasis on gathering has occasionally brought trustees into serious conflict with rural groups who stake out their "own" territories. The conflicts have not produced as many headlines as the marijuana growers in national forests in northern California, but they present a pervasive challenge to achieving the greatest return from these new resources. Even so, this entire area of management is very small potatoes when compared to the risk and potential of commercial development.

In many cases, commercial leases produce significantly higher returns per land area and per management dollar than traditional uses. And while commercial use revenues are not immune from macroeconomic cycles, they are potentially countercyclical to the economic cycles exhibited by natural resource commodity revenues. Commercial development of state trust lands also provides one of the few sources of rapidly escalating values for states that are not well-endowed with natural resource commodities. For example, between 1975 and 1990 the price of a standard 10,000-square-foot residential lot increased by a minimum of 200 percent in a number of western cities;

and in some it increased by as much as 900 percent to 1,500 percent.[45] The demand for recreational and retirement properties has caused similar patterns in rural land prices. Even when adjusted for inflation, the price increases were significant. And while commercial office real estate was overbuilt during the 1980s, resulting largely from 10-year cyclical trends and tax regulations, construction trends for the period beyond the year 2000 estimate a return to high growth rates.[46]

The range of potential commercial uses of state trust lands is broad.[47] Table 7-2 shows existing, proposed, and actual commercial uses in the states. Standard categories of commercial development range from single gas stations, stores, and recreation sites to large residential, commercial, industrial, or mixed-used developments occupying hundreds of acres.[48] States have focused on a limited number of these potential commercial uses, with different interests and emphases evident in different states. Many of these choices are restricted (as we saw in the permanent fund discussion) by state constitution. For example, North Dakota is prevented from leasing lands for commercial uses by the state constitution,[49] although the state does receive revenues from easements for pipelines, utility lines, and telecommunications sites. At the other extreme, both Arizona and Washington have large commercial leasing and development programs, and Washington's is supported by a "land bank" that temporarily holds land sales receipts pending purchase of replacement properties to reorient their land holdings toward commercial properties.[50] Arizona's Urban Lands Program seeks to prepare the state trust land for sale to developers instead of holding onto it and receiving annual receipts.[51] Between these extremes, a multiplicity of state trust land commercial leasing programs can be identified.

These programs produce a wide range of revenues. Figure 7-4 shows the revenues graphically, divided in each state between annual lease revenues and land sales revenues. It is differentiated between annual lease revenues and land sales receipts, to highlight the different strategies the various states pursue. For example, Figure 7-4 shows that Arizona and Washington receive both the greatest amount of annual leasing revenues and the highest land sales revenues.[52]

RELATIONSHIP BETWEEN RISK AND RETURN IN COMMERCIAL LEASES

Commercial leases fit well into portfolio theory as described in Chapter 3. This is because they have the potential to diversify the state's asset holdings, which in turn reduces the overall risk (measured as fluctuations in annual revenues). As with all other resources, the proportion of the value of the resource the state receives is directly related to the amount of risk it accepts in the production and management of the resource. This discussion examines diverse commercial leasing possibilities in light of portfolio theory concepts.

TABLE 7-2. Commercial uses of state trust lands

Use	AL	AZ	CA	CO	ID	MN	MT	NB	NM	ND	OK	OR	SD	TX	UT	WA	WI	WY
Recreational Facilities																		
Golf courses	E	E		C	C	E	E	E	E		P	C		C	P	E		E
Campgrounds (KOA, etc.)	E	E	P	E	E	E	E	E	E	E	C	C	E	P	P	E	E	E
Outfitter/guide camps	E	E		C	E		E	E	E			E			E	E		E
Cabin sites	E	E		P	P	E	E	E	E		E	C			E	E		E
Ski areas	E	E		P	P		E	E				E			E	E		
Developed sport, baseball and rodeo fields, auditoriums		C					E				E	C	E	E				E
Residential Developments																		
Single-family housing	E	E	E	E			E		C		C	C			E	E		E
Multi-family housing	E	E	E	C			E		C		C	C	E		E	E		E
Condominiums		E		P					C		C	C			E			
Commercial Developments																		
Downtown		E		E	P						C	C		P	C	E		
Office park	E	E		E	P			C	C		C	P		C	P	E		
Shopping center (retail)	E	E		P			P	P	C		E	P		E	P	E		
Freeway interchange (retail)	E	E		P	C				C		C	C		C	P	E	E	
Hotel/motel/resort	E	E		E	C		E	E	E	E	C	C		C	E	E		E
State government buildings	E	E		E	E		E	E	C	C	C	E		C	P	E		
Industrial Development																		
Industrial parks	E	E		E			E	C	C		E	P		E	P			E
Energy (oil, gas, electricity)	E	E					E	P	E		E	C			E			E
Discrete sites	E	E		E			E	E	E		E	C		C	E	E		E
Warehouses	E	E		E			E	E	E	P	E	C		C		E		
Communications Sites	E	E		E	E	E	E	E	E		E	E			E	E		E
Landfills/Waste Disposal	E	E		E	E	E	E	E	C		E	C		C	E	E	E	E

Codes: E = existing; P = proposed; C = considered.

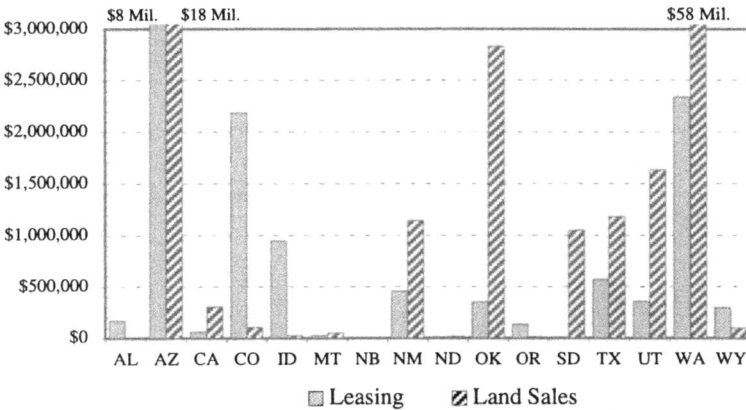

Figure 7-4. State trust land commercial leasing and land sales revenues.

Risk and Risk Premiums in Commercial Leasing. In Chapter 3, we identified three different types of risk: the risk associated with macroeconomic cycles; the risk associated with variations in returns received from a specific commodity or resource; and risks associated with particular leases. All three risk types occur in commercial leasing. Another risk—we might call it risk number 2.5—reflects the degree of state involvement in the actual development of commercial property. This is particularly important in commercial leasing, where states' involvement runs the gamut from minimal to extremely high. Figure 7-5 shows the relationship between risk and return in the various degrees of developmental involvement a state can choose to pursue.

Potential returns increase—but so do risks and costs—as the state becomes more active in developing its trust lands. At the higher levels of involvement shown in Figure 7-5, the state exposes itself to two forms of direct and future financial risk. First, the state incurs risk, in an amount potentially equal to the value of the property it holds, if it subordinates its fee interest to the leaseholder's mortgage for other development activities (such as construction of buildings and infrastructure). Second, the state exposes itself to financial demands above and beyond its fee interest if it actively participates as a working partner in the development. Most states prohibit their trust lands from being subordinated, and thus limit the trust's exposure to financial losses; however, this protection comes at the expense of potentially higher returns on asset value.

Problem of Subordination. For a state, subordination means agreeing to put the state's interest in its land in a lower position as a potential creditor than whoever is providing the mortgage for the building. If the lessee or

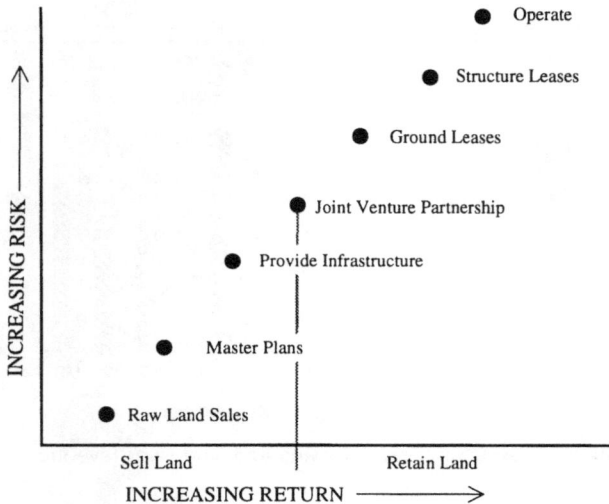

Figure 7-5. Schematic representation of the relationship between risk and return in various stages of commercial lands development.

mortgagee subsequently defaults to the lender, the lender has first priority to compensation from any funds received at liquidation. In the worst case, the state could suffer a complete loss of its asset value (investment) in this situation. Without a subordination agreement, the state retains first priority to compensation from any liquidated funds at foreclosure. Most state constitutions do not allow the trust's land or assets to be subordinated to others.[53] Only three—Alaska, California, and Oregon—do allow subordination of their interests, and then only for limited purposes.[54] States can partially overcome this limitation on subordination by becoming limited partners in real estate transactions. This reduces the return, but it also protects the trust from losses, including loss of land value.

DEVELOPMENT POSSIBILITIES

In spite of legal restrictions, states have a wide range of possibilities for approaching development of their commercial trust lands. The options are arranged in the following list in order of increasing risks and costs to the state:[55]

- *Sell raw land.* Selling directly to potential developers provides the quickest, least expensive way to dispose of trust lands. Once the lands are sold, all risks are assumed by the developer, including zoning, financing, and construction.
- *Master plan.* The state can receive additional revenues if its lands are sold

with an existing zoning and land use plan in place, and with the units of sale in developable-size parcels, instead of in the original single or quarter sections. This usually requires having the state prepare a master plan, defined by one state as "detailed descriptions of mixed land uses, zoning, annexation, open space and industrial and recreational centers. The land's income potential will increase tremendously if market-ready master plans are established prior to release of such property."[56] Master-planned sites are then usually sold to developers, who are responsible for the sale (and sometimes the construction) of the individual components of the project, as well as providing the infrastructure (roads and utilities).

Arizona uses master plans for residential and industrial park developments. Oregon prepares master plans for golf courses, state government buildings, and industrial parks (such as the one at Astoria). Texas uses master plans for most of its commercial developments.

- *Plan and construct infrastructure.* When the state provides the infrastructure, potential developers are relieved of this up-front cost; the arrangement also permits the state to sell individual, developable parcels instead of the tract as a whole. By selling individual parcels, the state accepts the risk that all parcels may not sell (or may not sell at an attractive price), and assumes the costs involved in planning and selling parcels, but it obtains the additional revenues received by the higher prices that the individual units of the development command.

Montana has provided infrastructure in the form of roads and utilities for a residential development of single-family homes outside Billings. Oregon provides infrastructure for uses ranging from golf courses to cabin sites to industrial developments. One method states may use to construct infrastructure is to join with a developer in a partnership. This method is used by Alaska for developing campgrounds, ski areas, warehouses, and communication sites.

- *Joint venture partnerships.* As a variant of the infrastructure option, the state may enter into a joint venture or limited partnership with a developer. The state contributes the land and (perhaps) construction of the infrastructure, and the developer handles the remainder of the project. In exchange for contributing the land, the state receives revenues representing a yield on the value of the land, possibly a percentage of the net or gross receipts during the lease period, and perhaps a portion of the proceeds from the ultimate sale of the development and/or its components. As a cost of entering into the venture, however, the state usually must subordinate its fee title ownership to the partnership and commonly is also be liable for debts of the project.

- *Ground leases.* The most common arrangement for commercial developments on state trust lands is the ground lease. All states (except North Dakota) use ground leases for some or all of their commercial developments, and some states (such as Oklahoma and Wyoming) use ground leases almost exclusively. In contrast to the previous options, under ground leases the state retains title to its land and leases development rights.

Therefore, states try to avoid ground leases for uses (such as single-family residences) where there is a socially ordained property right to ownership, and uses (such as landfills) where it is in the states' best interest to sever their property rights. Mortgage companies have reservations about some ground leases. If the state does not subordinate its interest, and the leaseholder subsequently defaults on the lease payment, the state can foreclose on the leaseholder's improvements. Mortgage companies typically do not like this scenario, preferring to be the first in line for proceeds from bankrupt developments.

- *Lease structures.* After the state constructs buildings, purchases them, or obtains them through foreclosure, it may make them available by lease to commercial tenants. In this situation the state is acting as landlord, and it accepts a range of responsibilities depending on the language of the lease. At the least risky end of the leasing spectrum, the state typically attempts to shift the burden of risk to the lessees by using "net leases" under which the tenant is responsible for paying property taxes, insurance, utilities, and maintenance (called "triple net leases"). Oregon leases buildings at its industrial park in the Port of Astoria; and Washington has an extensive leasing program for warehouses, retail outlets, and similar structures (see Table 7-2).

- *Conduct operations.* Very infrequently, a state actually builds and/or operates a business. This may occur in two cases. First, the state may be forced to foreclose on a sale contract and operate a business on an interim basis until it can be sold. The most prevalent type of development that states operate on a continuing basis is communications sites; Minnesota and Washington both operate such facilities. Minnesota also operates a golf course, and Washington operates various types of businesses—generally office parks and shopping centers. The second case occurs when the state constructs a building for its own use. The most common example of this practice is when the state land office constructs office buildings that are then leased to the state land office, other state agencies, or a combination of the two. Both Oregon and Nebraska currently do this.

DEGREE OF DEVELOPMENT FOR STATE TRUST LANDS

A few patterns emerge in commercial leasing based on the states' experiences. First, states are most likely to sell tracts for development if the prospective uses are unlikely to be compatible with long-term trust management—for example, landfills and home sites (either residential or cabin). In rapidly urbanizing areas and areas adjacent to freeways, states are increasingly likely to master-plan the development to increase its value. Master planning is a step that states can take to increase revenues even when they cannot subordinate their property interest or commit funds for infrastructure. Other degrees of involvement in commercial leasing usually depend on provisions in state laws and policies.

Table 7-3 shows the various ways states have decided to proceed. Generally, states sell trust lands to potential developers. Even states that have no commercial leasing program or that are prohibited from having one by state law (North Dakota), have provisions to sell trust lands. These provisions vary from state to state, but they often allow a potential purchaser to nominate tracts for sale. The state then determines whether it better serves the state's interest to sell or to retain and lease. This is the minimum level of risk and return. In specific instances, the state may have an explicit policy to reduce its exposure to risk by selling parcels. This practice is common when trust lands are designated for landfills and waste disposal. As long as the state disposes of its interest before the site is used for waste disposal, its liability for subsequent pollution is eliminated.

STATUTORY AND POLICY REVIEW OF PROVISIONS FOR TRUST LAND COMMERCIAL LEASES

A decision to engage in commercial real estate development requires the trustee to address three basic issues. First the trustee must identify lands suitable for such development. In this area, the states can take either a passive role, waiting for developers to come to them with proposals or nominations for land sales, or an active role, identifying lands that seem suitable for developers and seeking out partners. Second, if lands are suitable for commercial leases (as opposed to sales), the state must consider different means of interacting with the party that is going to obtain development rights. Third, the state must evaluate various lease provisions and terms, such as the length of the lease; whether (and how) rents are adjusted during the lease period; and how improvements to the property are approved, appraised, and transferred at the end of the lease.

Determining Land Suitability. States with legislation or an official board policy regarding commercial lands increase the visibility and incorporation of commercial concerns into their overall land and resource management programs. Table 7-4 shows the extent of state policies relating to commercial development programs.

Obtaining Development Rights. The major step where developers interact with the state land offices is when they attempt to obtain land. Table 7-5 shows which states use each of five different procedures. Two separate mechanisms are used by the states to determine what entity develops state

TABLE 7-3. Development mechanisms used in commercial programs for state trust lands

Use	AL	AZ	CA	CO	ID	MN	MT	NB	NM	ND	OK	OR	SD	TX	UT	WA	WI	WY
Recreational Facilities																		
Golf courses	J,G	G	G	S,G	G	O	J,G	S	G		G	S,M,I,J	G	S,M,G	J	G		G
Campgrounds (KOA, etc.)	G	G		G	G		G	G	G		G		G	G	G	G	G	G
Outfitter/guide camps	G			G	G	G	G	G			G		G		G			G
Cabin sites	G	S		G	G	G	G					I,J,B	G		G	G		
Ski Areas	J,G				G	G	G				G	S	G	S,M	G			G
Developed sport, baseball and rodeo fields, auditoriums		G					G				G			S,M				
Residential Developments																		
Single-family housing	S	M	S	S,M,J			S		S,J,G		S		J,B	S	S,M,I,J			G
Multi-family housing	S	S,M,G	S,G	S,G			G		S,J,G		G		J,B	S,M,G	J			G
Condominiums		M		G					S,J,G		G			S,M,G	S,J			
Commercial Developments																		
Downtown				G,B				S,G	S,J,G		G			S,M,G	O	G		
Office park		G		G				S	S,J,G		G	A		S,M,G	G	O		
Shopping center (retail)		G		G					S,J,G		G	A		S,M,G	J	O		
Freeway interchange (retail)		G		G			J,G	S	S,J,G		G				S	G		
Hotel/motel/resort		G		G				B	S,J,G		G		G,B	S,M,G	G	G	G	
State government buildings		G		G,B			G					S,M,I,B	B,O	S,M	G			G
Industrial Development																		
Industrial parks	G	M,G		G			G	G			G	M,I,J,G,B	J,G,B	S,M,G	J	G		G
Energy (oil, gas, electricity)	G	G					G	G			G		G		G			G
Discrete sites	G	G									G	I,G	G,B		G	O		G
Warehouses	J,G	G		G,B			G				G			S,M,G	G			G
Communications Sites	J,G	G		G	G	O	G		G		G			G	G	G,O		
Landfills/Waste Disposal	S	S		G	G	O	G		G		S,G				S		G	

Codes: S = land sale; M = master plan; I = provide infrastructure; J = joint venture; G = ground lease; B = building lease; O = operate; A = all except land sale.

TABLE 7-4. Mechanisms used to determine suitability for commercial development

Mechanism	States Using
State statute	ND
Land office policy	AZ, CA, ID, MN, NB, NM, OK, SD, WI
Individual parcel master plans	AL, CO, ID, NM, OR, TX, UT, WA
No legislation or policy	MT, WY

commercial trust lands: a developer approaches the state and nominates a specific parcel; or the state—through master plans, statute, or strategic plan—decides which of its lands has commercial potential and decides what developer should obtain the rights to develop it. The latter decision is usually made through an oral or written auction, but in some states negotiation may also be used.

Lease Terms. Lease terms are important because they specify how long the state is committed to an identified use, allow the lessee to plan for the future, and determine how frequently stateowned properties come onto the market. Rent adjustment measures determine whether the state's revenues keep up with inflation or other market-related indicators of fair market values for the state's assets. Table 7-6 shows the duration of commercial leases among the various states. In some states, such as New Mexico, leases longer than five years are prohibited unless advertised and auctioned.

Lease Improvements. One of the most important categories of provisions in commercial lease terms consists of provisions dealing with improvements. Improvements were first discussed in relation to agricultural leases in Chapter 4. In many respects, the same considerations raised with regard to agriculture apply to commercial leases as well. Important lease provisions, from both the state's and the lessee's point of view, include whether

TABLE 7-5. Mechanisms used to award development rights for commercial trust lands

Mechanism	States Using
Land Availability Determination	
Nomination	AL, CA, ID, MT, NB, NM, OR, UT, WA, WI, WY
Development proposals	AL, AZ, CO, NM, OK, OR, TX, UT
Sale or Lease Procedures	
Negotiation	AL, AZ, CA, CO, ID, MT, NM, OR, WA, WI
Oral auction	AL, AZ, CA, ID, MT, NB, NM, OR, OK, UT, WA, WY
Written sealed bids	AZ, CA, CO, ID, MT, OR, SD, TX, UT, WY

TABLE 7-6. Lease lengths for commercial trust land uses

Commercial Use	STATES' LEASE DURATION (YEARS)						
	< 10	10	15	20	25	30	> 30
Interim Uses	AL, WY		CO				
Recreational Facilities	AZ, WI	ID, MN, NB, WY		UT	WY		SD
Golf courses	AL				NM	AL	
Campgrounds (KOA, etc.)			CO	CA			
Outfitter/guide camps	WY						
Cabin sites	OK	MT					
Ski areas	MN						
Residential Developments		MN, WY			WY	CO	SD, UT
Single-family housing		MT					
Multi-family housing						TX	
Condominiums						TX	
Commercial Developments	CO	ID, MN, WY	AZ	AZ	WY	CO	SD, TX, UT, WA, WI
Office park				AL			
Shopping center (retail)						OK	AL
Freeway interchange (retail)			NM	AL		OK	
Hotel/motel/resort	MN					WI	
Industrial Development	CO	MN, WY			WY	CO	SD, TX, UT, WA, WI
Industrial parks							OK
Energy (oil, gas, electricity)						OK	
Discrete sites						OK	AL
Warehouses						OK	
Communications Sites		CO, ID		UT			
Landfills/Waste Disposal		ID					
Public and Charitable					NM, WY		AZ

prior approval to place the improvements is required; who owns the improvements at the end of the lease; and (if the state does not obtain ownership at lease termination) how the improvements are to be appraised to determine the original leaseholder's financial interest. Table 7-7 shows how the various states handle improvements on their commercial trust lands.

Improvements in commercial leases are as problematic to the states as improvements in grazing leases are (see discussion in Chapter 4). As in grazing leases, the method used to appraise the value of the improvements made by previous lessees depends in many ways on the parcel's future use by the state and/or the new lessee. If a similar use is intended, then appraising the depreciated value of the improvements is comparatively straightforward. If the new use is different than the previous use, however, appraisal of the improvements at the new "highest and best use" (which would be considered the new lessee's use) tends to reduce or eliminate the existing improvements' value for the previous lessee. Replacement value is always difficult, since the existing condition of the improvement may be marginal, and since the improvement may not be of much use to the new lessee. New

TABLE 7-7. State mechanisms for handling improvements on commercial leases

Mechanism	States Using
Prior Approval Required?	
Yes	AL, AZ, CA, CO, ID, MN, MT, NB, OK, OR, SD, TX, UT, WA, WY
No	WI, WY
Who Owns at End of Lease?	
State	AL, CA, CO, MN, NB, OK, TX, UT, WA, WI
Lessee	AZ, CO, ID, MT, NB, WY
Individually negotiated	CO, ID, MT, OR, SD
How Are Improvements Appraised?	
Replacement value	CA
Depreciated value	AL, AZ, CA, CO, ID, MT, NB, OR, SD, WY
Highest and best use	AZ, NB, OK, TX, UT, WY

Mexico has had problems with this in connection with a commercial lease for a motel in Albuquerque.

THE INTERESTING CASE OF TELECOMMUNICATIONS SITES

Telecommunications sites constitute an especially interesting subfield of commercial leasing. This subject is a bit off the beaten path, but it is worth a brief digression from our discussion of more typical real estate transactions. Although states have been leasing such sites since the 1950s, rapid development of what Vice President Al Gore popularized as the "information highway" has required managers to approach the issue with a new set of strategies and has involved them in an array of new issues.

All kinds of communications signals require mountaintop locations for transmitters and relay points. The market for such sites includes radio and television stations; pagers and radio communications for consumer and industrial service providers; and communications for police, ambulance, and similar public services. Location is the crucial variable in evaluating potential communications sites.

Controversy focuses on figuring out how much to charge for the sites. The value of a transmission site servicing a large television or beeper market like Los Angeles or Denver is considerably higher than the value of the same site utilized for transmitting radio signals to taxis in Paonia, Colorado. Pricing problems are further complicated by questions about whether sites for police and other public safety signals should have to be obtained through open competition in the same market. Finally, it is difficult to design lease and access systems that simultaneously permit full utilization of a site and ensure that the trust will benefit from development. If the first lessee of a communications site develops the infrastructure—roads, basic buildings, and equipment—under what terms and conditions should subsequent users be allowed to use the facilities so that the benefit is appropriately shared between the initial developer and the trust? It is particularly important to utilize each site fully because telecommunications facilities tend to be located on mountaintops and therefore have a significant aesthetic impact.

These difficult pricing problems are complicated by the fact that, in western states, the market is dominated by the federal government. Few privately owned sites exist that might provide comparable sales for appraisal. And as in so many fields, the federal government has decided not to charge fair market value. The Forest Service currently lets over 6,000 leases for communications facilities, and the Bureau of Land Management has granted 95 right-of-way authorizations for the same purpose. Many of these sites have been leased for decades (up to 40 years) and the federal fee structure has not been adjusted since the 1950s.

Under the Federal Land Policy and Management Act (FLPMA), the federal government is required to charge fair market value for telecommunications sites. However, Congress has become embroiled in a debate over how fair market value should be determined. The spat began in response to a 1985 Forest Service effort to draft regulations for setting fees on a regional rather than national basis. The agency surveyed more than 2,000 private leases and issued draft fee schedules for each region during 1986 and 1987. Forest Service regions 6 and 9 published final regulations for charging fair market value based on those market appraisals. The other regions ran into fierce opposition in Congress when they tried to publish their final fee structures in 1989. The new fees, involving increases as high as 2,000 percent of existing fees, have been blocked by language placed annually in the agency's appropriations bill.

The Forest Service conducted another market analysis in 1991, but the resulting reconstructed fee schedule was still not acceptable to Congress. The Secretaries of Agriculture and the Interior were instructed by Congress to establish a Radio and Television Broadcast Fee Advisory Committee. The committee, which issued its report in 1992, recommended that the Bureau of Land Management and Forest Service leasing procedures be made more similar. It also proposed a new fee schedule that would raise fees by 200 to 900 percent from their current levels. FLPMA allows the Bureau of Land Management to discount fair market value up to 100 percent for private interests providing a "public service." The advisory committee concluded that radio and TV operators provide such a public service, especially for rural areas. At present writing, a full spectrum of bills, some of which endorse fair market value and others of which support discounted pricing for various categories of telecommunications sites, are working their way through Congress. The 1993 Budget Reconciliation Act put a cap of 10 percent on any proposed increase in fees for federal telecommunications sites.[57]

This ambiguity at the federal level, in a market dominated by federal lands, has made it difficult for states to move aggressively in this promising new field. Only Utah has made a concerted effort to develop a comprehensive program in this area, and its plans have been confounded by federal fee-setting activities.

Land Exchanges

As with regard to telecommunications sites, state trustees' efforts to complete land exchanges are frequently confounded by conflicting priorities at the federal level. Land selections and exchanges with the federal government have, in fact, been a major feature of the school and trust lands program since its inception. The importance of land exchanges arises from two historic factors. First, beginning with the Ohio accession, states were authorized to select lands in lieu of granted sections that had been previously occupied. States joining the Union during the last decades of the nineteenth century were authorized to select alternative sections for granted lands included in expanding federal land reservations. Second, the lands were granted in scattered sections in each township, which makes management of the dispersed parcels difficult in any event. When, following passage of the Federal Land Policy and Management Act (FLPMA), it became clear that those state lands were permanently embedded in extensive federal land holdings, many of which were being evaluated for wilderness values, trustees' efforts to consolidate their holdings intensified. Unfortunately, state efforts to procure their in lieu sections and trade out of national parks, national forests, and Bureau of Land Management wilderness areas were frequently frustrated by the complex requirements of specific statutes authorizing federal agencies (particularly the Bureau of Land Management) to pass title or exchange lands.[58] Nothing before or after the passage of FLPMA has done much to make the process simpler. Some states (such as Washington) have succeeded in establishing purchase programs and land banks to facilitate the repositioning of trust assets primarily or exclusively involving state lands; but land exchanges involving the federal government continue to be a challenge.

The frustrations of the process, and its likely future evolution are well illustrated by events of the 1980s, beginning with a major legal and political battle in Utah.[59] Under its 1894 enabling act, Utah was entitled to select 223,000 acres of land in lieu of school sections that fell within federal reservations or had been taken up by private entry. Utah's efforts to make those selections were frustrated for more than thirty years by "administrative delay, disputes concerning valuation and changes in federal land management policy." Finally, in 1976, Utah sued the Secretary of the Interior to force recognition of state title to selected lands. Four years later, the U.S. Supreme

Court reversed the federal district and appellate court decisions and upheld the Interior Department's interpretation of Section 7 of the Taylor Grazing Act. According to the Supreme Court, the Taylor Act (enacted in 1934) modified the ancient in lieu selection provisions (which allowed the state to select an equal number of acres for the unavailable ones) and authorized the Secretary of the Interior to reject applications for replacement lands that were not also equal in value to the originally granted lands. Because the sites that Utah had selected were not equal in value to the ones they had been unable to occupy, the Utah state selections were disallowed.

The case gives a crude indication of some of the difficulties that may arise in any land exchange, whether the goal is to trade out of federal land or to acquire parcels for commercial development. It is no mean feat to find parcels to exchange that are equal in size and value. It is even more difficult to figure out how to appraise parcels, especially those that are land-locked within federal holdings such as national parks. Ought the value to be based on the utility of the land as grazing land, as a second home site, or as the location of a resort, or ought some other standard be applied? Moreover, the federal management agencies with whom states must deal have their own authorities, procedures, and requirements for making exchanges; and due to the complexity and likelihood of failure, they also have very little motivation to make the effort. They are especially unlikely to make the effort if, by doing nothing, they can effectively achieve their own goals on what remain (in title) state lands.

The Supreme Court defeat led the Governor of Utah to propose a legislative exchange of Utah's scattered school lands and its selection rights for consolidated and manageable blocks of federal lands. Project Bold, as the enterprise was known, first ran afoul of Bureau of Land Management authorities for land exchanges. Designed to expand and clarify its exchange authority, section 206 of FLPMA imposed so many requirements for land use planning and review prior to an exchange,[60] that the massive Project Bold proposal was never seriously pursued under normal administrative procedures. Instead, Utah's congressional delegation sought special legislation to consummate the massive land deal. In all, forty-five blocks of land involving 2.5 million acres of federal land were identified for acquisition by the state in exchange for 2.5 million acres of state inholdings. That proposal died in Congress in 1984, and the rest of the decade saw a series of lesser exchange proposals rise and fade without success.[61]

Meanwhile, frustrated by their inability to consummate exchanges of smaller parcels,[62] the states supported legislation to streamline the federal agencies' exchange procedures. The Federal Land Exchange Facilitation Act (FLEFA) passed in 1988. It was designed to streamline procedures, accelerate negotiations, and establish uniform rules for Forest Service and Bureau of Land Management exchanges. Its central features are mandatory timetables for progress on an exchange and a system of mandatory arbitration for establishing the value of the tracts involved. In 1989 the Forest Service and the Bureau of Land Management released draft regulations for exchanges under FLEFA. Incredibly, in response to a law intended to standardize the exchange process the two agencies proposed incompatible procedures. As of this writing, following several intervening trials and errors, the nation continues to await final, compatible regulations.

One might wonder, given the extraordinary difficulty of making exchanges, why any state would persist in trying to make them. Three reasons stand out. First, the state's scattered sections are frequently difficult to manage efficiently. Second, the state's trust mandate frequently draws the state into conflict with the priorities of its noisiest neighbors, the federal land management agencies. Although this has been a long-standing problem with the National Park Service, changes in Forest Service priorities and the development of a Bureau of Land Management wilderness program following passage of FLPMA have exacerbated conflicts. Again Utah ran most thoroughly afoul of this growing problem. In 1979, the state successfully sued the Secretary of the Interior to procure access for a mineral leaseholder to a checkerboarded state school section surrounded by a Bureau of Land Management wilderness study area. Although right of access was nominally assured, the bureau's exercise of its right to condition access has effectively prevented the lessee from developing the site.[63] Third, the states are increasingly likely to pursue exchanges to procure parcels valuable for commercial development.

The failure of the Project Bold exchange and (thus far) of the FLEFA reforms suggests that states are likely to pursue the aforementioned goals in the future quite apart from the tedious and problematic process of swapping one parcel for another, whether their pursuit be administrative or legislative. Utah finally gained some degree of satisfaction, not by exchanging parcels, but by trading landlocked sections and selection rights for mineral rights and revenues. Under the Utah School and Lands Improvement Act of 1993, the state exchanged almost 200,000 acres of land in national parks, national forests, and Indian reservations for less than 4,000 acres of land, unleased coal in four Forest Service– and Bureau of Land Management–managed areas totaling approximately 14,300 acres and $50 million in mineral revenues.[64] Similarly, Arizona successfully consummated a number of advantageous land exchanges with the Bureau of Land Management and other federal agencies during negotiation of land transactions necessitated by the Central Arizona Project. Most recently, California has completed long-desired land transactions—again not through any "normal" process, but as a part of larger land transactions resulting from passage of the California Desert Protection Act.

Frustrated by decades of fruitless efforts to go "by the book" to achieve important land exchanges, states are now pursuing their goals in the context of spectacular transactions, typically abetted by major federal programs, in which the exchanges become almost incidental. One major result of these activities is to make the lands—especially those in Utah and in the California desert—more visible.

NEW CONTROVERSIES

With new visibility comes controversy. Proceeding aggressively on a number of new resources and procedures has drawn more and more response from environmental groups and amenity interests that seemingly were unaware of these lands as recently as ten years ago. The controversies generally revolve around the public amenity value of the trust lands. On one hand, these controversies are couched in terms of the public's asserted right of access to their "public" lands—a line of argument generally pushed by hunters and anglers. On the other hand, the issue may be presented as one of maintaining the existing biological value and composition of the trust lands—usually couched in terms of protection of the trust corpus and sustainability. In this section, we briefly examine three controversies and their effects on trust management: the Endangered Species Act; recent efforts to open trust lands to recreational hunting; and increasing pressure to manage trust lands for preservation. We conclude with a discussion of trust lands and their role in defining sustainable resource management.

Endangered Species

The Endangered Species Act of 1973 is one of many laws of general applicability that affect trust resource management. Two sections of the ESA affect state programs: section 7, which requires consultation with the U.S. Fish and Wildlife Service if a federally funded or federally permitted action is proposed; and section 9, which requires a permit from the Fish and Wildlife Service if a proposed action has the potential to "take" a listed threatened or endangered species. Before we look at specific examples of the state trust interaction with the ESA, let us consider whether the ESA applies to state trust lands and, if so, why the provisions of the ESA supersede the terms of the prior Federal legislation that granted the lands to the states expressly to support public institutions.

The question of the relationship between the Endangered Species Act and the earlier federal grants to the states has arisen in almost every state. It is particularly grating in the Northwest, due to the controversy over spotted owls, and in the Southwest, where state trust lands proposed for residential developments are located in areas occupied by desert tortoises. Because of hazard posed by the state's timber program to the northern spotted owl, and vice versa, the Oregon Attorney General issued an opinion on applicability of the ESA to the common school trust's Elliot State Forest[65] finding that section 9 of the Act applies to states just as it does to private landowners. Nothing in the trust land's status either as state lands or as trust lands insulates them from laws of general applicability such as the Endangered Species Act.

Section 7 of the ESA requires consultation with the U.S. Fish and Wildlife Service prior to initiation of activities that are federally funded or permitted. The consultation process begins when the applicant (either the state or a federal agency) requests from the service a list of threatened or endangered species located within the proposed project area. Once this list is received, the applicant must prepare a biological assessment of the potential effect on the species of the proposed action. This assessment is sent to the service, which then issues a biological opinion on the proposal. The biological opinion may agree or disagree with the applicant's assessment, but in either case, if the project would expose the species or its critical habitat to harm, the service will recommend "reasonable and prudent" measures to eliminate the impacts. If no such reasonable and prudent measures are available, or if the applicant disagrees with the service's determinations, the section 7 consultation can be elevated in the Department of Interior hierarchy, finally reaching the Endangered Species Committee (the "God Squad") for ultimate resolution.

More commonly, a state's proposed action does not require a section 7 consultation because there is no federal "nexus." States are not clearly off the endangered species hook, however, because section 9 of the act requires a "taking" permit from the Fish and Wildlife Service if a proposed action affects a listed endangered animal (but not threatened animals, and not plants) or its habitat. Following the Supreme Court's ruling in *Babbitt v. Sweet Home Chapter*, 63 U.S. L.W. 4665 (1995), it is clear that courts will continue to follow their previous decisions that habitat destruction, as well as physical harm, constitutes "take" under section 9.[66] Generally, to obtain a permit, the applicant must prepare a habitat conservation plan (with attendant environmental documentation) that meets the Fish and Wildlife Service's specifications. Once the permit is received, as long as the Habitat Conservation Program (HCP) is followed, the applicant is allowed to conduct operations that might harm the listed species or damage its habitat.

Recreation and Hunting Access

While the federal government has become involved in wildlife management on trust lands through the Endangered Species Act, hunting and other rec-

TABLE 7-8. Hunting and recreational access policies

Policy	States Using
Access open	AZ, CA, ID, ND, SD, OR, UT, WA, WY
Access closed	NB, OK, TX
Access permit required	MT, NM
Access by lease	CO

reationists are exerting increasing pressure on trust managers to allow access to trust lands. Although the biggest conflict might be anticipated to involve areas where state lands are surrounded by federal lands with unrestricted access, most of the heat state managers have felt has been in states where lands open to hunting are scarce (either statewide or regionally within a state) or where trust lands are blocked up into large units. Surprisingly, access across trust lands to reach open federal lands is rarely a problem, largely because state lands are not usually separately fenced and posted. In contrast, where most of the surrounding land is posted, the state trust lands have a veneer of being "public" land that encourages sporting groups to demand that they be opened for access and generates counterpressures from the lessees (usually the surrounding owner whose lands are posted) to restrict access.

States have dealt with pressure for hunting and recreational use of trust lands in four ways, as shown in Table 7-8. First, the state may throw open all its lands, unless the land office specifically allows the lessee to restrict access. This stance is most typical of states where private land owners' rights to close land to hunting are restricted by state law. Where the norm is that virtually all rural land is open to hunting, state trustees comply, although they do close lands for administrative purposes. At the other extreme, the state may choose to prohibit everyone other than its officers and lessees from having access to its trust lands. When the state pursues this strategy, it may disallow the lessee to charge for hunting access, or it may allow the lessee to charge as long as the state receives a share of the revenues.

In the third alternative, the state may sell access permits to individuals—similar to hunting and fishing licenses—so that they can use legally accessible state trust lands. Persons without permits are excluded. Usually the beneficiaries receive the majority of the revenues from sales of these permits, although the permit seller is paid a fee as well, and the state land office may retain an additional sum to cover its expenses. The fourth strategy is to negotiate access leases either with other public agencies or with private individuals and clubs.

These third and fourth strategies provide an interesting basis for comparison, both in their effects and in their underlying philosophy. Colorado's and

Montana's access programs can serve as representative models. At the behest of the Montana legislature, the Montana Division of State Lands hired an economic consultant to determine how best to maximize revenues to the trust from recreational access. The economist determined that revenues would be maximized if the state charged a $35 per permit fee (instead of the then-current $5 permit), and that, based on willingness-to-pay surveys, the state would sell an estimated 12,000 permits at this fee level.[67] Thus approximately $420,000 per year of revenues would be received (if sales projections were met), while only 12,000 people would be accessing the trust lands. This is a case of maximizing revenues while restricting access. The purported benefit is that damage to trust resources as a result of public access is minimized while the trust receives the maximum revenues that the public—or a certain proportion of it—are willing to pay for the privilege of using trust lands.

In contrast, Colorado's hunting access program with the Division of Wildlife allows the division to specify a maximum of 500,000 acres of trust lands with legal access for public hunting areas. For this right, the division pays $500,000 annually ($1 per year per acre) and must prepare management plans for the designated areas. Access periods and conditions are determined site-by-site between the Land Board and the Division of Wildlife, but areas are generally open only during hunting seasons, and no camping is allowed, except on one 31,000-acre parcel at La Jara Reservoir. Unlike Montana's, Colorado's program maximizes public use of trust lands; at the same time, it provides the beneficiaries with revenues roughly equivalent to those produced by Montana's program.

There is no simple answer to the question of which is "better" for the state or for the trust. Montana's restrictive policy regarding access is designed to maximize revenue. Colorado's program is aimed at maximizing general public benefit—that is recreation access—while still providing revenues to beneficiaries. Significantly, both states receive financial benefits from providing recreational access—something none of the states in the open access and closed access categories achieve. Moreover, although Montana aims to maximize revenues, its program may not yield more net returns than Colorado's. We could complicate the issue by assessing the impact of the two programs on the long-term productivity of the trust, or we could perhaps simplify it by reading the trust documents: is the beneficiary the common schools or the people of the state? This small comparison suggests that, within the trust principles and the trustees' diverse interpretations of their mandate, there is room for considerable flexibility in pursuing a broad range of strategies regarding hunting and other recreation access programs.

Preservation for Aesthetic Reasons

It is unclear how far the issue of nonmonetary benefits and less-than-maximum benefits can be pushed in the trust context. Two recent court cases— one in Colorado and one in Utah—suggest that, under growing pressure from environmentalists, states may even permit aesthetic preservation to find its way onto the trustees' agenda.

Colorado courts took an aggressive approach to aesthetic preservation. A mining operation on state trust lands in the picturesque Flat Iron Mountains, which are visible to much of the affluent city of Boulder, was halted, after a long legal dispute, by the Colorado Supreme Court. The court's decision hinged on a Colorado reclamation statute that permitted counties to identify areas unsuitable for mining. When the Boulder County government identified a state trust land parcel as unsuitable under this law, the State Land Board unsuccessfully argued that the county should not be able to trump a trust purpose established by the state constitution. The decision in the *Conda* case[68] was hostile to the Land Board, and the publicity attendant to the long-fought case was extremely negative. Indeed, one could perhaps explain the board's subsequent public involvement in the decision to expand hunting and recreation access significantly as a response to the costly Boulder dispute.

Aesthetic preservationists elsewhere cannot count on Colorado's peculiar combination of a favorable statutory situation and an angry court. A Utah court discussed what may be the outer boundaries restraining preservationist impulses toward the trust lands in its 1993 decision in *National Parks and Conservation Association v. Board of State Lands*. The court noted that "we have emphasized the duty of the trustee to maximize the monetary return of the school trust lands. We turn now to an issue that is of great importance to this state. The question is, can such [unique scenic, archaeological, and paleontological] treasures be preserved without violating the terms of the school trust? We think so. Although the primary objective of the school land trust is to maximize the economic value of school trust lands, that does not mean that school lands should be administered to maximize economic return in the short run." The court went on to suggest that "it would be as much a violation of the state's fiduciary obligations to immediately sell all the state school lands as it would be to use the proceeds from the lands for a non-trust purpose. . . . The Division should recognize that some school lands have unique scenic . . . and archaeological values that would have little economic value on the open market. In some cases, it would be unconscionable not to preserve and protect these values." But the court stopped far short of saying that preservation goals trump the trustee's obligation to the beneficiary, instead suggesting that "[i]t may be possible for the Division to protect and preserve those values without diminishing the economic value of the land. For example, with appropriate restrictions it may be possible for livestock grazing and perhaps even mineral extraction to occur on a school section without damaging archaeological and paleontological sites. But when economic exploitation of such lands is not compatible with the non-economic values, the state may have to consider exchanging public trust lands or other state lands for school lands."[69]

Compensating the Trust for Areas Managed for Preservation

Three questions underlie the issue of management for preservation. The *Conda* case and the ESA examples suggest that, when the question is presented in the context of compliance with laws of general applicability, the trustees must comply with preservation programs, even if compliance substantially reduces the trust income.[70] Maintaining trust income is simply not an issue in this context. Two other permutations of the question, however, raise the revenues issue squarely. First, one could ask how far a preservation-oriented trustee may go, using discretion, in the direction of preservation programs that impose losses on the trust? To our knowledge, this precise issue has not been litigated. However, the *Skamania* and *Nigh* cases discussed in earlier chapters suggest that, if a beneficiary complains, the trustee's discretion either to forgo income or to incur costs is quite limited. Second, one could ask how far a preservationist-oriented citizen or citizen's group may push a reluctant or beneficiary-oriented trustee in the absence of a preservation statute of general applicability? Recent Idaho litigation, in which a citizen's group attempted to invoke the trustee's duty to maintain the productive capacity of the trust to stop a timber sale alleged to harm a watershed floundered: the plaintiffs were denied standing. This would seem to be a major barrier to litigation-based efforts to prod reluctant trustees in the direction of preservation.[71]

A second Idaho case, still pending, raises a potentially more promising approach to this same issue. Confronted by a state grazing lessee whose practices allegedly damaged watershed values, an Idaho conservation group attempted to outbid the lessee at renewal. For reasons imbedded in a fine-grained series of charges and countercharges over compliance with the Idaho Administrative Procedures Act, the Land Board turned down the conservationists, even though theirs was apparently not only the high bid but the only bid received during the lease auction.[72] One could envision similar efforts running afoul of requirements regarding the qualifications of bidders—that they have two years experience in ranching or a degree in range management—as discussed in Chapter 4. Nevertheless, the issue has not yet been fully joined. As it unfolds, it will teach us much about tradeoffs between development and preservation of resources, and the willingness of citizens to pay or forgo benefits to the trust in order to achieve preservation goals.

Under growing pressure from environmental interests, the courts and the trustees are beginning to find a place on school trust lands for subsidized recreation and hunting access, and even for aesthetic preservation. Trustees are on notice, we believe, that their mandate to maximize returns for the beneficiary does not free them from the growing public demand that profit be obtained by methods that are as aesthetically and environmentally sensitive as possible. The full range of public concerns and priorities, particularly as manifested in statutes such as the Endangered Species Act, will become part of the context in which the trustees' decisions are made and their undivided loyalty to the beneficiary is acted out. This does not mean that these lands will be converted, over time and under pressure, into multiple-use lands. But it does mean that the trust notion of protecting the corpus of the trust will grow increasingly large at the center of trust land management debates. The interplay between trust principles and management and the rapidly evolving discussion of sustainability or sustainable management is highly intriguing. We believe that the state trust lands have much to teach about sustainable resource management.

Sustainability

We saw in Chapter 5 that sustained yield management, as traditionally defined in the forestry context, is a narrow subset of the topics now being discussed under the general heading of sustainability. Whereas early foresters were concerned to sustain the production of a physical volume of wood or fiber, contemporary discussions focus on sustaining ecosystems, productive capacity, and human communities.

In this section we argue that trust lands management is peculiarly relevant to the growing national conversation about sustainable public lands management. First, we argue that institutional aspects of the trust provide a number of important guidelines for addressing institutional aspects of sustainable resource management. Much of the discussion of sustainability thus far has focused on defining it.[73] Our perambulation into trust resource management has convinced us that institutional design is at least as important as satisfactory definition to achieving long-term resource management goals. To underscore that conclusion, we return to our introduction to trust law and revisit the four basic themes discussed there: clarity, accountability, enforceability, and perpetuity. Using the structure afforded by those themes, we illustrate crucial aspects of trust management that seem central to designing institutions for sustainable management. Second, we point to a number of examples of trust land programs in which the trustee's obligation to preserve the productive capacity of the trust has justified redefinition of policies along nascent but significant lines of sustainability.

CLARITY

We believe that the school trust lands teach enormous lessons about institutional aspects of sustainable resources management. The clarity of the trust manager's mandate is crucial to our argument. The key distinction between trust land management and federal land management lies in the specificity of the trust goals. Unlike the very vague "multiple-use" mandate that guides management of Forest Service and, more recently, Bureau of Land Management lands—"the management of all the various renewable surface resources of the national forests so that they are utilized in the combination that will best meet the needs of the American people"[74]—the state trust lands are managed to achieve specific goals: raising money to support clearly identified beneficiaries. Translated into the language of sustainable management, these goals enable state trust land managers to be uncommonly clear about what they must sustain.

ACCOUNTABILITY

The clarity of the mandate and the trustee's obligation to keep records that permit the beneficiary to monitor the trustees' activity combine to make state trust resource management highly accountable. In our view, this accountability is also central to sustainability. We have been able to analyze state trust lands management in a way that, in our previous lives as aficionados of federal land management, we were never able to achieve. For example, we can say that, when inflation eats deposits in the permanent fund, it is not worth developing resources to produce those funds. Similarly, we can say that, under certain circumstances, the trustee is overinvesting in management of unproductive resources; we can do so because the goal—producing returns for the beneficiary—is clear. We need not be distracted by the managers' assertions that it is good for the community to overinvest. And the analysis is not confounded by data regarding expenditures and receipts that are put forward to conceal and justify overinvestment in management. The trustee is specifically accountable for keeping and producing numbers for the public that will tell the public what management is costing and what it is producing. We can tell when management's primary effort goes into sustaining or enhancing itself. Accountability—specifically, financial accountability—matters enormously to sustainability.

ENFORCEABILITY

A third key to the trust lands' lessons for sustainable resource management is enforceability. In each of the disputes we have mentioned in this book, management goals have been influenced and (ultimately) defined by the availability of the judicial forum to enforce trust principles. In key cases such as *Lassen, Skamania,* and *Nigh,* it is easy to become so enthralled by the issue of undivided loyalty that one misses another crucial fact: trust principles alter the nature of the judicial forum in which trust issues are heard. This is because the courts treat trustees with considerably less deference than they do administrators. Crudely stated, traditional principles of administrative review favor the administrator; but trust law bends toward protecting the beneficiary and the trustor's intentions from the trustee.[75]

On federal public lands, the administrator's advantage arises from the fact that the court must respect agency discretion: it cannot substitute its judgment for the administrator's, and it must defer to the administrator's expertise.[76] These presumptions are not always dispositive, and they certainly do not define a zone within which an administrator can depend on acting without close scrutiny from the judiciary; but they *are* the starting presumptions. The Court's willingness to take a "hard look" at administrative decisions ebbs and flows across time, place, and issue. Even when it crests, however, the Court must respect the agency, its expertise, and its discretion.

The shoe is on the other foot in the case of a trustee. The court specifically seeks to assess whether the trustee has met the "prudent person" standard: did the trustee act with prudence in handling the trust assets? The practical effect of any apparent or alleged expertise on the trustee's part is not to insulate his or her decision from scrutiny, but rather to require him or her to meet higher and higher standards of prudence.[77]

This slight tilt in the table does not mean that the trust always "wins." Lessees have won many cases against school land administrators, particularly when challenging a decision not to grant a lease renewal.[78] These cases are generally resolved in accordance with the parameters of normal administrative law, which afford no special protection either to beneficiaries or to trustees seeking to protect the trust. However, the potential exists for a different set of standards and outcomes: when the beneficiary (rather than the lessee) sues and alleges a breach of trust, trust principles are clearly the basis for judicial analysis. This gives both the trust and the diligent trustee an extra measure of clout. Trust principles are not always the fulcrum of the decision; but when they are invoked, they are enforceable. The special context provides the trust added protection from self-serving or politically or legislatively harassed administrators.

Explicit enforceability of the trust and its peculiar context for judicial decisionmaking are not a panacea. However, such enforceability clearly has the potential to protect long-term resource commitments from politically pressured legislatures and managers, and it provides another tool in managing for sustainability.

PERPETUITY

The three strands of trust management—clarity, accountability, and enforceability—contribute importantly to what we regard as instructive elements for designing institutions for sustainable resource management. The fourth and most crucial element, in our view, is perpetuity. The perpetual nature of the trust doctrine as applied to school lands provides the essence of the trusts' relevance to sustainability. The original school land grants did not clearly establish a perpetual trust, or even a trust of any lesser kind.[79] Indeed, early constitutions contemplated that the land would be sold, and early state programs frequently utilized the lands for such purposes as paying salaries for teachers.[80] At the outset, the grants were obviously meant to get school systems started; little thought was given to long-term management.[81]

Perpetuity became a component of the school trust when the "permanent school funds" were established.[82] Permanence in the school funds and in land management is a hallmark of the program and perhaps its most persuasive tie to current sustainability discussions. The discussions of clarity, accountability, and enforceability indicate that, under the trust lands regime it is possible to sustain the production of dollars. The three cases discussed in the remainder of this section are notable because each vindicates the beneficiary's claim against the trustee in the face of a clear legislative statement to the contrary.[83] In different resource settings and in two different states—agricultural leases in Oklahoma,[84] and mineral royalties in Arizona[85]—protection and "wise use" (at least of the value) of a resource were at risk. And in each case, trust principles yielded a consistent result that differed considerably from what one would predict in a traditional public resource case.

Trust principles were successfully used to attack cross-subsidization in *Oklahoma Education Association v. Nigh.*[86] The state legislature had directed the trustee to lease lands for agricultural use at a maximum rent of 3 percent of their appraised value—well below fair market value. Further, the trustee was to make loans from the permanent fund for first farm and ranch mortgages at a legislatively directed maximum of 8.5 percent interest.[87] The beneficiary sued to keep trust assets from being transferred to farmers. The court found that "the use of trust fund assets for the purpose of subsidizing farmers and ranchers is contrary to the provisions of the Oklahoma Constitution, and to the provisions of the Oklahoma Enabling Act."[88]

Trust principles similarly overcame leases let at rents below fair market value in *ASARCO v. Kadish,*[89] where the U.S. Supreme Court held that the state legislature could not establish a maximum (or flat) royalty fee for minerals produced from trust lands outside the competitive bidding process. The Court disallowed the legislatively prescribed maximums even though the state constitution clearly stated that the school lands shall be managed "as the State legislature may direct." If that "blanket authority" in the state constitution authorized the legislature to mandate below-market leasing, the Court reasoned, "it would allow minerals to be leased for little or no royalty, and thus would leave room for all the abuses that the establishment of a school trust was designed to prevent."[90]

Perhaps you can perpetuate dollars, then; but what about broader resource concerns? We see three possible arguments according to which perpetuity constitutes a higher priority than current income generation in trust lands management. First, the requirement to produce current income does not supersede the requirement to protect the corpus in perpetuity.[91] Second, ambiguity about future conditions transcends the requirement for current income and thus encourages conservative management styles. Third, rising resource prices may surpass income and resultant dividends from the permanent fund.[92] We see the emphasis on perpetuity both in court decisions and (increasingly) in the autonomous actions of state land trustees. We use some current management programs and court cases to demonstrate the range of practices.

In *Nigh*, the Oklahoma Supreme Court weighed the relative importance of conservation of the corpus and protection from waste against the desirability of maximizing revenues. The court found that "while it is true that reasonable precaution should be taken for the protection of the property within the trust, this does not mean the question of income becomes an unimportant factor. Conservation necessary to protect the value of the lands leased can be adequately controlled by lease provisions and conditions, and by reasonable conservation regulations imposed by Respondent Board."[93] Although the court emphasized returns, it rejected the defendant's argument that below-market fees and subsidized interest rates automatically encourage good land stewardship.[94]

Nonetheless, high returns are not the only priority. In 1988, in *Havasu Heights Ranch and Development Corp. v. State Land Department*, the Arizona appellate court agreed with the land office that it was better in some situations to do nothing than to lease lands for a particular use that might be incompatible with most or all future uses. Commissioners are required to make "best use" of lands,[95] but "keeping its options open may, under certain circumstances, be the 'best use' of the land."[96] The Court held that the state could withhold land from leasing if it believed that the land's future use value would be greater if left undeveloped (that is, unleased). The lessee does not have a compensable interest in the lease or in improvements if either of these would lessen the ultimate value of the property to the trust.[97]

As the *Havasu* case emphasizes, courts are not always required to enforce trust notions on retrograde trustees. Frequently, as in *Nigh* and in *Skamania* (discussed in Chapter 5), the courts use trust principles to protect trustees from legislatures. What is more important to our discussion of sustainability, however, is that trust principles guide the trustees in defining policies that ensure perpetuity. Trust managers rely on their duty to protect the corpus and to maintain its productivity in dealing with recalcitrant lessees, and they quote this duty in defending their programs. We look at Washington's timber programs and New Mexico's grazing program as examples of extending the trust mandate beyond simple current revenue maximization.

Washington incorporates sustainability in its forest management plans. This may result from the higher acreage of lands and revenues or from the higher level of controversy over harvest practices.[98] When questions arose about the sustainability of biological, economic, and social systems that depend on old growth timber, the state's Department of Natural Resources (DNR)—the trustee—established the Olympic Experimental State Forest to "be a 264,000-acre proving ground for theories and technology that hold promise for allowing sustainable timber production and important ecological values to exist side by side."[99] The experimental forest is not without immediate costs, since timber harvests will be deferred on spotted owl habitat covering 63,000 acres of the forest,[100] and another 3,000 acres of old growth will be sold from the trust for preservation.[101]

New Mexico's Range Stewardship Incentive Program provides an example of a state trustee forgoing income to preserve the corpus.[102] This is a case where protection of the corpus, especially the productive capacity of the lands to produce forage in the future, offsets the emphasis on current income received from grazing fees. Grazing fees are determined by a formula that incorporates the value of comparable private grazing rates per head of cattle—using adjustments based on beef and producer prices—and then multiplies this fee by the carrying capacity of the land to determine the total rental. Under the stewardship program, participating lessees have the range condition on their allotments monitored every five years by outside specialists. Lessees whose lands are in good or improved condition, with a stable or increasing trend, receive a 25 percent reduction in their fees.[103] The state land office expects that directly tying land condition to rental fees will provide incentives for good management.[104]

We see a direct relationship in the trust lands case between perpetual revenue production and the perpetual capacity to produce them. Thus, even in the trust lands case, perpetuity can mean more than just revenue production. By protecting the resources against special interest groups—whether they be lessees or legislatures—the trustees ultimately focus on protecting the lands themselves. The examples provided here show that this can be done by the trustees acting on their own or as a result of court decisions. But whichever occurs, the focus of the trust mandate remains on protecting the corpus in the long term, enabling it to remain a sustainable source of benefits.

Although the state land commissions' traditional emphasis on revenues has not endeared the school land traditions to environmentalists,[105] we believe that other components of the trust—its emphases on perpetuity and on the preservation of the corpus of the trust—lead to management that is certainly more conservative than some have feared, and plausibly more conservative than public resource management, which is not so constrained nor so straightforwardly directed. Part of the trustees' conservatism arises from the barriers that the trust presents to managers who might wish to manipulate the school lands for the benefit of the agency. Of course, the barriers are not perfect. We have seen, for example, that it is difficult analytically to distinguish between self-serving overinvestment and legitimate investment for long-term management. However, we do not see in school lands management the massive cross-subsidies between resources—for example the trading of timber for roads—that characterize federal lands management.[106] Authorization for the cross-subsidies that do occur—for example, the investment of permanent funds in first farm mortgages—is explicit in the terms of the trust document.[107] In cases of questionable activities, management actions must be justified by tying costs and gains to the beneficiary.

The trust system's combination of clarity, accountability, and mechanisms for enforcement, we believe, suggests important structural considerations for persons engaged in serious efforts to design institutions to achieve sustainable resource management. The school trust lands teach us that a commitment to sustainable resource management, however defined, is not enough: institutions and institutional design do matter. State school land management is not, we thoroughly recognize, a perfect model of sustainable land management or, for that matter, of trust management. It does, however, suggest what is possible in terms of enforceable accountability once the goals are clear. And it does signify the importance of making a commitment to perpetuity in evaluating day-to-day management programs.

CONCLUSIONS

More aggressive management and more aggressive responses from beneficiaries and from the environmental community will not put state lands consistently on the front pages, but they will make choices more interesting and more public, as these should be. The issues themselves are controversial, and the public should be involved in important decisions such as what the role of publicly owned resources should be in urban sprawl in Arizona, just as it already has become accustomed to debating the pros and cons of timber harvesting versus fishing versus aesthetic preservation.

Trustees, beneficiaries, and the general public have long ignored the permanent funds as a component of the trust portfolio. Clearly states would benefit if they allowed managers to pursue more diverse and modern investment strategies for the funds. Just as clearly the juxtaposition of fund and resource management would salubriously inform resource management decisions. One need not be a convinced preservationist to conclude that, if the development of a resource produces no benefit for the beneficiary, it ought not be undertaken.

This orientation is well applied to the growing public interest in water on state trust lands. The prospect that, in many pending adjudications, trust lands will lose their rights to water that is needed for trust purposes is not appealing. On the other hand, the effort to pursue and protect those rights is costly. There is certainly no justification for fighting for every drop, no matter how unjustly or imprudently it may have been lost. Thus, states are beginning to pursue and protect their rights and to develop programs that make economic sense. The public ought not allow rival water claimants to dissuade trustees from pursuing their long overdue sortie simply by upping the political ante. Here is a place where beneficiaries and newly active environmentalists can act in concert to support the trust.

The issue of commercial land development is even more problematic. Although it appeared during the 1980s that trustees ought to be playing a larger role in hot real estate markets, the picture is far harder to evaluate following the early 1990s recession. The truth of the matter, however, is that trustees have little choice when urban areas grow around state trust lands. In the case of telecommunications sites, one thing is indisputable: Congress does not benefit the states by pursuing a policy of less than fair market pricing for federal sites. In the area of condominiums and warehouses, the issue is more complex. High-risk ventures would seem to have no place in school trust land management. But an aggressive approach to public resource management does not have to be terribly risky. Many alternative options are available in this field, and many different ways of configuring state involvement are possible. The public ought to weigh and evaluate these options carefully. States are experimenting with different approaches, and the public ought to be attentive both to the fate of their school lands and to the lessons about public resource management that can be learned from them.

Indeed, we find the emerging and intensifying debate most riveting in this area of learning. Enhanced public scrutiny of trustee activity will, we believe, sharpen questions about trust management and about public resource management in general. In the area of general public benefits, the Utah court has invited trustees to find ways to protect archaeological and other treasures on trust lands. This area of trust management policy and law is wonderfully rich and exciting. The Utah court was clear that, as ever, the beneficiary remains the primary concern of the trustee. However, we look for diverse disputes in the future and for diverse and informative responses from the states. Already we see interesting and important variations in the different approaches that Montana and Colorado have taken to providing hunting and recreation access on trust lands. The trustees' embrace of the portfolio concept—together with their willingness to reposition their holdings—promises to make the field of land exchanges, purchases, and kindred transactions to achieve conservation and preservation extremely interesting in coming years. More broadly, in this area of new resources and increased scrutiny, we see a chance for new and interesting answers to fundamental questions about public resources management: what should be subsidized; what should not; who should pay fair market value; when should access be granted for free, and in those cases who should absorb the reduced value to the beneficiaries. These questions come clearly into focus on trust lands, where the beneficiary and the permanent funds sharpen tradeoffs, but the discussion is relevant to all publicly owned (and many privately owned) resources.

In the federal lands case, there is no residual claimant; in the state trust lands case, there is. We have seen (in Chapter 4) that, if grazing land lessees are subsidized by low fees or other emoluments, the beneficiary may force a change. But on the trust lands, we have a shoe on the other foot as well: if the price of grazing leases goes down because hikers are permitted access to the leasehold without charge, the beneficiary may squawk again. Different states are experimenting with different programs. The situation promises to be interesting, challenging to the trustees, and likely productive of new and interesting answers to old merely political power questions formerly settled strictly on the basis of political power.

We are especially taken with what the trust lands—with their commitment both to the beneficiary and to the long-term productivity of the corpus—have to teach us about sustainable resource management. Analysis of the four-part mandate—clarity, accountability, enforceability, and perpetuity—suggests that institutional structure is as important a consideration as the definition of sustainability. We make no representation that the trust lands are a model of sustainable resource management. We believe, however, that we can move toward the goal of developing such a model by understanding the experience of the state trust lands.

EPILOGUE

State trust lands are publicly owned and managed, but they are not "public lands" in the sense that we have grown accustomed to thinking about national parks and forests. They are, as was described in the Introduction and in Chapter 1, managed as trusts for clearly specified beneficiaries, principally the common schools. The trust manager's obligation to make the trust productive and to act with undivided loyalty to the beneficiary has led to confusion and some dismay, especially among those for whom making profit on public lands is anathema. State trust lands have been ignored in discussions of public resource management because they are frequently scattered, their management philosophy is out of step with the dominant model of what public lands "ought" to be, and their resource programs are difficult to discuss because of their enormous variability.

We argued in the Introduction that this is a costly error for two reasons. First, school lands are an important resource in most western states, even though in most jurisdictions the trust lands produce only a small fraction of annual state school expenditures. In some areas, the state lands are an integral and crucial part of farm economies and communities; in others, state timber programs are a major revenue and employment resource. In other instances, prudent land exchange programs, urban development, or the evolution of new resource needs has increased the economic value of state parcels previously valuable only for grazing. And the trust lands frequently contain surprisingly important environmental values. Because of constitutional language prohibiting any use of school lands in North Dakota other than "pasturage," the trust sections there have remained unplowed and now contain some of the last remaining major undisturbed areas of native prairie. Washington state forests contain nearly half of the old-growth stands on the Olympic Peninsula. School administrators, parents and friends of school children, legislators, taxpayers and environmentalists all ought to be paying more attention to the state trust lands. We have provided sufficient background, data, and analytic tools to enable concerned citizens and officials to begin asking useful, probing questions about their state's trust land management.

More broadly, the school lands are laboratories for techniques and management approaches that have much to teach us about public resources. Because the management mandate is peculiar—surely the trust idea is radically different from more familiar federal system multiple-use management—we can use the trust lands to ask important questions about public resources. And because the basic mechanism of management, the lease, is common to both state and federal public resource development programs, we can raise interesting questions about techniques and issues that underlie virtually all of our experience with public resource management. We summarize our conclusions about both trust management and its important lessons by focusing on three topics in this epilogue.

First, we draw attention to the centrality of the lease as an instrument of public resource management, both in theory, and in its diverse applications throughout the trust land states. The lease is both a focus for reasonable questions and a source of reasonable, interchangeable answers. In the myriad provisions utilized by states, we see a tool kit that those seeking to understand or reform management programs can explore and experiment with.

Second, we use the trust mandate—and our four-part mantra of clarity, accountability, enforceability, and perpetuity—to raise questions about public resource management. For many decades, economists have been urging critics of public resource management to embrace market mechanisms as a route to reform.[1] Most recently this discussion has focused on two familiar topics: first, critics argue that federal land managers lack proper incentives to manage resources efficiently; second, critics urge federal land managers to end subsidies and make every resource program pay its own way. Our discussion of the trust mandate lends considerable credence to this position. However, it also suggests that ending subsidies and creating proper incentives do not lie at the heart of the matter. Trust management exists in a clear institutional context that is far broader and more complex than can be encompassed by mere market mechanisms.

Finally, we address the political context of trust management. The tensions we have discussed throughout the volume—between lessees and the landowner, between the beneficiary and the general benefit, between present and future benefits—are, at bottom, political forces that shape all public resource management. Trust managers are not rendered immune to their environment by the trust mandate. The mandate does, however, define the process and the balance of power in interesting and important ways.

THE LEASE IN THEORY AND ON THE GROUND

Throughout this book, we have emphasized the fundamental differences between state trust lands and federal multiple-use lands. Here, we start by looking in the other direction. In order to demonstrate that lessons drawn from one category of lands are applicable to the other, we must first recognize a fundamental similarity that underlies all state and federal programs:[2]

the federal government and all state governments have uniformly decided not to invest directly in the development of publicly owned resources. Instead, both state and federal agencies rely on private entrepreneurs and private investment to produce most goods and services on public lands. We emphasize this common thread because most public lands management analysts emphasize statutory, economic, and cultural distinctions among management programs and agencies. Our study of state trust lands suggests that greater emphasis ought to be placed on the basic tool that underlies virtually all public commodity development programs: the lease.

The Lease in Theory

The three programs we have explored in detail—agricultural lands, timberlands, and mineral resources—all have at their core some form of lease, although in the case of timber it is more likely to be called a sales contract. The lease allocates the risks and benefits of resource development and extraction between the landowner and a private entrepreneur. This can be distinguished from the process adopted for hardrock minerals by some states and by the federal government: the location system allows the successful explorer to make most decisions about the timing and intensity of development without paying either rent or royalty.

Having decided not to invest in resource development, the landowner is obliged to develop programs and a process that are attractive to private investors while simultaneously meeting the landowner's overall management goals and constraints. There are three possibilities:

- The landowner can hire labor to produce the goods.
- The landowner can rent or sell total use of the resource to a private individual for cash.
- The landowner can share with the developer both the costs and the benefits of development.

States operate their trust programs within this range of development options. As we saw, few states directly hire labor to produce commodities from trust lands, although all states necessarily employ people to manage the trust lands. To greater or lesser degrees, however, all states use some form of the latter two development options. And the contractual mechanism used in both cases is the lease.

The basic similarity and familiarity of the lease instrument used on state and federal lands help us identify what is central in that process:

- Definition of the landowner's and lessee's rights and responsibilities
- Allocation of returns between the landowner and the developer

- Lease length and renewal terms at contract termination
- Decisions about access and the timing of development
- How improvements to the leasehold are approved, who owns them, and how their value will be appraised at lease termination
- How the lessee will vacate the property at lease termination

Within this general lease framework, a multitude of resource-specific practices have evolved. In Chapter 4, we described an "ideal" leasing system for agricultural lands, using the basic structure of the lease and its diverse application in the trust land states. Leasing in this area, we asserted, ought to begin by addressing issues of land capability; this would entail distinguishing parcels in which it is justifiable to invest, parcels that ought to be leased for less intensive agriculture, and those where lease provisions and depreciation schedules should encourage development for other uses. Some lands, we concluded, probably ought to be traded or sold. To conjure up our ideal scheme, we took techniques and tools from the myriad discussed in Chapter 4 and its appendix.

In looking at forestry activities (timber sales) on trust lands in Chapter 5, we addressed the issue of uncertainty in the availability of the resource due to environmental constraints and possible leasing developments to respond to this. In this regard, states have begun to consider dividing production into separate phases: first, the phase of logging and dragging trees to roads (yarding); and second, the phase of transporting to mills or central collection places. This division allows states additional flexibility to hire labor as needed. When the state undertakes this type of activity, it increases its own risks (labor must be compensated whether working or not), but it also receives potentially higher revenues in return (purchasers know exactly what they are buying, and its availability is guaranteed). Framing the problem in terms of the appropriate development mechanism and the relative apportionment of risk allows analysis to proceed in a more interesting light than the traditional approach does.

In Chapter 6, we examined leasing in terms of the relative risk apportioned between the landowner (the state) and the developer (the lessee). The potential yield of resources in mineral leasing is even more uncertain than for agriculture and forestry. As a result, a number of different procedures (with similarities to those used for other resources) have evolved for minerals leasing. Because of the generally high level of uncertainty associated with minerals leases, developers are rewarded for taking this risk by being given essentially perpetual leases ("held by production") on lucrative properties, as well as hardrock mineral royalty rates that usually allow deduction of some or all production costs. As in agricultural leases, our proposed first step in devising an ideal leasing system is for the states to assess the suitability of their trust lands for mineral development proactively rather than waiting to respond until after the demand for leases is high. States may also want to assess whether it is in their best interest to withhold portions of trust lands from leasing if resource prices are expected to increase in the future due to scarcity. Assessing this possibility involves explicitly linking trust mineral programs with permanent fund management, since the repository of mineral royalties is the permanent fund. We demonstrated how, in one state, the value of production was essentially lost as a result of permanent fund management practices. This observation, in conjunction with the perpetual nature of the lease, brought intergenerational equity considerations in mineral leasing into prominent focus.

Our ideal systems provide principles that should encourage readers to ask reasonable questions about leasing practices that concern them. Such questions do not require specialized knowledge about mining, ranching, farming, or linear algebra. For example, having seen the variety of state methods for evaluating agricultural land, we might well ask why State A does not do appraisals the same way State B does. At a more pressing level, perhaps, we might ask why the federal government does not do appraisals at all. And why are there so few variegations in the federal agency's agricultural lands category? If we look at the land rather than at the politics and the history, will we still be inclined to conclude that Bureau of Land Management lands are exclusively fit for use as grazing lands? Should the bureau, for example, lease any of its lands for irrigated agriculture? Similarly, knowing that the states routinely use diverse methods to determine the fair market value of lands in their care, we might well ask why the federal government imposes one grazing fee across the whole nation. Why does the federal government choose not to adopt a system for setting grazing fees appropriate to different market and ecological conditions? Perhaps it has a good reason, but we cannot think of it. Of course, Congress has passed a law that tells the federal agencies how to calculate the fee, but that does not mean that the policy makes any sense.

Having asked that question, we can move on to wondering why the federal government's grazing system does not provide for routine auctioning of leases. That seems to be a fairly standard approach to this type of land management at the state level; indeed, inherent in the idea of a lease is the notion of a term that expires under previously stated conditions. Some commentators have argued that leases should not "turn over"—that security of land tenure is the key to effective stewardship of lands. However, we know of no data that suggest that state lands are poorly cared for as a result of competitive bidding, and we are frequently reminded that federal lands are not consistently well cared for. Industry representatives who insist that their clients could not survive in a world where federal grazing permits were auctioned need to explain how the states' lessees manage to do so. Simply by understanding the basic structure of the contract—knowing that normally a lease has a specified term, after which it ends and a new one with new and appropriate terms and conditions must be drawn up—enables the outside observer to ask interesting and rewarding questions about the management of leased resources, whatever the jurisdiction.

Another area that invites exploration is that of bidder qualifications. In the abstract, what kinds of qualifications ought the landowner to look for? Surely they should include some criteria suggesting continuing ability to pay the rent and to use the resource without destroying it. But, when bidder qualifications are used to limit the potential market for a lease, problems arise in achieving fair market value. Moreover, as discussed in Chapter 7, bidder qualifications make it difficult for environmental groups interested in retiring or resting grazing areas to bid on open allotments at state lease auctions, regardless of the potential benefit to the lands of this "use."

Interestingly, such considerations do not arise in connection with management of federal lands. The Bureau of Land Management justifies its requirement that all permittees must have deeded land (a base property to which the livestock can return if the agency directs) as an environmental protection measure: the managers cannot protect federal range resources if there is no place other than federal land to confine the lessee's herd. However, this requirement makes it difficult for the agencies to establish a competitive leasing system. Indeed, the whole notion of bidding on a Bureau of Land Management allotment is itself speculative, since permits do not in any meaningful sense expire and are never available in an open auction.

The state trust land experience suggests that it does not have to be that way. Perhaps we would do better with a system—federal or state—that allows environmental groups to identify fragile areas, prioritize their interests in them, and purchase nonuse of them in the same way that resource developers can purchase access to develop. Perhaps not, but it is worth thinking about. One attractive aspect of allowing environmental interests to bid on grazing leases is that rest, retirement, or delay of development would not be subsidized. The "nonuser" would pay for the nonuse.

On the Ground: Leasing as Tool Kit

There are limits to how far one can go in toying with the logic of lease. The issues involved in leasing specific resources are much more complex than a general "what's going on here" question can fully explore. The individual resources themselves require different priorities in access arrangements. Different market realities and production requirements in agricultural and mineral leasing and timber sales are appropriately reflected in the lease arrangements. Cropland lessees, for example, are in the unique position of having to make investments to produce the resource they intend to harvest. Timber harvesters generally have no responsibility for producing the trees;

they simply acquire rights to harvest in a particular area for a specified period of time. Grazing leases fall somewhere between timber harvesters and row croppers on this spectrum. Both cropland and grazing leasing arise in a context where durability of access to the leased land is an issue. Consequently, public policy in agricultural leasing has focused not only on the partitioning of risk, investment, and return, but on defining the long-term relationship of the lessee to the land. Unlike the croplands lessee, and more like the timber harvester, the grazing lessee generally does not invest in the cultivation of the grass. However, in relation to improvements such as water developments and fences, both cropland and grazing leases are detailed and careful.

Mineral development is somewhat like cropland leasing in that it requires significant up-front investment. Mineral development is peculiar, however, in the extent to which investment must initially be undertaken in the face of very real ambiguity about whether the sought-after resource is present on the leased site in economically recoverable quantities. Thus, whereas the agricultural lessee makes investments in fencing and water developments, the mineral developer invests in information about the geologic structure of the leased land. Public mineral policy has sought to share that costly ambiguity in ways that encourage investment in geologic exploration while preventing speculative holding of leases.

Timber harvesters are less likely than a gold miner, for example, to be surprised or disappointed by the amount of timber on a sale area. And because the harvester does not require long-term access to the site in order to grow and then harvest the crop annually or to extract the resource fully, access is provided for a strictly defined and rather short term. Hence, issues such as improvements, speculative holding, and leasehold rights are less likely to come up in contemporary timber sales contracts. The policy concerns that surround state timber sales are more likely to focus on the environmental impacts of the harvest than on timing decisions, the cost of information regarding the resource, or improvements installed by the harvester.

Each leasing field has both a culture—here, an emphasis on diligent development; there, a focus on environmental impacts; elsewhere, a concentration on fees and fair market value—and requirements peculiar to the leasing of the particular resource. An important challenge facing the outsider is to understand where in the leasing process we are responding to cultural traditions that are incidental and changeable, and where real issues lie at the heart of a standard pattern. Recognizing that some of the realness of the issue is likely in any case to be in the eye of some particular beholder, we are nevertheless able to employ the diversity of state programs as an analytical tool to put some constraints on the effect of mere advocacy.

For example, we saw in Chapter 6 that the location system (where it exists in federal and state programs) is defended as a requirement for profitable operations by the mineral industry. Simultaneously, however, we see hardrock programs in many states that work well and profitably for both the landowner and the developer under a full-fledged leasing system. This suggests that there is nothing inherent in the hardrock mining business—either technically or economically—that requires the peculiar privileges granted to developers under the federal 1872 Mining Act. Observers will, we hope, be inspired to inquire further about the Pugh clause, for example, to learn what effect the existence of that oil and gas leasing provision has on bonus bids, subsequent royalties, the cost of information, and a host of other issues that impinge on the selection of particular lease provisions in the context of different goals.

Similarly, when viewing federal timber sales, we are struck by the frequency of charges that the federal government is selling its timber for less than the cost of producing it. Federal agencies frequently respond to debate about "below-cost timber sales" by recounting how difficult it is to account for all the costs and benefits of timber management. Listening to the Forest Service, one might get the idea that it is practically impossible to figure out how to set up an accounting system that adequately tracks receipts, investments, and returns. But we have seen in Chapters 2 and 5 that this is not the case at all. On state lands, questions about timber giveaways do not generally arise. When questions about the costs and benefit are presented, they can be sorted out fairly precisely with a degree of effort that is not especially onerous. The accounting issues that weigh so heavily on the Forest Service do not, we may safely conclude, inhere in the process of growing and cutting timber. They are an artifact of a particular approach to timber management whose continued application could be challenged on the basis of state experience with more efficient alternatives.

Two conclusions are suggested by our effort to understand what, in the abstract, a lease is good for and what some of the characteristics of different resource management systems that shape and define the issues covered in a lease are. First, variety in leasing systems is a good thing. Under different ecological and economic conditions, and given different priorities in different regions and jurisdictions, differences are necessary. The variations in lease terms in the relatively straightforward field of agricultural leasing are astounding. In the context of comparisons among sixteen different state programs, very little emerges as necessary or inevitable—the *sine qua non* of successful leasing. We will take that observation one step further and assert that national programs embodying one-size-fits-all lease terms are not a good idea. Lease terms reflect different economic and ecological conditions and different management priorities. One way to clarify goals and provide incentives to lessees to work toward them is to select lease terms to fit particular conditions and situations.

Second, borrowing is possible. We repeatedly invoke the vision of a tool kit to deal with the combination of what is common to all public resource management programs (leases) and the enormous variability we have encountered in examining lease terms and conditions. Lease terms and conditions are interchangeable parts. Since everyone is working within a common framework, managers can study each other's tools and borrow ones that are appropriate to different ecological and economic conditions.

THE TRUST MANDATE

Having drawn attention to the common basis provided by the state and federal governments' ubiquitous commitment to leasing, we need to recall the diversity of public resource management we have encountered. For far too long, we have proceeded as if the multiple-use concept—most particularly as practiced by the U.S. Forest Service—were the only feasible approach to resource development. The implicit dictum of a century of federal resource management is simple: forbid all resource development (as in a park or wilderness area), or follow the Forest Service's multiple-use model. As the Forest Service model becomes more and more widely recognized as a failure, or as falling apart, or both,[3] the quest for new visions of public resource management grows increasingly urgent. And as we begin to recognize that sustainable use, rather than destructive use or abstinent nonuse, is the most pressing challenge, the utility of the trust lands model becomes increasingly apparent.

It is futile to ignore or complain about the trustee's duty to make the trust productive for the beneficiary. Although the courts were slow (as were the managers) to apply the trust notion to school and related land grants strictly, this notion is now so thoroughly enshrined in state constitutions, case law, and management philosophy that major alterations seem unlikely. Seeking major changes also seems purposeless. The appropriate goal ought to be to understand the trust lands for what they are in the mix of western lands and resources and for what they can teach us.

Part of the necessity for this arises from the current emphasis on "ecosystem management." State trust lands are extensive throughout the West. We cannot manage the admixed federal, state, and private holdings that make up ecosystems, watersheds, or landscapes if we ignore the political and legal diversity that we encounter. State trust lands are a fundamental part of that diversity, and understanding why and how they are different is crucial. We are more impressed, however, by the opportunity the trust lands provide to analyze and experiment with cost-effective, efficient management of public resources.

Clarity

From the perspective of land management, the most important aspect of the trust is the clear mandate it provides as a guide to decision making about resource allocations and priorities. The trustee's obligation of undivided loyalty to the beneficiary lies the core of that mandate and is the source of much of the trust lands' controversial peculiarities.

For-profit management is widely perceived as being environmentally destructive. Yet the trust mandate has proved useful as an antidote to the historic domination that grazing lessees and timber purchasers enjoy in public resource management. Given that environmental advocates consider commodity interests to be insufficiently controlled on federal lands, the experience on state trust lands ought to prove both instructive and challenging to them. In instance after instance, unalloyed commitment to the trust beneficiaries has been dispositive in redirecting lessee-oriented management. When state legislatures have intervened to obligate the trust managers to lease minerals and agricultural lands at below fair market value, the courts disallowed it.

Indeed, one striking thing about the history of trust land management is how successfully a few well-placed law suits have redefined the dominant themes of trust land management. As we saw in Chapter 1 (concerning rights-of-way), in Chapter 4 (concerning agricultural land leasing), in Chapter 5 (concerning defaults on timber sale contracts), and yet again in Chapter 6 (concerning minimum prices for mineral leases), court decisions hewing to simple clear trust principles have repeatedly and literally turned state programs around, simply by reiterating in clear terms the legally prescribed dominant goal of management.

We continue to be amazed at how little is required to achieve fundamental change in agency orientation when the goals are clearly specified. We conclude that the trust mandate provides useful clues for a more fruitful balancing of environmental and industry priorities in public resource debates than is currently available in the power struggles over federal lands.

The clarity of the trust mandate is also useful in directing discussions toward what uses should be subsidized and what uses should pay fair market value. We have discussed this most explicitly in Chapter 5, when addressing the conflict between using trust resources for the general public benefit and using them for the beneficiary's benefit. The same topic came up again in Chapter 7, in connection with the status of hunting and recreation as new uses of trust resources. The question of subsidized general public benefit is far easier to define in the trust context than with regard to federal public lands.

Clearly, uncompensated use of trust resources for highways is impermissible. However, the efforts of states to achieve generally beneficial goals in the context of raising funds for a specific beneficiary opens an unusually enlightening window into the true costs of multiple-use management. The Montana solution—maximizing returns while limiting access—might be attractive to hunters and to environmentalists. The key here is that the trust lands context permits this discussion to be held at all. Clarity of mandate, in association with trust requirements for accountability and the prospective enforceability of the mandate, allow managers and auditors to separate legitimate multiple use from illegitimate private benefit.

Accountability

The second aspect of the trust mandate we have emphasized is accountability: trustees are required to keep records and to disclose their activities fully to the beneficiary. The most important issue on which we have been able to hold trust land managers consistently accountable in our analyses is the matter of whether their management programs are benefiting the manager.

This occurs frequently on Forest Service lands, critics complain.[4] One aspect of the problem is that the Forest Service subsidizes certain activities by using revenues from an income-producing activity to subsidize non-monetary, nonpriced activities.[5] For example, timber receipts are used to fund activities such as road construction and insect and disease control.[6]

Alternatively, the agency may balance costs for commodity production programs against nonquantifiable or nonmonetary benefits, such as recreation or "community stability." This cross-subsidization can continue undetected because of inadequate cost accounting.[7] Critics frequently have argued that the agency is the principle beneficiary of its own management programs—an allegation that neither the Forest Service nor anyone else is in a position to confirm or refute with hard numbers. We have demonstrated that, on trust lands, thanks to the accountability requirements, we can identify benefit to the managers.

For example, we noted in Chapter 5 that only in four states (at most) is timber worth managing on trust lands. We can make that assessment because the states provide data about expenses, receipts, and the productivity of their timber management programs, both per employee and per acre. Under a different set of management priorities, the content of the phrase "worth it" would not be defined in terms of monetary returns. One might, for example, give up a little in cash returns in order to achieve higher-quality riparian areas. Our experience with trust lands, however, makes us want to sound a note of caution against such apparently well-intended fuzzy lines of accountability. Unless some other clear way to account for the gains in riparian area quality can be specified, the fuzziness will likely benefit not the ecosystem but the manager. The central advantage of trust lands record keeping—its emphasis on money as a criterion notwithstanding—is that it facilitates removing the manager from the equation as the principle benefi-ciary of public resource management.

A review of the various types of data the different states gather, main-tain, and publish should provide guidance to those looking for systems that would permit more detailed analysis of who is paying for and who is actu-ally benefiting from public resource management programs. The data com-mon to all our study states have given us the opportunity to analyze trust-ees' decisions—about staffing levels, lease terms, time horizons, and general public benefits—in a way that is not possible in connection with other public resource categories.

Enforceability

Accountability in connection with a clear mandate makes legal enforcement of trust mandates possible. Three enforceability issues are especially impor-tant to consider in trust management. The first is "who specifically is the trustee?" We found in Chapter 1 that the state is trustee—or more directly in some states, the Board of Land Commissioners are the trustees. The resolu-tion of this issue has important consequences on enforceability because it determines whether individual land office staff and managers have fiduci-ary trust duties, as well as establishing the extent of their discretion to act outside trust mandates.

The second enforceability issue is "who has standing to sue over trust management?" The initial test to determine standing is whether the plaintiff has suffered harm as a result of an agency action. Certainly, lessees in all cases have standing to sue over decisions made by the land managers. In addition, beneficiaries have standing to sue; however, the definition of *bene-ficiary* is less settled than the definition of *lessees*. Other potential litigants range from state departments of education (Utah presents a good example of their involvement), to individual counties and school districts (for in-stance, the *Skamania* case); to state educational organizations (as in *ASARCO v. Kadish* and *Oklahoma Education Association v. Nigh*); to individual parents and teachers, and finally to members of the general public. We have seen in-stances where courts recognized standing down to the level of educational associations. Parents and the general public have had much more difficulty obtaining standing.

Finally, as we discussed in Chapter 7, the third enforceability issue is "is the trustee acting with undivided loyalty to the beneficiary?" But this question raises two additional issues. The first involves determining true benefit to the trust versus general public benefits—specifically, public bene-fits that affect beneficiaries such as local governments (the *Skamania* case provides a good model for this discussion). The second issue, delved into in Chapters 6 and 7, involves determining whether current generations are being benefited at the expense of future generations. We know of no cases that have litigated this question, but it brings up the fourth fundamental characteristic of trust management.

Perpetuity

Perpetuity seems to have at least two dimensions: perpetuating the productive capacity of the trust, and perpetuating the permanent funds.

The trust mandate to act with undivided loyalty to the beneficiary is easier to discuss and to evaluate than is the equally clear mandate to preserve the productive capacity of the trust. Both in law and in science, the latter obligation is less well defined. Most of the litigation of the last several decades has been focused on protecting the beneficiaries from the lessees. It remains to be seen whether the productive capacity issue will be as thoroughly addressed by the courts. However, as we saw in Chapters 5 and 7, environmental groups throughout the West are beginning to address the issue.

We are not aware of any inquiries into whether riparian areas, the productive capacity of the soil, or range trends and conditions are better on state trust lands than on comparable parcels managed under other regimes.[8] Hence, we can not evaluate the effectiveness of trustees' efforts to protect the productive capacity of the trust, nor can we compare it to federal or private regimes. Nonetheless, we can look indirectly at the states' successes and failures in this area, and we can ask questions about policies, incentives, and (most particularly) institutional arrangements that appear to be conducive to sustainable resource management. We argued at the end of Chapter 7 that the institutional aspects of sustainability are as important as the definitional ones focusing on what should be sustained, and that the trust lands have much to teach everyone interested in this area. We also believe that this area is ripe for further analysis.

Another particular aspect of trust lands, the permanent fund, facilitates discussion of intergenerational equity. Mineral management and the existence of the permanent funds have allowed us to be uncommonly precise in our discussion of mineral development decisions on trust lands. When receipts placed in the permanent fund rapidly lose their value to inflation, the question of whether to extract the minerals or to leave them in the ground seems fairly easy to resolve. However, when the alternative funding mechanisms for the schools are either to increase local property taxes or to increase state general taxes, the issue becomes muddied again.

Finally, the existence of the trust encourages managers to treat resources as a portfolio of assets that change over time. New assets—water, commercial lands, recreation, and so on—become valuable, and their value must be factored into trust management. We see the portfolio concept, in conjunction with the trust perpetuity mandate, as requiring that managers constantly reevaluate the resources under their care to ensure that the resources are protected in their current form and that the value of the overall trust corpus is maintained.

THE POLITICAL CONTEXT

Emphasis on the trust mandate should not tempt readers to view trust land management as apolitical—an antiseptic undertaking tangential to the intense disputes that afflict public resource management elsewhere. Nothing could be further from the truth. Each of the chapters of this book is structured by explicitly and unavoidably political themes: the tension between the lessee and the manager; the tension between the need to serve the beneficiary's benefit and pressures for general public benefits; the tension between current and future benefits; the increasing public response to increasingly aggressive management. All of this may take place at the margins of public lands and education policy struggles, but the decisions reached cannot be insulated from the political debates of our time. Trust land managers are under intense and growing political pressure.

Our analyses shed some interesting light on the political context of trust management, echoing a huge body of literature in political science that suggests that the political structure and setting of state decisions does not significantly influence outcomes. We have been less successful than we had originally hoped in demonstrating the importance to policy outcome of obvious structural differences tied to key political differences.

For example, we have been unable to demonstrate—or even to suggest enticingly—that whether the land commissioner is elected or appointed is tied to a discernible pattern of policy outcomes or priorities. On the other hand, we have repeatedly seen that funding priorities (that is, is the operation profit-maximizing as opposed to cost-constrained?) matter significantly. Clearer still, the source of operating funds appears to matter: is the land office funded by the legislature out of appropriations or with a percentage of receipts. This issue appears to play a role in staffing decisions, since managers tend to add staff in settings where funds are readily available, without consistent regard for its contribution to trust returns. Further, the relationship of number of staff to returns in specific resource programs has been most revealing. We also encountered considerable anecdotal evidence and observations to support the notion that the participation of the beneficiary in decision making is important. Certainly, a beneficiary sufficiently involved to initiate litigation, as in *Skamania, Nigh,* or *Lassen,* is of crucial importance in defining not only outcomes but the terms of the debate. Even so, minute institutional variations are far less critical than individuals presently engaged in redesigning grazing advisory groups et al. would have us believe.

We want to be careful, therefore, not to overstate the importance of the trust mandate as an antidote to political reality: the trust mandate does not insulate trust managers from political pressure or prevent them from making politically expedient responses to such pressure.

CONCLUSIONS

This book has been about state trust lands. Our observations about other public lands have been, with few exceptions, implicit or abbreviated. Therefore, we do not want to draw major conclusions with regard to federal land management beyond the lessons that various examples of doing the same thing differently can squarely and fairly teach. Nevertheless, two general points seem noteworthy.

First, the trust provides a system: not a perfect system, but clear guidelines for achieving something that has been a long-sought goal of federal land management reformers. One way to understand the body of trust law is as a method for removing—or minimizing—the manager as the beneficiary of management. We have seen that in some states this system does not always work. Nevertheless, the data are available to make analysis possible. Many discussions of incentives to bureaucrats proceed with an excessively religious overlay: simple application of market mechanisms will solve the problems of federal resource management. Our discussion of trust lands suggests that this is probably not true. Organizational structure, enforcement mechanisms, record keeping, and clarity of goals are all crucial to establishing accountability in trust land management. But there are clearly valuable payoffs. One reason that only four of the states have a significant timber management program is that those are the only states in which the resource justifies the investment. We cannot argue that the Forest Service should only manage timber in those same four states, because Forest Service data are not adequate to answer basic questions. However, the juxtaposition is at least suggestive.

Second, we believe that it is legitimate to ask "how can the states sell what the feds are giving away?" We think it is time that this issue be raised in a broader context. Members of Congress and of the Senate from western states have traditionally proceeded as if federal resource giveaways were to the advantage of the western states and their citizens. Here is a concrete example where the opposite is true. In grazing, in telecommunications sites, and in hardrock mining, very clear costs are imposed on state programs by federal below-market pricing. As state trustees venture further into marketing recreation, hunting, and (perhaps) water, this issue will become more important. State trust lands provide an opportunity and some data for reexamining this ancient political assumption of porkbarrel benefits.

State trust lands are interesting in themselves and warrant further exploration. It may be, however, that the most productive route of inquiry, at least in the near term, is the lens they provide for exploring our nation's public resource management experiences and traditions. Trust land management is our nation's most ancient and durable resource policy. Important tools for thinking about what is working and what is not can be found in well-documented experiences under the state lands' trust mandate. With all resource management agencies—federal, state, and local—searching for ways to operate more efficiently, downsizing, and looking for opportunities to gain returns from resource management programs, the time is right for a resurgence of attention to these long ignored lands.

NOTES

INTRODUCTION

1. And later 36s and then 2s and 32s. See Fairfax et al., *The School Trust Lands: A Fresh Look at Conventional Wisdom*, 22 ENVIRONMENTAL LAW 797 (1992) [hereinafter cited as *Conventional Wisdom*], at 813–14.

2. For a history of the grants of land and their trust nature, see *id., passim*.

3. Here we weave together RESTATEMENT (SECOND) OF TRUSTS (1959) §§ 2, 3, and 4, and the less turgid prose of G. T. BOGERT, TRUSTS (1987), at 1–2 [hereinafter cited as BOGERT].

4. See RESTATEMENT (SECOND) OF TRUSTS, §§ 170–83.

5. *Id.* at § 24(1).

6. *Id.* at § 24(2). We are not particularly interested in the notion of an implied trust here. With inconsequential exceptions, the idea is that the accession documents are the trust instrument and that no implication of trust is required.

7. *Id.* at § 24(2).

8. *Id.* at § 25(b).

9. *Id.* at § 25(a).

10. *Id.* at §§ 25, 112.

11. BOGERT at 5.

12. RESTATEMENT (SECOND) OF TRUSTS, §§ 170–83.

13. As we discuss in Chapter 4, the general rule is that a trustee may tolerate uncompensated use only if it does not impose costs on the beneficiary. Undivided loyalty does not mean that an investment or activity is disallowed if it coincidentally benefits someone other than the beneficiary, but it does bar programs that impose costs or reduce benefits in order to achieve a collateral or general benefit. See Oklahoma Education Association v. Nigh, 642 P.2d 230 (Okla. 1982); County of Skamania v. State, 685 P.2d 576 (Wash. 1984); and Ervien v. United States, 251 U.S. 41 (1919) for examples.

14. RESTATEMENT (SECOND) OF TRUSTS, §§ 172, 173, 179.1–2.

15. Or others with an identifiable interest. *Id.*, § 172. See especially the Arizona and New Mexico situations. "Nothing herein contained shall be taken as in limitation of the power of the State or of any citizen thereof to enforce the provisions of this Act." New Mexico–Arizona Enabling Act, as Amended, § 28 (Act of June 20, 1910, 36 Stat. 557, ch. 310). Cited in Lassen v. Arizona Highway Dep't, 385 U.S. 458, 472, app. to opinion (1967), reversing State of Arizona ex. rel Arizona Highway Department v. Lassen, 407 P.2d 747 (1965). Other states are more problematical, see *Conventional Wisdom* n.194 and accompanying text. Most recently, see Plaintiffs' Brief in Opposition to Motion for Summary Judgment at 26–47, Selkirk-Priest Basin Assoc. v. Idaho (1st Dist., Idaho, Bonner Co.) (No. CV-92-0037, Oct. 9, 1992).

16. "If by the terms of the trust, the trust is to continue only until the expiration of a certain period or until the happening of a certain event, the trust will be terminated upon the expiration of the period or the happening of the event." RESTATEMENT (SECOND) OF TRUSTS, § 334.

17. This is the *cy pres* doctrine of charitable trusts. *Conventional Wisdom* at 875–77 and references therein.

18. See H. TAYLOR, THE EDUCATIONAL SIGNIFICANCE OF THE EARLY FEDERAL LAND ORDINANCES 123 (1922). See also *Conventional Wisdom*.

19. *Conventional Wisdom* at 807; F. SWIFT, HISTORY OF PUBLIC PERMANENT COMMON SCHOOL FUNDS IN THE UNITED STATES 1795–1905, at 107 *passim*, 111 (1911). In Mississippi, school funds invested in railroads were lost when the roads were destroyed during the Civil War. See Papasan v. Allain, 478 U.S. 265 (1986).

20. See *Conventional Wisdom* at 824, n.94, for a discussion of the technical names of what are ubiquitously referred to as permanent school funds.

21. Examples of common language are "shall be held by the said state in trust. . . . No mortgage or other encumbrance of the said lands . . . shall be valid in favor of any person. . . . Said lands shall not be sold or leased . . . except to the highest and best bidder at a public auction. . . . All lands, leaseholds, timber and other products of land before being offered shall be appraised at their true value, and no sale or other disposal thereof shall be made for a consideration less than the value so ascertained. . . ." New Mexico–Arizona Enabling Act, as Amended, § 10 (Act of June 20, 1910, 36 Stat. 557, ch. 310). See also *Conventional Wisdom* at 811–12, 820 *passim*.

22. The original work on this project, in which we struggled to decide whether the category state trust lands was analytically useful, was undertaken with the assistance of Paul Klein, who argued strongly that it is.

23. The figures for the federal lands are taken from LOOMIS, INTEGRATED PUBLIC LANDS MANAGEMENT 19 (1993); the state lands figures are from the ANNUAL DIRECTORY OF THE WESTERN STATE LANDS COMMISSIONERS ASSOCIATION (1989–1994).

24. WSCLA member states are Arizona, Arkansas, California, Colorado, Hawaii, Idaho, Minnesota, Montana, Nebraska, Nevada, New Mexico, North Dakota, Oklahoma, Oregon, South Dakota, Texas, Utah, Washington, Wisconsin, and Wyoming.

25. But see Papasan v. Allain, 478 U.S. 265 (1986), which suggests the contrary.

1. HISTORY OF THE SCHOOL LAND GRANT PROGRAM

1. Actually, the notion of granting land to support common schools is much older. One enthusiastic scholar who discounted the importance of the program's colonial heritage mused that the beginnings of land grants for schools perhaps began in ancient times; he was, however, able to penetrate no deeper into the English mists than the reign of Henry V. See TAYLOR, THE EDUCATIONAL SIGNIFICANCE OF THE EARLY FEDERAL LAND ORDINANCES. Teachers College, Columbia University Contributions to Education no. 118 (1922) [hereinafter cited as TAYLOR]. Another scholar noted that after the monasteries were destroyed by Henry VIII and Edward VI, many grammar schools were lost in England and it became common for individuals to endow schools with land. SCHAFER, THE ORIGIN OF THE SYSTEM OF LAND GRANTS FOR EDUCA-

TION. Bulletin of the University of Wisconsin [Madison], no. 63, History Series, vol 1, no. 1 (1902), at 8–10. For present purposes it is sufficient to note that the idea of granting, donating, or bequeathing land in support of schools was common throughout the colonial period. It was, however, most characteristic of the northeastern states, especially Massachusetts, New York, Connecticut, and New Hampshire, "where it developed steadily in the direction of a public land grant system." *Id.* at 11. For a fulsome listing, much of it overlapping, of colonial programs, see also, COMMISSIONER OF EDUCATION, REPORT OF THE COMMISSIONER OF EDUCATION FOR THE YEAR 1895–96: THE AMERICAN COMMON SCHOOL IN THE SOUTHERN STATES DURING THE FIRST HALF CENTURY OF THE REPUBLIC, 1790–1840 (1897); DIXON, THE ADMINISTRATION OF STATE PERMANENT SCHOOL FUNDS: AS ILLUSTRATED BY A STUDY OF THE MANAGEMENT OF THE UTAH ENDOWMENT. Southern California Education Monographs, no. 9, (1936) [hereinafter cited as DIXON]; GREEN, CONSTITUTIONAL DEVELOPMENT IN THE SOUTH ATLANTIC STATES, 1776–1860: A STUDY IN THE EVOLUTION OF DEMOCRACY (1930, 1966); HIBBARD, A HISTORY OF THE PUBLIC LAND POLICIES (1924) [hereinafter cited as HIBBARD]; KNIGHT, HISTORY AND MANAGEMENT OF LAND GRANTS FOR EDUCATION IN THE NORTHWEST TERRITORY (OHIO, INDIANA, ILLINOIS, MICHIGAN, WISCONSIN) (1885) [hereinafter cited as KNIGHT]; SWIFT, HISTORY OF PUBLIC PERMANENT COMMON SCHOOL FUNDS IN THE UNITED STATES 1795–1905 (1911) [hereinafter cited as SWIFT, 1911]; SWIFT, STUDIES IN PUBLIC SCHOOL FINANCE: THE WEST–CALIFORNIA AND COLORADO, Research Publications of the University of Minnesota Education Series no. 1 (1922); SWIFT, FEDERAL AND STATE POLICIES IN PUBLIC SCHOOL FINANCE IN THE UNITED STATES (1931) [hereinafter cited as SWIFT, 1931]. And for a series of charts tracking different provisions in state constitutions circa 1930, see Koch, Constitutional Provisions for Common School Funds in the Several States (Master's Thesis, Ohio State University, 1930) [hereinafter cited as Koch]. Unfortunately, for present purposes, Koch's thesis does not contain the original constitutions and therefore is not a consistently reliable guide to what states originally agreed to.

2. The analysis of the accession process in this section is almost wholly the work of Karen Bradley, History Department, University of California, Berkeley.

3. The Virginia land cession obviously resolved many issues, but it also created a number of new problems. The original thirteen colonies vigorously pursued enormous, overlapping claims to all the land between the Appalachians and the Mississippi. Following the Revolution, they gradually ceded their claims to the central government. Virginia's claim was the most extensive and its cession was the one most central in the process under discussion here. There is an enormous literature on the subject. See HIBBARD; ROBBINS, OUR LANDED HERITAGE: THE PUBLIC DOMAIN 1776–1936 (1942); and GATES, HISTORY OF PUBLIC LAND LAW DEVELOPMENT [a report prepared for the Public Land Law Review Commission] (1968); and the references cited, particularly in the latter [hereinafter, cited as GATES]. The terms of the Virginia cession are key to almost everything that follows in American political and social history: *inter alia*, the ceded land was to be laid out into states; the states formed were to have a republican form of government and were to be admitted to the Union; all land not taken up by military bounty claims was to be "common fund for all the states."

4. When the 1785 and 1787 ordinances passed, the nation was still operating under the Articles of Confederation; the federal Constitution did not come into effect until 1789. For an exhilarating discussion of key issues in the 1780s see ONUF, STATE-

HOOD AND NATION: A HISTORY OF THE NORTHWEST ORDINANCE (1987, 1992) [hereinafter cited as ONUF, STATEHOOD AND NATION].

5. The most important strand of these policies is the "equal footing" doctrine, which has become so ingrained that many people erroneously look for it in the Constitution. Both the Land Ordinance of 1785 and the Northwest Ordinance of 1787 acknowledged the importance of public schools, but the 1785 law defined a specific process by which schools would be supported. Passed on May 20, 1785, the ordinance made specific provisions for education. "There shall be reserved the lot No. 16, of every township," it decreed, "for the maintenance of public schools." See ONUF, STATEHOOD AND NATION, at 22–24. Reference to schools in the Ordinance of 1787 was less concrete and more in the nature of a statement of principles: the ordinance asserted that "religion, morality and knowledge, being necessary to good government and the happiness of mankind, schools and the means of education shall forever be encouraged." In practice, of course, the dictates of the two acts were entwined, since new states could not gain the land for public schools that had been set aside in the 1785 Ordinance without satisfying the prerequisites for statehood defined by the Northwest Ordinance.

6. The survey "organizes land into six-by-six mile townships divided into thirty-six sections of one square mile each." Again, there is an enormous literature. See, for example JOHNSON, ORDER UPON THE LAND: THE U.S. RECTANGULAR SURVEY AND THE UPPER MISSISSIPPI COUNTRY (1976); TREATT, THE NATIONAL LAND SYSTEM: 1785–1920 (1910) [hereinafter cited as TREATT]. Many recent authors discuss the survey in terms of straight lines, which nature abhors as much as it does vacuums. Property lines and fence lines followed the survey lines, and farmers plowed along the fence line, hence, the Dust Bowl. Reality and the literature are more complex, but you get the picture. More relevant here, Treatt discusses the decision as a regional sociological conflict between the South and the New England states and views the survey and sale notion as a victory for the New England approach to ordering both land and community life (see especially chapter 2). There are also whiffs throughout the literature that the Southeast was not really wholly enthusiastic about common or free schools, preferring to concentrate resources on educating the sons of the aristocracy. Daughters everywhere are a more ambiguous subject, and whether education for all included them depends considerably on where and when.

7. In reality, American settlers had been moving and would continue to move West, with or without congressional guidance. Even before the Revolution began, significant numbers of settlers moved West, especially into the region of present-day Kentucky, West Virginia, and western Pennsylvania.

8. BILLINGTON, WESTWARD EXPANSION: A HISTORY OF THE AMERICAN FRONTIER, (1960), at 217.

9. TANSILL, ADMISSION OF STATES INTO THE UNION: A BRIEF SUMMARY OF PROCEDURES, Library of Congress Congressional Research Service, #F 2200 70–156 GGR (1960, 1970), at 3.

10. Whether or not Congress was obligated to accept the state or could negotiate further was a subject of much debate, which ultimately was resolved clearly in the direction of congressional discretion. See ONUF, STATEHOOD AND NATION, at 76–85.

11. ONUF, in STATEHOOD AND NATION, is emphatic regarding congressional determination that land sales would cover the costs of western government and would eventually pay off the national debt. See especially chapters 1 and 2.

12. Vermont was carved out of New York's lands and became a state in 1791. Kentucky and Tennessee were carved out of the western land cessions of Virginia and North Carolina respectively.

13. The phase-one states also provide a basis of comparison with subsequent states, because no federal land lay within their borders. Phase-one states had to organize their own tax base to support schools and other public functions. In subsequent states, by contrast, the federal government owned large tracts of land, and was called upon to contribute to the development of public institutions.

14. The ceding states were Virginia, North Carolina, South Carolina, New York, Georgia, Connecticut, and Massachusetts. See ORFIELD, FEDERAL LAND GRANTS TO THE STATES WITH SPECIAL REFERENCE TO MINNESOTA (1915), at 33 [hereinafter cited as ORFIELD]. Virginia's land cession was the last, accepted by Congress in 1783. See *Conventional Wisdom* [*supra*, Introduction, note 1], at 804.

15. See ONUF, STATEHOOD AND NATION, Ch. 4.

16. Except that Ohio and Michigan had some long-standing boundary disputes, and Michigan's admission was predicated on their resolution. See SOULE, THE SOUTHERN AND WESTERN BOUNDARIES OF MICHIGAN, Publications of the Michigan Political Science Association, vol II, no. 2, (May 1896) [hereinafter cited as SOULE, 1896]. See also ONUF, STATEHOOD AND NATION, ch. 5.

17. JORDAN, LITWACK, ET AL., THE UNITED STATES: CONQUERING A CONTINENT, 6th ed., vol. 1 (1987), at 192 [hereinafter cited as JORDAN, LITWACK, ET AL.].

18. POTTER, THE IMPENDING CRISIS (1976), focuses on the central role the Compromise of 1850 played in heightening sectional strife. A good brief narrative of the Kansas-Nebraska Act and Bloody Kansas is given in JORDAN, LITWACK, ET AL. at 329–31.

19. If Nevada had followed the guidelines established by the Northwest Ordinance, its population would have had to be 60,000, the federal ration of the number of people to a single Congressman, before it qualified for admission to the Union. In 1860, Nevada's population was only 6,857. See GATES at 309.

20. *Id.* at 299.

21. The "Turner Thesis" is everywhere discussed. For a recent version see LIMERICK, THE LEGACY OF CONQUEST: THE UNBROKEN PAST OF THE AMERICAN WEST (1987), at 20ff.

22. See IVISON BLAKEMAN & CO. (publishers), THE NEW STATES: A SKETCH OF THE HISTORY AND DEVELOPMENT OF THE STATES OF NORTH DAKOTA, SOUTH DAKOTA, MONTANA AND WASHINGTON . . . (1889).

23. New Mexico, Arizona, Oklahoma [together with Indian Territory], and Utah.

24. Harriet E. Rogers, The Organization of the Territory of Arizona (MA thesis, U.C. Berkeley, 1923); Marie Y. Troiel, Certain Phases of the Land Problem in New Mexico and Arizona (MA thesis, U.C. Berkeley, 1924); R. W. LARSON, NEW MEXICO'S QUEST FOR STATEHOOD, 1846–1912 (1968) [hereinafter cited as LARSON, 1968]; LARSON, THE "AMERICANIZATION" OF UTAH FOR STATEHOOD (1971) [hereinafter cited as LARSON, 1971]; LYMAN, POLITICAL DELIVERANCE: THE MORMON QUEST FOR UTAH STATEHOOD (1986) [hereinafter cited as LYMAN].

25. CONGRESSIONAL QUARTERLY SERVICE, CONGRESS AND THE NATION: 1945–1964 (1965), at 1948. This section is based on this source's treatment of the topic, at 1497–1503.

26. Kazutaka Saiki, Historical Perspective on Land Tenure in Hawaii. Western States Land Commissioners Association Meeting, Honolulu, July 1994.

27. The major sources for this section are THORPE, THE FEDERAL AND STATE CONSTI-TUTIONS, COLONIAL CHARTERS, AND OTHER ORGANIC LAWS OF THE STATES AND COLONIES NOW OR HERETOFORE FORMING THE UNITED STATES OF AMERICA [7 vols.] (1909), printed pursuant to an act of Congress as House Doc. 357, 59th Cong., 2d Sess. [hereinafter cited as THORPE], and SHEPARD'S CITATIONS, DIGEST OF PUBLIC LAND LAWS (1968) [prepared for the Public Land Law Review Commission].

28. Not, of course, if you are most interested in Alaska, Hawaii, Guam, U.S. Virgin Islands, or Puerto Rico.

29. Regarding why a state might wish to join the Union, see ONUF, STATEHOOD AND NATION, especially chapter 4.

30. The discussion in the next section of the chapter emphasizes evolution in the land grant program. It is interesting to note, therefore, that the commitment of in lieu selections never wavered and varied only slightly over the whole period.

31. THORPE, vol. 5, at 2899.

32. *Id.* at 2899.

33. GATES at 289–90. More fundamentally still, the legal terms of Ohio's admission were contested from the start. The Federalist governor of the Territory, Arthur St. Clair, argued vociferously that Congress was overstepping the boundaries of its power when it "enabled" Ohio to hold a constitutional convention, as Ohio's authority to do so independently was already written into the Northwest Ordinance. As Mathias Orfield points out, the Ohio precedent is therefore important because Ohio effectively trumped these protests when it overrode them to enter the Union: until Ohio actually took its public land grants, there was no assurance that the grants would actually be made, nor was there a clear rule about what powers vis-a-vis public lands Congress could exercise. "With this act land grants for the support of schools may be said to have become firmly established as a national policy." ORFIELD at 38.

34. States admitted without enabling acts were Arkansas, California, Florida, Idaho, Iowa, Kansas, Kentucky, Maine, Michigan, Oregon, Tennessee, Texas, Vermont, West Virginia, Wyoming. See Procedures Followed by States Admitted into the Union Without Congressional Enabling Acts (Legislative Reference Bureau, Territory of Hawaii, # 372, Feb. 15, 1949), at 1.

35. On Utah statehood problems, see LARSON, 1971, and LYMAN. On the politics of California and Texas statehood, see GATES at 299–304. On Texas land issues, see MONTEJANO, ANGLOS AND MEXICANS IN THE MAKING OF TEXAS (1987), and MILLER, THE PUBLIC LANDS OF TEXAS 1519–1970 (1972). On Michigan's border problems, see Anna May Soule, "International Boundary of Michigan" (M.L. thesis, University of Michigan, 1895), and SOULE, 1896.

36. "As early as 1850," historian Robert Larson argues, "the territory's fate was affected by national issues." LARSON, 1968, at 301. The New Mexico accession was further confounded by racism, which played out specifically in the area of land grants and selections. School and other public land grants could not be selected until the Spanish–Mexican land grant question was settled, because, where school sections fell on the Spanish–Mexican grants, in lieu land would have to be chosen. This is not an appropriate place to discuss at any length the interplay between Spanish land grants and school lands. However, there is a surprisingly extensive literature on the subject. See, for example, LARSON, 1968, at 176; Westphall, *Fraud and Implications of*

Fraud in the Land Grants of New Mexico NEW MEXICO HISTORICAL REVIEW (1974), at 190–93; CONGRESSIONAL RECORD, House, 1898, at 1369.

37. CONGRESSIONAL RECORD, House, 1898, at 1369–70.

38. 36 Stat. 557 (1910).

39. The money was to be paid to a "permanent inviolable fund, the interest of which only shall be expended for the support of the common schools within the said state." Recall that Ohio "got" 5 percent, which the federal government was to spend in the state on roads and highways. During the intervening accessions the figure rose to 5 percent and the strings were removed, only to be reintroduced in the Arizona–New Mexico statute, this time in favor of the permanent school fund.

40. This provision is unique to Arizona and New Mexico. It may partially explain why key U.S. Supreme Court decisions are unusually likely to involve cases about those two states. The general trust rule is that, once a trust is established, the settlor has a very limited role in its administration. However, the U.S. government is not a typical settlor.

41. THORPE, published in 1909, does not contain the pertinent original Arizona and New Mexico documents. Here we rely on SECRETARY OF STATE, THE CONSTITUTION OF THE STATE OF NEW MEXICO ADOPTED BY THE CONSTITUTIONAL CONVENTION HELD AT SANTA FE, N.M., FROM OCTOBER 3 TO NOVEMBER 21, 1910, AND AS AMENDED, NOVEMBER 6TH, 1911 (1912).

42. *Id.,* art. 12, §§ 2 and 7.

43. Investment policy in the states was, to use Dixon's word, "confused": "On the one hand existed the notion that the money was intended to be used to build up the state and develop her resources, while it was contended, on the other hand, that the purpose of the trust was to aid the institutions endowed." DIXON at 92–93.

44. See SWIFT, 1911, at 124. Some of the impetus for protecting the permanent fund and its purpose may have come from the fact that many of the funds were diverted to other purposes during the Civil War, to support the conduct of the war. In addition, many of the railroads and other internal improvements in which the funds were invested, especially in the South, were destroyed during the war. See *id.* at 150. Railroad investments lost in the Civil War and never replaced were the subject of recent litigation in Mississippi. See Papasan v. Allain, 478 U.S. 265 (1986).

45. See Fairfax, *Interstate Bargaining over Revenue Sharing and Payments in Lieu of Taxes: Federalism as If States Mattered,* in FEDERAL LANDS POLICY (Foss ed. 1987), and the references cited therein.

46. See TREATT, Chapter 11, for a discussion of "quid pro quo."

47. Oklahoma, which joined the Union in 1907, was, as Gates notes, "treated differently." Oklahoma received sections 16 and 36 "for schools, section 13 of Indian lands, when opened, were to be one-third for the University of Oklahoma and its associated preparatory school, one-third for normal schools, and one-third for a colored A & M school. Section 33 of the Indian lands was assigned to charitable and penal institutions." Arizona and Oklahoma also received $5 million in lieu of the school sections that they would not have in the Indian Territory. Oklahoma wound up with only 4.6 percent of its total acreage, which compares unfavorably with the 11 percent it would have received if it had gotten four sections like the others. "On the other hand the Oklahoma lands were likely to produce revenue much earlier than those of Arizona, partly because of their minerals and because they had greater value as farms." See GATES at 314–15.

48. The climate of the North American continent, which becomes dramatically drier west of the one hundredth meridian, created new challenges both for hopeful settlers and for Congress's land grant formula. One section of desert land per township would not create enough revenue to support public schools in the West—as it would in Ohio, for example—so western states demanded more public land grants. Starting in 1853, when California received its school lands (three years after statehood), western states were allotted two sections per township for the support of public schools and proportionately more for other public land projects as well.

49. If the courts were to compare the restrictions on the salt land grants to those accompanying the school land grants, they would observe that, with regard to the former, Congress offered clear and restrictive policy direction to the states from the outset and then increased these over time.

50. TREATT and GATES are the places to begin if you want the full grant story. That additional background might lead the reader to wonder in the next section why the school land grants, but not others, were transformed into "trusts." Throughout the process, for example, Congress was much more restrictive regarding salt licks than school lands. See THORPE, vol. 5, at 2899 to compare Ohio enabling act language regarding the two.

51. See SWIFT, 1931, at 6.

52. That is, persons who occupied and improved land prior to sale or survey. Squatters' claims were generally honored, if sometimes reluctantly or belatedly.

53. The difference between in lieu lands and section grants is more significant than it might first appear. The section grants included whatever happened to fall within the specified lines. The in lieu lands were located by the grantee or, more usually (as things worked out) by the likely purchaser. Hence, they were almost guaranteed to be marketable or valuable, because they were not selected unless they were. The state typically did not select in lieu lands unless they had been identified first by a purchaser.

54. Although differently stated, the same principle was applied to Oklahoma.

55. See HIBBARD at 313–14.

56. See Ivanhoe Mining Co. v. Keystone Mining Co., 102 U.S. 167 (1880), at 174–75.

57. ROBINSON, LAND IN CALIFORNIA (1948), at 190–91.

58. Congress frequently directed that the school sections be reserved from entry well in advance of the statehood debate. Squatters occupied the school lands in spite of the reservation, however, and their claims were uniformly honored. This early reservation may therefore be most significant if reserved water rights ever attach to state trust lands. Many of the reservation dates are well in advance of the time of statehood. See also HIBBARD at 312ff.

59. See *id.* at 309–10.

60. SWIFT, 1911, at 107ff has the most detailed discussion of this progression.

61. The problems encountered by townships are detailed in numerous sources. See particularly SWIFT, 1911, at 115ff; TAYLOR at 85ff. Taylor notes that the earlier settlers' educational work was hampered by physical hardship, Indian hostility, general poverty, scarcity of money, scattered population, difficulty in getting teachers, and lack of social coherence (at 115ff).

62. This is not the place, we have reluctantly concluded, to share all that we have

learned about the evolution of free, general public education and the strong popular (and later, professional) movement that defined its goals. The best short treatment of the subject relevant here is Tyack & James, *State Government and American Public Education: Exploring the "Primeval Forest."* 26 HISTORY OF EDUCATION QUARTERLY 39 (1986), or the longer version: TYACK, JAMES, & BENAVOT, LAW AND THE SHAPING OF PUBLIC EDUCATION 1785–1954 (1987). See also WELTER, POPULAR EDUCATION AND DEMOCRATIC THOUGHT IN AMERICA (1962) and KAESTLE, PILLARS OF THE REPUBLIC: COMMON SCHOOLS AND AMERICAN SOCIETY 1780–1860 (1983). A less analytical more celebratory phase of reporting is represented by CUBBERLY, PUBLIC EDUCATION IN THE UNITED STATES: A STUDY AND INTERPRETATION OF AMERICAN EDUCATIONAL HISTORY (1934).

63. TAYLOR at 93.

64. KNIGHT at 65. Interestingly, Knight cites the 1821–1822 Indiana Senate Journal for the following: "The system has been adopted in many parts of the United States . . . of leasing lands either permanently or for a life or lives. But the same beneficial results have not been here as in Europe." KNIGHT at 65, n.5.

65. At the federal level, the shift was not was not explicit or final until 1976. Involved in the process is everything from the rise of science and scientific bureaucracies in government, to the beginning of the Progressive era, to the closing of the frontier, to the death of the last passenger pigeon. See GATES; and PEFFER, THE CLOSING OF THE PUBLIC DOMAIN (1950) for starters. See also Fairfax, *Coming of Age in the Bureau of Land Management: Range Management in Search of a Gospel,* in DEVELOPING STRATEGIES FOR RANGELAND MANAGEMENT, NATIONAL ACADEMY OF SCIENCES [a National Research Council report prepared by the Committee on Developing Strategies for Rangeland Management] (1984), at 1689. A key indicator, without so stating, that the federal government was going to retain far more extensive land holdings than the park and forest reservations previously authorized was the passage of the Mineral Lands Leasing Act of 1920. Because the lands had been withdrawn from entry and, therefore, from patent, leasing was necessary to access the resources (primarily coal). But the subtext of the leasing system, now frequently overlooked, is that the lands would be retained in federal ownership. See FAIRFAX & YALE, THE FEDERAL LANDS: A GUIDE TO PLANNING MANAGEMENT AND STATE REVENUES (1987).

66. Koch also notes that all aspects of state constitutions simply got longer and longer over time.

67. See SWIFT, 1911, at 124; and note 44 *supra.*

68. Grosetta v. Choate, 51 Ariz. 248, 75 P.2d 1031 (1938); Ross v. Trustees of the University of Wyoming, 222 P. 3 (1924). Note that *Ross* is a university—not a school— lands case.

69. State v. Lassen, 407 P.2d 747 (1965), *rev'd,* Lassen v. Arizona Highway Dep't, 385 U.S. 458 (1966).

70. Ide v. United States, 263 U.S. 497 (1923), at 502.

71. U.S. v. Fuller, 20 F. Supp. 839 (D. Idaho 1937).

72. 385 U.S. 458 (1966).

73. *Id.* at 461.

74. *Id.* at 465.

75. *Id.* at 469.

76. United States v. 78.61 Acres of Land in Dawes & Sioux Counties, 265 F. Supp. 564 (1967), at 566. The court noted that the Nebraska enabling act "did not contain

the express restrictions which were incorporated in later, similar acts," and cited *Lassen*. "Nevertheless," the court continued, "the grant was undoubtedly in trust for a specific purpose as was recognized by the Supreme Court of Nebraska." But the language the court cited for that conclusion contains nothing about trusts: "The provision of the enabling act making the grant, and of the Constitution of 1866 setting apart and pledging the principal and income from such grant . . . and the subsequent act admitting the state into the Union under such Constitution constituted a contract between the state and the national government relating to such grants. [T]he state was and still is under a contractual as well as constitutional obligation to refrain from disposition or alienation of the use of this property except as allowed by the enabling act and the Constitution." State ex rel. Johnson v. Central Nebraska Public Power & Irr. Dist., 143 Neb. 153, 8 N.W. 2d 841, 847–48 (1943). Ellipses are as cited in 78.61 Acres. A contract regarding means of disposal is not, obviously, a trust. The court then went on to discuss *Lassen*.

77. United States v. 78.61 Acres of Land in Dawes & Sioux Counties, 265 F. Supp. 564 (1967), at 567.

78. *Id.*

79. United States v. 111.2 Acres of Land in Ferry County, 293 F. Supp. 1042 (E.D. Wash. 1968), aff'd 435 F.2d 561 (9th Cir. 1970).

80. Trust principles became "familiar" late in the nineteenth century. A course in trusts was not taught in American law schools until a Professor Ames initiated the first course at Harvard in 1882. His casebook on the subject, first published in that same year, contained 200 cases, 175 of which were English cases. See Scott, *Fifty Years of Trusts*, 50 HARVARD LAW REVIEW 60 (1936).

81. It is not clear how much of the domination of Arizona and New Mexico cases to attribute to this provision. The first federal prosecution, Ervien v. United States, 251 U.S. 41 (1919), was not long in coming. The Supreme Court was explicitly reluctant to hold that a state law allowing use of trust receipts to advertise New Mexico lands generally was a "breach of the trust" (at 48), but it affirmed an Eighth Circuit Court of Appeals opinion so stating. The key case in the contemporary interpretation of the school grants, Lassen v. Arizona Highway Department, 385 U.S. 458 (1967), contains an explicit discussion of trust obligations but did not directly involve the U.S. Attorney General. The United States was granted special leave to argue the case as an amicus curiae however.

82. This is true in spite of the fact that the Supreme Court has been uncommonly careful to avoid sweeping generalizations and is unusually well informed about the grant process. Nonetheless, the Supreme Court noted in its *Lassen* decision that it had agreed to hear the case "because of the importance of the issues to other states which received the grants." *Id.* at 461.

83. Discussed in *Conventional Wisdom*, nn. 86–95 and text accompanying.

84. 685 P.2d 576 (Wash. 1984). The facts involve timber purchase contracts entered into by the State Department of Natural Resources, which manages the school lands in part by selling harvest rights to timber on state lands. The contracts were entered into during the period January 1978 to July 1980. At that time, purchasers expected the value of timber to rise, and bid quite high for timber that, in the natural course of events they would harvest several years hence. When timber prices plummeted, the state legislature in Washington passed a statute that, among other things, allowed

the purchasers to terminate their contracts if they forfeited their original small deposit. *Id.* at 578–79. The legislature justified its action, vis-a-vis the trust, on grounds that it had acted in both the long- and short-term interest of the trust: it protected the trust by preventing bankruptcies and disruption within the market for its assets. *Id.* at 581. Skamania County sued the state, alleging that the legislative act was "a breach of the state's fiduciary duties to the trust and a violation of several state and federal constitutional provisions." *Id.* at 579.

85. *Id.* at 582.

86. *Id.* at 580: "the Supreme Court, interpreting the Arizona Enabling Act, held that Arizona could not transfer easements across trust lands without compensation to the trust. The Court stated that the Arizona Enabling Act contains 'a specific enumeration of the purposes for which the lands were granted and the enumeration is necessarily exclusive of any other purpose.'" *Lassen*, as the *Skamania* court noted, was actually citing Ervien v. United States, 251 U.S. 41, 47 (1919). Whether *Ervien* supports the *Skamania* court's point is unclear following a reading of the subsequent paragraphs in the 1919 decision.

87. 293 F. Supp. 1042 (E.D. Wash. 1968), *aff'd*, 435 F.2d 561 (9th Cir. 1970).

88. "There have been intimations that school land trusts are merely honorary, that there is a 'sacred obligation imposed on (the state's) public faith,' but no legal obligation. These intimations have been dispelled by *Lassen* v. *Arizona* . . . This trust is real, not illusory." *Id.* at 580. Both the *111.2 Acres* court and the *Skamania* court also cite State ex rel. Hellar v. Young, 21 Wash. 391, 58 P. 220 (1899), as a case "in which courts have applied private trust principles to federal land grant trusts" [*Skamania* at 580] or for the notion that "Section 10 of the Enabling Act and Article XVI, section 1 of the Washington Constitution constitute a declaration of trust." [*111.2 Acres* at 1049]. *Hellar* in fact does neither of those things. It does not mention Section 10 of the Enabling Act or Article 16 of the Constitution, although it does discuss parts of Section 5 of the Enabling Act on one page. Nor does it discuss trust principles or even mention the word *trust* beyond one simple sentence ("but the permanent school fund of this state must be regarded as a trust fund," at 221) in a decision holding that warrants drawn by the auditor of the state upon the state's general fund cannot be paid out of the permanent fund when there is no money in the general fund "legally available to pay the warrant." *Id.* at 220–21.

89. THORPE, vol. 7, at 4000. Clearly "all the people" must remain within the context of the purpose of the grant as expressed in the enabling act. Don Lee Fraser, former Supervisor of the Washington Department of Natural Resources, comments as follows: "It was our impression that in earlier grants to other states . . . the 16's and 36's were to support school within the township. Washington's constitution made it clear that this was not the case." Personal Communication, March 13, 1991. This issue is not peculiar to Washington. See Jerke v. State Department of Lands, 597 P.2d 49 (Mont. 1979), at 50, and cases cited therein.

90. One possibility is that the broader reference to "all the people" may expand the range of people who could gain standing to sue to enforce the trust. In many jurisdictions, the courts have taken a surprisingly narrow view of this issue.

91. Unlike *Lassen*, the earlier and equally widely cited *Ervien* case appears to put little reliance on trust principles. Instead, it draws on the authority of the federal government to make specific grants for specific purposes (at 48). Nevertheless, it is a

leading trust case, along with Lassen. Compare with Papasan v. Allain, 478 U.S. 265 (1986). The application of trust principles is also selective, emphasizing undivided loyalty and maximum returns, and rarely (if ever) protection of the trust property. See Beaver, *Management of Wyoming's State Trust Lands from 1890–1990: A Running Battle Between Good Politics and the Law* 26 LAND AND WATER LAW REVIEW 69 (1992), at 1.

2. USING A SYSTEM ORIENTATION

1. This view of the trust asset is not the prevailing one, although it is used in Washington (WASHINGTON, DEPARTMENT OF NATURAL RESOURCES, FINAL TRANSITION LANDS POLICY PLAN [1988], at 33ff) [hereinafter cited as FINAL TRANSITION LANDS POLICY PLAN].

2. This chapter focuses on contemporary state trust land management, during the period from 1970 to the present. We describe each of the major component parts of the trust system, using 1993 information, where available. Because the majority of the land offices' expenditures go to staffing, state-by-state employment patterns are studied. Since agency personnel receive different salaries among the states, a more uniform measure based on full-time equivalent (FTE) employment is used.

3. For simplicity we use the term "state land office," although the actual name varies from state to state.

4. Another difference between these states is in the number of commissioners: Colorado has three, while Utah has eleven members.

5. However, the New Mexico State Land Office has recently come into conflict with the state attorney general over the issue of its authority to conduct land exchanges. Presentation by Art Waskey, general counsel for the New Mexico State Land Office at the winter meeting of the Western States Land Commissioners Association, Breckenridge, CO, January 8–11, 1990.

6. Comments from Rowena Rogers, former President of the Colorado Land Board, in response to the survey questionnaire. The land board also requested an attorney general's opinion outlining the areas of authority of the Department of Natural Resources vis-a-vis the State Land Office and Land Board.

7. Both these situations occur in Utah, and the first also occurs in Wyoming.

8. The employment levels and funding mechanisms for the agency managing the permanent funds are not included here since the agencey usually receives legislatively appropriated general funds for its operations. Many court cases dealing with management of the permanent funds have arisen over the years in specific states, principally Idaho and Montana. The feedback mechanism between funding for these activities, and their performance should not be discounted however.

9. Two items of information are important for identifying state land office staffing patterns: the number (and type) of employees managing the various resources (or equivalently, the amount of payroll); and the relationship between staffing patterns and the mechanisms used to fund the agency. The first information permits estimation of management intensity per unit of output or area, and thus provides a mechanism for comparing intensity among states and owners. The second item relates to the feedback mechanism, if any, between revenue generation from the trust lands and the managing agency's budget. This second item is discussed in detail in

Chapter 3. In the present section, we simply provide the basic information needed to conduct the analysis in Table 2-1, which shows the number of full-time equivalent (FTE) employees in the states' trust land management programs.

10. In most states, the apportionment of staff time to the various programs is difficult to document, at best, and is frequently impossible. Table 2-1 provides the best information that we have been able to achieve working with the state land offices over the past five years.

11. In Figure 2-1 this is represented by the shaded line running from the renewable resource rents to the agency management account.

12. These "county" forest lands are peculiar to Oregon and will be discussed in Chapter 5.

13. OREGON DEPARTMENT OF FORESTRY, FOREST LOG 59(1) (August–September 1989) at 6. Comparative percentages of sales are not discussed. Whether the cost recovery is on a sale-by-sale basis, by management area (75% of common school forested lands are in the Elliot State Forest in Clatrop County), or on a program-wide basis is not stated.

14. This is represented by the shaded dashed line in Figure 2-1 running from the nonrenewable resource revenues to the agency management account.

15. WASHINGTON DEPARTMENT OF NATURAL RESOURCES, PROPOSED FOREST LAND MANAGEMENT PROGRAM (1983), at 29 [hereinafter cited as PROPOSED FOREST LAND MANAGEMENT PROGRAM].

16. *Id.* at 28.

17. REVISED CODE OF WASHINGTON § 76.12.

18. IDAHO DEPARTMENT OF LANDS, IDAHO FORESTRY OPPORTUNITIES 1980–1990 (March 1988), at 9 [hereinafter cited as IDAHO FORESTRY OPPORTUNITIES]. IDAHO CODE ANNOTATED § 58–140 requires that funds derived from specific activities, such as timber, be used only to improve the productivity and revenue generation of that activity. For timber, allowable activities are timber management, protection, and reforestation.

19. IDAHO DEPARTMENT OF LANDS, FOURTEENTH ANNUAL REPORT 1987–1988 (June 30, 1989), at 7.

20. Office of the [Montana] Legislative Auditor, Department of State Lands: Report on Examination of Financial Statements, Two Fiscal Years Ended June 30, 1983. Report 83-20 (1983), at 3–10. This program was established in 1967 by the legislature (MONTANA CODE ANNOTATED § 77-1-604). Section 77-1-605 allows funds to be used to improve productivity of timberlands.

21. *Id.* at 10.

22. The primary source of information for this subsection is a ten-state study of state trust and sovereign lands: Souder & Fairfax, Western States Survey Responses. (State Lands Project, Department of Forestry and Resource Management, University of California, Berkeley, December 1989) [hereafter cited as Western States Survey Responses].

23. Utah, like Arizona and New Mexico, received four sections, a large proportion of which consisted of low quality land that was hard to sell; but the state did not have such extensive disposition restrictions.

24. The major exceptions are Oregon (which manages land for the counties), and Washington (which manages forest board lands that directly benefit the counties, as discussed in Chapter 5), and states that received other lands through tax defaults (Minnesota and Michigan).

25. In comparison to the other states, Arizona, New Mexico, and Oklahoma have also retained much of their college and university grant lands, although Montana and Idaho have each kept more than 200,000 acres of land for these beneficiaries.

26. In looking at the acreage figures in Table 2-4, any given parcel of state trust land may be simultaneously leased for a variety of uses.

27. See FINAL TRANSITION LANDS POLICY PLAN, for a discussion of Washington's program.

28. See Fairfax & Souder, Working Paper 90-4 (1990), on file at University of California, Berkeley, Forestry Department, for a complete enumeration.

29. All net income (both rentals and royalties) from school and in lieu lands is now placed in the state teachers' retirement fund (ANNOTATED CALIFORNIA CODE–PUBLIC RESOURCES § 6217.5 and EDUCATION § 24702(a)), while net receipts from land sales go into the State Land Bank to purchase replacement lands PUBLIC RESOURCES § 6217.7). There are two exceptions to this division. First, royalties (or their in lieu replacement) for the two sections within the Elk Hills Naval Petroleum Reserve go into the State Land Bank, (with the interest only going into the teachers' retirement fund. Second, geothermal indemnity lands (PUBLIC RESOURCES § 3826) income is divided 50 percent to the Geothermal Resources Development Account (30 percent to the Renewable Resources Investment Fund; 30 percent as grants to local jurisdictions, and 40 percent to the county where the revenues were generated; while the other 50 percent goes to the teachers' retirement fund (PUBLIC RESOURCES § 3826 and EDUCATION § 24702).

30. As noted in Chapter 1, states have added a number of other categories of revenues to the permanent school fund over the years. For example, Washington's original constitution specified, in Article 16, that, in addition to relying on proceeds from the granted lands, the fund would be derived from appropriations and donations by the state, donations and bequests by individuals, proceeds of escheated and forfeited lands, funds accumulated in the treasury, and the 5 percent from federal land sales that returned to the state.

31. Land sales made before passage of the Jones Act in 1927 (which gave the states legal title to their school sections classified as mineral in character, instead of requiring them to obtain in lieu lands) did not include sale of the mineral rights along with the surface lands. Thus, states that came into the Union during the phase-two period (California, Colorado, Nevada, and Oregon, especially) sold whatever unknown minerals were on their lands, often retaining only a one-sixteenth royalty right, if any. This problem was especially prevalent in states whose lands were valued for surface uses, while the value of the subsurface resources was unknown or masked for fraudulent purposes. In states where surface rights were not in demand, settlement and land claims did not occur on a large scale until either the restrictions on purchasing lands were stricter (New Mexico) or the Jones Act had been enacted (Utah and Wyoming). Basically, if there wasn't water, nobody wanted the lands. See TOWNLEY, ALFALFA COUNTRY: NEVADA LAND, WATER AND POLITICS IN THE NINETEENTH CENTURY (1976), for a description of Nevada's early problems with selling its trust lands. For states "lucky" enough to have lands that nobody wanted before 1927, the Jones Act allowed the mineral values to be captured for the trust. This occurred in most states after the OPEC oil embargoes in 1973 pushed the prices for petroleum products up and spurred demand for state leases. See Chapter 3 for further discussion of price

trends in crude oil and coal and their effects on trust revenues going into permanent funds.

32. This was accomplished via a court case pitting the state auditor against the state land commissioner. Jensen v. Dinehart, 645 P.2d 32 (1982). The effects of this decision are discussed further in Chapter 4. Utah's example provides a case study for Chapter 3.

33. ASARCO v. Kadish 109 S. Ct. 2037; 104 L. Ed. 2d 696 (1989).

34. There are two exceptions to this case: Utah in 1981 allowed its beneficiaries to withdrawal principal from their permanent funds in the face of a one-third cut in their appropriations from the legislature; and states that have a land banking process (Arizona, California, and Washington) allow proceeds from the sale of trust lands to be retained in a special account that is used to purchase other lands for the beneficiaries.

35. This possibility was pointed out by Rick Lopez, Assistant Commissioner of Commercial Resources and Exchanges, New Mexico State Land Office during an interview, August 2, 1988.

36. This differentiation is further elaborated in the discussion of land office funding mechanisms later in this chapter.

37. See Table 2-2 for administrative costs for permanent fund management where the money goes to the state land office. In most states, the state investment agency also deducts money for managing the permanent fund. The extent of these deductions is unknown; payments from the permanent fund to the beneficiaries reported here are *net* payments, after any management fees are deducted.

38. Office of the [Montana] Legislative Auditor. Performance Audit: State-owned and Leased Land. Report 82P-17 (June 1983), at 6, 7. Basic language is in Article 10, Section 5 of the 1972 Constitution of Montana. Note however, that D. H. Jackson, Economic Returns and the Management of Montana's Trust Forest Lands (prepared at the request of the Joint Interim Subcommittee No. 2 of the Montana Legislature, December 5, 1983), at 2, based on work by Virginia Griffing at the University of Montana School of Law, states that the proceeds from timber go into a beneficiaries' permanent fund, owing to the concept from English common law that timber is affixed to the land as opposed to being a renewable resource.

39. IDAHO FORESTRY OPPORTUNITIES at 3.

40. MONTANA CONSTITUTION art. X, § 5.

41. PROPOSED FOREST LAND MANAGEMENT PROGRAM, at 29.

42. This has the effect of heightening public awareness of the contributions of the trust lands to the common schools. The current Land Commissioner, Curtis Johnson, is a former high school principal who ran for and was elected to the office because he was concerned about the revenues the schools were receiving. Interview with Curtis Johnson, South Dakota Commissioner of School and Public Lands, Pierre, South Dakota, December 1991.

3. EVALUATING TRUST LANDS MANAGEMENT DECISIONS

1. Production economics is also known by the term "Theory of the Firm" and is the purview of microeconomics. Microeconomics texts provide varying levels of dis-

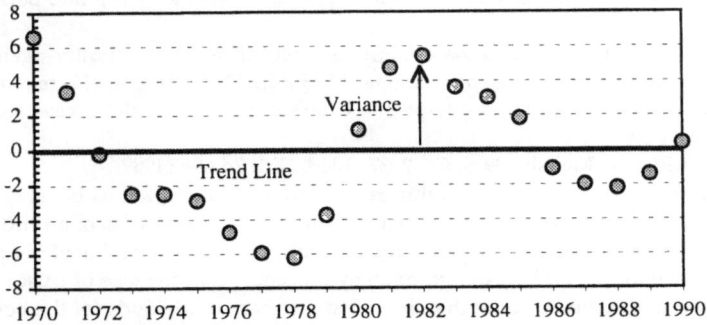

Figure N-1. Variance of actual values in relation to a long-term trend line.

cussion. For an introduction, see D. MCCLOSKY, THE APPLIED THEORY OF PRICE (1982). Those wishing a more advanced discussion might consult W. NICHOLSON, MICROECONOMIC THEORY: BASIC PRINCIPLES AND EXTENSIONS (3d ed. 1985), Part III.

2. The discussion of risk and its measurement is necessarily brief in this chapter. For more information, basic business texts on financial management will provide an adequate introduction. We used BREALEY & MYERS, PRINCIPLES OF CORPORATE FINANCE (2d. ed. 1984) , chapters 7, 8, and 9 [hereinafter cited as BREALEY & MYERS].

3. Variance is simply the difference between the expected value and the actual value for a single activity, without looking at the interaction among different activities. Variance is usually determined by looking at past trends. While this view is simplistic, it can provide insights to help predict future developments. The first step in calculating the variance is to determine the trend over time. There are a number of possible ways to do this, and most electronic spreadsheet programs have routines for performing them. The simplest method is to fit a straight line through the approximate middle of all the actual values. This identifies the trend. Once this has been done, the variance at each measured point is the difference between the expected value from the trend line and the actual value that occurred. Figure N-1 shows a trend line for the period from 1970 to 1990 and the variance (actually, deviation) at the value for the year 1982. The variation for the entire period from 1970 to 1990 is essentially determined by taking the average of the square of the deviations. The exact formula for calculating the variance over a period of time (or number of observations) is

$$\text{Variance } (\tilde{r}_m) = \frac{1}{N-1} \sum_{t=1}^{N} (\tilde{r}_{mt} - \tilde{r}_m)^2,$$

where

$\tilde{r}_{mt}$ = Market return in period t

r_m = Mean of the values of $\tilde{r}_{mt}$ [that is, the trend]

N = Number of measurements.

The variance of the actual versus the expected results over time or space provides an indication of risk. The results of an individual action vary more from the average or trend if there is a high level of variance than if there is a low level.

4. Covariance is the way to measure the interaction or comparative effects of vari-

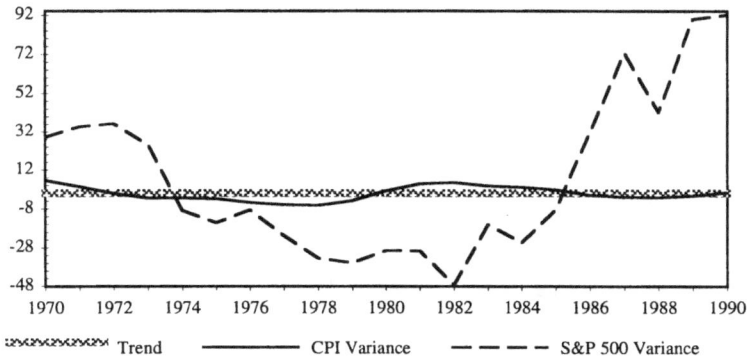

Figure N-2. An example of the covariance of two economic indexes around their long-term trend lines, 1970–1990.

ations in a number of activities. Unlike the variance and standard deviation for a single activity, the covariance between two activities can be negative. An example illustrating covariance is shown in Figure N-2. In Figure N-2, the variances of two common macroeconomic indexes—the Consumer Price Index (CPI-U) and the Standard and Poor's Index of the average of 500 stock prices (S&P 500)—are plotted against their own trends. As Figure N-2 indicates, the variance of the S&P 500 is greater than that of the CPI. The covariance between the CPI and the S&P 500 is calculated by multiplying the differences in actual versus expected (trend) values for the two indexes. The covariance of an individual observation at time t would then be

$$\text{Covariance (CPI, S\&P)}_t = (\text{CPI}_{\text{actual, }t} - \text{CPI}_{\text{trend, }t})(\text{S\&P}_{\text{actual, }t} - \text{S\&P}_{\text{trend, }t})$$

Then the total variance over a period is

$$\text{Covariance (CPI, S\&P)} =$$
$$\frac{1}{N-1}\sum_{t=1}^{N}\left[(\text{CPI}_{\text{actual, }t} - \text{CPI}_{\text{trend, }t})(\text{S\&P}_{\text{actual, }t} - \text{S\&P}_{\text{trend, }t})\right].$$

Over the period from 1970 to 1990, the variance of the CPI was 13, while the variance of the S&P 500 was 1,772. The standard deviations (positive square roots) corresponding to these two indexes were, respectively, 3.7 and 42. From these two numbers, we can conclude that stock prices vary by approximately an order of magnitude more than do consumer prices—an important item of risk information to weigh if stocks are used as investments. The covariance provides an estimate of the relative risk of activities in combination and by reference to their own variances.

5. The beta of an activity is its own variance in relation to the variance of all the activities.

6. The difference in the return between these two activities—one risky and one riskless—is called *risk premium*. The example we used in note 4 compared the Con-

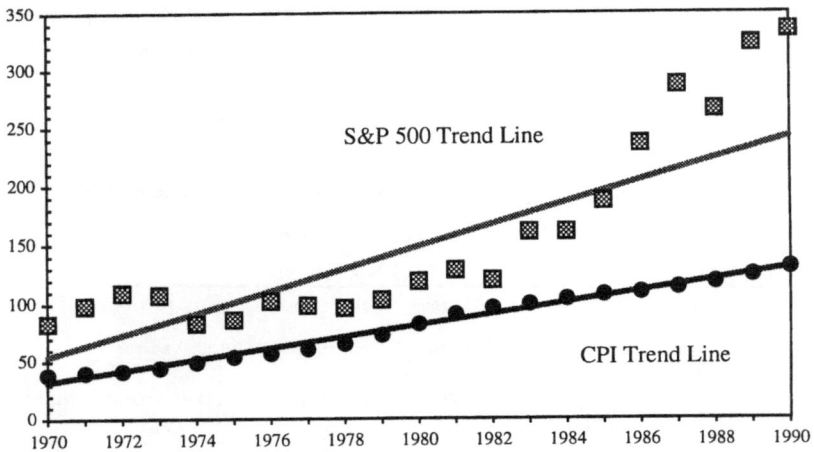

Figure N-3. Risk premium received for stocks compared to consumer prices, 1970–1990.

sumer Price Index with stock market variation and showed that the risk associated with investments in the stock market is quite a bit higher than that of consumer prices. We should expect then that there would be a risk premium resulting from stock investments, as shown in Figure N-3. In Figure N-3, the solid lines show the trend lines for the CPI and for the S&P 500, with individual actual measurements at corresponding points. The average risk premium gained by investing in the stock market is the distance between the two lines or (over the period from 1970 to 1990), the area between the trend lines. The individual annual risk premium for the stock market is the distance—or relative price difference—between the square markers (representing stock market averages) and the solid circles (representing consumer prices). If the risk premium is high enough, the *potential* return from the activity offsets the associated additional risk. Beta is used as a proxy for risk. Risk premiums are calculated by means of a method called the *capital asset pricing model*. This model says that the risk premium varies in accordance with the beta of the activity. The expected risk premium $(r - r_f)$ equals the beta (β) of the activity times the expected risk premium of the market as a whole $(r_m - r_f)$, where r is a risky investment and r_f is a risk-free investment (such as Treasury bills or government bonds). This is calculated as $r - r_f = \beta(r_m - r_f)$. See BREALEY & MYERS at 129–31.

7. Here we are talking only about financial risks, and not about environmental or other types of risk.

8. The U.S. Bureau of the Census publishes two useful sources of information on the status of the economy as a whole and of specific data by investment or commodity type. These are the biennial *Business Statistics* (the latest of which is *Business Statistics, 1963–1991* (1993)), and the monthly *Survey of Current Business*. The former is a compilation of data found in the latter.

9. It is possible to develop an idea of the trend in these indicators, as well as to

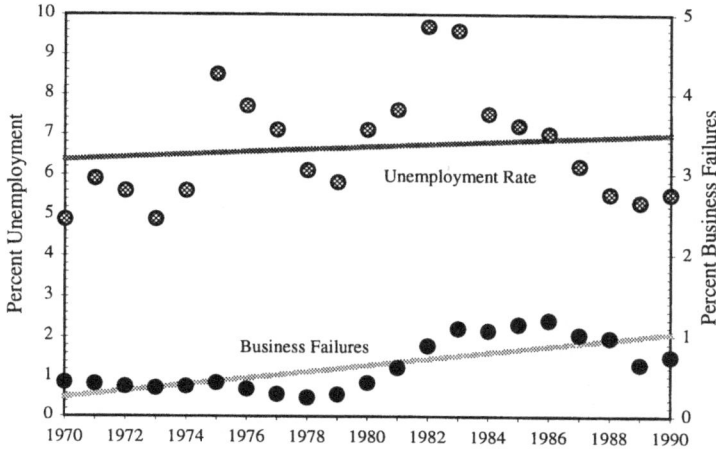

Figure N-4. Two indicators of macroeconomic cycles.

describe their variation. In Figure N-3, the lower line is the Consumer Price Index; the slope of this line, 4.9, is the long-term rate of inflation, which averaged about 5 percent over the years 1970–1990. Recessions are much more difficult to describe. In Figure N-4, the unemployment rate and the rate of business failures are used to illustrate whether the economy is in recession or expansion, as described in the accompanying text.

10. We will use the information in Figure N-5 for crude oil and Douglas fir price indexes to perform a simple analysis. Examination of the cycle of variation between

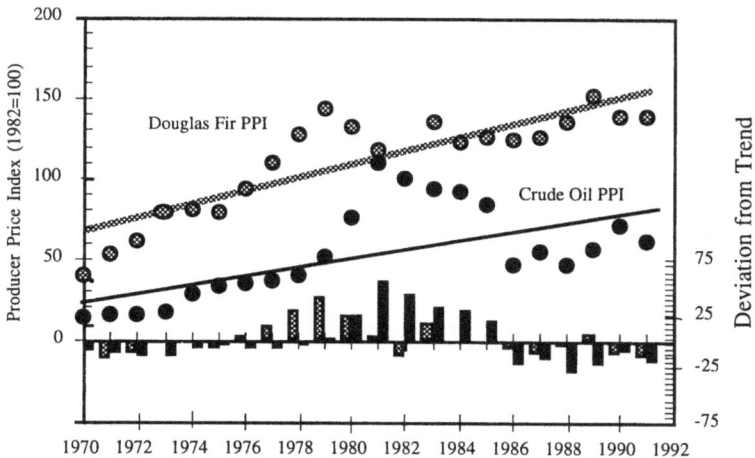

Figure N-5. Trend and variation in producer price indexes for crude oil and lumber.

lumber and crude oil and their respective trend lines shows that they appear to vary together; that is, when the producer price of Douglas fir rises above its trend line, the producer price crude oil behaves similarly, but with a lag of approximately two years. The basic data for these two producer price time series show that crude oil varied an average of 13 percent above and below its trend line, with an increased price trend approximating 13 percent per year. On the other hand, Douglas fir lumber varied an average of 39 percent above and below its price trend line, which increasing at an average rate of 6.4 percent per year. Thus, while the price rose faster on average for crude oil, the fluctuations in its price around its long-term trend were considerably less than the ones that occurred in Douglas fir lumber prices, even though the average price increase in Douglas fir was half that of crude oil. From a risk standpoint, investments in timber production appear to be less favorable than those in oil production, at least over this period of time and taken individually, because their variance is higher and their average price increase is less. More important in portfolio theory is the covariance between the two commodities: if their covariance is low, they have the ability to reduce overall variation by balancing each others' price fluctuations. The covariance between lumber and crude oil is 87.4 (a unitless measure), while the correlation coefficient between the two producer price indexes is 25 percent. This means that these two commodities tend to cycle together, although there is little correlation between their average prices.

11. Commonly used terms include "for the benefit of the schools," or "for the generation of revenues." See *Conventional Wisdom* [*supra*, Introduction, note 1], (1992) for a listing, by state, of the original federal enabling act and state constitution language for each trust arrangement. For a discussion, see the dissent in Oklahoma Education Association v. Nigh, 642 P.2d 230 (1982), a case discussed in Chapter 7.

12. For revenues, gross and net (minus expenditures) receipts indicate returns to the trust. Management efficiency is characterized by four key factors: expenditures; expenditures as a percentage of revenues; expenditure per acre; and return per employee (the labor factor from the activity analysis). Two other areas were examined to control for other possible sources of variation between states. First, land quality was expressed in three ways: as total acres leased; as acres leased by resource use, and as gross revenues per acre (both total and by resource use—the land factor). Second, any effects of state land office organization were tested by classifying whether the land commissioner is elected (New Mexico, Washington), whether the land board is active in the day-to-day management of the office (California, Colorado, Oregon, Utah), and whether the land office is highly influenced by the state executive or another state office (Idaho, Montana, Wyoming).

13. We are talking here about the *ceteris paribus* conditions for personnel assignment *within* a state, not between states. Within a state, revenues produced per employee should be roughly equivalent across programs, unless—through a planning process—explicit offsets are recognized between current revenues and potential future ones that would result from "investing" personnel in other activities. If all things are not equal, the state should undertake a program to rectify the inequalities.

14. This is because the elasticity of substitution is zero among factors. Factor prices may play a role in the choice of alternative production processes. See CHIANG, FUNDAMENTAL METHODS OF MATHEMATICAL ECONOMICS (3d ed., 1984) at 704ff [hereinafter cited as CHIANG] for technical details.

15. In this respect, the activity analysis production function provides the input matrix for commonly used linear programming optimization techniques. See CHIANG at 701ff; and DORFMAN ET AL., LINEAR PROGRAMMING AND ECONOMIC ANALYSIS (1958) at 346ff [hereinafter cited as DORFMAN ET AL.] for linear programming formulations of the activity analysis model.

16. Subject to minimum legal compliance measures, which may be high enough to warrant divestment of the land type or parcel requiring undue amounts of effort or monetary expenditures.

17. Such would be the case when staff is needed to survey and monument state trust lands as a means of preventing adverse possession.

18. For more detail, see J. A. Souder, Economic Strategies for the Management of School and Institutional Trust Lands: A Comparative Study of Ten Western States (unpublished Ph.D. dissertation, University of California, Berkeley, 1990) [hereinafter cited as *Economic Strategies*].

19. The percentages themselves are derived from the ratios of pairs of labor factor returns, and as such are unitless:

$$(\$/FTE_{LHS}/\$/FTE_{RHS}) \times 100.$$

The interpretation of the percentages is that a unit of labor in the left-hand-side (LHS) use returns X% of the revenues of a unit of labor allocated to the program on the right-hand side (RHS).

20. The basic source for this material is *Economic Strategies* at 83–92, particularly table 4-6 at 85.

21. We must accept two assumptions prior to applying this criterion: wage rates must be equal across the programs or must be adjusted to reflect any differences; and the marginal contribution of labor is assumed to be the same across the programs. Staff levels for nonrenewable resources were adjusted downward 20 percent to account for wage differentials between surface versus mineral management personnel, as required by the first assumption. This differential is based on data obtained for salaries in the California State Lands Commission (Cal. Gov., California Budget: Supplement–Salaries and Wages 1989–90, R39-R41 (submitted to the California Legislature 1989–1990 Regular Session)) and received conceptual concurrence from Kevin Carter, Unit Manager for Trust & Asset Management, Utah Division of State Lands and Forestry, during an interview in Salt Lake City, Utah, on July 24, 1991. We have also used the average contribution, rather than the marginal contribution, for the labor factor; because this violates the second assumption—and the fact that revenues fluctuate much more on an annual basis than do personnel levels—a strict interpretation should be avoided. Regardless, the information obtained from this analysis point to some very interesting management problems within the state land offices.

22. Efficiency criteria indicate whether the state land office is allocating personnel to produce maximum revenues—an objective at least in the short term. Whether a state is allocating personnel to achieve resource sustainability requires a longitudinal analysis. Sustained production of revenues (the state trust lands management objective) requires that assets—both land and labor—be employed for the best long-term benefit. It may be that personnel are engaged in long-term management programs

that have yet to produce revenues. In these cases, prospective future revenues should be discounted to the present to examine efficiencies, or longer-term average revenues should be used as a metric, or other justification should be provided. What is important is that there be a standard by which the managing agency is required to justify its personnel allocations to the beneficiary.

23. Where marginal revenue product is the marginal revenue times the marginal product for an input. If the firm is a price-taker, the marginal revenue is considered the market price.

24. Unlike the U.S. Forest Service, with its cumbersome mandate and unsuitable data system, trust land managers have a clear mandate and clear criteria for getting marginal lands out of production. See generally, SOCIETY OF AMERICAN FORESTERS, REPORT OF THE BELOW-COST TIMBER SALES TASK FORCE: FISCAL AND SOCIAL RESPONSIBILITY IN NATIONAL FOREST MANAGEMENT (1986) [hereinafter cited as AMERICAN FORESTERS].

25. We are not alone in identifying accountability as crucial to oversight of land management: Utah's state auditor found that the procedures used by the land office were insufficient to determine whether the latter was efficiently managing the state's trust assets. Office of the Legislative Auditor General, A Performance Audit of the Division of State Lands and Forestry. Report No. 92-09 (November 1992) at ii, 13–18.

26. This has traditionally been a problem in federal lands management. See AMERICAN FORESTERS at 17ff. Whether all trust lands must be managed was examined by the California attorney general, who found that "there is no compulsion on the state to sell or lease any of the lands." Op. Att'y General 63-48 (June 5, 1963) at 211.

27. THEIL, A SYSTEM-WIDE APPROACH TO MICROECONOMICS (1980) at 219.

28. One possible exception to this would be raw logs sold by the Department of Natural Resources into the export market from Washington state, due to their size, species, and availability characteristics.

29. DORFMAN ET AL. at 227.

30. Trona—a mineral composed of hydrous sodium carbonate and bicarbonate—is found in or under dry lake beds and is used in the production of glass.

31. Good explanations of economic growth theory are found in DORFMAN ET AL.; TAKAYAMA MATHEMATICAL ECONOMICS (1985) [hereinafter cited as TAKAYAMA]; and (especially for natural resource–based systems, P. S. DASGUPTA & G. HEAL, ECONOMIC THEORY AND EXHAUSTIBLE RESOURCES (1979) [hereinafter cited as DASGUPTA & HEAL].

32. Specifying an ending capital stock for the planning horizon can also be used to determine the amount of wealth passed to future generations.

33. One place to start is MISHAN, COST-BENEFIT ANALYSIS (3d ed., 1976), at 165–272.

34. The three equations specify the production function, the capital accumulation function, and the population growth rate. The production function can be generalized as

$$Y_t = F(L_t, K_t)$$

so the production (Y_t) at time t is the result of using a combination of labor (L_t) at time t and of capital (K_t) at time t in the production function(s) F.

The rate of capital accumulation at time t is a function of the previous period's capital level (K_t), and the amount of new capital added ($Y_t - X_t$)—that is, production minus consumption—less the rate of depreciation of the existing capital stock (m), in the relationship

$$\dot{K}_t - \mu K_t = Y_t - X_t,$$

where $\dot{K}_t \equiv dK_t/dt$, the instantaneous growth rate of capital, is equal to the change in capital at time t. The instantaneous growth in labor, L_t, is defined as

$$\frac{\dot{L}_t}{L_t} = n,$$

where n is the population growth rate. Based on TAKAYAMA at 432ff and 444.

35. Using population growth as a proxy for beneficiary demand growth, the preceding three relationships can be combined and expressed in per-capita terms as the fundamental equation for an aggregate growth model:

$$k_t = f(k_t) - \lambda k_t - x_t,$$

where k_t is the per-capita capital growth rate and $\lambda \equiv n + \mu$.

This last equation can be interpreted as indicating that per-capita accumulation at time t is a function of the productivity of the capital $f(k_t)$ based on the per-capita capital level (k_t), less the depreciation rate (μ) and the population growth (n), minus the amount of consumption (x_t). These variables then form the choices available to society regarding consumption of the revenues of the trust (x_t) versus increasing the amount of capital (k_t) available to produce future benefits. Putting the model in per-capita terms allows the expectations for future beneficiary needs to be explicitly incorporated. In the main-text discussion that follows, the major choices available to the states are the amount of capital, the amount of production (that is, revenues) retained to increase the capital stock versus the amount consumed for current operations. TAKAYAMA at 435.

36. The subsistence level of consumption under this path sometimes causes it to be called the "Stalinist" path.

37. Figure N-6 shows the differences in capital stocks and in consumption between these two extreme paths.

38. This is due to the declining marginal productivity of capital that is implied by the leveling off of the subsistence capital growth path in Figure N-6 (note 37).

39. The main reference here is TAKAYAMA at 410ff.

40. *Id.* at 432ff.

41. This is assuming a Cobb–Douglas world, where production (Y) is a function of capital (K) and labor (L) in the form $Y = K^\alpha L^\beta$ and where, in constant returns to scale, $\alpha + \beta = 1$.

42. This requires that the marginal productivity of capital be equal to the rate of population growth plus the rate of depreciation. TAKAYAMA at 440ff.

43. In the case of the trust lands, we know the first two items (capital and population growth); and historically, at least, technological changes can be estimated.

44. TAKAYAMA at 559ff.

45. The exceptions to this are in Washington, where the Washington Department of Natural Resources takes 25 percent of royalty revenue as management expenses, and in Utah, where 20 percent of royalties and 20 percent of permanent fund dividends are available for land office management expenses. See Table 2-2 and its references for a complete description.

46. At the same time, the capital stock in the form of standing trees is no longer

Capital Accumulation Paths

Income and Capital Consumption Paths

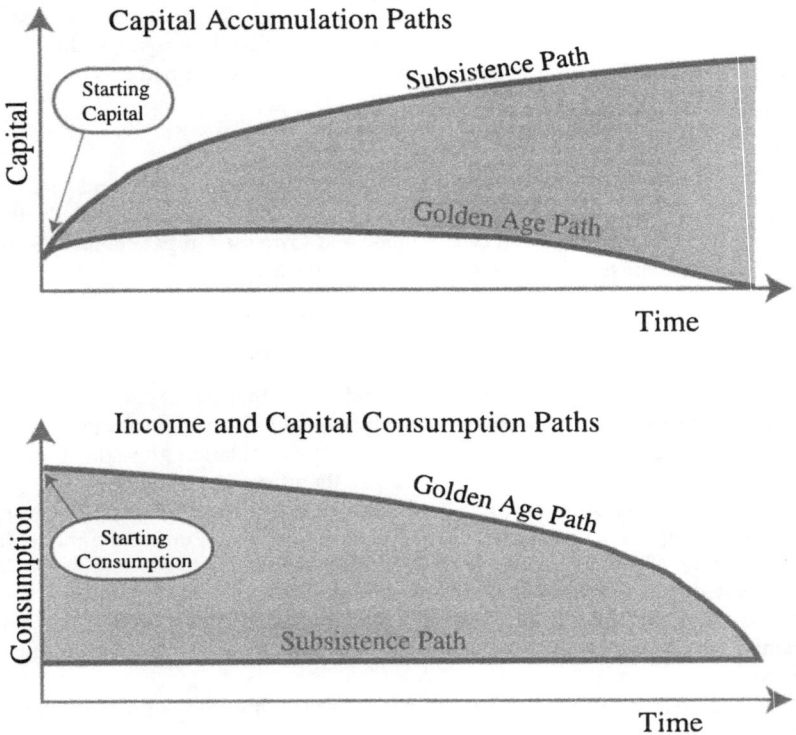

Figure N-6. Possible paths for capital growth and consumption.

present, having been cut and sold. The importance of the disposition of timber revenues to the permanent fund will become clear when decisions to allocate revenues to increase the productive capital of the trust lands are considered.

47. See Figure N-6 (note 37).

48. See *Conventional Wisdom* for details.

49. The basic reference used for these models is BLANCHARD & FISCHER, *Lectures on Macro-economics* (1989), chapter 2 [hereinafter cited as BLANCHARD & FISCHER].

50. Ramsey, *A Mathematical Theory of Saving*, ECONOMIC JOURNAL 38(152): 543–59 (1928).

51. BLANCHARD & FISCHER at 39. Refer to the previous discussion of production functions in this chapter for discussion of the terms used here.

52. Ramsey's original formulation of the growth model did not include a positive discount rate, giving rise to the school of welfare economics called "classical utilitarianism." See DASGUPTA & HEAL at 260ff for a historical perspective, and at 286ff for its implication in exhaustible resource exploitation rates.

53. The Ramsey model has the added advantage—compared to most other macro-

economic growth theory models—of not including in its formulation the ability of the government to increase the money supply. This is beneficial in the state trust lands framework for two reasons: first, it simplifies the analysis; and second, it mirrors the states' lack of authority to print money.

54. DASGUPTA & HEAL at 381.

55. Jensen v. Dinehart, 645 P 2d 32 (1983).

56. 44 Stat. 1026, 43 U.S.C. § 870 *et seq.*

57. The difference between $66 million and $20 million also accounts for the 1983 mineral royalties in addition to the accumulated royalties through 1982.

58. This assumes that the nominal interest rate received on the permanent fund was 8.5 percent—the average received by the permanent fund over the years 1982 to 1989 (excluding 1983). This calculation is net of the 20 percent state land office maintenance fee. Without this, the annual cost to the beneficiary is $6 million.

4. CROPLAND AND GRAZING LEASES

1. Oklahoma Education Association v. Nigh, 642 P.2d 230 (Okla. 1982).

2. Calculated from Oklahoma annual reports.

3. Solt, *Trust Lands Leases,*, TOTEM 31 (Summer 1989): 4–5. TOTEM is published by the Washington Department of Natural Resources.

4. See generally TOTEM 31 (Summer 1989).

5. TOTEM 24(5) (September/October 1982).

6. Mackey et al., Capital Project Tracking & Portfolio Analysis (Washington Department of Natural Resources, Olympia, July 1988) cites P.L. 91-310 (July 7, 1970) as allowing the trust lands to exceed the acreage limitation [hereinafter cited as Mackey et al.].

7. Buchholtz, *Transformations,* TOTEM 31 (Summer 1989): 12.

8. *Id.*

9. Interview with Patrick Hennessey, Agricultural Leasing Section Manager, Washington Department of Natural Resources in Olympia, WA June 12, 1991.

10. Mackey, et al. at 5.

11. *Id.*

12. Telephone interview with Mark Grassel, Acting Agricultural Leasing Section Manager, Washington Department of Natural Resources, June 4, 1992.

13. State of Montana, Report of the Commissioner of State Lands and Investments to the Honorable Elmer Holt, Governor. Iver M. Bandjord, Commissioner of State Lands and Investments (1936), at 40.

14. *Id.* at 41.

15. Utah attempted the same type of statewide consolidation with Project Bold in the 1980s that Montana's commissioner had proposed in the 1930s. The failure of Project Bold demonstrated the difficulties inherent in trying to adjust land holdings for thousands of parcels at once (discussed in Chapter 7).

16. Oregon Division of State Lands Internal Memo from Jeff Kroft to Gus Gustafson (Director) and others, January 11, 1993. Subject: "Summary of Land Board Items Relating to Grazing Issues."

17. Interview with Burt Lewis, Grazing Lands Manager, Oregon Division of State Lands, in Bend, Oregon, on April 1, 1992.

18. OREGON DIVISION OF STATE LANDS, RANGELAND MANAGEMENT PROGRAM, FACTS—QUESTIONS & ANSWERS (n.d. [1993]). After consolidation, the division manages the 44 blocked units and another 129 unblocked parcels, of which 28,500 acres are wetland grazing leases, 12,300 acres are inholdings in the Hart and Malheur National Wildlife Refuges, and 32,000 acres are in isolated parcels of 640 acres or less each that have been classified for disposal. OREGON DIVISION OF STATE LANDS, RANGELAND RESOURCES SECTION, CORE MANAGEMENT UNITS BLOCKED (1991). This is generally referred to as the "Cowboy Notebook," and is hereinafter cited as such.

19. "Cowboy Notebook."

20. Land Board fee policy allows for an increase or decease of 10¢ per AUM if the price of beef increases or decreases by $10.00 per hundredweight.

21. The state's grazing managers did not bill the ranchers for the increased forage available on their leases unless its value exceeded the amount of repayment for the improvements. So while it may appear that the lessees were paying relatively high forage fees because of their repayment of state-financed improvement costs, they were in fact only paying the base grazing fee if the tradeoffs are taken into account. The rationale offered by Oregon's grazing managers was that this subsidy encouraged the lessees to contribute about an equal amount of their own money to improve the leases. Discussions with A. K. Majors and Burt Lewis at the Oregon Division of State Lands Grazing Fee Advisory Committee Meeting in Bend, Oregon, on June 30, 1993.

22. This process was underway as this chapter was being written and is nearing completion as it goes to press.

23. Oklahoma Education Association v. Nigh 642 P.2d 230, 235 (Okla. 1982).

24. Interview with John Taylor (now retired), then director of the Real Estate Management Division, Commissioners of the Land Office, in Oklahoma City, July 1992. See generally OKLAHOMA ADMINISTRATIVE CODE § 385:25, Surface Leasing for Agricultural and Commercial Purposes.

25. Id. § 385:25-39-3.

26. Id. § 385:25-3-1(7). Oral bids are used at the expiration of routine leases. If the lands remain unleased or if the lessee defaults after the oral auction, sealed bids are accepted for the re-lease of the lands. Letter from Keith Kuhlman, Director, Real Estate Management Division, Commissioners of the Land Office, to Jon A. Souder, May 19, 1993.

27. OKLAHOMA ADMINISTRATIVE CODE § 385:25-17-8

28. Telephone interview with Keith Kuhlman, Director, Real Estate Management Division, Commissioners of the Land Office, June 1993.

29. AMERICAN INSTITUTE OF REAL ESTATE APPRAISERS. THE APPRAISAL OF REAL ESTATE, 8th ed. (1983), at 42ff.

30. This division of theoretical models is evident from the literature, but it was specifically noted in Bartlett et al., Grazing Lease and Fee Arrangements of Western Governments and Agencies for Study of Western State, Local Governments, and Other Federal Agencies Grazing Leasing Arrangements and User Charges (Final Report, USDA Forest Service Contract No. 53-31872-18, Department of Range Science, Colorado State University, Fort Collins, 1983.

31. Public Rangelands Improvement Act (PRIA) of October 25, 1984, § 6(a); P.L. 95-514; 92 Stat. 1806.

32. See generally HAZELL & NORTON. MATHEMATICAL PROGRAMMING FOR ECONOMIC ANALYSIS IN AGRICULTURE (1986).

33. Secretary of Agriculture and Secretary of Interior, Grazing Fee Review and Evaluation: Final Report 1979–1986 (Department of Agriculture, Forest Service and Department of Interior, Bureau of Land Management, February 1986), at 45ff.

34. See, for example, discussion in H. GEORGE, PROGRESS AND POVERTY (1880), at 368ff.

35. Most studies of the relationships among lessees, owners, and government policies have taken place outside the United States. In the Philippines: MANGAHAS ET AL. TENANTS, LESSEES, OWNERS: WELFARE IMPLICATIONS OF TENURE CHANGE (Quezon City: Ateneo de Manila University Press, 1976). In China (Taiwan): CHEUNG, THE THEORY OF SHARE TENANCY WITH SPECIAL APPLICATION TO ASIAN AGRICULTURE AND THE FIRST PHASE OF TAIWAN LAND REFORM (1976) [hereinafter cited as THEORY OF SHARE TENANCY].

Sharecropping received bad press from its implementation in the South: "There are great differences in economic status and degree of dependency between the several types of tenants. Highest on the ladder are the renters and the cash tenants, who rent their farms for a fixed sum of money. Cash tenants usually can be regarded as independent entrepreneurs—or at least they are not in most cases far removed from such a position. All other kinds of arrangements entitle the landlord to a certain share of the main cash crop, for instance, one-fourth, one-third, one-half, sometimes even as much as three-fourths. Those tenants who receive one-half (or less) of the crop are the sharecroppers. The cash tenants usually furnish all the work, stock, feed, fertilizer, and tools themselves. The other groups generally furnish less and less of these things the lower their tenure status. Those lowest down on the scale have little or nothing but their labor to offer." [MYRDAL, AN AMERICAN DILEMMA (1944), vol. 1, at 236–37.

36. Interview with Jeff Hagener, Lands Administrator, Montana State Land Department, Helena, Montana, June 23, 1992.

37. Based on THEORY OF SHARE TENANCY. A theoretical section is also found in Cheung, *Private Property Rights and Sharecropping,* 76 JOURNAL OF POLITICAL ECONOMY 1107 (1968); and Cheung, *Transaction Costs, Risk Aversion, and the Choice of Contractual Arrangements,* 19 JOURNAL OF LAW AND ECONOMICS 23 (1969).

38. Presentation by Jerry A. Warner, Executive Vice President and Chief Management Officer, Farmers National Company, at the Western State Land Commissioners Association 1993 Summer Meeting in Omaha, Nebraska, July 26, 1993.

39. There is an extensive literature on federal grazing policies. For an elaborate discussion of the Taylor Grazing Act, which began regulation of grazing on the non–Forest Service federal lands, see PEFFER, CLOSING THE PUBLIC DOMAIN (1959). An extensive series of law review articles by George Coggins and his students provide one perspective of the entire process: Coggins et al., *The Law of Public Rangeland Management I: The Extent and Distribution of Federal Power,* 12 ENVIRONMENTAL LAW 535 (1982) [hereinafter cited as *Coggins I*]; Coggins and Lindeberg-Johnson, *The Law of Public Rangeland Management II: The Commons and the Taylor Act,* 13 ENVIRONMENTAL LAW 1 (1982) [hereinafter cited as *Coggins II*]; Coggins, *The Law of Public Rangeland Manage-*

ment III: A Survey of Creeping Regulation at the Periphery, 1934–1982, 13 ENVIRONMENTAL LAW 295 (1983) [hereinafter cited as *Coggins III*]; Coggins, *The Law of Public Rangeland Management IV: FLPMA, PRIA, and the Multiple Use Mandate,* 14 ENVIRONMENTAL LAW 1 (1983) [hereinafter cited as *Coggins IV*]; and Coggins, *The Law of Public Rangelands Management V: Prescriptions for Reform,* 14 ENVIRONMENTAL LAW 497 (1984) [hereinafter cited as *Coggins V*]. See also the references cited within the Coggins series.

40. "'Base property' means: (1) Land that has the capability to produce crops or forage that can be used to support authorized livestock for a specified period of the year, or (2) water that is suitable for consumption by livestock and is available and accessible, to the authorized livestock when the public lands are used for livestock grazing." 43 C.F.R. Ch. II (10-1-87 ed.) § 4100.0-5.

41. DANA & FAIRFAX, FOREST AND RANGE POLICY (1980), at 102; for an earlier window into the pattern, see Omechavarria v. Idaho, 246 U.S. 343 (1918).

42. WASHINGTON ADMINISTRATIVE CODE § 332-20-050.

43. In an Idaho case involving a watershed conservation group's efforts to bid on a grazing lease in order to protect riparian areas, the basic qualifications of a bidder have become a visible issue. See Chapter 7 *infra.*

44. States that do not advertise their leases are Arizona, California, Colorado, Idaho, Montana, New Mexico, Oregon, Utah, Washington, and Wyoming. References to codes and regulations in the various states are:

Arizona:	Doesn't appear to be have competitive bidding. Strong preference system.
California:	CALIFORNIA CODE OF REGULATIONS, title 2, div. 3, ch. 1, art. 2, § 2000(d).
Idaho:	Rule 3. Applications and Processing. Idaho Administrative Procedures Act § 20.13 (1988). Covers "Conflict Bids" where there is more than one applicant for a lease. However, the Department is not compelled to advertise the fact that leases are coming up for renewal.
Montana:	Montana Code Annotated § 77-6-202. Competitive bids on unleased tracts only.
New Mexico:	NMSLO, "SLO Rule 8 Relating to Agricultural Leases," § 8.003(D) Application to Lease. First person to file on "open" acreage usually gets the lease; however, the commissioner may decide to have competitive bid.
Utah:	"When two or more permit applications have been received for the same land, the following procedures shall be followed: 1. The division shall award the permit to the applicant that has an established federal grazing allotment, lease, or owns the land surrounding or adjacent to the tract applied for, provided that the allotment includes the state land under application. 2. When no applicant is the adjacent federal allotment holder or private land owner, the grazing permit shall be awarded to the highest bidder, with the minimum bid starting at the current AUM fee." Rule R632-50-4. Conflict Filings of Applications. Utah Division of State Lands. "Rules Governing the Management and Use of State Lands in Utah," 17th ed., October 1989.

| Washington: | WASHINGTON STATUTES ANNOTATED § 79.01.242(2). Washington can either negotiate a lease, or let the lease at competitive auction. In either case, notice must be given. |
| Wyoming: | Wyoming Board of Land Commissioners, "Rules and Regulations of the Board of Land Commissioners." Chapter IV, Rules and Regulations for Grazing and Agricultural Leasing § 5(d). |

45. Notification requirements for the various states are found in:

Nebraska:	NEBRASKA ADMINISTRATIVE RULES § 77.3.004.
North Dakota:	NORTH DAKOTA CENTURY CODE § 15-04-09.
South Dakota:	SOUTH DAKOTA CODIFIED LAWS § 5-5-5.
Texas:	TEXAS NATURAL RESOURCES CODE § 51.122.
Utah:	Utah Division of State Lands, Rule R632-30-5.2(d).
Washington:	WASHINGTON STATUTES ANNOTATED § 79.01.252.

46. In Chapter 7 we discuss managing permanent funds so that investments keep pace with inflation. In a long-term lease it is also important for the rental to keep pace with inflation.

47. State ex rel. Ebke v. Board of Educational Lands and Funds, 47 N.W. 2d 520 (1951), 154 Neb. 244, 596 (1952).

48. Propst v. Board of Educational Lands and Funds, 55 N.W. 2d 653, 156 Neb. 226 (1952), *cert. denied*, 346 U.S. 823 (1953). See also State v. Platte Valley Public Power & Irr. Dist., 23 N.W. 2d 300, 147 Neb. 289, 166 A.L.R. 1196 (1946).

49. Hogan v. Greenfield, 122 P.2d 850 (1942), 58 Wyo. 13.

50. New Mexico courts have found that the state cannot give an absolute right of renewal (Ellison v. Ellison, 146 P.2d 173, 48 N.M. 80 [1944]), but it may give a preferred right of renewal as long as it is not exclusive or absolute (State ex rel. McElroy v. Vesely, 52 P.2d 1090, 40 N.M. 19 [1935]).

51. Absolute preference rights are found in these states:

Arizona:	ARIZONA STATUTES § 37-291
Louisiana:	LOUISIANA REVISED STATUTES ANNOTATED § 41:1217. Length of preference right depends on the value of improvements the lessee has placed on lands, ranging from ten to thirty years.
Oregon:	Oregon's leasing rules are currently being revised.
Washington:	For permit range, preference right is absolute unless canceled by department or terminated by lessee. WASHINGTON ADMINISTRATIVE CODE § 332-20-180.
Wyoming:	WYOMING STATUTES § 36-5-105(a).

52. States that allow the existing lessee to match the highest bid are:

Montana:	MONTANA CODE ANNOTATED § 77-6-205(2).
New Mexico:	NEW MEXICO STATUTES ANNOTATED § 8.012(A)(3). NMSLO, "SLO Rule 8 Regarding Agricultural Leases."
Utah:	R632-50-4. Conflict Filings of Applications. Utah Division of State Lands, "Rules Governing the Management and Use of State Lands in Utah," 17th ed., October 1989.
Washington:	WASHINGTON ADMINISTRATIVE CODE § 332-20-210.

53. There is a large literature on auctions and bidding behavior. Case law relating to bidding for state trust land leases is sparser:

Arizona: Manning v. Perry, 62 P.2d 693 (1936).

Montana: Toomey v. State Board of Land Com'rs, 81 P.2d 407, 106 Mont. 547 (1938), over whether oral auction is required by the constitution for sale of interests or estate in land versus the land itself. Notice provisions for sales are not applicable to interests or estates in the lands.

Nebraska: Anderson v. Board of Educational Lands and Funds, 256 N.W. 2d 318, 198 Neb. 793, regarding requirement for public auction.

54. States using written bids are:

Louisiana: LOUISIANA REVISED STATUTES ANNOTATED § 41:1214(A).

Montana: MONTANA ADMINISTRATIVE RULES § 26.3.142(2)(c).

New Mexico: NMSLO, "SLO Rule 8 Relating to Agricultural Leases." For "open acreage" only.

Utah: Rule R632-30-5.2(d). Applications for Lands Under Permit and Preference Rights. Utah Division of State Lands, "Rules Governing the Management and Use of State Lands in Utah," 17th ed., October 1989.

55. States using oral auctions are:

Idaho: IDAHO CODE § 58-310.

Nebraska: NEBRASKA ADMINISTRATIVE RULES § 97.3.008.

North Dakota: NORTH DAKOTA CENTURY CODE § 15-04-10, 1991 Pocket Supplement.

Oklahoma: OKLAHOMA REVISED STATUTES § 64-101. Oklahoma uses oral auctions for its fall leases. If the tracts remain unleased or if the lessee defaults, they are re-leased in the spring with written, sealed bids.

South Dakota: SOUTH DAKOTA CODIFIED LAWS § 5-5-6.

56. MONTANA CODE ANNOTATED § 77-6-202.

57. For its competitive bids, Montana uses highest amount per AUM. *Id.*

58. Interview with Keith Kuhlman, Director, Real Estate Management Division, Oklahoma Commissioners of the Land Office, in Coeur d'Alene, Idaho, September 1992. Letter from Keith Kuhlman to Jon Souder, May 19, 1993.

59. Interview with Jeff Hagener, Surface Management Supervisor, Montana Department of Lands, in Helena, Montana, June 1992.

60. BLACK'S LAW DICTIONARY 462 (abridged 5th ed., 1983) [hereinafter cited as BLACK'S LAW DICTIONARY].

61. Most of the case law dealing with leasehold interests has resulted from eminent domain cases, where a governmental agency has taken the underlying property for public use. When the cases go to court, both the landlord and the tenant are trying to obtain their fair share of the value of the property and the value of its use (by the tenant). The latter, termed *leasehold value*, depends on whether the lessee is getting below-market rent for the lease and whether the lessee is compensated for improvements at termination of the lease. *Id.* at 462. How leases are written and sold

determines the extent of leasehold value. For instance, leases can be written with a "no bonus clause" so that the lessee is only compensated for the value of improvements and prepaid rent, but not for any leasehold interest resulting from below-market rents. *Id.* at 544.

62. 73A C.J.S. *Public Lands* § 95(d) (1983).

63. In *In re Leasing of State Lands*, 32 P. 986 (1893), a Colorado court held that a five-year limitation on the length of a grazing lease was within the legislature's power to set.

64. States that lease agricultural and grazing lands for five-year terms are:

New Mexico: NEW MEXICO STATUTES 1978 ANNOTATED § 19-7-30.
North Dakota: NORTH DAKOTA CENTURY CODE § 15-04-01.
Oklahoma: OKLAHOMA STATUTES ANNOTATED § 64-259. 1992 Cumulative Annual Pocket Part.
South Dakota: SOUTH DAKOTA CODIFIED LAWS § 5-5-11.
Washington: WASHINGTON REVISED CODE §§ 79.01.096 and 79.12.570. Agricultural leases can be given for periods ranging from ten to twenty-five years, depending on the crop grown.

States that have ten-year lease terms, and their regulatory cites, are:

Arizona: ARIZONA REVISED STATUTES § 37-281(A).
California: CALIFORNIA CODE OF REGULATIONS, title 2, div. 3, ch. 1, art. 2, § 2004. Agricultural leases can be for twenty-five years.
Idaho: IDAHO CODE § 58-307.
Louisiana: LOUISIANA REVISED STATUTES Annotated § 41:1217.
Mississippi: MISSISSIPPI CODE ANNOTATED § 29-3-81. Agricultural leases are for five years, with the exception of rice. Pasturage is for ten years.
Montana: MONTANA ADMINISTRATIVE RULES § 26.3.11(1).
Nebraska: Based on an analysis of the "Board of Educational Lands and Funds, Minutes of Meeting, October 18, 1991, at 20–42, leases for agricultural and grazing use are sold for periods ranging from five to twelve years, with ten years the usual maximum. The only twelve-year leases were in Morrill County.
Texas: TEXAS NATURAL RESOURCES CODE § 51.121.
Wyoming: WYOMING STATUTES § 36-5-102.

Citations for other than five- or ten-year leases are:

Utah: UTAH CODE ANNOTATED § 65A-9-2(1).

65. Although this may be changing, given the current uncertainty over tenure and grazing fees and the tightening of collateral standards for federally insured banks. Ranchers at a recent meeting of the Oregon Division of State Land's "Grazing Fee Advisory Committee" stated that bankers were refusing to consider either federal or state grazing leases as collateral for loans.

66. This practice tends to mirror the federal rules that allow collateral assignment. 43 C.F.R. Ch. II (10-1-87 ed.) § 4130.8.

67. Definition of *collateral security*, BLACK'S LAW DICTIONARY at 137.

68. See 73A C.J.S. *Public Lands* § 99 (1983), which states that collateral assignments must be allowed.

69. States that prohibit collateral assignments are:

North Dakota: Cannot use lease as collateral: no equity in the lease beyond the lease; bankers are not usually eager to use a four- to five-year lease on a longer-term loan; and if commisioners are doing their job, there is no value left to mortgage. Interview with Tim Kingstad, Commissioner, North Dakota State Land Department, in Bismarck, North Dakota (November 11, 1991). [Notes on file at State Lands Project].

South Dakota: Policy is not to allow collateral assignments. Interview with Curtis Johnson, Commissioner, South Dakota Office of School and Public Lands, in Pierre, South Dakota (November 13, 1991). [Notes on file at State Lands Project].

70. *Subleasing*, in the federal context, is defined as: "The act of a permittee or lessee entering into an agreement that either (1) allows someone other than the permittee or lessee to graze livestock on the public lands without controlling the base property supporting the permit or lease or (2) allows grazing on the public lands by livestock that are not owned or controlled by the permittee or lessee." [43 C.F.R. Ch. II (10-1-87 ed.) § 4100.0-5].

"Control" means being responsible for and providing care and management of base property and/or livestock, and differentiates between subleasing and "pasturage" agreements.

71. The federal government does not allow subleasing, but it does permit pasturage agreements. 43 C.F.R. Ch. II (10-1-87 ed.) § 4140.1(a)(6).

72. BLACK'S LAW DICTIONARY at 62.

73. *Id.* at 386.

74. North Dakota State Land Department, "Land Lease," Clause 4, Permanent Improvements. SFN 14791 (12-87). TEXAS NATURAL RESOURCES CODE § 51.130.

75. "Cowboy Notebook."

76. Utah Division of State Lands, "Rules Governing the Management and Use of State Lands in Utah," 17th ed., October 1989.

77. Telephone interview with Mark Grassel, Acting Agricultural Leasing Section Manager, Washington Department of Natural Resources, Olympia, June 4, 1992.

78. Code cites for removal of improvements are:

Arizona: ARIZONA STATUTES § 37-292 [1981 ed.]
Nebraska: NEBRASKA ADMINISTRATIVE RULES § 97.7.002.03.
North Dakota: NORTH DAKOTA CENTURY CODE § 15-08-26.
South Dakota: SOUTH DAKOTA CODIFIED LAWS § 5-5-22.
Texas: TEXAS NATURAL RESOURCES CODE § 51.130.
Washington: WASHINGTON STATUTES ANNOTATED § 79.01.092.
Wyoming: WYOMING STATUTES § 36-5-11.

79. Commissioners of the Land Office, "Oklahoma School Land Trust Surface Agricultural Lease Contract," Clause 3.11, Removal of Improvements. CLO Form 5-1, May 31, 1990.

80. Colorado State Land Board, "Lease of State Land," Clause 6(b).

81. How improvements are appraised varies by state. Some states require that the prior lessee be compensated for the undepreciated value of the improvements:

North Dakota: NORTH DAKOTA CENTURY CODE § 15-08-26. Based on original cost.
Oregon: Oregon Division of State Lands, "Grazing Lease," § 8.5, Compensation for Improvements. Based on current value.

Other states use the depreciated replacement value to determine compensation for improvements, in some cases (Nebraska) not allowing for more than the original cost:

Colorado: Colorado State Land Board, "Lease of State Land," Clause 6. Based on the depreciated cost.
Idaho: Idaho Administrative Procedures Act § 20.13, Rule 24(a), Appraisal of Improvements (1988). Current new replacement cost less actual depreciation.
Nebraska: NEBRASKA ADMINISTRATIVE RULES § 97.7.002.
New Mexico: New Mexico State Land Office, "SLO Rule 8 Regarding Agricultural Leases," § 8.015(B). Replacement cost less depreciation.

The remaining states use the existing fair market value determined by an appraisal:

Arizona: ARIZONA STATUTES § 37-322.
Mississippi: MISSISSIPPI CODE ANNOTATED § 29-3-43.
Montana: MONTANA CODE ANNOTATED § 77-6-306.
South Dakota: SOUTH DAKOTA CODIFIED LAWS § 5-5-29.

82. This topic, called "surface damages," is covered in Chapter 6.

83. AMERICAN INSTITUTE OF REAL ESTATE APPRAISERS, THE APPRAISAL OF REAL ESTATE, 8th ed. (1983), at 545.

84. States that explicitly deny a leasehold interest are:

Colorado: Colorado State Land Board, "Lease of State Land," Additional Conditions (typed in). Revision of July 1987.
Utah: Utah Division of State Lands, "Rules Governing the Management and Use of State Lands in Utah," Rule R632-50-7, Grazing Permits—Legal Effect. 17th ed., October 1989.

85. States requiring lessee to pay leasehold taxes on the interests in the lease are:

South Dakota: SOUTH DAKOTA CODIFIED LAWS § 5-11-1.1
Washington: Washington Department of Natural Resources, "Master of Masters Worksheet" [lease form] § 5.03 Taxes (January 2, 1990).

86. Administrative Rules of Montana § 26.3.138(2).

87. Washington Department of Natural Resources, Draft Agricultural and Grazing Lands Program—Policy Plan (August 5, 1988), at 27.

88. Interview with Patrick Hennessey, Agricultural Leasing Section Manager, Washington Department of Natural Resources, in Olympia, Washington, on June 12, 1991.

89. The basic source for understanding the federal PRIA formula is the 1986 Grazing Fee Review and Evaluation: Final Report 1979–1985 (Report from the Secre-

tary of Agriculture and the Secretary of the Interior, USDA–Forest Service and USDI–Bureau of Land Management) [hereinafter cited as *Grazing Fee Review and Evaluation*].

90. The chapter appendix shows the exact method used by each state.

91. The USDA and state departments of agriculture report livestock prices in a variety of different categories: total beef marketed, steers, fattened calves. Prices differ by category, but not substantially.

92. J. A. Souder and S. K. Fairfax, Western States Survey Responses (Department of Forestry and Resource Management, University of California, Berkeley, 1989) [hereinafter cited as Western States Survey Responses].

93. Land bank funds are discussed in Chapters 5 and 7.

94. Act of October 25, 1984, § 6(a); P.L. 95-514; 92 Stat. 1806.

95. Grazing Fee Review and Evaluation.

96. See *id.*, Appendix A.1, for a discussion of the 1966 Western Livestock Grazing Survey.

97. *Id.* at 77–78, Figure B.4.

98. *Id.* at 17, Figure 3.1.

99. The source for the beef price data used in the PRIA formula is the same December issue of the USDA's *Agricultural Prices.* However, the individual state reports can be found in the USDA, Statistical Reporting Service, Crop Reporting Board's Livestock Slaughter, which publishes in April an annual summary of the previous year's monthly data by state.

100. See *Grazing Fee Review and Evaluation.*

101. The regression equations resulting from the statistical analyses essentially back-calculated the difference in private forage fees, by subtracting the value of the services provided by private landowners compared to the value of the services provided by the state and then weighting various price indexes to make the two fees comparable.

102. In the Idaho system, changes in the BCPI have almost double the weight of changes in the PPI, while the FVI index of private forage rates is minimally weighed (0.13). The most weight (0.74) in the formula is accorded to the current fee.

103. "The rental rate per animal unit month is determined by adding the beef price index and the forage value index, subtracting the prices paid index, dividing by one hundred and multiplying by a base fee of ninety-five cents." ARIZONA REVISED STATUTES ANNOTATED § 37-285(B). "In this section: 1. 'Base fee' means the fee derived from the one dollar twenty-three cent fair market value base fee established by the 1966 western livestock grazing survey for federal lands adopted by Congress (P.L. 95-514 Oct. 25, 1978) less twenty-eight cents for range improvement investment and taxes paid on improvements by grazing lessees on state land. 2. 'Beef price index' means an index of the weighted average annual price for beef cattle, excluding calves, for the eleven western states as compared with a specific base period equal to one hundred, as compiled by the United States department of agriculture statistical reporting service. 3. 'Eleven western states' means Arizona, California, Colorado, Idaho, Montana, Nevada, New Mexico, Oregon, Utah, Washington and Wyoming. 4. 'Forage value index' means the index computed annually by the United States department of agriculture economic research service of the relative change in the previous year's average monthly rate per head for pasturing cattle on privately owned

land in the eleven western states, using the base period of 1964 through 1968 as equal to one hundred with each animal unit month equal to three dollars sixty-five cents. 5. 'Prices paid index' means an index of prices paid by farmers for commodities and services, interest, taxes and farm wages, as compiled by the United States department of agriculture statistical reporting service, compared to a specific base period equal to one hundred." ARIZONA REVISED STATUTES ANNOTATED § 37-285(E) (1990 Suppl.).

104. CALIFORNIA CODE OF REGULATIONS, Title 2, Division 3, Chapter 1, Article 2, § 2003(a)(6).

105. Interview with Lee Otteni, Assistant Commissioner for Surface Resources, New Mexico, July 2, 1992.

106. New Mexico State Land Office, "SLO Rule 8 Relating to Agricultural Leases," § 8.005, Rent, provides that:

"A. All land used for the grazing of native forage, that have not been bid on or classified as cultivated, shall have a rental determined and based on the following formula: Regular Billing: Annual Rental = $0.0474 Base Value × Carrying Capacity (CC) × Economic Variable Index (EVI). The rental charged for the acreage participating in the Range Stewardship Incentive Program will be based on the formula set out above, less a 25% discount. The 25% discount also applies to bids and or offers.

"B. In no event shall the annual rental using this formula be decreased or increased by more than thirty-three and one-third percent (33.3%) for each successive year of the lease term.

"C. The EVI in any particular year, October 1 through September 30, (i.e., year "t") is the ratio of the value of a State Land Office Adjustment Factor for that year (SLOAF$_t$) and the value of that same Adjustment Factor calculated for the base year 1987 (SLOAF$_{87}$). The SLOAF for any year is determined by a mathematical combination of the prior year's value for the western states Forage Value Index (FVI), the Beef Cattle Price Index (BCPI), and the Prices Paid Index (PPI). Each of these indices are published annually by the United States Department of Agriculture (USDA). The specific mathematical expression for the SLOAF in any year (e.g., year = $t + 1$) is given by the following equation:

$$SLOAF_{t+1} = -14.92 + (1.57 \times FVI_t) + (0.26 \times BCPI_t) - (0.67 \times PPI_t).$$

Range Stewardship Incentive Rental Formula:

$$SLOAF_{t+1} = [-14.92 + (1.57 \times FVI_t) + (0.26 \times BCPI_t) - (0.67 \times PPI_t)] \times (0.75).$$

"D. The specific value of this Adjustment Factor for any year will be determined by the Commissioner relying on the USDA published indice values for the preceding year."

107. Personal communication, Kevin Carter, Unit Manager, Trust and Asset Manager, Utah, January 5, 1993.

108. UTAH CODE ANNOTATED § 65A-9-4.

109. Western States Survey Responses.

110. MONTANA CODE ANNOTATED § 77-6-507.

111. SOUTH DAKOTA CODIFIED LAWS § 5-5-10.1(3).

112. *Id.* § 5-5-10.4.

113. Interview with Curtis Johnson, Commissioner, South Dakota Office of School and Public Lands, in Pierre, South Dakota (November 13, 1991).

114. *Id.*

115. See WASHINGTON ADMINISTRATIVE CODE § 322-22 for details. Source: Personal Communication (telephone) with Mark Grassel, Acting Agricultural Leasing Section Manager, Washington Department of Natural Resources, Olympia, Washington, June 4, 1992.

116. WASHINGTON ADMINISTRATIVE CODE (1989 ed.) § 322-20-230. Statutory cite is WASHINGTON REVISED CODE § 79.28.050 and § 79.28.040.

117. Western States Survey Responses.

118. Agricultural Statistic Service, Agricultural Prices (Bulletin Pr-1). This is commonly known as the "June Enumerative Survey," even though it is now conducted in the spring.

119. COLORADO STATE BOARD OF LAND COMMISSIONERS, AGRICULTURE AND GRAZING NEWSLETTER (August 1990).

120. Nebraska Board of Educational Lands and Funds. *1992 Rent Book.* Lincoln, NB. June 13, 1991.

121. NORTH DAKOTA CENTURY CODE § 15-04-07.

122. North Dakota State Land Department, Surface Management Division, Summary of the Fair Market Value Method of Establishing Minimum Bids on North Dakota State School Lands. (Bismarck, North Dakota, revision June 28,1990.

123. TEXAS NATURAL RESOURCE CODE § 51.121.

124. *Id.* § 51.124.

125. WYOMING STATE LAND AND FARM LOAN OFFICE, WESTERN STATE LAND SURFACE LEASING SUMMARY OF SELECTED FACTORS (Summer 1988), at 11.

126. WYOMING STATUTES § 36-2-106.

127. Western State Survey Responses.

128. WYOMING BOARD OF LAND COMMISSIONERS, RULES AND REGULATIONS OF THE BOARD OF LAND COMMISSIONERS, chapter 4, Rules and Regulations for Grazing and Agricultural Leasing § 6(b).

129. Personal communication, Paul Cleary, Assistant Commissioner, Wyoming State Land Office.

5. TRUST LAND FORESTRY

1. Most old-growth timber is, in fact, located on public lands. Harvesting did not begin in earnest on those lands until after World War II.

2. Of course, this does not always create a conflict. When and how the trust must be compensated for amenity and preservation uses will be discussed in more detail in Chapter 7.

3. This unusual situation arose in three ways. First, large-scale in lieu land selections and land exchanges with the Forest Service in the 1920s gave some states the opportunity to select contiguous blocks of lands in return for parcels that were in-

cluded in the newly created national forests. Second, tax forfeitures during the 1930s left states, particularly Washington and Oregon, managing revested timber lands. Third, several states—again, most notably, Washington and Oregon—have actively pursued land exchange programs with private timberland owners and the federal government.

4. J. A. Souder and S. K. Fairfax, Western States Survey Responses (State Lands Project, Department of Forestry and Resource Management. University of California, Berkeley, December 1989), at 5 [hereinafter cited as Western States Survey Responses].

5. And in Washington, other "junior" tax districts, such as libraries, and fire departments, are also included as beneficiaries of state management.

6. *Timberlands* are defined as lands that are producing or are capable of producing 20 cubic feet per year per acre of industrial wood that are not withdrawn from timber production by statute or administrative action. See Waddell et al., Forest Statistics of the United States, 1987 (Resource Bulletin PNW-RB-168, Pacific Northwest Research Station, USDA Forest Service, Portland, Oregon, 1989).

7. Removals, not price or sales volume, directly determines revenue from year to year. Purchasers have two to three years to remove the timber they have purchased, and they generally take advantage of market shifts in the context of their own unique supply structure.

8. We obviously recognize importance of Alaska's holdings. Nevertheless we focus on the four contiguous northwestern states because they have comparable history, legal status, and data availability.

9. The productivity measure of average harvest per acre can be called "yield per acre," since it represents the volume harvested and not the volume grown (or potential growth) per acre. As such, it reflects the current inventory of the state's forest lands, compared to their productivity.

10. See Western Survey Responses. See also PUTER, LOOTERS OF THE PUBLIC DO-MAIN (1908), UZES, CHAINING THE LAND: A HISTORY OF SURVEYING IN CALIFORNIA (1977), and TOWNLEY, ALFALFA COUNTRY: NEVADA LAND, WATER AND POLITICS IN THE NINETEENTH CENTURY (1976), for discussions of Oregon, California, and Nevada, respectively.

11. See LEVESQUE, A CHRONICLE OF THE TILLAMOOK COUNTY FOREST TRUST LANDS (1985) [hereinafter cited as LEVESQUE].

12. See Western States Survey Responses.

13. WASHINGTON REVISED CODE § 76.12.

14. 685 P. 2d 576, 102 Wash. 2d 127 (1976).

15. Pat McElroy, personal communication, October 12, 1994. Lengthy and fascinating letter on file with authors. Thank you, Pat!

16. Jones, *State Forest Lands*, in LETTERMAN (ed.), ASSESSMENT OF OREGON'S FORESTS (1988), at 50.

17. WASHINGTON DEPARTMENT OF NATURAL RESOURCES, PROPOSED FOREST LAND MANAGEMENT PROGRAM 1984–1993 (November 1983), at v [hereinafter cited as PROPOSED FOREST LAND MANAGEMENT PROGRAM].

18. Colorado does not, because its trust forestlands are managed under contract with the Colorado Forest Service; New Mexico does not, because it has no forestry program in the State Land Office. In the other states, the trust forest management

agency also fights forest fires and—except in Arizona, California, Montana and New Mexico—regulates private timber harvests.

19. PROPOSED FOREST LAND MANAGEMENT PROGRAM at 29.

20. Office of the Legislative Auditor. Performance Audit: State-owned and Leased Land (Report 82P-17, State of Montana, Office of the Legislative Auditor, June 1983), at 6, 7 [hereinafter cited as Performance Audit]. The basic language is in Article 10, Section 5, of the 1972 Constitution of Montana.

21. MONTANA CONSTITUTION, art. 10, § 5.

22. IDAHO DEPARTMENT OF LANDS, IDAHO FORESTRY OPPORTUNITIES 1980-1990 (March 1988), at 3 [hereinafter cited as IDAHO FORESTRY OPPORTUNITIES].

23. OREGON REVISED STATUTES § 327.410.

24. Id. § 530.110. All revenues from lands acquired under the Forest Rehabilitation Act are retained until the bonds have been repaid. Id. §§ 530.210 et seq.

25. OREGON DEPARTMENT OF FORESTRY, FOREST LOG (August-September 1989), at 6. Comparative percentages of sales are not discussed. Whether the cost recovery is organized on a sale-by-sale basis, or by management area (75 percent of common school forested lands are in the Elliot State Forest in Clatrop County), or on a program-wide basis is not stated.

26. IDAHO FORESTRY OPPORTUNITIES at 9. IDAHO CODE ANNOTATED § 58-140 requires that funds derived from specific activities, such as timber, be used only to improve the productivity and revenue generation of that activity. For timber, allowable activities are timber management, protection, and reforestation.

27. IDAHO DEPARTMENT OF LANDS, FOURTEENTH ANNUAL REPORT 1987-1988 (June 30, 1989), at 7.

28. Office of the Legislative Auditor, Department of State Lands: Report on Examination of Financial Statements, Two Fiscal Years Ended June 30, 1983 (Report 83-20, Report to the Legislature, State of Montana, Office of the Legislative Auditor, 1983), at 3-10 [hereinafter cited as Two Fiscal Years]. The program was established in 1967 by the legislature (MONTANA CODE ANNOTATED § 77-1-604). Id. § 77-1-605 allows funds to be used to improve productivity of timberlands.

29. Two Fiscal Years at 10.

30. County of Skamania et al. v. State of Washington, 685 P.2d 576 (1984) [hereinafter cited as Skamania].

31. See MANTHEY, THE BUBBLE THAT BURST . . . (1984) for a discussion of this same situation in federal timber sales program.

32. Skamania at 578.

33. One especially interesting aspect of this case is that, not surprisingly, the same timber speculators also appealed to Congress for relief from the same misreading of the future direction of the market in connection with their bidding on federal timber. The Congress also obliged. Without the trust mandate, however, there was no barrier to implementation of the industry's political victory. If we live long enough, we are going to go back and figure out how much money the trust mandate saved the state—it was a considerable amount—and compare that with the federal losses.

34. Skamania at 582.

35. Id. at 581, 583.

36. Id. at 582.

37. *Id.* at 581.

38. *Id.* at 582 citing Gladden Farms, Inc. v. State, 633 P.2d 325, 129 Ariz. 516 (1981).

39. *Id.* at 582.

40. *Id.* at 583.

41. Lassen v. Arizona ex rel. Arizona Highway Dept., 385 U.S. 458 (1967).

42. *Skamania* at 582, citing *Gladden Farms*, at 521.

43. *Skamania* at 582 [italics in original]. This appears in fact to be an important misrepresentation of the decision in Ervien v. United States, 251 U. S. 41 (1919) at 47, which states that there is "in the Enabling Act a specific enumeration of the purposes for which the lands were granted and the enumeration is necessarily exclusive of any other purpose."

44. For an extreme formulation of the opposite position see Segner v. State Inv. Bd., no. 587-489319, slip op. Ramsey County Dist. Ct., Minnesota, August 11, 1988, discussed in *Conventional Wisdom* [*supra*, Introduction, note 1], n.284 and text accompanying at 870.

45. Rick Pederson, consultant to the Colorado Land Board noted in a speech to the Western State Lands Commissioners that private trustees are allowed to make charitable donations if they have a reasonable basis for assuming that their action will enhance the standing and profitability of the trust in the community where it does business. WSCLA Meeting, January 1992.

46. In this emphasis, *Skamania* seems far more strident than Oklahoma Education Association v. Nigh, 642 P.2d 230 (Okla. 1982), with which it is frequently read and compared.

47. Board of Natural Resources of the State of Washington v. Brown, 992 F.2d 937 (1993) [hereinafter cited as *Brown*]. This case began its life under a previous Secretary of Commerce and is therefore sometimes referred to as Mosbacher.

48. The case is also interesting because it appears to eliminate some of the hurdles that plaintiffs in state trust lands cases have had to surmount to gain standing. The *Brown* court appears to have overcome a number of government objections to plaintiffs bringing the case. Compare *Brown*, at 5ff. with *Conventional Wisdom*, n.194 and text accompanying at 850.

49. 16 U.S.C. § 620.

50. *Brown* at 941.

51. *Id.* at 944.

52. This is, of course, as clearly a general public benefit as a highway or a hiking trail.

53. *Brown* at 941.

54. *Id.* at 944, citing Case v. Bowls, 327 U.S. 92 (1946) at 100.

55. *Brown* at 944.

56. *Id.* at 947.

57. For a more comprehensive discussion of this issue, see *Conventional Wisdom*, 861–68.

58. See Western Survey Responses, at 18 *passim*.

59. MONTANA CONSTITUTION, art. X, § 11.

60. WASHINGTON CONSTITUTION, art. XVI, § 1.

61. IDAHO CONSTITUTION, art. IX, § 8.

62. 139 P. 557, 25 Idaho 654 (1914).

63. OREGON CONSTITUTION, art. VIII, § 5(2). Amended by HJR No. 7, 1967, and adopted by the people May 28, 1968.

64. OREGON REVISED STATUTES § 530.490.

65. T. R. Waggener, Some Economic Implications of Sustained Yield as a Forest Regulation Model. Report No. 6, Institute of Forest Products. (College of Forest Resources. University of Washington. Seattle, WA. 1969), at 8 [hereinafter cited as Waggener].

66. 74 Stat. 215; 16 U.S.C. §§ 528–531.

67. WASHINGTON REVISED CODE § 79.68.010. [Emphasis added.]

68. WASHINGTON REVISED CODE § 79.68.020.

69. OREGON REVISED STATUTES § 530.500.

70. See *Conventional Wisdom, passim.*

71. Waggener at 8.

72. *Id.* See also Washington Department of Natural Resources, Timberlands Acquisition Plan: Commissioner of Public Lands Brian Boyle—DNR request legislation—SB 65536 and HB 2804. (press release, Washington Department of Natural Resources, Olympia, Washington undated [1989–1990]); and Washington Department of Natural Resources, Free Trade, the Forests and the Future: A Position Paper on Log Exports by Washington Commissioner of Public Lands Brian Boyle (September 1989).

73. *Id.*

74. Western States Survey Responses at 81. See also Jerke v. Department of State Lands, 597 P.2d 49 (1979).

75. Jackson, Economic Returns and the Management of Montana's Forest Resources. (prepared at the request of the Joint Interim Subcommittee No. 2 of the Montana Legislature, December 1983).

76. MONTANA DEPARTMENT OF STATE LANDS, FOREST MANAGEMENT STANDARDS AND GUIDELINES (Forestry Division, March 1988), at 1–3.

77. PROPOSED FOREST LAND MANAGEMENT PROGRAM. Codified as WASHINGTON REVISED CODE §§ 79.68.030, 79.68.040.

78. IDAHO CONSTITUTION, art. IX, § 8, cited in IDAHO FORESTRY OPPORTUNITIES. Notice, however, that the version of the Idaho constitution included with the annotated code does not have the phrase "long term" included in § 8.

79. *Id.* at 10. See also GRUENHAGEN ET AL., PAYETTE LAKES AREA FOREST INVENTORY REPORT, 1987 REMEASUREMENT (Idaho Department of Lands, May 1989).

80. See, for example, OREGON STATE FORESTRY DEPARTMENT, LONG RANGE TIMBER MANAGEMENT PLAN, SOUTHERN OREGON REGION STATE FORESTS (Report 3-0-2-220, August 1987), at 10.

81. *Id.* at 10, 11.

82. DAVIS & JOHNSON, FOREST MANAGEMENT (3d ed. 1987), at 41 [hereinafter cited as DAVIS & JOHNSON].

83. *Id.*

84. Western States Survey Responses at 81.

85. Part of the reason for this is that the quality of the lands owned by the common schools in the Elliot State Forest is lower than that of the lands held by the state for the county as beneficiary.

86. It also has the effect of inducing the Forest Service to come up with novel schemes (such as improved growing stock) that purport to increase future yields, and various accounting measures euphemistically called "allowable cut effects" and "departures" from even flow and long-term sustained-yield harvest limitations. See DAVIS & JOHNSON 691–711.

87. Western States Survey Responses at 83.

88. This practice was particularly egregious in the late 1970s and early 1980s, when inflation and timber prices were high; but then both fell, leaving both federal and state timber purchasers with contracts at above-market prices.

89. Washington passes these risks to the purchaser upon confirmation of the sale, usually within 30 days of the sale. Pat McElroy, personal communication, October 12, 1994.

90. WASHINGTON DEPARTMENT OF NATURAL RESOURCES, TRANSITION LANDS POLICY PLAN [final] (1988) [hereinafter cited as TRANSITION LANDS POLICY PLAN]. Land sales and land bank legislation is found in WASHINGTON REVISED CODE § 79.66.

91. See LEVESQUE. The Oregon Department of Forestry operates under the provisions of OREGON REVISED STATUTES chapter 526. Public lands are regulated under chapter 274.

92. Western States Survey Responses at 49, 50.

93. *Id.* at 50, 58, 59.

94. *Id.* at 48, 51, 55, 59.

95. "The legislature finds that from time to time it may be desirable for the Department of Natural Resources to sell state lands which have low potential for natural resources management or low income-generating potential or which, because of geographic location, or other factors, are inefficient for the department to manage. However, it is also important to acquire lands for long-term management to replace those sold so that the publicly owned land base will not be depleted and the publicly owned forest land base will not be reduced." WASHINGTON REVISED CODE § 79.66.010. The Land Bank is allowed to accumulate a maximum of 1,500 acres before transfer to a specific trust beneficiary. WASHINGTON REVISED CODE § 79.66.020.

96. OREGON REVISED STATUTES § 273.413 (1), (2).

97. IDAHO CODE ANNOTATED § 58.133.

98. *Id.* § 58.503.

99. MONTANA CODE ANNOTATED § 77-2-203.

100. *Id.* § 77-2-201.

101. TRANSITION LANDS POLICY PLAN at vii.

102. WASHINGTON REVISED CODE § 79.01.244.

103. *Id.* § 79.68.050.

104. OREGON REVISED STATUTES § 273.051(2)(b).

105. Western States Survey Responses at 63.

106. MONTANA CODE ANNOTATED § 77-1-203. Recommendations for enhanced multiple-use management are found in Performance Audit.

107. MONTANA DEPARTMENT OF STATE LANDS, INTERIM GRIZZLY BEAR MANAGEMENT STANDARDS AND GUIDELINES (Forestry Division, December 1988).

108. Western States Survey Responses at 63.

109. IDAHO CODE ANNOTATED § 58-133.

110. *Id.*

6. MINERAL RESOURCES

1. For further discussion of the distinctions among these categories, see FAIRFAX & YALE, FEDERAL LANDS: A GUIDE TO PLANNING, MANAGEMENT, AND STATE REVENUES (1987), particularly chapters 4 and 5 [hereinafter cited as FAIRFAX & YALE].

2. For more information on minerals, consult an economic geology text. We used JENSEN & BATEMAN, ECONOMIC MINERAL DEPOSITS (3d ed. 1981).

3. 61 Stat. 681; 30 U.S.C. §§ 601–602, 611.

4. See also Common Varieties Act of 1955, 30 U.S.C. § 611; 7 C.F.R. 15.

5. Two general sources appear to be essential starting point for further reading: R. W. Swenson, *Legal Aspects of Mineral Resources Exploitation* in GATES, ed., HISTORY OF PUBLIC LAND LAW DEVELOPMENT (1968), ch. 23, written for the Public Land Law Review Commission; and LESHY, THE MINING LAW: A STUDY IN PERPETUAL MOTION (1987) [hereinafter cited as LESHY]. For less law and more human and land history, see SMITH, MINING AMERICA: THE INDUSTRY AND THE ENVIRONMENT, 1800–1980 (1987).

6. In 1993, the Department of Interior changed from requiring $100 per year of work to requiring a payment of $100 to the U.S. government to hold the lease.

7. It is therefore not immediately clear why a locator would choose to "go to patent." Historically, eastern banks were hesitant to lend development capital on such apparently flimsy title as a valid mining claim; and this encouraged loan seekers to patent their claims. Currently, the developer makes a choice about the risk of invalidation of the claim, and balances the cost of environmental compliance on federal (unpatented) vs. state (patented) lands.

8. The basic reference is Marsh & Sherwood, *Metamorphosis in Mining Law: Federal Legislation and Regulatory Amendment and Implementation of the General Mining Law since 1955*, 26 ROCKY MOUNTAIN MINERAL LAW INSTITUTE 209 (1980).

9. Upheld in United States v. Weiss, 642 F.2d 296 (1981).

10. See generally LESHY, ch. 10.

11. See, generally *id*. at 29–39.

12. FAIRFAX & YALE at 11ff.

13. See Fairfax & Andrews: *Debate Within and Debate Without: NEPA and the Redefinition of the Prudent Man Rule*, 19 NATURAL RESOURCES JOURNAL 505 (1979).

14. See United States v. Locke, 471 U.S. 84 (1985).

15. For a general discussion, see LESHY, ch. 14 and 17.

16. An excellent source for tracking diverse proposals at any point or over time is *Public Lands News*. (1010 Vermont Avenue, Suite 708, Washington, D.C. 20005).

17. A good introduction to mineral resources from an economic perspective is Harris & Skinner, *The Assessment of Long-term Supplies of Minerals*, in SMITH & KRUTILLA, eds., EXPLORATIONS IN NATURAL RESOURCE ECONOMICS (1982).

18. The distinction between "known" and "unknown" geological areas is crucial in federal leasing policy, because the returns to the developer and the state's share are determined by whether the tract is leased as one or the other. See Akrla Exploration Co. v. Texas Oil & Gas Corp., 734 F.2d 347 (8th Cir. 1984).

19. The concept of *ad coelum* was modified in traditional mining practice and in the 1872 General Mining Law to allow ownership of mineral veins or lodes occurring on a specific parcel even if they extended laterally outside the surface boundaries.

20. MCDONALD, THE LEASING OF FEDERAL LANDS FOR FOSSIL FUELS PRODUCTION (1979), at 62.

21. In Oklahoma, however, any unleased mineral owner or any owner of a working interest of a lease may request that a unit be involuntarily pooled. Letter from Doug Morgan, Attorney/Assistant Director of Minerals Management, Commissioners of the Land Office, to Jon A. Souder, August 2, 1994.

22. Extensive discussion of bonus bidding, both in theory and in application to offshore oil and gas leases, is provided in MEAD ET AL., OFFSHORE LANDS: OIL AND GAS LEASING AND CONSERVATION ON THE OUTER CONTINENTAL SHELF (1985) [hereinafter cited as MEAD ET AL.].

23. Opponents also contend that bonus payments discriminate against small businesses that do not have the capital to make large up-front payments.

24. However, lessees often continue operating beyond the point where "the marginal revenue from production equals the marginal cost to produce." Mines, particularly large ones, cannot generally be started or stopped easily. Many mining companies continue to run mines for many months—even years—at a loss, in anticipation of improved commodity prices. Comment by Jeff Kroft, Policy Development Specialist, Oregon Division of State Lands. Letter of October 21, 1994.

25. Following this line of reasoning, if bonus payments are considered fixed costs that do not influence marginal production decisions, then production is maximized by having what is called a "pure" bonus lease under which no royalties are charged and the entire return to the resource owner is based on the bonus bid. In this case, the entire risk of the lease is assumed by the lessee, and the consequent returns to the resource owner are less, on average, than if the risk is shared. See our discussion of risk and return in Chapter 3. Pure bonus bids are discussed in MEAD ET AL. at 48.

26. Letter from Doug Morgan, Attorney/Assistant Director of Minerals Management, Commissioners of the [Oklahoma] Land Office, to Jon A. Souder, August 2, 1994.

27. A classic introduction to the theory of mineral economics, particularly relating to production costs, mineral quality, and the timing of development and exploration is Herfindahl, *Depletion and Economic Theory*, originally published in GAFFNEY, ed., EXTRACTIVE RESOURCES AND TAXATION (1967), and reprinted in BROOKS, ed., RESOURCE ECONOMICS: SELECTED WORKS OF ORRIS C. HERFINDAHL (1974).

28. See LOWE, OIL AND GAS LAW IN A NUT SHELL, at 178–90 (2d ed. 1988).

29. See Idaho Department of Lands, "State of Idaho State Land Lease," Clause 15, Easements, Attachment B.

30. MONTANA ADMINISTRATIVE RULES § 26.3.162.

31. Interview with Curtis Johnson, Commissioner, South Dakota Office of School and Public Lands, Pierre, South Dakota (November 13, 1991). The code cite is SOUTH DAKOTA CODIFIED LAWS § 5-7-17.1.

32. Interview with Rick Larson, Minerals Leasing Manager, North Dakota State Land Department, Bismarck, North Dakota (November 11, 1991).

33. Sovereign lands include the bed and banks of navigable rivers and the outer continental shelf. They were not granted by the federal government to the states; state title to them is an attribute of state sovereignty.

34. SOUTH DAKOTA CODIFIED LAWS § 5-7-52.

35. Telephone conversation between Jon Souder and Gary Carlson, Minerals Resources Manager, New Mexico State Land Office, September 14, 1993.

36. OREGON ADMINISTRATIVE RULES § 141-71-640.

37. Idaho Administrative Procedures Act § 20.09 (November 1, 1989, but marked "Unofficial").

38. Letter from Doug Morgan, Attorney/Assistant Director of Minerals Management, Commissioners of the [Oklahoma] Land Office, to Jon A. Souder, August 2, 1994.

39. Notice in Figure 6-9 that the scales change by an order of magnitude depending on whether the graph is used to represent the permanent fund or the annual payments. Notice, too, that the revenues are reported in current (rather than constant) dollars.

7. EMERGING STRATEGIES AND ISSUES

1. Oregon Attorney General's Opinion No. 8223, July 24, 1992.

2. Utah HB No. 416, filed 2-24-93, Melvin R. Brown.

3. Utah HB No. 416, passed 3-03-93. Same bill number, now calling for a study by an Advisory Board for School and Institutional Trust Lands.

4. Such as Oklahoma Education Association v. Nigh, 642 P.2d 230 (Okla. 1982), discussed *supra* Chapter 4, and County of Skamania et al. v. State of Washington, 685 P.2d 576 (Wash. 1984), discussed *supra* Chapter 5.

5. Paul Degraffenreid, General Counsel, Commissioners of the Land Office, Oklahoma, personal communication. WSLCA Meeting, July 1994.

6. The funds' real value can be determined by dividing the nominal (that is, reported) value by a price index, such as the Gross National Product (GNP) deflator. See *supra* Chapter 3 for a discussion of how to do this.

7. And as was discussed *supra* Chapter 4, there is always the "issue of when is a good time for the trust to cash in on its inflation hedge, the retained lands? What good does it do to retain an asset whose value tracks inflation if you never capture its value?" asked Clint Beaver of Wyoming in commenting on an earlier draft of this chapter.

8. It is interesting to speculate, however, that state land offices in states lacking direct linkages have tried to integrate at least some permanent fund functions, such as land banks, to store the proceeds of land sales temporarily, pending purchase of replacement lands. Other states—for example, New Mexico and Texas—have taken natural gas in kind for supply to public institution beneficiaries.

9. Interest rates determined by fitting a least-squares trend line through a state's net implicit interest payments for 1970–1990. The net implicit interest rate is determined by dividing the dividends distributed from the permanent fund to the beneficiaries by the amount of the permanent fund for each of the 21 years.

10. See State Investment Council, Statement of Objectives for the State Permanent Fund, Rule 85-3 (September 30, 1985). Historically, investments in stocks have been problematic for the states. See SWIFT, A HISTORY OF PUBLIC PERMANENT COMMON SCHOOL FUNDS IN THE UNITED STATES, 1795–1905, at 132, 149–53 (1911). See cites therein under index entry "Securities, poor, unsafe, worthless."

11. MONTANA CONSTITUTION, art. X, § 5.

12. Interview with Tim Kingstad, Commissioner, North Dakota State Land Department, Bismarck, North Dakota, November 12, 1991.

13. See CLARK, THE INTERNATIONAL CRISIS (1993).

14. The Forest Service's mandate, as expressed in the Creative Act of 1891, ch. 561, 26 Stat. 1103, is "to improve and protect the forests . . . secur[e] favorable conditions of water flows, and to furnish a continuous supply of timber . . ." 16 U.S.C. § 475.

See also SCHIFF, FIRE AND WATER: HERESY IN THE U.S. FOREST SERVICE, (1960) for early chicanery in dealing with the topic.

15. MONTANA CODE ANNOTATED §§ 77-6-115, 77-6-310, 77-6-302.

16. MONTANA ADMINISTRATIVE RULES § 26-3.123. This 1979 regulation states that "any water rights hereafter secured by the lessee shall be secured in the name of the State of Montana."

17. Approximately 4.1 million acres of state trust lands are used for grazing, and 4,750 acres are used for dry land agriculture (spring wheat, barley, hay).

18. A private citizen in Montana can obtain access to water across another's land without an easement, but a private citizen needs an easement to cross state lands.

19. Filing of instream stock water rights and domestic well use rights were optional in the adjudication process (no one knows whether these rights will be protected, as there has not been a test case); thus, the DSL did not file for these rights. The DSL is considering legal action to enforce instream stock water rights against the diverting and dewatering of streams for other purposes. Preference of an instream stock watering right over a prior appropriation right would add a bit of riparianism to a strictly prior appropriation state.

20. The oldest of the twenty-three water rights had a priority date of October 1, 1883.

21. Described in Department of State Lands v. Pettibone, 702 P.2d 948, 216 Mont. 361, (1985), at 950 [hereinafter cited as *Pettibone*].

22. *Pettibone*.

23. This potential loss represents approximately $250,000 year in revenues.

24. Brief of Amicus Curiae filed by Lon J. Maxwell, Montana Department of State Lands, at 3.

25. Abandonment of water rights also collides with the public trust of MONTANA CONSTITUTION, art. X, § 3, according to the brief.

26. The court ruled that the late claims were abandoned under MONTANA CODE ANNOTATED § 85-2-226.

27. Winters v. United States, 207 U.S. 564 (1908).

28. Fairfax & Soderstrom, Institutional Change in Water Management: Consequences of State Trust Land Claims and Participation (USGS Final Report 14-08-0001-G1891, August 3, 1990).

29. Brief of Amicus Curiae filed by Albert W. Stone, 1984, in the Supreme Court of the State of Montana, in connection with the *Pettibone* case.

30. COLORADO CONSTITUTION, art. XVI, § 6.

31. *Nontributary groundwater* is defined as underground water that lies outside a designated groundwater basin and that, when withdrawn, does not deplete the flow of a natural stream within 100 yards by greater than one-tenth of 1 percent of the annual amount of withdrawal. COLORADO REVISED STATUTES § 37-90-103(10.5).

32. See BECK, ed., WATER AND WATER RIGHTS, vol. 6, (1991), at 60–63.

33. *Id.*

34. Oppenlander v. Left Hand Ditch Co., 31 P. 854, 18 Colo. 142 (1892).

35. Ditches are also considered improvements, and the lessee must be compensated for them when the lease terminates. Some surface water rights may be required to remain attached permanently to irrigated state lands. These surface water rights continue to be owned by the lessee, but they cannot be transferred off state trust lands without approval of the BLC.

36. The following clause has been added to all leases prepared in recent years: "If the lessee shall initiate or establish any water right for the leased premise, for which the point of surface diversion or groundwater withdrawal is on the leased premises, such right shall, upon termination of the lease, become property of the lessor without cost" (Surface Leases, State School Lands, Laws, Rules, Regulations, Policies, 1969). This clause does not include water rights for water with a point of diversion or withdrawal off state trust lands but applied to state trust lands.

37. The BLC possesses 75 tracts of irrigated land. This is a small amount of land, but the land produces relatively high revenues compared to other uses. The BLC also owns some ditch rights outright, usually as the result of land foreclosure; these water rights are called "closed water stock."

38. The BLC has right of first refusal to buy collateral water stock from the lessee when a lease is terminated. The BLC has yet to buy any collateral water stock from a lessee. The BLC reports that funds needed to buy these water rights could come from the Land and Water Management Fund.

39. State law requires surface ownership of land before one can acquire rights to groundwater under the land, unless the landowner transfers the right. Thus, groundwater has not usually been diverted from state trust land and applied to adjacent private land, as surface water has.

40. See Radosevich et al., *Colorado Water Laws*, in RADOSEVICH ET AL., SAN LUIS VALLEY WATER PROBLEMS: A LEGAL PERSPECTIVE (Colorado Water Resources Research Institute Publication, 1979).

41. Interview with Bob Mailander, Colorado Land Commissioner, July 20, 1992.

42. At present, the BLC charges the same fee for agricultural land with a collateral water stock right as it does for land with a closed water stock right.

43. In a troubling twist, the lessee also works for the state as a hydrogeological consultant.

44. The study recommended six other well sites for development, but the BLC encountered local protest when it applied to develop these sites. The BLC decided to drop these six well permits due to local opposition. Local communities perceived the state as interfering or competing with private water interests in the area.

45. Cities in the western United States with reported lot price increases for 1975 to 1990 include Albuquerque (222%), Boulder (274%), Phoenix (200%), Portland (213%), Salt Lake City (205%), San Diego (900%), San Jose (1,486%), Seattle (869%), and Tacoma (207%). URBAN LANDS INSTITUTE, RESIDENTIAL DEVELOPMENT HANDBOOK (2d ed., 1990), Table 1-3, at 4.

46. URBAN LANDS INSTITUTE, MIXED-USE DEVELOPMENT HANDBOOK (1987), at 313–14.

47. Descriptions of potential commercial land uses can be found in the Urban Lands Institute's community builders handbook series (Urban Lands Institute, 625 Indiana Avenue, N.W., Washington, D.C. 20004-2930). Books in the community builders handbook series are: RESIDENTIAL DEVELOPMENT HANDBOOK (2d ed., 1990); MIXED-USE DEVELOPMENT HANDBOOK (1987); SHOPPING CENTER DEVELOPMENT HANDBOOK (2d ed., 1985); RECREATIONAL DEVELOPMENT HANDBOOK (1981); OFFICE DEVELOPMENT HANDBOOK (1982); and HOTEL/MOTEL DEVELOPMENT (1984). These handbooks are updated periodically; contact the Urban Lands Institute for the latest list. More detailed information on the financial aspects of development is available in HINES, SHOPPING CENTER DEVELOPMENT AND INVESTMENT (1988) [hereinafter cited as HINES].

48. The New Mexico State Land Office, for example, has prepared (or is preparing) master plans for land parcels as large as 15,000 acres in the vicinity of major urban areas (Albuquerque, Las Cruces, and Santa Fe). New Mexico State Land Office, Annual Report, 78th Fiscal Year, July 1, 1989 to June 30, 1990 (Santa Fe, October, 1990), at 21 [hereinafter cited as NMSLO, 78th Fiscal Year].

49. Art. IX, § 161 of the original NORTH DAKOTA CONSTITUTION specified that educational granted lands "shall only be leased for pasturage and meadow purposes. . . ."

50. WASHINGTON REVISED CODE § 79.66.

51. Arizona's Urban Lands Program is described in an occasional publication, *Urban Lands Newsletter.*

52. Washington's revenues are primarily from commercial leases, including office buildings, warehouses, and even motels.

53. In states that do not allow subordination, at least one strategy has been developed to protect the mortgage company. This strategy, written into the ground lease contract, allows the mortgage company to cure defaults if the lessee does not pay. This strategy protects the mortgage company's interest by preventing the lease from being canceled by the state. After curing the lessee's default, the mortgage company can either negotiate with its mortgagor, the ground lessee, or liquidate the project by selling to a fourth party, without having the state cancel the lease. This strategy works in the trust's interest, too, because it places the responsibility for guaranteeing lease payments on the mortgage company, thus increasing the possibility that beneficial use will be made of the property.

54. Specific survey responses to subordination are as follows:

Alaska: Subordination is allowed for single- and multiple-family housing
                and for landfills/waste disposal sites.
California: Subordination is allowed for campgrounds.
Oregon: Subordination is allowed for cabin site leases, state government
                buildings, and industrial parks.

55. This section is based primarily on HINES at 29, 74–75, and 342.

56. NMSLO, 78th Fiscal Year, at 21.

57. The best way to follow this saga is to read *Public Land News* for the several years in question.

58. The classic pre-FLPMA study is Wheatley, Study of Land Acquisitions and Exchanges Related to Retention and Management or Disposition of Federal Public Lands (1970)—a study done for the Public Lands Law Review Commission. See also Anderson, *Public Land Exchanges, Sales, and Purchases Under the Federal Land Policy and Management Act of 1976*, 1979 UTAH LAW REVIEW 657 (1979) [hereinafter cited as Anderson]. Anderson argued convincingly (and presciently) that, although FLPMA provisions were designed to resolve the major barriers to land exchanges by clarifying and consolidating Bureau of Land Management authority in the area, the new powers to enlarge the bureau's ability to act were sufficiently qualified that "private parties will begin to seek specific congressional authorization for transactions." (at 659).

59. What follows is based on and quoted from Dragoo, *"Utah's Project Bold Land Exchange"* 16 NATURAL RESOURCES LAW NEWSLETTER 14(1) (Winter 1984) at 14 [herein-

after cited as Dragoo]. See also Tomsic, *The Loss of the States' Right to Indemnify Preempted School Land Grants on the Basis of Equal Acreage: Andrus v. Utah*, 1981 UTAH LAW REVIEW 409 (1981). The Supreme Court's opinion in this legal controversy appears in Andrus v. Utah, 446 U.S. 500 (1980).

60. Dragoo at 15. See, more extensively, Anderson at 659.

61. See, for example, *A New Front in the Utah Land War*, HIGH COUNTRY NEWS (7-18-88), at 6.

62. For an interesting view of the problems that have typically arisen, see C. Beaver, *Wyoming School Trust Lands Trapped Inside Grand Teton National Park—Alternative Solutions for the Commissioner of Public Lands*, 20 LAND AND WATER LAW REVIEW 207 (1985).

63. See State of Utah v. Andrus (Cotter), 486 F. Supp. 995 (1979).

64. Kevin Carter, Utah State Land Commission, personal communication, July 1994. An exception to this suggestion may be emerging in the California Desert Protection Act. Various versions of the pending bill provide for a rather standard exchange of California school lands within the proposed new park for federal lands outside the park to be identified by the Secretary of the Interior and selected by the state.

65. William Cook, Assistant Attorney General of Oregon, presentation at the Western States Land Commissioners Association meeting in Bend, Oregon, January 12, 1994.

66. For a statement of the previous rule, see Palila v. Hawaii Department of Land and Natural Resources, 852 F.2d 1106 (1988). But see Sweet Home Chapter v. Babbitt, 17 F.3d 1463 (D.C. Cir. 1994), preceded by Sweet Home Chapter v. Babbitt, 1 F.3d 1 (D.C. Cir. 1993).

67. See J. Duffield, B. Anderson, and C. Neher, Economic Analysis of the Values of Surface Uses of State Lands—Summary Report. Report for Montana Department of State Lands (February 1993), at 39.

68. Colorado State Board of Land Commissioners v. Colorado Mined Land Reclamation Board, 809 P.2d 974 (Col. 1991).

69. National Parks and Conservation Association v. Board of State Lands, (No. 880022, June 24, 1993), at 17.

70. The general rule is stated in Case v. Bowles, 327 U.S. 92 (1945) and restated most recently in Board of Natural Resources v. Brown 922 F.2d 937 (1993).

71. See *Conventional Wisdom* [*supra*, Introduction note 1], n.284 and text accompanying.

72. Idaho Watersheds Project, Inc. v. State Board of Land Commissioners (Case No. CV-94-1171, 5th District, Idaho, Blaine County, 1994).

73. See Selkirk-Priest Basin Association, Inc. v. Idaho, CV-92-00371 (1st District, Idaho, 1992). This general point is discussed in Souder et al., *State School Lands and Sustainable Resources Management: The Quest for Guiding Principles*, 34 NATURAL RESOURCES JOURNAL 271 (1994), at 276.

74. Multiple-Use Sustained Yield Act of 1960, 16 U.S.C. § 531-4(a) [emphasis added]. George Coggins has tried to say that *multiple use* means something and imposes some enforceable standards, but other commentators and the courts demur. See Coggins, *Of Succotash Syndromes and Vacuous Platitudes: The Meaning of "Multiple Use, Sustained Yield" for Public Land Management*, 53 UNIVERSITY OF COLORADO LAW RE-

VIEW 229 (1982); but see also McCloskey, *Natural Resources–National Forests–The Multiple-Use Sustained Yield Act of 1960,* 41 OREGON LAW REVIEW 49 (1961); and Dorothy Thomas Foundation v. Hardin, 317 F. Supp. 1072 (W.D. N.C. 1970).

75. This discussion obviously applies to issues on which the trustee is challenged as such (typically, by a beneficiary). When a lessee challenges an administrative decision, trust principles frequently are not even mentioned.

76. Scenic Hudson Preservation Conference v. FPC, 453 F.2d 463 (2d Cir. 1971), *cert. denied,* 407 U.S. 926 (1972), is the classic statement of what gets weighed in this context.

77. A friend of the family or surviving spouse, for example, will pass muster with the court if he or she evinces ordinary prudence in handling trust assets. A trustee that claims skill in handling resources, such as a bank, will be held to a higher standard of care. G. T. BOGERT, TRUSTS (1987), at 93.

78. See, for example, Kerrigan v. Miller, 84 P.2d 724 (Wyo. 1938) and references cited.

79. See TAYLOR, THE EDUCATIONAL SIGNIFICANCE OF THE EARLY FEDERAL LAND ORDINANCES (1922), at 123.

80. *Conventional Wisdom* at 807; F. SWIFT, HISTORY OF PUBLIC PERMANENT COMMON SCHOOL FUNDS IN THE UNITED STATES 1795–1905 (1911), at 107 *passim,* 111.

81. *Conventional Wisdom* at 806–7.

82. The earliest school land grants, as the "old northwest" states between Ohio and Michigan joined the Union, were made to townships to support schools in each township. In 1849, during the Michigan accession, the state became the grant recipient. This constituted an explicit embrace of perpetuity because the state was obligated to set up a fund, known ever after as a "permanent school fund" and a formula for disbursing the receipts. (See *Conventional Wisdom* at 824, n.94, for a discussion of the technical names of what are ubiquitously referred to as "permanent school funds.") Thereafter, states enacted increasingly elaborate provisions for supplementing the fund and for protecting it against loss and diversion. Examples of common language are "shall be held by the said state in trust . . . . No mortgage or other encumbrance of the said lands . . . shall be valid in favor of any person . . . . Said lands shall not be sold or leased . . . except to the highest and best bidder at a public auction . . . . All lands, leaseholds, timber and other products of land before being offered shall be appraised at their true value, and no sale or other disposal thereof shall be made for a consideration less than the value so ascertained . . . ." New Mexico-Arizona Enabling Act, as Amended, § 10 (Act of June 20, 1910, 36 Stat. 557, ch. 310). See also *Conventional Wisdom* at 811–12, 820 *passim.*

83. When we discuss perpetuity later in this chapter, we recall that a trust is durable and not easily altered by legislatures under transient political pressure.

84. Oklahoma Education Association v. Nigh, 642 P.2d 230 (Okla. 1982) [hereinafter cited as *Nigh*], discussed *supra* Chapter 4.

85. ASARCO v. Kadish, 109 S. Ct. 2037 (1989) [herinafter cited as *Kadish*].

86. See *Nigh* at 235, 236. Contrast with NRDC v. Hodel, CIV #S 86-054-8-EJ6 (1986). Cross-subsidization is, of course, a key component in producing below-cost timber sales on Forest Service lands.

87. *Nigh* at 235.

88. *Id.* at 236.

89. *Kadish* at 2052. See also Kadish v. Arizona State Land Department, 747 P.2d 1183, 155 Ariz. 484 (1987) for the Arizona Supreme Court's original decision overruling the existing Arizona mineral leasing statute.

90. *Kadish* at 2052, citing § 1(b) of the Jones Act, 44 Stat. 1026. This is based on the procedural requirements for leases under § 28 of the New Mexico–Arizona Enabling Act of June 20, 1910. Arizona's mineral leasing regulations were overturned because, even after the Jones Act, they were not in conformity with § 28. In contrast, soon after passage of the Jones Act, New Mexico successfully petitioned Congress to allow it to change its mineral leasing procedures so that advertisement, appraisal, and bidding procedures (all required under general leases) were not required for mineral leases. *Kadish* at 2052, n.5, citing Joint Resolution no. 7, ch. 28, 45 Stat. 58 (1927). Thus, New Mexico, by changing its enabling act and constitution, was able to lease minerals legally under terms equivalent to those found to violate the original enabling act that brought both states into the Union. In fact, Arizona revised its enabling act in 1936 and 1951 to remove the original leasing requirements from hydrocarbon minerals; it just didn't do the same for hardrock minerals. Act of June 5, 1936, ch. 517, 49 Stat. 1477, and Act of June 2, 1951, 65 Stat. 51, cited in *Kadish* at 2050, 2053.

91. *Nigh* at 238.

92. See Souder, Economic Strategies for the Management of School and Institutional Trust Lands: A Comparative Study of Ten Western States (unpublished Ph.D. dissertation, University of California, Berkeley, 1990), at 140–46.

93. *Nigh* at 237–38.

94. *Id.* at 238.

95. Havasu Heights Ranch and Development Corporation v. State Land Department, 764 P.2d 37, 42 (Ariz. App. 1988).

96. *Id.* at 42.

97. *Id.* at 41, 43.

98. Washington has about 1.8 million acres of commercial timber land (WASHINGTON DEPARTMENT OF NATURAL RESOURCES, PROPOSED FOREST LAND MANAGEMENT PROGRAM 1984–1993 (November 1983) at 22), while Oregon has 735,000 acres managed by the state (Jones, *State Forest Lands*, in LETTERMAN (ed.), ASSESSMENT OF OREGON'S FORESTS (1988), at 50). Most of Oregon's state-owned forest lands came to the state as a result of tax defaults after forest fires. In contrast, Washington, particularly on the Olympic Peninsula, has 200,000 acres of old growth. As a result, the level of controversy over management of timber on state trust lands is higher in Washington than in Oregon.

99. Crickenberger, *Management Philosophy Quickly Puts Winning Techniques to Work*, 33 TOTEM 16 (Winter 1991).

100. The cost of this deferral in terms of timber volumes is estimated to be 1,000 board-feet per year per acre, or 63 million board-feet per year for the entire area. Pat McElroy, Deputy Supervisor, Washington Department of Natural Resources, personal communication, November 18, 1992.

101. Notice that, in the 3,000 acres, the trust is receiving fair market value for the lands and timber. Money from the real estate portion of the sale is used to purchase replacement land, while the revenues from the timber go to the beneficiaries. Partridge, *Breakthrough Concept Offers Creative Alternative, New Optimism*, 33 TOTEM 6 (Winter 1991).

102. NEW MEXICO STATE LAND OFFICE, RANGE STEWARDSHIP INCENTIVE PROGRAM (document on file with the authors, n.d.) and NEW MEXICO STATE LAND OFFICE, STATE LAND OFFICE RULE 8, 7–8, 19 (Draft #4, June 22, 1992).

103. The grazing fee system used for this program has not had a court test.

104. Interestingly, this feature has been incorporated into the BLM's new proposals for federal grazing fees. *'Incentive-Based' Grazing Fees Proposed,* ALBUQUERQUE JOURNAL (October 30, 1992).

105. See Patric, Trust Land Administration in the Western States, (Public Lands Institute Report, 1981) for a comparison of federal and state trust land provisions for access and multiple use.

106. This issue is specifically addressed under the topic "below-cost timber sales." See SOCIETY OF AMERICAN FORESTERS, REPORT OF THE BELOW-COST TIMBER SALES TASK FORCE: FISCAL AND SOCIAL RESPONSIBILITY IN NATIONAL FOREST MANAGEMENT (1986) and Wolf, *National Forest Timber Sales and the Legacy of Gifford Pinchot: Managing a Forest and Making It Pay,* 60 UNIVERSITY OF COLORADO LAW REVIEW 1037 (1989).

107. But see *Nigh* at 237, 243 (Simms, J., diss.) (Okla. 1982) and our discussion of this dissenting opinion in *Conventional Wisdom* at 865, 868–73.

EPILOGUE

1. R. O'TOOLE, REFORMING THE FOREST SERVICE (1987) [hereinafter cited as O'TOOLE] is the most prominent critic of the Forest Service. See R. Johnson, *The Budget Maximization Hypothesis and the USDA Forest Service,* 1 RENEWABLE RESOURCES JOURNAL 8 (1983) and OFFICE OF TECHNOLOGY ASSESSMENT, FOREST SERVICE PLANNING: ACCOMMODATING USES, PRODUCING OUTPUTS, AND SUSTAINING ECOSYSTEMS (1992) at 43–49 *passim* [hereinafter cited as OTA Report].

2. For present purposes, we halt our discussion with the observation linking state and federal lands. Obviously, however, this same emphasis on leasing provides a clear and important way to break down the supposed (and we think vastly overplayed) distinctions between public and private land management. See also Sax, *The Claim for Retention of the Public Lands,* in BRUBAKER, ed., RETHINKING THE FEDERAL LANDS (1984), ch. 6.

3. NELSON, forthcoming, summarizes an enormous body of work—his and others'—that reaches this conclusion.

4. See also Reich, *The Public and the Nation's Forests,* 50 CALIFORNIA LAW REVIEW 381 (1962).

5. O'TOOLE at 119–22, 127–30, 187.

6. *Id.* at 72. OTA Report at 147. See also H.R. Rep. No. 593, 99th Cong., 2d Sess., "Federal Grazing Program: All Is Not Well on the Range" 5–10 (1986). See also OTA Report at 148–50, 154–57.

7. O'TOOLE at 28 *passim.* OTA Report at 154 discusses this in terms of "off-budget" funding. See also R. Wolf, *National Forest Timber Sales and the Legacy of Gifford Pinchot: Managing a Forest and Making It Pay,* 60 UNIVERSITY OF COLORADO LAW REVIEW 1037 (1989) for a detailed history.

8. This issue is discussed indirectly in SCHULTZ, FORESTRY BEST MANAGEMENT

PRACTICES IMPLEMENTATION MONITORING (Montana Department of State Lands, 1992), cited in Leal, *Making Money on Timber Sales: A Federal and State Comparison*, in ANDERSON, ed., MULTIPLE CONFLICTS OVER MULTIPLE USES (1994). Schultz's work indicates that the state does a better job of protecting land from the impacts of timber harvesting than do the federal government agencies.

BIBLIOGRAPHIC ESSAY

We started our work by confidently asserting that there was no literature to speak of on the subject of school trust lands. Because that statement has turned out to be demonstrably incorrect, we feel some obligation to provide a small essay that supplements the material found in the footnotes, particularly in Chapter 2 regarding data sources. We have learned a few tricks and we want to share them.

The best place to start an inquiry into state trust lands, and practically anything else related to public resources for that matter, is Paul Gate's *History of Public Land Law Development*, which he prepared for the Public Land Law Review Commission (1968). The best general treatment of land grants generally is the one by Mathias N. Orfield, *Federal Land Grants to the States With Special Reference to Minnesota* (1915). Any difficulty you may encounter in locating it is more than rewarded in the reading. Two other wonderful general volumes are Payson J. Treatt's *The National Land System: 1785–1920* (1910, available in microfiche [Chicago, Il: Library Resources, 1970]), and Hildegard B. Johnson's *Order Upon the Land: The U.S. Rectangular Survey and the Upper Mississippi Country* (1976). Finally, for a reasonable first approximation of a description of federal programs that produce revenues in which states have an interest and which might be compared with state programs, see Sally Fairfax and Carolyn Yale, *The Federal Lands* (Island Press, 1987).

Gate's treatment of the accession process, focusing briefly on each state, is also indispensable. When confronting that mammoth tome, however, it is nice to have some guidance. The best general introduction to the accession process—and the grants to each state at statehood—is in Chapter 12. Because we are so deeply immersed in present understandings of public lands, post-Kleppe, as federal lands, it is particularly important for modern scholars to have a feel for the role of the states and general public understanding of the western territories under the Articles of Confederation, which is, after all, when the land grant program began. Therefore, Chapters 1 and 2 are particularly helpful. On this same topic, it is also imperative to get hold of Peter Onuf's *Statehood and Nation: A History of the Northwest Ordinance* (1992).

On the state trust lands specifically, the best place to start is in dissertation abstracts, the state archives, or the libraries of the major graduate-degree granting institutions in the state. We found a wealth of information in diverse dissertations and more particularly in master's theses. If you have an interest in a particular state program, do not overlook this important source of already compiled information. The best of the breed, and useful to anyone interested in forest management, is Tom Waggener's doctoral dissertation, "Some Economic Implications of Sustained Yield as a Forest Regulation Model" (published as Report No. 6, Institute of Forest Products [College of Forest Resources. University of Washington, 1969]). The last major studies on state trust lands and funds, particularly their educational significance, were conducted in the 1910s through 1930s by Fletcher H. Swift, particularly his *History of Public Permanent Common School Funds in the United States; 1795–1905* (1911).

Another wonderful place to start looking at the history of the trust lands is in a whole raft of analyses concerned with the effect of the trust lands on education finance. These were done at the beginning of the twentieth century by Henry Taylor, George Knight, and Joseph Schafer (cited in footnote 1, Chapter 1 of this volume). Because Utah historically allocated a small percentage of its trust earnings to analysis of trust management (now there is provision to delight an academic!), there is an unusually rich early literature on that state. Henry Dixon's *The Administration of State Permanent School Funds: As Illustrated by a Study of the Management of the Utah Endowment, Southern California Education Monographs; No. 9* (1936) is the most useful of many.

Two recent volumes that came to our attention too late to be used in this volume but that deserve attention are *Multiple Conflicts Over Multiple Uses* (1994), edited by Terry L. Anderson, and *Timberland Investments: A Portfolio Perspective* (1992) by F. Christian Zinkhan, William R. Sizemore, Goeorge H. Mason, and Thomas J. Ebner. Zinkhan et al.'s book provides the best analysis of the application of portfolio theory to natural resources that we have found. The classic timber production economic analysis is Walter Mead's *Competition and Oligopsony in the Douglas Fir Lumber Industry* (1966). The ideas in Mead's book are as fresh today as when it was written. For oil and gas leasing, our initial resource, albeit somewhat dated, was Stephen L. McDonald's *The Leasing of Federal Lands for Fossil Fuels Production* (1979). John Leshy's *The Mining Law: A Study in Perpetual Motion* (1987) is a good place to start to understand hardrock minerals issues.

Finally, we want to call to attention the volume *Permanent School Fund in South Dakota and the Beadle Club* (1976), which was prepared by members of the still quite active organization that honors General W. H. H. Beadle and other South Dakotans who have made a major contribution to public education in that state. Beadle worked assiduously in many western jurisdictions to protect the school lands and funds. *Permanent School Fund* tells a wonderful tale, emphasizing that the school lands are an important part of both the history of education and the history of public lands. Perhaps now more than ever, we need reminding that we cannot take for granted public education and public lands: vigilance is necessary and heroic.

INDEX

www.ingramcontent.com/pod-product-compliance
Lightning Source LLC
Chambersburg PA
CBHW030635270326
41929CB00007B/89